D0893692

Index to Pennsylvania's
COLONIAL RECORDS
Series

Compiled by Dr. Mary Dunn

Prepared for Publication by Martha Reamy

*With a Foreword by Jonathan R. Stayer
of the Pennsylvania Historical and
Museum Commission*

Copyright © 1992
Genealogical Publishing Co., Inc.
1001 N. Calvert Street
Baltimore, Maryland
All Rights Reserved
Second printing 1993
Third printing 1996
Library of Congress Catalogue Card Number 91-77068
International Standard Book Number 0-8063-1332-3
Made in the United States of America

Published by authority of the Friends
of the Uniontown Public Library

The publisher gratefully acknowledges the contribution
of Mrs. Martha Reamy in indexing Volume XIII of the
Colonial Records and incorporating her work with
Dr. Dunn's.

Dr. Mary Dunn

 orn October 25, 1908, Dr. Mary Dunn was a dedicated educator and a civic-minded person who touched the lives of many until her death on May 6, 1984. A native of Uniontown, Pennsylvania, she was a graduate of Uniontown public schools, Indiana University of Pennsylvania, and Penn State University. She received her doctorate in elementary education from the University of Pittsburgh. Following her thirty-one-year career in Uniontown schools as an elementary teacher and principal, she became a professor at California State University and Waynesburg College.

Dr. Dunn was also a member and former elder of Trinity United Presbyterian Church, corresponding secretary of Friends of the Uniontown Public Library, a member of Rho of Delta Kappa Gamma, an honorary educational society, and "Teacher of the Year" of both Fayette County and Pennsylvania.

Her index to the *Colonial Records* of Pennsylvania, in manuscript at the Uniontown Public Library, is published in affectionate memory by authority of the Friends of the Uniontown Public Library.

FOREWORD

By Jonathan R. Stayer

Head, Reference Section
Division of Archives & Manuscripts
Pennsylvania Historical and Museum Commission

 ennsylvania's *Colonial Records* represent the beginning of the Commonwealth's endeavors to publish some of its most historically significant primary sources. The sixteen-volume set presents in printed form William Penn's charter and rules of government as well as the chronological minutes of Pennsylvania's governing bodies from the time of the founder until the period of the State's 1790 Constitution. Executive bodies represented and inclusive dates are:

Provincial Council, 10 March 1682/3 – 9 December 1775
Committee of Safety, 30 June 1775 – 22 July 1776
Council of Safety, 24 July 1776 – 21 April 1777
*   and 17 October 1777 – 4 December 1777*
Supreme Executive Council, 4 March 1777 – 20 December 1790

The Provincial Council advised the Governor and fulfilled his executive duties in his absence. At the time of the American Revolution, Pennsylvania's General Assembly established a Committee or Council of Safety which acquired the colony's executive powers. The Supreme Executive Council assumed this authority under the Commonwealth's 1776 Constitution, while the Council of Safety was reconvened concurrently in October 1777 for two months to deal with pressing military matters. In 1790, in accordance with a new constitution, a popularly elected Governor replaced the Council.

Each succeeding executive body maintained minutes of its meetings and of reports, messages from the General Assembly and the Governor, and other items submitted for its consideration. Following the establishment in 1903 of the State Archives in Harrisburg, the original minute books were deposited there, where they continue to be preserved. The Archives microfilmed both the original and the related *Colonial Records* volumes as parts of two filming projects: [RG-21] "Records of the Provincial Council, 1682-1776" (1966), and [RG-27] "Records of Pennsylvania's Revolutionary Governments, 1775-1790" (1978). Duplicate rolls and explanatory guides are available for purchase from the State Archives.

Recognizing the historical importance of these records, a joint committee of the Historical Society of Pennsylvania and the American Philosophical Society, headed by Peter S. Du Ponceau, urged the State Legislature, in 1837, to preserve the Commonwealth's provincial records by publishing them. The General Assembly responded favorably, passing the Act of 4 April 1837 which authorized the printing of "the Minutes of the Council of the Proprietary Government" from 1681 to 1717 at a cost not in excess of three thousand dollars.

Three volumes, covering the dates 10 March 1682/3 – 23 January 1735/6, were produced between 1838 and 1840. Owing to financial difficulties, the State did not fund additional volumes at that time. These three books may be recognized as the first edition of the *Colonial Records* and the foundation of the *Pennsylvania Archives* series.

In 1851, Governor William E. Johnston sought to resume publication, and his desire was supported by the legislature. From 1851 to 1853, the State reprinted the three original volumes and published thirteen others, resulting in the sixteen volumes now known as the *Colonial Records*. The reprinted books appear with page numbers different from those of the 1838-40 set and so constitute a second edition. (A microfiche copy of this edition, #PS261 – #PS263, may be purchased from University Microfilms International, 300 North Zeeb Road, Ann Arbor, MI 48106-1346.) Researchers should be aware of this discrepancy when checking references and preparing citations. The present index refers to the second edition.

While the *Colonial Records* contain only the executive minutes, related papers such as letters and petitions were published in the First Series of the *Pennsylvania Archives*. Arranged primarily in chronological order, these items often bear cross-referenced notations to the *Colonial Records*. Thus, a petition, letter or report mentioned in the executive minutes might be transcribed in full in the First Series.

Originals of some of the transcribed items and other documents which were never published are held by the State Archives. Papers from the proprietary period, 1682-1776, are filed as Record Group 21, Records of the Provincial Council; while Record Group 27 contains records of Pennsylvania's Revolutionary governments, 1775-1790. Both groups have been microfilmed as mentioned previously (see reading list for guides).

Other colonial materials are scattered throughout the ten series of the *Pennsylvania Archives*. Church, military, land and tax records appear in the Second, Third and Fifth Series. The Fourth Series contains the messages and proclamations of the Lieutenant Governors and Governors from 1681 to 1903. The journals of the provincial General Assembly were published in the Eighth Series. The *Guide to the Published Archives of Pennsylvania* (Harrisburg: Pennsylvania Historical and Museum Commission, 1949; reprinted 1976), prepared by Henry H. Eddy and Martha L. Simonetti, provides detailed information and a subject guide to the entire collection of *Pennsylvania Archives*.

Although Volumes 12 through 16 included rudimentary tables of contents, no index to the *Colonial Records* was prepared until Samuel Hazard compiled a *General Index to the Colonial Records . . . and to the Pennsylvania Archives . . .* which the State published in 1860. Primarily a listing of subjects and names of prominent persons, names of individuals mentioned *inter alia* often will be found only under the type of record. Hence, the subject entry for "Letters" is several pages long as the names of correspondents appear beneath that heading. While somewhat useful for historians, this method of indexing generally frustrates genealogists. Subsequent guides and descriptive aids (see reading list) provide alternative subject listings, but no complete name index was available until this present publication.

Because Pennsylvania's colonial governments often became entangled in the personal lives of their citizens, the *Colonial Records* provide much information about individuals whose names may not appear in other records of the period. For the earliest years of the Penns' proprietorship, these volumes are particularly useful in filling the record gap. Permitting access to the series in greater detail than ever before possible, this index provides researchers—especially genealogists—the opportunity to identify persons of specific interest who may otherwise be lost to posterity.

For Further Reading and Research

A Guide to the Genealogical/Local History Section of the State Library of Pennsylvania. Harrisburg: State Library of Pennsylvania, Pennsylvania Department of Education, 1989.

Ames, Herman V. "Report on the Public Archives of Pennsylvania," *Annual Report of the American Historical Association . . . 1900* 2 (1900): 267-93.

Baumann, Roland M. "Dr. Shenk's Missing Series of the Published Pennsylvania Archives," *Pennsylvania Magazine of History and Biography* 103 (1979): 415-31.

_____ , comp. & ed. *Guide to the Microfilm of the Records of Pennsylvania's Revolutionary Governments, 1775-1790, in the Pennsylvania State Archives*. Harrisburg: Pennsylvania Historical and Museum Commission, 1978.

_____ . "The Pennsylvania State Archives and Research Opportunities in the Era of the American Revolution," *Pennsylvania Heritage* 2 (1976): 11-16.

Eddy, Henry Howard. "The Archival Program of Pennsylvania," *American Archivist* 12 (1949): 255-66.

*_____ , and Simonetti, Martha L. *Guide to the Published Archives of Pennsylvania*. Harrisburg: Pennsylvania Historical and Museum Commission, 1949; reprinted 1976.

Evans, Frank B. "The Many Faces of the Pennsylvania Archives," *American Archivist* 27 (1964): 269-83.

Hasse, Adelaide R. *Materials for a Bibliography of the Public Archives of the Thirteen Original States*. New York: Argonaut Press, 1966.

Hoenstine, Floyd G. *Guide to Genealogical and Historical Research in Pennsylvania*. Revised and enlarged. Hollidaysburg, PA: By the Author, 1978. See pages 87-96.

Kent, Donald H., project director. *Guide to the Microfilm of the Records of the Provincial Council, 1682-1776, in the Pennsylvania State Archives*. Harrisburg: Pennsylvania Historical and Museum Commission, 1966.

*Morris, Jean S., comp. *Use of the Published Pennsylvania Archives in Genealogical Research*. Pittsburgh: Western Pennsylvania Genealogical Society, 1978.

*Schlegel, Marvin W. "The Pennsylvania Archives," *Pennsylvania History* 8 (1941): 219-27.

*Item of particular usefulness to genealogists.

1

2

3

4

5

ASSERHARTUR 5:353
ASSOGHQUA 5:318
ASSUCHQUAY (ASSUEHQUAY) 5:388, 390
ASSUEHQUA 5:393
ASSWAGARAT 8:176
ASTON, --- 7:17
--- (Capt.) 6:764
George 3:227, 230, 263, 522-523
(See ASSHETON); 4:504; 5:186;
7:59
ATACKQUOSSON 6:551
ATHEPOTY 5:685
ATHOLL, --- (Duke of) 5:66
ATIRUNTA 6:199
ATKINS, Christopher 8:58-59, 156
Edmund 7:598-600, 604, 608, 622,
626, 628-631
John 3:218-219; 6:253-254
Samll. 1:165, 207, 339, 344,
476-477, 479, 500, 509, 511-512
ATKINSON, Anne 15:548
Cornelius 7:155; 14:465
Elizabeth 11:673
George 14:214, 366
Humphrey 14:365
James 1:182, 185; 2:24, 34
John 14:571
Joseph 11:123
Theodore 6:57, 64, 67, 72-73, 82,
91, 93, 96
Thomas 14:516
William 3:140, 289, 332, 370, 387,
416, 465, 520, 575, 615; 4:247,
309, 352, 470
Wilton 11:84, 528; 12:112, 374,
437
AT(T)LEE, --- 13:555
--- (Col.) 13:61
--- (Lt.) 14:132
--- (Mr.) 13:217-218, 410, 431,
483, 509, 734, 746
J. 13:182
John 10:442; 14:607
Samuel 10:538, 569, 573, 585, 605,
622, 627-628, 649, 651, 656,
673-674, 678, 689, 704, 734,
745, 756, 782; 11:444, 568, 694,
747; 12:170, 220, 279, 437, 480,
628, 644, 659; 14:1-3, 5-6, 8-9,
11, 16, 18, 25-40, 42-45, 47,
54, 103, 105-119, 121-122, 130,
135-148, 150-153, 170-172,
174-183, 185-186, 188, 190, 194,
196, 205-206, 311, 378, 410,
509, 556, 600
Samuel J.(ohn) 13:243, 383, 393,
415, 420, 497, 697, 722, 724,
726-727, 729, 731-732, 734-748,
750-753, 773-776; 15:94, 98
William 11:72, 96, 102, 104-107,
114, 116, 153, 155, 196, 202,
215, 270-271, 320-321, 414, 510,
585, 600, 603, 630, 673; 12:69,
138, 303, 331, 593
William Augustus 13:526; 14:175,
314, 319; 15:160, 166, 193, 204,
243, 262, 291, 375, 379, 398,
434, 459, 490, 559, 561, 577,
645; 16:17, 54, 68, 87, 114-115,
123, 174, 177, 189, 192, 242,
326, 349, 400, 465, 544, 546
William Richardson 16:172, 174,
176, 218, 444, 450
ATLER, John Adam 3:386
ATONDHEYDHAW 3:435
ATTLISON, Robert 13:717

ATTMORE, William 13:503, 771;
14:600; 15:16
ATTSCHECHOKATHA 6:524
ATTWOOD, William 3:239
ATWOOD, Mary 12:68
AUBELL, Jacob 11:19
AUCHMUTY, Ar. Gates 6:648
AUCHSOCHQUAW 3:435
AUCKLEY, John 13:86
AUDIBERT, --- (Mr.) 12:661
Philip 13:7
AUDRAIN, Peter 14:514
AUFRERE, Geo. 9:2, 47-48, 50-52
AUGHLERBAUGH, Henry 15:324
AUGUIRRE, Juan Joseph (Don) 15:284
AUGUSTUS, --- 6:749; 7:118-119,
166, 285-287, 357, 482
--- (Capt.) 8:132, 144
AULAY (AULEY), Cornelius 11:363
AULD, Jacob 13:262; 14:455; 15:428;
16:43, 49, 64
Mussenden 7:500
AULL, Robert 5:186
AULT, Aibgail 12:11
AURAND, John 11:218
AURANDT, Daniel 16:195
AUSTIN (AUSTEN), Isaac 12:492, 524,
439, 585; 13:518; 14:314; 16:387
Sarah 10:774
Stephen 14:47-48
Thomas 10:472-473, 477-478, 485
William 11:494, 745; 12:492, 524,
539, 584-585; 16:387
AUTENREIT, William Frederick (Dr.)
9:173 (See Handenreid)
AUYHARUNGQUAS 6:125
AVANOS, --- (Capt.) 7:478
AVERIE (ALIAS BRIDGMAN) 1:510
AVERY, --- (Capt.) 1:531, 550, 554,
559, 580
John 12:52
Sarah 1:84
AWAHELAH 1:448
AWANNEMEAK 4:420-421, 447
AWEAYKOMAN 3:321
AWEHELA (alias James Davis) 8:211
AWENNOOL 3:123
AWINNE, Onus 8:293
AWL, Robert 14:453
AX, Jacob 12:240
AXE, --- (Lt.) 13:189
AXTELL, Thomas 16:42
AYAQUACHAN 3:150
AYRES, --- (Capt.) 10:689, 761
--- (Col.) 11:278, 527
AYYMAIKAN 13:467
AZEAS, Peter 13:63

BAAS, Jeremiah 2:240
BAASLER, Ulrich 3:466
BAAST, George 3:454
BAB, Hans Conrats 4:59
BABB, Peter 16:267
Thomas 12:463
BABEER, --- (Monsieur) 6:10, 12
BABEMEYER, Frederick 3:410
BABIN, Simon 7:240
St. Pierre 7:240
BACCHUS, Thomas 14:407-408, 438
BACHE, --- (Lt.) 10:287-288
Benjamin Franklin 16:409

8

9

BARGE, John **5**:193, 325
BARGE (SEE CORNMAN &) **10**:754
BARK, Isaac **11**:515-517, 677
 Susan **16**:165
BARK(E)STEAD, Joshua **1**:168, 174,
 298-299
BARKER, Jane **14**:378
 John **1**:227; **13**:729
 Joseph **14**:310
 Leatherbury **11**:59, 190
 Michael **14**:378, 382-383
 Tho. **2**:153
 Thomas **1**:29, 202
 William **11**:59
BARKLEY, Hugh **13**:266
 John **5**:247; **13**:708; **16**:538
 Thomas **10**:328
BARKMAN, Jacob **13**:72
BARKMIRE, Daniel **13**:554; **14**:94, 423
BARLET, --- (Adj.) **13**:190
BARN(E)S, John **3**:158, 177-178;
 9:203, 339
BARNARD, --- (Capt.) **5**:115
 John **4**:750
BARNES, --- (Capt.) **7**:459
 --- (Mr.) **11**:80
 Abraham **6**:58, 67, 83, 92
 Barnaby **9**:241
 Cornelius **14**:114
 James **11**:21, 27, 602
 Jno. **1**:87, 95, 125-133, 135,
 137-138, 140-143, 149, 151, 153,
 155-156, 160-167, 173, 175-185,
 188-191, 194-199, 201, 203-206,
 211, 322, 439-440
 Simon **13**:153
 Stephen **5**:119, 125, 134, 140, 268
 Thomas, Jr. **13**:520
 William **13**:778; **14**:82, 417
BARNET (BARNEL), Charles **10**:718
 Henry O. **12**:506, 714
 Hugh **13**:615; **14**:103, 425
 Jacob **14**:615
 Margaret **14**:171, 323
 William **10**:181
BARNETT, Joseph **15**:11
 Lazarus **13**:474
 William **16**:32
BARNETZ, Jacob **14**:127, 421
BARNEY, --- (Capt.) **13**:275
 Joshua **13**:283, 340, 382
BARNHILL, --- (Mr.) **11**:74
 John **11**:24, 640
 Robert **15**:653
BARNHOLD, Henry **13**:187
BARNITZ, Jacob **13**:701, 709; **14**:455,
 584-585, 663; **16**:443-444
BARNS, James **12**:317
 John **14**:656
BARNSLEY, John **11**:281
 Thomas **9**:235, 672, 704
BARON & HURST **15**:28
BARONET, Bowman **7**:220
BARONS, Benjamin **7**:44, 116
BARR (BARRE), --- (Mr.) **13**:357
 Adam **13**:521
 Alexander **13**:351, 558, 730; **15**:540
 Andrew **14**:81, 102, 439
 Catharine **11**:27
 Edward **14**:224
 George **4**:468
 James **10**:724, 726; **13**:521, 621;
 14:605; **15**:550
 John **9**:199, 285, 333; **13**:756;
 14:91, 124, 129, 421, 433
 Robert **13**:621; **14**:4

BARR (BARRE), Samuel **13**:389
 Thomas **10**:529; **14**:124, 127, 434
 William **15**:109, 122, 306
BARRESTEIN, Matthes **3**:456
BARRET, Philip **10**:270
 Timothy **11**:40, 56, 93
BARRETT, Edward **12**:271
 William **14**:260
BARRINGTON, --- (Viscount) **8**:40,
 552, 557; **9**:629, 637, 640
BARRIT, Lemuel (Samuel) **9**:304-306,
 345
BARRON, James **11**:281
BARROW, --- (Mr.) **8**:322
 Robert **1**:521
 Samuel **3**:50; **11**:610, 612
BARROWELLY, Martin **7**:562
BARRY, --- (Capt.) **10**:526, 528,
 545-546, 583; **11**:700
 John **14**:196, 439; **15**:389
 Richard **13**:315
 Theodore **14**:298, 305, 433
BARRYSFORD, James **4**:228, 230
BARSTOW, Michael **11**:21
BART, Jacob **3**:517
BARTEL, Nicholaus **3**:456
BARTELLS, Henry **2**:494
 Senwes **2**:493
BARTHOLOMEW, --- (Col.) **16**:251
 Ann **13**:429
 B. **13**:739
 Benjamin **10**:280, 296-298, 306-307,
 341-342, 367, 373-374, 380, 448,
 459, 486, 490, 578, 600, 655,
 711, 754; **11**:34, 36, 77-78, 450;
 13:639, 714; **14**:62, 99, 437
 Edward **10**:654, 657, 725, 736;
 11:536; **14**:308, 403, 405, 461;
 15:33, 72, 261; **16**:311, 393, 446
 Geo. **1**:166-167
 Henry **11**:305-306
 John **3**:542, 587, 590; **11**:37;
 12:435, 448, 512; **13**:633; **16**:433
 Lactitia **13**:394
 Mary **1**:86, 88
 William **15**:282
BARTLESON, Ezra **10**:449
 Sephus **11**:118
BARTLETT, Johan Wolk **3**:455
 John **12**:27-28, 383
 Nicholas **1**:75, 77
BARTLING, Chrisleib **13**:35
 Christleib **13**:81, 366
 Christlieb **15**:77
BARTON, George **15**:396
 Job **13**:139
 John **11**:281
 Joseph **13**:139
 S. (Rev.) **11**:565, 579
 Thomas **6**:675; **11**:514, 516-517;
 13:139
 Thomas (Rev.) **12**:339, 357
 William **12**:47, 256, 314, 317, 339,
 357, 745; **13**:20, 36, 302, 547;
 15:66, 72, 542
BARTOW, Thomas **13**:390; **15**:377, 388
BARTRAM (BARTRUM), Alexander
 11:482, 484-485, 745; **12**:175,
 323, 425; **13**:175-176, 361, 498,
 748; **14**:292; **15**:143, 153, 172,
 185, 192, 223, 272; **16**:283
 George **11**:17
 James **12**:726
 Jane **12**:425; **13**:294
 Jno. **1**:607
 John **5**:107, 131

BARTRAM (BARTRUM), Martha 12:525
  Moses 10:671, 677
BARUMAN, Walter 4:72
BASDEN, Joseph 11:772-773
BASELR, Henrick 3:458
BASIL, Johan Jerig 4:59
BASILION, Peter 1:397 (See
  Bisalion)
  Richard 1:397
BASKELL, William 5:247
BASS, Robert 10:292, 305, 489
BASSERT, Baltzar 3:593
BASSET, William 12:383
BASSETT, Francis 1:538-539, 541
  Mary Magdalen 1:538-539
  Sesannah 1:538-539
  Susanna Magdalen 1:538-539
BASTIAN, Adam 3:368
  Andrew 3:367
  Johannes 3:453
  John Frederick 14:480
  Lorentz 3:453
BATCHELOR, James 10:384
BATES, John 11:136
  Joseph 12:335
BATHO, Charles 7:62; 9:514, 672
BATHS, Charles 8:576
BATHUNE, John 10:581
BATHURST, --- (Lord) 5:618
BATT, Thomas 9:515
BATTELL, William 3:254, 260, 289
BATTELLI, Matteo 13:744
BATTIN, William 3:193
BATTLE, French 5:248, 597, 662
BATTON, John 14:62, 102, 410
BATWELL, --- (Rev.) 12:296
BAUBIN, Baptiste 7:240
BAUCHMAN, Christian 11:349
BAUDER, Hans Jacob 3:455
BAUMAN, Joseph Christop 3:417
BAUOR, Johan Cristofall 3:410
BAUR, Christopher 11:745
BAUSEMAN, Frederick 14:362
BAUSMAN, William 11:223, 330, 336
BAUTLETT, John 11:262
BAVAN, John 1:167
BAWCOMB, Peter 1:57
BAWCUM, Peter 1:106
BAWER, Jacob 13:716; 14:144;
  15:194, 565
BAWERS, John 16:374
BAWSMAN, William 10:520
BAXTER (BAXTON), Elizabeth 15:10,
  322, 413; 16:388, 412
  Mice 10:461
  Thomas 14:191, 195, 421
  William 10:764, 766, 771; 11:17,
    37, 139; 15:10
BAY, Jacob 12:326
  Thomas 13:133
  William 13:412
BAY(N)TON, --- (Mr.) 9:302, 304
BAYARD, --- (Col.) 13:97, 127, 144,
  160
--- (Maj.) 13:189
--- (Mr.) 13:87, 90-96, 98-104,
  106, 109-111, 114, 116-117,
  120-121, 123, 125, 128, 131-133,
  135-140, 142-143, 145, 147-150,
  157, 159-160, 162-164, 166-175,
  178-182, 186-187, 193, 200-201,
  203, 206-208, 213, 215, 218,
  232-235, 237-243, 245, 250-257,
  262, 266, 268, 270-276, 280-284,
  286, 288-289, 299-305, 308,
  310-311, 313-316, 318-319,->

BAYARD, --- (Mr.) (continued)
  13:323-326, 328-332- 334-343,
  345, 347-348, 350-354, 356-357,
  362-370, 372-374, 376, 379,
  381-385
  Craig 14:521
  James 13:139-140; 15:194
  John 10:297, 422, 440, 467, 469,
    605, 717-733, 735-742, 744-747,
    749-750, 752-756, 758-762,
    764-766, 770-771, 773-775,
    777-780, 783-784; 11:1, 2, 4-5,
    8-16, 20, 25, 27-29, 32-33, 39,
    57, 99, 105, 108, 111, 115,
    117-120, 124-125, 128, 131, 135,
    181, 210, 213, 216, 317,
    325-326, 332, 341-343, 347,
    349-351, 353, 365, 384, 386,
    434, 450, 524, 633, 661, 734;
    12:131, 135, 164, 279, 414-415,
    417, 525, 608; 13:86, 112, 152,
    242, 313, 366, 388, 535, 543,
    550, 578, 770; 14:229, 249-250,
    446, 463, 619, 668; 15:37, 40,
    95, 124, 155, 198
  Stephen 10:374; 11:47, 67, 119,
    180, 463, 500; 13:717, 755;
    14:90, 290, 412, 508, 532
BAYARD & HODGE 10:477, 511
BAYER, Jacob 16:367
BAYERS (BYERS), John 16:359, 395,
  487
BAYLEY (BAYLER, BAILIE, BAYLY), ---
  (Lt.) 6:490
--- (Mr.) 11:409
  Francis 11:191, 368, 460-462, 472,
    474, 563, 679
  Jacob 16:31
  James 11:398, 449
  Jonathan 1:548
  Margaret 15:319
BAYLIE, Jonathan 1:490
BAYLIS, Robert 5:245
BAYLOR (BAILOR), George 14:259
BAYNTON, Ann 1:536-537
  John 7:499, 518, 715; 8:19, 41,
    69, 81, 84, 163, 335; 14:403,
    621, 654; 15:321, 416-417, 435
  Peter 1:536-537; 4:517, 526;
    15:159
BAYONA, Ezekiel 16:121
BAYS, Thomas 10:235
  William 10:235
BAZELEE, John 10:749; 11:11
BEA, John 10:446
BEACH, --- (Capt.) 10:329
  Edmund 10:743, 752
  George 10:218
  Leriah 15:279-280
BEACKLEY, Christian 15:455; 16:136
BEAKES, Saml. 2:397
  Stephen 1:517
BEAKS, Wm. 1:129
BEAL(E), Thomas 16:198, 543
BEALE, Thomas 11:97; 13:7; 14:401;
  15:105
BEALL, --- (Capt.) 7:603
BEAM, Abraham 13:72
  Daniel 16:460
BEAN, Andrew 10:704
  Jesse 11:514, 516-517
BEANES, --- (Dr.) 11:123
  Thos. 2:239
BEANS, Colmore 11:107
  Seth 11:281
BEAR, George 3:466; 4:134

BEAR, Hans Jacob 3:390
 Jacob 4:72, 248, 267
 John 3:390
BEARD, --- (Dr.) 16:537
 James 11:373
 John 5:247; 11:220; 14:237
 John (alias James) 11:641-642
 Samuel 16:162
BEARDSLIE, Alexr. 1:382
BEARIS, Christian 14:427
BEARON, John 14:312
BEARSTRICKER, Andrew 12:626
BEASLER, Frederick 3:466
BEASLEY (BEASLY), Stephen 11:31,
 199, 750; 13:554; 14:86, 406,
 408, 428, 436
BEATON, John 11:230, 262, 444, 543;
 12:193, 334, 449, 460, 647, 703;
 13:316; 14:486
BEATSON, William 4:250, 253
BEATTON, John 13:254
BEATTY (BEATY), --- (Col.) 12:101,
 324
 Charles C. 10:450
 David 12:353; 14:208, 256; 15:227,
 474, 615
 Ercurius 13:717; 15:437
 Erkurius 13:568
 Erkurius (Ercurias) 14:150, 165,
 173, 178, 190, 401-402, 440, 533
 James 14:293, 300, 412
 John 10:447, 768; 13:589; 14:63,
 86, 103, 148, 292, 299, 413,
 420, 427, 465, 526
 Rachel 16:411
 Reading 13:115
 Reading (Dr.) 12:534, 622; 13:554,
 715
 Reading Z. 14:95, 440
 Robt. 9:102-103
 William 15:131, 363; 16:451
BEATY, Charles (Rev.) 7:754-756
 James 11:718
 Peter 13:14
BEAUDUE, --- (Capt.) 14:240
BEAUMONT, John 12:754
BEAVEN, Jon. 1:320
BEAVER, --- 6:155, 159, 781-782;
 9:9, 215-216, 221-222, 226-228,
 233, 253, 525, 537
 Benjamin 16:102
 King (Augus) 8:189, 305-306, 308,
 312-313, 383-384, 386, 389-391,
 434, 618, 655, 676, 690, 707,
 721-723, 725, 735, 737, 739-740,
 750-752, 776, 778
 Michael 14:261
BEAZOR, John 1:48
BECHTLUFF, Tobias 3:455
BECK, --- (Capt.) 13:189, 191
 Andrew 11:152-153, 157-159,
 162-164, 166, 168-169, 184
 Cath. 11:584
 John 11:241
 Marcus 13:273
 Matthias 3:519
 Philip 15:421
 Roger 13:334
BECKELEY, Thomas 4:468
BECKER (BICKER), --- (Capt.) 12:240
 Frederich 3:517
 Henry 10:449; 11:34-35, 68, 131,
 135, 138, 152, 179-180, 456
 Johannes 3:455
 John 12:618
 Nicholas 16:257

BECKER (BICKER), Philip 10:774
 William 14:237
BECKETT, Joseph 14:313
BECKLEY, John 16:439-440
BECKWORK, --- (Capt.) 6:490
BECTAR, Caspar 3:417
BECTEL, George 11:668
BEDDE, --- (Lt.) 8:386
BEDFORD, --- (Col.) 10:669
 --- (Duke of) 5:228, 329-331,
 359-361, 379-380, 411-412, 417,
 457, 515; 6:356; 9:13
 --- (Mr.) 13:675, 752-753
 Gunning 11:26, 152, 205, 546, 607;
 13:579, 590, 745; 14:6, 110,
 645; 15:401, 538, 574; 16:53,
 251
 John 3:293
 Peter 13:543
BEDKIN, Henry 14:626, 645
BEDLOW, Henry 10:93
BEDSKIN, Henry 12:568
BEDWELL, Robt. 1:48, 83, 168
 Tho. 1:580, 595, 599
 Thomas 2:136
BEDWELL & WATLER(S) 10:608, 712,
 754
BEDWELL (BEDWILL), Thomas 10:519,
 549, 589, 595
BEDWORTH, William 14:615
BEE, --- (Mr.) 12:693
BEECHER, Felte 3:368
BEEK(S), Adam 11:211, 214
BEEKMAN (BECKMAN), Colo. 3:204
 John 6:61, 63
 Mary 13:531
 William 14:149
BEELER, Joseph 10:212, 273
 Samuel 14:58
BEER, Abraham 4:100
 Enoch 15:642
 Enock 14:442
BEESON, Henry 14:567; 15:109, 121,
 303, 584; 16:202, 257, 518
BEEVENS (BEVANS), --- (Lt.) 12:303,
 316, 449
BEEZLEY, --- (Capt.) 12:452-453
BEGTOL, Dirik 3:328
BEHEN, Conradt 3:453
BEHIR, George Philip 3:458
BEHN, Johannes 3:429
BEICHLER, Matthias 3:519
BEIGEL, Hans Jerig 3:329
 Jacob 3:329
BEL(L)AMY, Charles 5:598
BELCHER, --- (Gov.) 6:19, 410,
 462-463, 680
 Benjamin 11:151
 J. (Gov.) 5:111, 256, 266
 Jonathan 4:226, 241
BELCHTER, Jonathan (Gov.) 7:124,
 164, 166-167, 385-386, 467, 566,
 606, 634
BELERTH, Johan Jacob 3:432
BELITS, Laurence 3:329
BELL, --- 13:587
 --- (Capt.) 4:498
 --- (Col.) 14:298, 305, 433
 --- (Mr.) 7:168, 483, 501; 13:485
 Henry 3:112
 James 12:315; 16:255
 John 3:38; 6:266; 7:187; 8:576;
 12:188; 15:267
 Jonathan 10:218
 Josiah 12:781

BELL, Patterson 11:330, 339, 479,
504, 624; 16:85
Peter 15:119
Robert 11:201; 14:38; 16:148
Samuel 11:514, 516-517; 12:315
Thomas 10:701, 711; 11:2, 161-162,
164-169
William 5:210; 11:515-516, 518;
12:45, 130; 13:7, 448, 529, 537,
557, 570; 14:101, 431, 443;
15:325-326, 445, 520, 644;
16:40, 199, 210, 466
Zephaniah 16:411
BELLAIN, Jno. 1:110
BELLAMIE, John 1:376
BELLAMONT, --- (Lord) 1:559
BELLAMY (BELLANY), Jno. 1:76-78,
89, 118
William 11:156-157, 167
BELLASES 1:179
BELLEMONT, --- (Earl of) 1:578, 580
(Also Bellamont & Bellomont)
BELLETRE, --- (Monsieur) 5:549
BELLEW, --- (Capt.) 10:595-596, 606
BELLIN, --- (Monsieur) 5:758
BELLMAN, Hans George 3:457
BELLMEYER (BILLMEYER), Andrew
15:150-170, 173-182, 190, 192,
194-195, 197-200, 226-230,
232-238, 240-245, 247-263, 284
BELLOW, James 14:217
BELMAN, George 12:608
BELOW, John 1:148
BELT, --- 6:613-614, 640, 648,
762-763, 779, 784 (See
TOHASHWUGHTONIONTY)
BELT (The), David 7:1, 3, 5, 33-34,
47-50, 64
BELTZ, John 15:648
BELTZNER, Simon 3:458
BEM (BEN) 7:172,207
BEMINCO, --- 9:280
BENDELOW, Barbara 13:443
BENDER, George 3:432
Hans Adam 3:458
Hans George 3:410
Hans Jacob 3:287
Joseph 13:681
Peter 14:224
BENDLER, Christian 3:432
John 3:431
BENEBECK, Conrad 11:164
BENEDICT, George 12:627; 16:121
BENESET, Daniel 7:62
James 7:394
BENEZET, Anthony 7:717, 720; 14:499
Caleb North 13:743
Daniel 6:170-171, 175; 8:436, 575;
9:205; 13:172
Daniel, Jr. 13:390
James 6:171; 11:187, 194, 282,
340; 14:153; 15:269, 272
John 10:281
Philip 5:174; 15:558
Samuel 11:131, 135, 138, 177,
179-180; 13:639; 14:153, 198,
212; 15:269, 271, 441; 16:83
BENGAL, Daniel 3:329
BENHAM, Robert 15:646
BENI, Abraham 3:284
BENIZET, Samuel 10:447
BENJAMIN 8:126-128, 151, 156-158,
161
BENJAMIN, --- 7:205, 220
BENKER, Christopher 3:328
BENLIE, Hans 3:328

BENN, James 3:519
BENNAWISKER, --- 9:233
BENNER, George 12:619; 13:204;
15:14
Jacob 13:204; 14:657; 15:387;
16:452
BENNET(T), --- (Justice) 10:86
Charity 13:534
Edmd. 1:109, 129, 285, 322, 607
George 5:193, 326
Henry 2:539, 543
Ishmael 14:223
Jacob 11:281; 14:237; 15:98, 566
James 13:618, 663; 15:136, 143-144
John 2:82, 86, 106; 15:25; 16:187
Joshua 9:711-712
Lenah 15:475
Mary 15:143-144
Richard 3:554
Thomas 5:194; 9:584, 711-712
William 10:42; 13:534, 720;
14:214, 237-238; 15:566; 16:192,
521
BENNETT, --- 14:555
Abraham 11:257; 12:326
Barnet 13:181
Caleb 16:494, 498, 512
Charles (Dr.) 10:547
Jacob 12:306; 16:191-192, 200,
490, 521
James 13:612; 14:292-293, 299-300
John 12:544; 13:134
Joshua 11:652
Margaret 16:159
Mathias (Matthew) 14:85, 418
Simon 11:266
William 11:281; 13:181, 392, 720
BENNIT, John 3:387
BENSEL, Charles 10:46
Charles (Dr.) 10:580, 596, 637
BENSIL, George 12:589
BENSON, John 14:242
John (alias John BRINKLOE) 9:173
Robert 14:245
BENSTEAD, Alexander 11:98, 135;
12:356; 13:778; 14:87, 428
BENT, George 12:560
BENTER, Hisbert 3:368
BENTLEY, Henry 13:636; 14:86, 416
BENTLY, George 5:210
Sashbazer 16:212
BENTZ, Henry 12:562
BENWISAKER, --- 9:232
BENZIER, Christ. Thos. 7:190
BERBESDORF, Georg. Frederick 3:329
BERDSEYE, Nathan 9:571
BERGAHOFF, Nicholas 14:83, 411
BERGEMER, Wilhelm 3:432
BERGEN, --- 12:437
Elizabeth 12:198, 206-207, 220
BERGER, John Adam 9:601
Regina Magdalena 9:601
BERGSTOTTER, Joseph 11:28
BERGSTROSER, John Georg. 3:414
BERGUHOFF, Nicholas 13:709
BERINGER, --- (Widow) 6:547
BERKEL, Hans Jacob 3:520
Jacob 3:520
BERKELEY, --- (Lord) 5:618
BERKELY (BERKLEY, BARKLEY), ---
(Earl of) 3:70
--- (Lord) 6:556; 7:277; 8:438,
552, 557
BERKENHOUT, --- (Dr.) 11:567,
569-570, 576, 584
BERKER, --- (Col.) 11:272

BERKMAN, William 15:286
BERLIN, Abraham 11:52, 260
BERNARD, Fra. (Gov.) 8:139-140,
  150, 153, 156, 178-179, 181,
  183, 187, 190, 193, 201-202,
  205, 208, 216-220, 222, 743
  James 16:191, 494
  Nicholas 13:64
BERNDHEISEL, Johan 3:432
  Wendel 3:432
BERNE, Wilhelm 3:456
BERNIE, Lawrence 10:612
BERNTHEISEL, Henry 16:109
BERRET, Henrich 3:432
  Johannes 3:284
BERRETT, Timothy 11:201
BERRIE, Wm. 1:607
BERRIMAN, Jemima 15:482
  Richard 15:482
BERRINGTON (BAHRINGER, BARRINGER),
  David 9:199, 285, 333, 398
BERRIS, Christopher 13:756; 14:87
BERRY, --- 7:154
  Bartholomew 13:668; 14:89, 422
  James 4:681-682; 16:432
  Sam 3:288, 332, 370, 387, 416,
  575, 615
  Thomas 3:254
  Wm. 1:115, 134, 140, 147, 149,
  158-159, 165, 168, 170
BERRYHILL, Alexander 15:100
BERTROUG, James 9:767-768
BERWICK, Edward 5:378
BESAKER, Jacob 3:455
BESALION, Louis 2:18
  P. 2:18 (See BEZALION)
BESINGER, Andreas 3:517
BESLER, John 14:405; 15:115
BESSER, Christopher 3:459
BEST, Abraham 14:611, 615
  Humphrey 1:89
  Joseph 11:773; 12:33
BETAM, Jacob 16:335
BETCHEL, John 7:460
BETCHER, Benjamin 11:158
BETECKER, --- (Capt.) 14:595
BETHEL, --- (Capt.) 10:431; 11:44
  --- (Maj.) 13:191, 212, 228-229
  Elizabeth 12:773
  Robert 13:5-6
  Samuel 3:465, 575; 4:280
BETHELL, John 2:397-398
  Robert 12:687
BETHWELL, Samuel 3:521
BETTER, Christopher 3:385
BETTIN, Adam 10:448
BETTINGER (BITTINGER), Nicholas
  14:608
BETTS, Jno. 1:83-84, 322, 340, 451,
  493
BETTY, (wife of Capt. John)
  9:103-104
  William, Jr. 4:102-103, 108-109
  William, Sr. 4:102-103, 108-109
BETZ, Adam 15:384, 419
BEUTNITZ, Justus 16:323
BEVAN, Awbray (Awbrey) 4:309, 352,
  469, 500, 601
  Davis 9:57, 199; 11:89; 12:62;
  13:217; 15:518
  John 1:155, 209, 567-569, 601-602
  Joseph 4:209, 224
BEVANS, Welder 13:716
  Willm. 2:160
BEVELL, Simon 3:570
BEVENS, Welder 14:299, 608

BEVERAGE, David 11:544
BEVERHOUT, --- (Mr.) 12:7
BEVERLY, William 4:698
BEVINS, Wilder 13:676
BEWL(E)Y, John 2:69, 95-96, 104,
  117-118
BEWLEY, John 1:534-535, 543, 553
BEWZILL, --- (Mr.) 6:498
BEYELEY, John 11:47
BEYER, Andreas 3:414
  Christopher 3:413
  Dewalt 4:59
  Jacob 3:331
  Johan Adam 3:414
  Johan Christo. 3:454
  Johan Jacob 3:414
  Johan Philip 3:413
  John Adam 3:518
  Joseph 3:415
  Valentine 3:453
BEYERS, Godfrey 12:29
  John 13:216
BEYSON, James 14:313
BEYSS, Johan Michl. 3:517
BEZAC, Edw. 1:95
BEZAILLION, Mitchel 2:386, 389
BEZALION, Peter 2:100, 145, 186,
  403-404, 509, 531 (See BESALION)
BIBB, William 13:595
BICKER (BICKAR), Henry 10:446;
  12:215
  Walter 10:449, 453
BICKHAM, --- (Mr.) 16:44
  George 11:21, 31-33, 35, 37, 40,
  42-44, 49, 52-53, 56, 59-66,
  69-70, 72-76, 78-91, 95-114,
  117-123, 126-128; 14:230
  James 9:386, 419, 673; 11:96, 181,
  421
BICKHEIM, George 13:307
BICKING, Frederick 13:306
BICKINGS, Frederick 12:323
BICKLEY, Abr. 2:473, 480
  Daniel 15:68; 16:483
  Samuel 4:602, 748
BIDD(I)ESON, George 14:97, 425
BIDDES, John 12:262
BIDDLE, --- (Ens.) 8:271
  --- (Mr.) 13:752-753
  Adam 14:612
  Charles 13:547; 14:231-232,
  242-250, 252-263, 265-270, 274,
  276-279, 281-285, 287-291,
  307-311, 313-318, 321-322,
  326-327, 342, 344-348, 356-365,
  367-369, 371, 373-387, 393-396,
  398-402, 404-406, 441-452,
  455-456, 462-465, 470-474,
  476-484, 486-489, 491-510,
  512-514, 516-519, 522, 524,
  526-554, 556-568, 570-571,
  573-574, 577-582, 584-590, 593,
  595-604, 606, 616-643, 645-653,
  656-662, 664-667, 670-672;
  15:1-3, 5-12, 14-17, 21-81,
  84-97, 99, 101-116, 118-154,
  160-180, 182-185, 187-190, 202,
  204, 206, 209, 212, 218,
  220-221, 243, 245, 247, 249-278,
  280, 282-285, 288-292, 297, 301,
  313-314, 319, 488-489, 544, 592,
  596, 639, 656; 16:3, 117, 127,
  145, 204, 219b, 244, 285, 291,
  327, 368-370, 397, 410, 422,
  465, 498, 523-526

14

BIDDLE, Clement **10:**331, 418, 424,
427, 489, 491, 497-498, 549-550,
600, 634, 638, 640, 649, 657,
659, 664, 672, 707, 739; **11:**18,
95, 104; **12:**392, 537, 539;
13:53, 67, 71, 136, 197, 296,
331, 358, 386, 706; **14:**551;
15:17, 63, 115, 257, 323, 349,
363, 381, 387, 438, 448, 481,
496-497, 503, 509, 540-541, 613;
16:76, 286-287
Edward **6:**705; **10:**213, 215, 225,
239, 280, 374, 442-443, 445-446,
448; **11:**617, 633
Elihu **13:**439
James **6:**705; **9:**205, 672, 699, 769,
771; **10:**46, 373-375, 377-378,
382, 384-385, 388-390, 395-396,
398-400, 406-407, 410, 414-417,
419-423, 425-426, 429, 436-439,
441-446, 448-449, 451-452,
456-461, 463, 466, 468-478,
480-481, 489-491, 493, 495,
498-499, 501-502, 504-507, 509,
511-515, 517, 519, 523-527,
530-537, 542-543, 547-551,
554-557, 560-563, 566-567, 570,
572-574, 578, 580-581, 585,
589-590, 592-593, 595-600, 612,
614-617, 619-620, 623, 627-629,
631-633, 635-639, 642-643,
647-648; **11:**30, 45, 146; **14:**506;
15:595-596, 607; **16:**220
Jemmy **6:**705
John **12:**539; **14:**499, 568; **15:**30,
322; **16:**8, 184, 204, 208
John, Jr. **11:**68, 745
Nicholas **10:**296, 379, 425-426
Owen **10:**280, 282-292, 294-302,
304-307, 312-315, 322-323,
327-333, 341-342, 344, 346-347,
351-357, 360-363, 365, 367,
371-375, 377-378, 380-382,
384-385, 387-388, 390, 395-396,
398-401, 403-408, 410-412,
414-417, 419-420, 422, 429, 431,
433-434, 436-437, 439, 441-446,
448-449, 451, 453, 456-458, 460,
463-478, 480-484, 486-491,
493-496, 498-499, 501-502,
504-507, 509, 511-514, 517,
519-527, 529-537, 539-540,
542-544, 549-550, 552-557,
559-562, 566-567, 569-570,
572-575, 578, 580-581, 585-586,
590-590, 592-602, 604, 607, 612,
614-615, 617, 619-621, 623,
626-629, 632-633, 635-637,
639-644, 647, 651, 653-660, 662,
664-666, 668, 670-675, 677-678,
680, 682-683, 687, 689, 692-705,
707-710, 720-723, 726, 733,
735-738, 740, 742, 744-747,
749-750, 753-756, 758-759,
761-762, 764-766, 769-771,
777-781, 783; **11:**3-9, 12-19,
22-25, 27-30, 32, 34, 36-37,
39-45, 47-51, 53-55, 57-64,
67-69, 72-73, 76, 78, 84, 86-88,
93, 95, 97, 118, 120, 125-128,
130-133, 135, 138-143, 145, 181,
194, 201, 211, 335, 476, 695;
12:65, 228, 300, 305, 539;
13:192; **14:**264
BIDDLE & DEHAVEN **10:**528
BIDDLESON, George **13:**568

BIDGOOD, William **15:**45
BIDKIN, Henry **15:**180
BIDLEY, William **11:**58
BIELER, Catharine **13:**445
BIETRAB, Hans Jacob **4:**73
BIG WOLF **9:**220
BIGBY, Richard **7:**275, 387
BIGGER, Peacock **5:**175
BIGGLE(S), John Adam **14:**298, 304,
412
BIGGS, Robert **15:**5
Thomas **14:**312
William **16:**449
BIGHAM, James **12:**508
John **12:**303, 316, 449, 599, 618,
675, 683, 761
BIGLAND, William **10:**295
BIGLER, Marcus **3:**519
BIHLMEIR, John Leonard **3:**415
BILES (BYLES), Charles **4:**247
John **11:**12, 760
Langho(u)rn(e) **5:**193, 388, 573
Martha **16:**309, 320
Samuel **10:**100, 211, 270; **11:**482,
484-485, 745; **16:**309, 320, 390,
507
Thomas **3:**260, 289; **11:**495-496, 732
William **2:**9, 106, 122, 127, 186,
200-201, 397, 398; **3:**28, 31,
108, 241; **4:**244, 313; **16:**320
William, Jr. **2:**183
Wm. **1:**47, 57-72, 79-82, 84, 86-89,
92-94, 111, 129, 164, 169, 177,
320, 454, 465, 469, 481,
483-486, 488, 491, 503, 507,
514, 536, 539, 541, 547, 551,
553, 555, 557-559, 561, 563,
565, 567-568, 571-572, 578, 589,
591, 593-596, 600, 604, 612-613,
617
BILL SACK **9:**103
BILLER, Martin **3:**432
BILLEW, Nicholas **16:**260
BILLIG, Johan Arnold **3:**520
BILLIGAR, Daniel **3:**458
BILLINGS, Joseph **9:**647
BILLINGTON, Thomas **14:**79, 105
BILLMEYER, Andrew **16:**194, 492
BILLY **8:**457
BIMER, George **13:**636; **14:**133
BINCKES, George **13:**639
BINDERS, --- (Mr.) **11:**157
BINGHAM, --- (Mr.) **6:**481
Henry **10:**676
James **3:**416; **12:**134
William **5:**174; **13:**389; **15:**189,
274, 328, 339, 655
BINGLEY, Edward **10:**609
BINKS, --- (Mr.) **10:**333
BINKSON, Andrew **1:**168, 334
BINNEY, Barnabas **13:**122, 718
Barnabas (Dr.) **13:**557; **14:**86, 413,
455, 544; **15:**46, 618, 621-622
BINSIVASINA **9:**229
BIRCH, --- (Dr.) **2:**628
Mathew (Mathiew) **1:**534, 543,
559-561, 563
BIRD (BURD), Benjamin **11:**112
James **10:**701
Mark **9:**440, 674; **10:**584, 673, 691,
696-697, 699, 703, 772; **11:**633;
12:139, 508, 680, 750
Mary **12:**343
William **6:**503; **8:**562; **10:**448
BIRK, Alexander **11:**155
BIRMINGHAM, Rd. **2:**614-615, 630

BLOEMAN, John 3:329
BLOND, --- (Col.) 11:637
BLONNFIELD, --- 9:509
BLOOM, Jacob 3:454
 Stephen 15:100-101
BLOSS (BLOSSIN), George 14:261-262
BLUE, Uriah 15:113
 William 11:101
BLUM, Stephen 7:119
BLUMSTON(E), John 1:86-87, 110,
 129, 134, 138, 140, 151, 323,
 503
BLUNDELL, Robert 4:229-230
BLUNSTED, John 1:48
BLUNSTON(E), John 2:18, 26-30, 32,
 34, 61, 87, 89, 91, 94-95,
 104-105, 107-109, 122, 132, 138,
 153, 156-157, 200, 206, 509;
 15:478
 John, Jr. 2:596
 Jno. 1:140, 152-153, 169, 178-179,
 263-264, 320, 324, 331, 333,
 335, 438, 493, 507, 517-518,
 520, 568, 570, 590, 601, 607,
 609, 617, 621-623
 Nicholas 1:607
 Samuel 3:263, 305, 331, 345, 356,
 358, 470, 472, 475, 509-510;
 4:56-58, 63, 69-70, 105, 147,
 149-152, 155-156, 188, 190, 194,
 280-282, 313, 523
BLYTH, Benjamin 11:358, 566
 David 11:614
 William 9:414-415, 421-422, 424,
 429, 436, 438, 443-444
BLYTHE, Benjamin 12:322; 13:246,
 522; 14:600; 16:106
 Jacob 16:102
 Samuel 12:473
 William 7:6
BO(U)QUET, --- (Col.) 7:358, 361,
 374, 376, 380, 471, 525-526, 563
BOARST, Michael 3:367
BOATMAN, George 11:514, 516-517
BOBIN, Is. 3:204
BOCHER, Leban 13:567
BOCK, Leonard 3:415
BOCKIUS (BOCHIUS), Godfrey 12:448
 Peter 12:638
BODEN, --- (Mr.) 14:77, 104
BODIE, William 4:273-276
BODITT, Jacob 1:561
BODLYS (BODLEY), William 11:130,
 140; 12:440
BODMAN, Ulrich 3:466
BOE(H)M (BAEHIN, BEAHM), Joseph
 13:754
 Joseph, Jr. 13:725
 Philip 11:17, 40, 47, 53, 81, 83,
 194, 215, 279, 365, 395, 451,
 488, 567, 588, 597, 600, 718,
 767; 12:55, 135, 243, 261, 424,
 427, 506; 14:639, 659, 668
BOELHAM, Wm. 1:29
BOERUM, Simon 10:291
BOGARD, --- (Lt.) 10:595-596
BOGARDUS, Petrus 6:377
BOGART, Jacob 8:577; 9:235, 672;
 10:162
 James 5:209
 Nicholas 3:290, 455
BOGER, Johan Philip 3:432
 Martin 3:413
 Paulus 3:432
 Richard 10:545, 547, 551, 601,
 622, 627

BOGER, Samuel 13:568
BOGG, John 9:702; 10:116
BOGGART, John 10:769
BOGGS, Alexander 13:282
 Andrew 5:247
 James 14:373; 15:42
 John 11:98, 111, 330, 340, 367,
 479, 504, 609; 12:166, 489, 519;
 13:133-134, 396, 591; 14:95,
 140, 370, 419, 574; 15:13, 59,
 301, 399, 592; 16:32, 73, 215
 Martha 14:373
 Mary 16:539
 William 16:540
BOGLER, Leban 14:432
BOGS, John 10:719
BOHER, Adam 4:60
BOHRER, Elias 10:511
BOICE, John 15:475
BOIDEN, James 3:260
BOLDOF, Casper 11:89
BOLESBY, Thomas 13:37
BOLINGBROKE, --- (Lord) 2:576
BOLLARD, David 2:456, 458
 James 14:143
BOLLEN, John 13:213
BOLLINGER, Peter 11:374
BOLLON, Conrad 3:453
BOLTON, --- (Duke of) 4:298,
 484-485; 6:264
 Aubigney 4:471
 Joseph 11:513, 516-517
BOM, Cornelius 1:174
BOMBENGER, Charles 12:601
BOMGARTNER, Johan. Fredr. 3:453
BOMPER, --- (Mr.) 7:774
BOND, George 4:102
 John 15:135, 143, 144-145
 Joseph 3:28
 Phineas 11:284, 288-290, 296, 300,
 525; 15:6, 8, 93, 187, 215,
 408-410, 416, 419, 517, 520
 Thomas 4:498, 525, 529, 568, 587,
 674; 13:554, 718; 14:102, 414,
 544, 613-614
 Thomas (Dr.) 5:100, 109, 112,
 121-122, 175, 410; 6:170, 173,
 175; 10:452, 458, 512, 633, 639,
 763; 11:300; 12:139, 144, 617
 Thomas, Jr. 9:459; 13:102, 115
 Williamina 15:6, 8
BONDHAM, William 14:256
BONE, Joseph 11:490
BONHAM, Ephraim 10:671, 677;
 11:218; 12:297
 William 12:110; 13:19, 346
BONNER, Rudolph 3:453
BONNETT, Jaques 3:516
BONNIL, Robert 2:448
BONSAL(L), Benjamin 15:478
 Jesse 12:420, 461
 Jos. 10:734
 Joseph 4:313, 482
 Richard 11:579
 Sarah 11:579; 13:460
BONSALL (SEE CLARKSON &) 14:478
BONSEL(L), --- (Justice) 7:354,
 356, 391
BONSELL (BONSALL), Joseph 5:3, 108,
 203, 301, 303, 387, 572
BONUM, Hans 3:417
BOOG, Jerig 3:329
BOOKS, Johan 4:72
BOOM(E), Hawkins 11:97, 704
BOON(E), --- (Mr.) 5:709
 Andrew 10:699

17

BOON(E), George 3:491; 4:54, 312,
482, 762
Hawkins 10:741; 14:64, 74, 436
James 5:612
John 14:104
Somonom 12:188
William 5:597, 662; 6:144, 638
Wm. 7:266
BOOR, Joseph 5:60
BOORS, Gisbertus 3:414
Johannes 3:414
BOOSHUNG, Hans 3:415
BOOT, Joannes 3:328
BOOTH, --- (Capt.) 11:168
Benjamin 12:751; 13:23
Joseph 1:490, 601; 2:34, 83, 426
Joseph, Jr. 3:254
BOOTZ, Johan George 3:452
BOOZER, Jacob 14:611
BOQUET, Henry (Col.) 9:30, 34-35,
42, 144, 183, 197, 206-210,
212-214, 216, 219-224, 226-234,
238-239, 249-250, 252-253, 255,
257-260, 262, 265-266, 269, 283
BOQUINVILLE, --- (Col.) 8:505
BORASS, James 13:709; 14:194, 412
BORDEN, Joseph 12:197, 600
BORDLEY, --- 4:115
BORDON, --- (Widow) 1:559
Joseph 13:239
BORE, Lassey (Lassee) 3:491, 531
BOREA, Peter 14:382
BOREMAN, Edward 12:29
John 12:747
BORGAN, Yost 14:422
BORGAR, John 14:124, 128, 435
Yost 13:679
BORGARE, Yost 14:84
BORGER, Peter 16:195
BORK (BURK), Lawrence 6:650; 8:143,
147
BORKE, Thomas 5:556
BORLAND, John 1:560
BORSTLER, Hans George 3:457
BORTENER, Baltzar 3:456
BORTNER, Jacob 12:601
BORTON, --- (Col.) 7:127
BORY, Mary 13:539
BOSCAWEN(S), --- (Adm.) 6:451, 454,
456, 461, 463, 468, 480, 521,
587, 592, 712, 729; 7:240
Ed. (Adm.) 8:163-166, 170
BOSHART, Henrich 3:597
Jacob 3:593
BOSHEARS, Zacharias 14:311
BOSLEY, John 15:96
BOSS, --- (Lt.) 12:633, 675, 693
George 13:202, 709; 14:100, 417
Peter 1:365-366
BOSWALT, Jacob 13:602; 14:432
BOSWELL, Jane 12:391, 684
BOSWORTH, Henry 5:94
BOTETOURT, --- (Lord) 10:237
BOTIKOFER, Nicholaus 3:597
BOTNER, Elias 10:681, 734; 11:31,
57, 127, 129
Elizabeth 13:530
BOTT, Johan Balzar 3:453
Reinhard 12:146, 513
BOTTING, Henry 14:297, 304, 412
BOTTOMLY, Joseph 14:198
BOUCHER, Hans Ulrich 3:455
BOUD, Thomas 7:266, 510; 11:68
BOUDE, Thomas 6:144, 638; 10:449;
13:716; 14:124, 127, 431
BOUDES, --- (Dr.) 5:327

BOUDINOT(T), --- (Mr.) 13:61, 576,
618
Elias 11:402; 13:502
BOUGER, --- (Capt.) 10:663
BOUGH, George 13:453
Martin 16:401
BOULT, John 1:145
BOULTON, Everald 2:596
Everard 3:28
BOUMAT, Louis 1:81
BOUQUET, --- (Col.) 8:234, 270,
284, 294, 388, 777
BOURG, Paul 7:240
BOURKE, James 14:227-228
BOURNE, --- (Dr.) 6:169-170
--- (Maj.) 6:447
Thomas 5:175
BOUSER, Henry 11:281
William 14:89
BOUSMAN (BAUSMAN), Jacob 16:204,
450-451
BOUSSER, Christian 3:519
Matthias 3:519
Matthias, Jr. 3:519
BOUSZACK, Peter 13:696
BOUTCHER, Samuel 13:77
BOUVIERE, Francis Charles 6:224-225
BOVARD, James 14:465
BOW, William 14:294, 301, 426
BOW(S)MAN, Martin 12:372, 406
BOWD, Grimstone 2:151
BOWDE (BOUDE), Samuel (Dr.)
6:653-654
BOWDIN, James 14:517, 525
BOWEN, --- (Capt.) 13:479
John 4:269
John L. 14:296
Stephen 15:118
Thomas B. 13:676, 715; 14:150,
165, 173, 178, 401-402, 428, 430
Thomas Bartholomew 11:20, 96, 440
William 11:28
BOWER(S), Adam 14:492
Bartholomew B. 14:99
Giles 9:513-514 (See POWELL)
Hans Martin 3:457
Jacob 10:643; 13:632, 695; 14:94,
101-102, 414-415, 422, 434, 436
Johan Martin 3:454
John J. 14:303
Michael 11:74, 107
Nicholas 12:48
Thomas 6:703
BOWERLANE, Catharine 14:320
BOWERS, --- (Capt.) 12:774
Jacob 16:135
William 11:63, 88, 153, 159
BOWES, Martin 16:104 (See John
RYAN)
BOWIE, --- (Dr.) 11:79, 123
BOWL(E)Y, --- (Mr.) 12:12
BOWLAND, Thomas 13:758; 14:93, 421
BOWLE, Joseph 1:115
BOWLES, Leonard 12:92
BOWLEY (SEE LUX &) 12:12
BOWLING, Edward 12:280
John 16:232
BOWLINGS, Mary 13:37
BOWMAN, --- (Capt.) 10:529, 692
Albrecht 3:290
Benjamin 13:535
Daniel 3:288
Dorts 3:417
Elijah 12:626
Hans Jerig 3:284

BOWMAN, Henry **1**:48, 63, 166, 168, 180, 224, 226, 228
Jacob **3**:288, 368, 570; **13**:501; **15**:486
Johannes **3**:453
John **11**:753; **12**:9
Mary **15**:119
Samuel **7**:459; **11**:381-382, 385; **12**:277-278
William **13**:604; **14**:91, 425
BOWNE, --- (Capt.) **5**:111, 250; **8**:155
BOWON, William **11**:375
BOWONE, --- (Maj.) **6**:447
BOWRNE, Thomas **15**:440
BOWSER, William **13**:709; **14**:417
BOWSMAN, William **10**:53, 267
BOWYER, Michael **11**:307, 488
Thomas **12**:599
BOYCE, Elias **11**:465
BOYCE (BOY'S), Nathan (Nathaniel) **10**:327, 353, 423, 426, 514, 557, 636, 720
BOYD, (W.) John **13**:753-754, 760-764, 766, 768-776
--- **11**:775
--- (Capt.) **13**:119, 121, 145, 151, 359, 427, 448, 484, 585, 593
--- (Col.) **11**:381
--- (Lt.) **12**:88-89
--- (Maj.) **13**:661
--- (Mr.) **12**:361-362, 649; **13**:485, 670, 673
Adam **10**:505
Alexander **11**:111; **12**:502, 525, 569; **13**:491, 547; **14**:42, 403, 521; **15**:50, 52-53, 317-318, 536-537, 571, 576
Alexander & Co. **16**:391
Andrew **10**:666; **11**:103, 233, 445, 496, 511, 589, 662, 672, 707, 761; **12**:46, 298, 445, 451, 513, 733; **13**:458, 580, 725, 735; **14**:93, 238, 418; **16**:464, 533
Augustus **7**:187
Catherine **12**:21
Elizabeth **13**:603
James **12**:131, 164, 178, 494, 512, 542, 624; **13**:392, 415, 502; **14**:441, 452
Jaret **15**:428
John **5**:186; **7**:187, 482; **10**:690, 708, 717, 756; **11**:80, 418-419, 489, 511, 530, 681; **12**:355, 623, 679; **13**:461, 471, 473-474, 477, 580, 583, 729, 731, 751-752; **14**:2-6, 8-11, 15-16, 18, 23-38, 40-60, 65-72, 82, 108, 114-119, 121-122, 130, 135-141, 144-146, 149-169, 176, 182-186, 188, 196-204, 218-219, 223, 225-226, 233-240, 242-248, 250-258, 281-283, 285, 287-291, 307-311, 313-327, 342, 344-348, 356-365, 367-369, 371-387, 393-396, 398-402, 404-406, 410, 443-445, 447, 450-452, 455-466, 492-493, 495-497, 501, 511-514, 516-518, 522, 524, 526-530, 532, 534-543, 550, 553-554, 556-562, 566-568, 570-571, 573-575, 577-582, 584-593, 595-604, 606, 616-643, 646-651, 655-661, 663-665, 667-672; **15**:1-9, 18-23, 26-41, 43-60, 62-63, 68-74, 76, 78-81, 84-93, 95-96; **16**:231, 237, 494

BOYD, M. **11**:39, 48, 61, 83, 139, 563, 589
Matthew **15**:40
Robert **9**:601, 673; **11**:589
Samuel **4**:313, 483; **9**:689, 778; **10**:56, 101, 211, 270, 772; **12**:647, 703; **13**:44, 88; **14**:447; **16**:178, 182, 209b, 260, 274
Sarah **13**:755
Sarah (Mrs.) **14**:82
Sceny **12**:494, 542
Stephen **14**:600
Thomas **10**:678, 681, 765; **11**:130, 181, 251, 318, 339, 398, 446-447, 589; **13**:755; **14**:82, 177-178, 189, 192, 410; **16**:30
William **5**:210; **9**:205; **10**:757; **11**:676; **12**:349, 355, 362, 405; **13**:368, 542; **14**:82, 196, 269, 410
BOYDE, Barnaby **11**:165
Thomas **13**:635
BOYDEN, James **1**:48, 87
BOYEN (BOYER), James **10**:9, 217
BOYER, --- (Capt.) **6**:490
A. **15**:76
Abraham **12**:110
Andreas **3**:518
Conrad **14**:230, 555
Frederick **14**:417
Hans **8**:728
Henry **13**:346
Jacob **13**:554; **14**:94, 416; **16**:192
James **9**:645
John **13**:340
Lelian **14**:100
Michael **10**:726; **11**:10, 107, 117, 138, 201, 214, 242, 268, 279; **14**:371
Peter **10**:643; **14**:431
Philip **13**:554; **14**:88, 428
Samuel **14**:305, 434
BOYL FAMILY **6**:411
BOYLAN, James **10**:745
BOYLAN (BOYLEN), Adam **15**:92, 196
BOYLE, Alexander **10**:769
James **14**:80, 86, 610
John **14**:292, 299, 411; **16**:461
Peter **11**:181
BOYLING, Adam **13**:360
BOYLS, --- (Maj.) **12**:356
BOYRIE, --- (Monsieur) **8**:713-714
BOYS, --- (Capt.) **13**:17, 54
Elias **12**:354; **13**:81, 307; **14**:230, 250; **15**:322
Nathan **11**:640, 657, 692, 717, 727, 750, 777; **12**:82, 134, 190, 216, 223, 250-251, 274, 314, 325, 340-341, 354, 376, 392, 406, 440, 452-453, 457, 463, 482, 489, 518, 521, 525, 549, 576, 600, 627, 629, 657, 686, 718-719; **13**:14, 43, 48, 149, 151, 165, 250, 554; **14**:87, 89, 406, 408, 410, 420, 430, 436, 555
BOYSAL, Van **14**:260
BOZART, Philip **7**:493-494, 620
BRAC(E)Y, Thomas **1**:48, 59, 96
BRACEYS, Robert **1**:83
BRACHEY, Robert **12**:147
BRACKEN, William **10**:78, 142
BRACKEN (BRAKIN), James **11**:483-485
BRACKENRIDGE, --- (Mr.) **15**:121
James **14**:208
Jane **14**:276

BRACKENRIDGE, Robert **11**:282
BRACY, Robert, Sr. **1**:48
BRADDICK, Nicholas **2**:89
BRADDOCK, --- (Gen.) **4**:7, 12; **7**:10,
  19-20, 24-25, 64, 179-180, 342,
  360, 445, 592, 601, 632; **8**:257,
  284, 322
  Edward (Gen.) **6**:286, 294, 298-299,
    302-308, 318, 320-321, 331-335,
    338, 358, 365, 371-372, 375,
    377-378, 380, 382-384, 389,
    394-395, 397-401, 404, 406, 408,
    412-413, 415, 420-421, 424-432,
    436-437, 442, 445-446, 452,
    455-456, 461-464, 466, 469-472,
    474-476, 480-484, 486-487, 489,
    494-499, 502, 510, 512, 514-515,
    517, 519-520, 524, 547, 549,
    560, 562, 565, 593, 599-600,
    614, 622, 634, 644, 671, 686,
    700, 727, 730, 733, 768, 777
  Mary **11**:758
  Middleton **11**:758
BRADEN, --- (Mr.) **14**:620
BRADFORD, --- **11**:654; **15**:366, 392,
  444
  --- (Mr.) **7**:467, 715; **13**:188
  Andrew **3**:143, 145, 369
  Isaac **4**:209, 224
  Joseph **11**:408; **14**:298, 305, 432
  Thomas **10**:420, 471, 548; **11**:286;
    12:21, 23, 29, 37, 49, 53, 55,
    111-112, 125, 230, 236, 241,
    253, 353, 368, 422, 494, 675;
    13:252, 667, 729; **14**:34, 37, 54,
    197, 642; **15**:150, 187, 384, 639
  Thos. B. **2**:410
  William **5**:174; **8**:439-440; **10**:302,
    304, 321-322, 327, 342, 359,
    366, 371, 420, 471, 521, 531,
    548; **13**:137
  William C. **11**:9, 442, 448, 451,
    464, 469-470, 475, 511, 521,
    582, 588, 591, 639, 660, 678,
    704, 728, 780; **12**:44, 48, 65,
    90, 159, 170, 185, 192, 208,
    227, 585; **16**:66
  William, Jr. **11**:2, 127, 182-183,
    193-194, 210, 283, 286-287, 289,
    292, 295, 365-366, 387, 701,
    775; **12**:390, 550, 702; **13**:37,
    73, 128, 136, 166, 241, 266,
    280, 310, 319, 407, 420-421,
    440-441, 447, 452, 458, 474,
    482, 496, 591, 639; **14**:35, 52,
    141, 143, 156, 159, 279, 308,
    448, 550, 624; **15**:37, 71, 116,
    146, 207, 211, 227, 277, 330,
    372, 420, 446, 484-485, 629,
    631, 655; **16**:21, 114, 128, 153,
    188, 220b, 226, 253, 391, 420,
    450, 527, 546
  Wm. **1**:82, 165, 366-367
BRADFORD (SEE DUNLAP &) **12**:197
BRADHURST, Benjamin **13**:547
BRADIN, Nathaniel **14**:362
BRADING, Nathaniel **14**:571, 577
BRADLEY, Abraham **16**:317
  Daniel **13**:705; **14**:556-557; **15**:101,
    297; **16**:399
  Edward **4**:459
  Hugh **14**:610
  John **12**:187
  Samuel **12**:540; **13**:419; **14**:146, 170
  William **11**:152, 157, 160-165, 167;
    16:335

BRADNON, --- **7**:417
BRADOCK, Abner **16**:38
  Francis **16**:38
BRADSHALL, Jno. **1**:174
BRADSHAW, James **1**:157, 161, 164
  John **1**:168, 517-518, 524
  Robert **11**:282, 363
  Saml. **2**:277
  Samuel **15**:478
  William **7**:405
BRADSTREET, --- (Col.) **7**:102
  Jn. **6**:412, 427-428, 446, 453
BRADY, --- (Lt.) **12**:435-436
  Andrew **14**:568
  John **10**:752; **11**:97; **16**:288
  Joseph **11**:313, 330, 479, 504
  Samuel **11**:578; **16**:464
  William **11**:41
BRAFT, John Sebastian **3**:386
BRAINES, Thomas **2**:100
BRAISER, Jacob **10**:705
BRAMHALL, Thomas **11**:513, 516
BRAND, --- **5**:471, 685-686
  George **15**:571, 576
  Hans Wilhelm **3**:454
  John **11**:136
  Michael **3**:455
  Samuel **3**:432
BRANDEL, Catherine **16**:463
BRANDEN, Thomas **10**:741
BRANDINGHAM, Robert **1**:559, 562,
  566, 578
BRANDON, James **13**:53
  John **16**:521
BRANDT, Nicholas **6**:291
  Samuel **10**:110
  Valentine **10**:110
BRANN, William **13**:727-728
BRANNAN, John **14**:613
BRANNON (BRANNAN), Benjamin
  11:219-220, 231, 242, 270, 282;
    12:651, 727; **13**:392, 415, 691,
    748; **14**:72, 512-513, 586;
    15:175, 198
  James **14**:615
  John **12**:188; **15**:347
BRANSCOME, Thom **1**:323
BRANSON, Abraham **16**:240
  Benjamin **14**:201
  Henry **15**:570
  Stout **13**:589
  Walter **3**:612
  William **4**:270-271; **9**:632
BRANT, Abram **6**:291
BRANTON, Moses **9**:657
BRASEY (BRASSY), Thomas **15**:63, 440
BRASSIE, Tho. **1**:263
BRASSY, Robert **1**:77
BRATELLI, Matteo **13**:720, 725, 727
BRATTELLI, Matteho **13**:735
  Matteo **13**:743
  Mattes **13**:704
BRATTON, William **10**:451; **11**:569,
  684; **13**:666
BRAUGH, Daniel **6**:648
BRAUUN, Johan Daniel **4**:59
BRAXTON, --- **12**:63-64
BRAY, George **14**:506
  James **15**:254
  John **11**:9, 35, 41, 44, 77, 105,
    109, 513, 516-517
BRAYMAN, Joseph **1**:443
BREADING, Nathaniel **16**:210b-212b,
  214b-223b, 226-227, 230-233,
  235-236, 238-244, 251-252,
  254-264, 267-274, 276, ->

BREADING, Nathaniel (continued)
16:278-291, 293, 295-306,
312-313, 406, 408-429, 432-435,
439, 441-442, 452, 454, 500-501,
507, 509-511, 513-528, 535-540,
543, 545-546
BREADY, Samuel 13:714
BREAKLE, David 14:506
BREARLY, David 13:3, 74, 474; 16:14
BRECHBEIL, Wendel 3:432
BRECHBIEL, Jacob 3:467
BRECHBIL, John 3:432
BRECHBILL, Bendu 3:467
Hans 3:467
Hans Peter 3:467
BRECHER, John Nicol. 3:386
BRECHT, Peter 10:100, 211, 270,
491, 560
BRECKLEY, David 12:399
BRECKLY, Christopher 3:432
David 15:499
Hans Jacob 3:432
Mathias 3:432
Ulrick 3:432
BREED, Gerhsam 9:571
BREENNER, Ralph 10:447
BREGELL, Friedrick 4:59
BREIDENHART, Christopher 11:18
BREINIG, George 14:629, 637; 15:363
BREINING, George 16:361
BRENAN, George 5:210
BRENHOLTZE, Christian 3:607
BRENINGHER, Conrad 14:468
BRENNAN, Amy 8:628
BRENNER, Hans Casper 3:515
BRENTAL (BRINTALL), Henry
11:381-382
BRERETON, --- 6:490
--- (Capt.) 2:148
--- (Mrs.) 6:522
BRETT, Robert 1:377, 381, 442-444
BRETZ, Jacob 12:601
BREUNINGER, Baltzer 3:520
BREWER, Elisha 15:502; 16:296
BREWSTER, --- (Capt.) 11:156
Sam. 11:297
BRIAN, --- (Col.) 10:675
Ann 12:776
Mary 9:666
BRIANT, Mary 12:663
BRICE, John 13:714; 14:298, 305,
429
Sarah 15:11
BRICKELL, Martin 14:611
BRICKER, Peter 3:455
BRIDGER, Leo. 11:151
BRIDGES, John 16:425
Robert 10:630, 659, 735; 11:80,
640, 748; 13:109, 320; 14:367,
587, 606
BRIDGMAN (See AVERIE) 1:510
BRIENT(U)ALL, Joseph 4:85, 247, 313
BRIENTNAL, Joseph 3:614
BRIETENBACH, Micahel 14:8
BRIG(G)S, Jno. 1:123, 164-165, 174
Samuel 16:88, 346
BRIGG, Jno. 1:104, 114
BRIGGS, --- (Mr.) 11:1
Anne 13:725
Charles 6:304
John 11:514, 516-517; 13:590, 725;
16:543
BRIGHT, Jacob 11:56, 536; 13:102,
183; 16:451
Joseph 15:155

BRIGHT, Michael 10:430, 491, 652;
14:480; 15:34, 84, 386
BRIGHT & SALTER 15:34
BRIGHTWELL, John 8:750
BRIGMAN, Ch. 13:327
BRIGS, John 10:753, 759
BRIHTON, Moses 11:213
BRIMM, Andreas 4:60
BRIMMER, Hans George 3:517
BRIN(C)KLOE, John 2:31, 34, 50,
129, 136
BRINCKLE, John 9:698
BRINCKLOE (BRINKLO), John 1:458,
481, 483-486, 488, 491, 493,
495, 500, 502, 504-505, 507-508,
601, 615; 9:173
BRINDLE, Jacob 11:386
John 11:385
BRINER, Johan George 3:455
BRINGHURST, James 10:701; 12:238
BRINGSTON, Andrews 1:48
BRINHARB, Peter 4:72
BRININGER, Frederick 14:421
BRINK, Henry 14:222-223, 320
John 14:224
William 14:167, 172, 311, 319-320,
495
BRINKER, Andreas 3:597
BRINKET, Thomas 1:80
BRINKHALTER, Peter 10:728
BRINKHURST, --- 15:93-94
BRINKLAIR, John 1:48
BRINKLAND, James 13:368
BRINKLE, John 6:136
BRINKLER, Joannes 3:367
BRINKLOE (BRUNKLOE), Jon. 1:158,
160-161, 168, 170, 179, 320,
322-326, 335-339, 342, 344-345,
418, 451
BRINKLOW, Jno. 1:83, 149
John 3:254
BRINKSON, Andrew 1:87
BRINSIUS, Geo. Mich. 3:386
BRINTELL, David 1:87
BRINTON (BRENTON), Caleb 14:471
Edward 5:572; 8:573; 9:205
Joseph 3:381; 4:279, 482; 5:387
Owen 5:3
BRISBANE, John 15:48
BRISHAN, John 10:447
BRISTELL, Hans Peter 3:515
BRISTOL, (Negro slave) 15:347
--- (Earl of) 10:103
Benjamin 11:159
James 10:778
BRISTOL (NEGRO SLAVE) 13:640
BRISTON, --- (Earl of) 9:761
BRISTOW, John 1:196-198, 203-206,
208-222, 224-229, 234, 258,
261-262, 266-267, 269-270, 272,
274-275, 277, 281-282, 285-286,
291-292, 298, 300-302, 304-305,
307, 310, 312, 317, 320-321,
324, 370, 375, 438
BRIT(T)ON, John 10:451, 562, 593,
612, 672, 705, 712, 754
Thomas 12:149, 202, 265; 15:542,
554
BRITAIN, James 13:369
Jesse 14:47
John 11:244
Joseph 12:405
BRITELMAN, Dolls. 3:385
BRITON, Thomas 16:483
BRITT, --- (Mr.) 16:503
Elizabeth 12:342

BRITT, Mary **13**:272
BRITT (BRETT), George **12**:342, 436
BRITTON, John **11**:33, 96; **12**:55;
   14:583
BROADES, William **13**:515
BROADHEAD, --- **6**:756-760, 764
 Charles **6**:751-754; **7**:322, 326, 328
 Daniel **5**:113, 388, 489-490, 573,
   736, 757, 774; **10**:442, 444, 448,
   629, 722, 727, 743, 749, 751,
   767; **11**:180, 457, 459, 519, 531;
   12:25, 31, 81, 84, 167, 173,
   215, 245, 286, 331, 346, 377,
   397, 435, 445, 470, 498, 530,
   586, 640, 735, 747; **13**:544, 643,
   715, 758; **14**:62-63, 85, 99, 126,
   190, 194, 414, 423, 435; **15**:383,
   458, 584
 Daniel, Jr. **16**:44, 138, 208, 210,
   214, 216, 224, 211b-212b,
   223b-224b, 225, 229, 231, 256,
   261, 280, 288, 292, 311, 317,
   385, 390, 461, 541
 Luke **11**:98
BROADLY, Paul **7**:242
BROADNAX, Thomas **14**:611
BROADSTOCK, William **14**:293, 300,
   415
BROADSTREET, --- (Col.) **7**:284
 John (Col.) **9**:193-194, 196-197,
   208-211, 213, 215-218, 221, 530
BROADWOOD, James **14**:81, 100, 432
BROCK, John **15**:63, 440, 478
 Ralph **15**:440, 478
 Rebecca **16**:421
 Rudolph **3**:517
 William (alias William SMITH)
   15:164
BROCK(E), Jon **1**:320, 375
BROCKDEN, --- (Mr.) **7**:464
 Charles **5**:345; **9**:397
BRODERICK, David **14**:190, 194, 415
BRODHEAD, Dan'l. **9**:206, 308, 746
 Daniel **6**:253-254
 Garret **9**:660, 732; **10**:50, 156
 Luke **16**:335
BRODIE, Alexander **16**:496
BRODY, Samuel **12**:632
BROKEN THIGH **6**:762, 779-780; **7**:64
BROMALL, --- (Mr.) **10**:684
BRONNER, Felix **3**:459
BROOK, John **13**:722
 Samuel **3**:486, 490
BROOK(E)S, Bowyer **11**:3, 494
BROOKE, Benjamin **10**:705
 Chidley **1**:401
 Edward **3**:246
 Henry **2**:99, 448; **3**:143-145, 147,
   156-158, 160, 162-163, 165, 225,
   228-229, 238, 240, 250-251,
   253-254, 256-259, 261, 263,
   269-270, 384, 389-390, 393, 395,
   399-400, 464, 467, 474, 478,
   491-492, 574, 577, 579, 585,
   588-589, 591, 594
 James **10**:706; **12**:483
 John **16**:122
BROOKE (BROOKS), Matthew **11**:21, 23
BROOKES, Edward **12**:553
 Jam. **1**:320
 John **11**:340
BROOKHOUSE, Rudolph **14**:163
BROOKS, --- **11**:315
 David **14**:155
 Edward **3**:218-219; **5**:29

BROOKS, John **10**:358-359, 361-362,
   367, 371-373, 378, 380, 385,
   403, 408-409, 451, 503, 698;
   12:411
 Jonathan **14**:562
 Joseph **14**:612
 Thomas **10**:496
 William **13**:624; **14**:84, 416; **16**:333
BROOKS (BROOKE), William **11**:328,
   330, 339
BROOM, Leonard **13**:757
BROOM (BROON), Leonard **14**:49, 430
BROOMHEAD, Josephus **14**:293, 300,
   416
BROOMS, Nicholas **15**:77
BROONBACK (BROOMBACK), Benjamin
   10:694, 705
BROSINGER, Johannes **4**:59
BROSIUS, Nicholas **14**:403, 486;
   15:40; **16**:92, 131, 369, 371-372
BROTHERS, Alice **12**:670
 John **16**:547
BROUCH, Johan Mathias **4**:60
BROUGHTON, Tho. **4**:166
BROUNWART, Matthias **3**:453
BROWER, Henry **12**:88-89
 John I. **14**:431
BROWLEE, Arthur **4**:102
BROWM(E), William **12**:110, 134, 164,
   185, 518, 525, 527, 559
BROWN, --- **11**:347; **15**:576
 --- (Adjutant) **10**:451
 --- (Capt.) **11**:278
 --- (Col.) **13**:222
 --- (Maj.) **13**:661
 --- (Mr.) **5**:304; **11**:185; **12**:186,
   754; **13**:369
 Alexander **8**:260; **11**:70; **13**:694
 Anderson **6**:419
 Andrew **15**:566; **16**:222b, 493
 Benjamin **11**:514, 516-517
 Christopher **3**:367
 David **7**:559; **11**:665; **12**:356
 Eleanor **16**:349
 Elijah **11**:283, 288, 296, 309, 460,
   472
 Esther **5**:384
 George **5**:210
 Henry **12**:627; **15**:294
 J. **11**:60
 James **5**:384; **6**:271-273; **10**:269,
   506; **11**:366, 515; **13**:118;
   14:297, 304, 308, 417; **16**:79,
   547
 Jeremiah **5**:385
 Johan Martin **3**:520
 John **1**:304; **6**:136; **10**:476; **11**:32,
   60, 153, 344-349, 394, 406-407,
   453, 459, 513, 516-517, 742,
   774; **13**:139, 283, 668, 755;
   15:423, 426-427, 432
 Jonathan **16**:258
 Jos. **13**:327
 Joseph **11**:753; **15**:8; **16**:283
 Joseph (Dr.) **13**:569; **14**:99, 427,
   506
 Leonard **14**:99
 Mary **11**:150; **13**:171
 Mercer **3**:256, 381
 Patrick **14**:298, 305, 428
 Peter **9**:469, 521; **10**:719, 750;
   11:19; **14**:227-228, 268
 Richard **10**:736, 766; **11**:43, 48,
   66, 134, 303
 Robert **13**:593, 723, 737; **14**:98,
   250, 418, 556; **15**:100

BROWN, Rudolph **3**:456
Samuel **5**:444, 469; **16**:283
Sarah **16**:310
Silvanus **13**:599
Sylvanus **14**:100, 432
Thomas **5**:210; **9**:508; **13**:14; **15**:8;
16:85, 210
William **5**:384; **9**:732; **10**:451, 456,
488, 504-505, 548, 596, 606,
687-688, 725, 752, 766, 775;
11:5, 22-23, 32, 229, 366,
418-419, 514, 516-517, 534, 633,
691; **13**:88, 110, 112, 133, 371,
393, 396, 415, 420, 425-426,
437, 722, 726, 737; **14**:101, 236,
250, 298, 305, 344, 413, 433,
485, 556, 577, 580-582, 584-592,
602-604, 606, 616-635, 638-643,
646; **15**:7-9, 11-12, 14-25,
28-33, 36-37, 39-42, 65-69,
72-76, 78-81, 84-93, 95-97, 99,
101-106, 128-170, 186-190,
193-195, 197-200, 202-204,
206-209, 211-222, 256-267,
269-285, 288-289, 291-292, 395;
16:168, 199, 224, 266, 538, 543
William (Dr.) **13**:755
BROWN & SHORTALL **16**:8, 121
BROWN(E), Daniel **1**:48, 322, 493
James **1**:207, 568, 580; **14**:554
John **14**:90, 124, 128-129, 154,
199, 234, 243, 382, 410, 435-436
William **13**:269
BROWNE, --- (Col.) **6**:272
--- (Gov.) **13**:524
Anne **13**:523
John **13**:565
Joseph **12**:85
Margaret **12**:225
Mary **12**:181, 773; **13**:565
Nathaniel **12**:391
Peter **15**:98
Samuel Montgomery **12**:664
Thomas **13**:153
William **13**:247, 270
BROWNFIELD, Robert **14**:654
BROWNLEE, James **16**:434
Joseph **11**:98, 181
BROWNLOW, --- (Capt.) **5**:281-282
BROXON, B. **10**:725
BROYLE, Philip **13**:674
BRUBAKER, John **3**:472
BRUCE, Alexander **15**:310
John **10**:668; **12**:5
BRUCKI, Jacob **3**:517
BRUDENELL, Ja. **4**:472-473, 475
BRUELASHER, Jacob **3**:328
BRULEMAN, Jno. **8**:506
BRUMMER, Jacob **3**:328
BRUNB, Johannes **4**:60
BRUNEAU, --- (Capt.) **5**:264
BRUNER, George **12**:70
Henry **3**:593
BRUNINGER, Veith **3**:414
BRUNNER, Daniel **15**:481
Hans Jacob **3**:417
Johan Henrich **4**:59
Paulus **4**:59
BRUNSON, Stout **14**:91, 425
BRUNTON, Elizabeth **16**:214b
BRUSLAM, Hugh **5**:104
BRUSTER, --- (Capt.) **11**:41, 47
BRUTON, Joseph **12**:188
BRYAN, --- (Judge) **13**:219
--- (Mr.) **13**:331
Charles, Sr. **5**:248

BRYAN, Edward **13**:710; **14**:193, 420
Francis **11**:464
George **9**:205, 288, 672, 699;
10:46, 610, 728; **11**:173-175,
177, 182, 184, 186-187, 195-197,
200, 202, 214-217, 219, 221-223,
225-226, 228-238, 241-243,
245-253, 255-265, 267-268,
270-278, 280, 282-283, 285-287,
290-295, 297, 300, 302-304, 306,
308-309, 311-312, 314-322,
357-376, 381, 383-385, 387-393,
395-396, 398-400, 402-403,
407-412, 414-415, 417-418, 425,
462-463, 468-472, 475-479, 481,
486, 488-490, 492, 495, 497,
499, 501-503, 506, 508, 512,
518-520, 522, 526-531, 533-536,
539, 541-548, 550-554, 556-567,
569, 571-574, 576-596, 598-600,
606-609, 612-620, 622-626,
628-639, 641-653, 655-667,
672-674, 676-680, 682-685,
690-691, 693-694, 696-699, 701,
710, 714-724, 727-728, 732-733,
735, 738, 740-741, 743-744, 745,
747-749, 751-762, 764, 766-767,
769, 771, 773, 775-776, 778-779,
781, 783; **12**:1, 3-5, 7-11,
16-17, 31, 33-35, 37, 39-40,
42-46, 48-50, 55, 60, 62-64,
66-71, 73-74, 76-77, 79, 92-94,
100-102, 104, 106-109, 111-114,
117, 119, 121, 123-131, 156,
159-160, 164, 173, 177, 186,
200, 211, 213, 232, 250, 275,
303, 305, 367, 409, 423, 428,
470, 704, 726, 772; **13**:3, 215,
220, 228, 231, 372, 500, 513,
543, 578; **14**:42, 117, 123, 135,
210, 276, 543, 607, 668; **15**:45,
56, 89, 114, 138, 189-190, 204,
211, 220, 237, 248, 256, 260,
265, 281, 360, 379, 419, 452,
479, 501, 505, 507, 549, 561,
619, 631, 636; **16**:39, 55, 87,
105, 114, 128, 161, 165, 171,
232, 240, 312, 389, 448, 465,
546
Jacob **6**:293
James (See O'BRYAN) **11**:645
Joel **11**:513, 516-517
John **10**:100, 211, 270; **12**:2;
13:608; **14**:97, 425; **15**:140
Justice **13**:614, 619
Mary **12**:590
Philip **13**:748
Samuel **13**:22; **14**:163, 211-212
Thomas **14**:603
BRYAN (See MC NAMAIRA), Morgan O.
15:27
BRYANT, --- **14**:1-8, 112
Rebecca **12**:494
BRYCE (BRICE), John **10**:464, 501,
760; **13**:582; **14**:126, 418;
16:298-299
BRYSON, James **11**:476
Samuel **13**:624, 716; **14**:101, 437
BRYSON (BRISON), James **15**:548, 550
BU(C)KLEY, Sam **1**:84-88
BUCHANAN (BUCHANNAN), --- (Capt.)
12:355
--- (Mr.) **7**:231
Alexander **10**:129
Arthur **3**:612-613; **4**:135; **11**:506;
12:322

23

24

BURCHILL, William **13**:778; **14**:133, 438
BURCKHOLTER, Ulrich **3**:432
BURCORT (BURKHORT), Philip **6**:170-171
BURD (BIRD), --- (Maj.) **7**:161, 281, 436, 453, 550, 597, 619, 622, 734, 736, 772
--- (Mr.) **16**:335
Benjamin **13**:730; **16**:239, 315
Edward **11**:566, 603, 605, 631; **13**:183, 532; **14**:482, 628-629; **15**:44, 160, 226, 237, 262, 282, 302, 328, 379, 392, 398, 413, 432, 459, 494-495, 577, 623; **16**:17, 68, 114, 122-123, 192, 232, 276, 350, 544
James **4**:7; **9**:27, 29-30, 59, 61, 172, 419, 438, 603, 673; **6**:131, 369, 377, 397, 402, 404, 431, 433-437, 452-453, 460, 466-467, 476, 484-485, 493, 498-499, 502, 515, 555, 641, 667, 730, 733
James (Col.) **8**:234, 310, 776-778
John **11**:214, 282, 363, 379, 455, 493, 610-611, 633, 742, 773; **12**:147, 164, 400, 544, 631, 740, 754
BURDEN, David **11**:156
J. R. **1**:16
BURDESWAY, Vandel **10**:739
BURDIN, Charles **14**:312
BURDINE, John **15**:124-125
BURFORD, George **16**:51, 76, 146
BURG, Conrad **16**:334
BURGARDT, Jacob **16**:535
BURGE, --- (Mr.) **5**:235, 245
David **11**:610-612; **13**:361
Samuel **12**:612
BURGER, Martin **3**:386
Nicholas **3**:524
BURGES, James (alias STENCHEON) **14**:477
BURGESS, Elizabeth **13**:87
Ellis **14**:507, 526, 536
William **16**:295
BURGH, Conrad **14**:64, 130, 433
John **11**:444
BURGHALTER, Ulrick **3**:519
BURGHART, Johan Frederick **3**:457
Jurig **3**:456
BURGIN, Elizabeth **12**:106
BURGOYNE, --- (Gen.) **13**:432
BURH, John **15**:637
BURINOL (BURINAL), --- **8**:311-312
BURK, Frederick **6**:170-171
William **9**:571
BURK (BANKS), Sarah **11**:161-162, 164-165
BURK(E), Benjamin **5**:232, 246, 255, 262-263
BURKART (BURKHARD), Andrew **11**:128, 602
BURKE, Boudes **12**:13, 21
Edmund **13**:758; **14**:84, 90, 425, 433
Edward **12**:534, 587, 774
Esther **10**:4694, 710; **11**:21
James **14**:407-408, 439
John **10**:668, 721; **11**:423-424, 610-612; **12**:673; **13**:272
Thomas **14**:292, 299, 415
BURKELOE, Samuel **9**:334
BURKET, John **16**:482
Rachel **11**:584
BURKETT, John **11**:610

BURKHALTER (BURKHOLDER), --- (Mr.) **15**:533
Peter **12**:298; **14**:250, 270, 556
BURKHARD, Carolus **3**:518
Daniel **10**:634, 649
David **3**:518
Hans **3**:518
BURKHART, Martin **13**:271
Nicholas **13**:207
BURKHOLDER (BUCKHOLDER), Peter **11**:365, 451, 525; **13**:102; **15**:90, 100, 168
BURKON, Henry **9**:509
BURLEY, Henry **12**:53
Thos. **2**:24
BURN, James (See JONES, Philip) **15**:80, 206
BURN(E)S, James **14**:292-293, 299-300, 414
BURNE, Michael **5**:155, 158, 163
Patrick **5**:155, 158, 163
BURNE (BYRNE), Laughlin **14**:97, 424
BURNES, Robert **11**:163
BURNET, Charles **11**:152
John **11**:514, 516-517
William **3**:119, 134, 136, 203-204
BURNEY, Hugh **15**:412
Thomas **5**:599-601, 635
Thomas (alias Thomas JOHNSON) **12**:87, 89, 267, 272
BURNHOLDER, Peter **13**:91
BURNIAN, Jno. **2**:102
BURNIE, John **13**:599; **14**:90, 413
BURNS, --- **5**:573
Alexander **16**:38
Andrew **14**:608
Francis (John) **16**:187
George **11**:513, 516-517; **13**:687-688
James **13**:647; **16**:189
John **15**:32
Joseph **12**:469
Larry **12**:275-276
Lazarus **14**:612
Levi **13**:638
Levy (Levi) **14**:86, 425
Mary **13**:72
Robert **10**:765
Samuel **13**:204
Thomas **11**:513, 516, 518
Timothy **13**:562; **14**:611
William **14**:475
BURNSIDE, James **5**:729; **16**:137
BURQUETT, Bastian **14**:541
BURR, Hudson **11**:610
BURRALL, Jonathan **12**:382; **14**:28
BURREES, Thomas **11**:109
BURRELL, Benjamin **13**:441
BURROUGHS, John **3**:356
Samuel **14**:357
BURROW(E), Samuel **11**:514, 516-517
BURROWS, Jeremiah **11**:7
John **3**:81; **10**:225, 227; **13**:594
Lawrence **13**:548
Samuel **13**:594
BURSON, Andrew **14**:361
BURT, Esther **3**:285
John **3**:285-287, 313-314, 326
BURTLE, David **11**:152
BURTLES, Ann **12**:482
BURTON (BURTEN), --- (Col.) **6**:488-490
Anthony **2**:596; **3**:28
Benjamin **9**:203; **10**:81, 217
Jno. **1**:84
Robert **1**:601; **11**:59, 190
Robt. **2**:129

BURTON (BURTEN), William **15**:310
Woolsey **3**:254, 259, 270
BURY (BERRY), Christian **3**:432
Jacob **16**:439, 510
BUSBIE (BUZBY), Richard **1**:500, 502
BUSBY, --- (Lt.) **12**:207
Benjamin **12**:333; **13**:569; **14**:97,
419
BUSBY (BUZBY), Richard **3**:218-219
BUSH, --- (Capt.) **10**:563
Charles **5**:194
David **5**:194, 234; **7**:405, 559
George **11**:488; **13**:717; **14**:84, 88,
402, 413, 416, 418, 421, 431
Henry **15**:640; **16**:192
Johan Jacob **4**:72
John **12**:356; **13**:202, 456, 714;
15:122
Lewis **10**:451
Mathias **12**:185, 525
Matthias **11**:268, 276
Solomon **11**:240; **12**:140, 151, 187,
537, 604, 753; **13**:567; **14**:126,
396, 410, 511, 571
BUSHE, --- (Capt.) **7**:283
BUSK, William **9**:571
BUSKIRK, --- (Capt.) **13**:189
BUSS, Jacob **12**:140
Johan Jacob **3**:452
BUSSE(E), --- (Capt.) **7**:302, 658;
8:140
BUSSEY, Christian (Dr.) **6**:760
BUSTEED (BUSTEAD), Morgan **10**:298,
412, 438-439, 462, 500, 622-623,
641
BUTCHER, John **11**:513, 516-517;
12:447,621
Jonathan **10**:713
Martin **14**:430
Zach **4**:185
BUTLER, --- **13**:603
--- (Capt.) **7**:128
--- (Col.) **10**:445; **13**:608, 657
--- (Lord) **15**:193, 300, 577;
16:17, 204-205, 209-212,
214-216, 218-220, 222-224,
209b-212b, 214b, 267-274, 276,
278-291, 293, 295-307, 309-313,
315-316, 318, 320-321, 386,
388-390, 392-396, 399-406,
408-409, 412, 414, 427-429,
432-435, 439, 441-442, 445-447,
449-456, 458-459, 461-465,
477-478, 496-501, 507, 509-525,
527-528, 534-535, 537-540, 543,
545
--- (Lt.) **6**:609-610; **11**:42, 451
--- (Mr.) **13**:2
Anthony **11**:245, 279, 303; **12**:139;
15:478, 541, 554, 634, 651, 653;
16:5, 300
Benjamin **5**:209
Charles **1**:386
Edward **13**:591, 716; **14**:85, 608
James **13**:643; **14**:84, 415
Johannes **4**:60
John **9**:280, 497; **11**:490; **13**:745;
14:153; **15**:119, 138
Joseph **15**:571, 576
Patrick **13**:602; **14**:92, 419
Percival **13**:716; **14**:609
Richard **11**:143, 180, 267, 465,
468, 492, 550, 555, 690, 732;
12:10, 37, 255, 428, 596;
13:418, 425, 503-504, 654, 717;
14:126, 165, 431; ->

BUTLER, Richard (continued) **15**:551,
553, 555, 582, 598, 604-606,
618; **16**:36-37, 45, 95, 177, 372,
375, 423-424, 502, 508, 537
Sarah **15**:624-625
Simon **4**:313, 482; **5**:3, 209, 388,
573; **6**:638; **7**:437
Thomas **14**:61, 85, 439; **15**:442,
481, 485
Walter **5**:624; **13**:304
William **11**:179-180; **13**:604, 668,
713; **14**:92, 300, 373, 419, 608;
15:42, 73, 512, 598, 602; **16**:45,
308
Zebulon **9**:675, 677, 682, 767-771;
10:151, 153-154, 274; **13**:763;
14:120; **15**:193, 264, 325, 484,
489, 493, 505, 526, 577
Zebulun **16**:29, 317, 464
BUTLER & POTTS **10**:770
BUTRICK, Nancy **14**:173
BUTTENGER, Nicholas **10**:690
BUTTERWORTH, Jno. **1**:131
BUTTLER, William **10**:447, 449
BUXTON, John **13**:778; **14**:126, 410;
16:333
BUYERS, --- (Mr.) **13**:121, 492, 494
John **12**:305, 491; **13**:446-447, 493,
638, 686; **14**:116, 120, 319-320,
493, 538
BUZBY (BUZBIE), John **1**:332, 380
BUZZARD, Frederick **13**:520; **14**:34
BY(L)E, Nathaniel **2**:520, 543
BYARD, Samuel **16**:363
B(A)YARDS, John **7**:637; **9**:201, 417
BYER, Casel **14**:600
Hans Melchior **4**:60
BYER(S), Andrew **11**:267-268
BYERLE, Johan Jacob **3**:459
BYERLY, Frederick **14**:64, 87, 418
BYERS, --- (Mr.) **6**:436; **13**:123,
125, 128, 131-133, 135-138, 140,
142-143, 145, 147-150, 157,
159-160, 162-164, 166-175,
177-182, 186-188, 195-196, 198,
200-201, 203, 205-208, 210-211,
214-216, 218-219, 221, 222-223,
228, 231, 313, 317-319, 323-326,
328-332, 334-343, 345, 347-348,
350-360, 362, 385-386, 388, 390
Jno. **9**:487, 673, 704, 732
John **11**:107, 365; **13**:120, 133,
152-153, 185, 217, 227, 360,
410, 585-589, 591-592, 594-595,
597-603, 605-607, 609-611, 613,
615, 617-623, 625-628, 630-635,
637-641, 645-647, 666, 668, 670,
761-763, 766, 768, 771-776;
14:1-2, 6, 8-9, 11, 25-29,
32-33, 36-38, 41-60, 65-71;
16:395
BYLES, Daniel **5**:135
Samuel **13**:599
Thomas **10**:447; **13**:596; **14**:125, 430
Wm. **1**:179, 181-183 (See Biles)
BYRD, --- (Col.) **8**:297
BYRN, Thomas **10**:713
BYRN(E)S, James **14**:306, 435
BYRNE, James **15**:245
Laughlin **13**:586
Michael **9**:497
Redman **13**:193
BYRNES, James **12**:730; **13**:235
BYRON, Eleanor **16**:417
BYSON, Samuel **16**:183, 211b

CABLE, Abraham **11**:303, 716; **15**:24;
   16:533
 John **11**:514, 516-517
CABOT, Sebastian **6**:100
CACAWICHI(C)KY **4**:747
CACHANATKREKA **6**:568
CACHAWATSIKY **4**:648-649
CACHKAWATCHIKY **6**:160
CACHRADODON **5**:686
CACHYACKO **6**:291
CACKAWATCHEKY **5**:351-352
CACOWATCHIKE (CACOWATCHICO) **4**:336,
   588
CADARIANIAHA **5**:317
CADARIANIRKA **5**:318
CADENHEAD, John **13**:755, 760, 764
CADERMAN, Jacob **6**:704
CADSEDAN-HIUNT **5**:438
CADWALADER (CADWALLADER), John
   3:107; **10**:260, 282-288, 290-292,
   294, 296-301, 312-315, 323,
   328-336, 338-341, 343-344, 347,
   351-353, 357-358, 360, 362-363,
   365, 367, 371, 373-375, 377,
   379-382, 384, 386-390, 395-396,
   398-403, 406-407, 412, 415-417,
   419-421, 438-439, 441-443,
   445-448, 451-453, 455-460,
   464-465, 467-477, 481, 483,
   505-507, 509, 511, 515, 517,
   519-521, 525-527, 543, 548, 554,
   557, 559, 566-567, 570, 572-575,
   577-578, 580, 582-583, 585-586,
   589, 594, 607-608, 610-615,
   628-629, 631-632, 635-637, 642,
   749, 754, 768; **11**:26-27, 29, 62,
   65, 104, 199; **16**:184
 Lambert **10**:281, 444-445, 767;
   11:94, 110, 112, 114, 131, 137,
   143, 179-180, 300, 495
 Robert **10**:442
 Thomas **7**:18, 33, 37, 46, 55-56,
   58-61, 64, 70, 78, 83, 87,
   96-97, 110, 120, 122, 130, 135,
   151, 153, 163, 186, 192, 202,
   220, 236, 246-247, 249, 251,
   256-257, 265-266, 296, 305, 354,
   361, 374, 391, 393, 401, 403,
   406-407, 409-410, 412, 416, 429,
   441, 443, 459, 463-465, 468,
   484, 495, 552, 560, 595, 618,
   637, 714, 716-718, 722-723, 727,
   734, 739, 750, 759, 776; **8**:19,
   24, 26, 35, 37, 40, 42, 58,
   63-64, 66, 70, 77, 79-81, 86,
   89, 100, 101, 112, 116, 124-125,
   139, 146, 161-162, 223-224,
   231-232, 236, 259, 263, 269,
   288, 297, 299, 301, 304, 315,
   319, 323, 329, 337, 339, 342,
   347, 353, 357, 360, 362, 372,
   397-398, 402, 407, 409, 630,
   655, 665, 670, 677, 713, 715,
   719, 721; **9**:23, 25, 30-31,
   36-37, 44, 77, 100, 123, 128,
   132, 135, 146, 170, 172-173,
   188, 192, 201-202, 205-206, 235,
   238, 316, 389, 392, 547-548,
   602-603, 704, 733, 735, 737,
   739, 745-746, 752, 759-760, 767,
   776-778, 782; **16**:184

CADWALADER (CADWALLADER), Thomas
   (Dr.) **6**:666, 670, 672, 685, 688,
   696, 711, 728-729, 742-743, 751,
   755-756, 762, 765, 769-770, 773,
   776, 778; **10**:1, 45, 90, 111,
   180, 452, 458
CADY, Zebulon **15**:489, 603, 628
 Zebulun **16**:11
CAERIEJAS (CARILJAS), Francisco
   (Don) **8**:234-235
CAGER, Richard **4**:468
CAGHERA, Canrach **8**:457
CAGLE, Anthony **16**:106-107
CAGNELIN, Deitrich **4**:72
 Jean **4**:72
 Sebastien **4**:72
CAGONGSANIYONG **3**:271
CAHESHCAROWANOTO (CAHESHCAROWNO)
   4:660-662, 778
CAHEY, John **11**:91
CAHICHTODO **3**:439
CAHOON, George **5**:441-442
CAHUWASEY **5**:685
CAIN, James **14**:64, 88, 428, 615
 John **14**:193, 415; **16**:512
CAINER, Michael **13**:63
CAINLATE, John **14**:190
CAIRL, Margaret **13**:283
CAIRNS, Christopher **12**:252
CAJADIES **5**:136
CAJUA SACHIM **5**:548
CAKAKEY **8**:723
CAKANONEKOANOS **8**:176
CAKUNDAWANNA **2**:547
CAL(L)HOON, William **14**:294, 301,
   427
CALAHAN, Daniel **10**:465
CALB, Martin **3**:329
CALBERTSON, --- (Capt.) **11**:99
CALDER **3**:550
CALDER, James **6**:174
CALDWELL, --- **14**:637
 --- (Mr.) **14**:621
 Andre **12**:324-325
 Andrew **4**:109; **9**:203, 339; **10**:9,
   456, 480, 489, 494, 496,
   519-520, 571, 581, 587, 651;
   13:100, 153, 389, 561, 718;
   14:409, 440; **15**:606
 Charles **11**:446-447, 488
 David **11**:633, 664
 J. **11**:702
 James **9**:689, 778; **10**:574; **13**:306,
   309, 320; **15**:43
 John **4**:152; **13**:328, 368, 597, 744
 Nicholas **14**:614
 Noble **14**:107, 111
 Robert **11**:751; **13**:555; **14**:90, 428
 Samuel **11**:299, 309, 394; **12**:137,
   465, 591, 630, 689; **13**:279-281,
   325, 328, 764; **14**:4, 68, 105,
   241, 403; **15**:116, 322, 417, 434,
   473, 558; **16**:114, 364, 461
 Sarah **15**:606
 William **3**:615; **4**:86, 247, 309;
   10:778; **11**:515-517
CALDWELL (SEE MEASE &) **11**:10,
   47-50-52, 54, 56, 60-61, 64-66,
   88-89, 119, 683; **12**:679
CALE, Lodowick **6**:171
CALEB, Caleb **2**:45
CALENDER, --- (Mr.) **6**:46
 Apt. **8**:455
CALGAN, Richard **13**:680
CALHAGHEHEROT **3**:45
CALHOON, Alexander **14**:157

CALHOON, George 12:17
  James 14:297, 304, 412, 612
CALHOON (CALHOUN), Andrew 9:201,
  487, 673, 732
CALHOUN (CALHOON), George 11:2, 15
CALL, Christopher 12:92
  Eb'r. 10:333
  William 12:92
CALLADY, William 13:737
CALLAGHAN, Edward 13:679
  William 14:533; 15:119
CALLAGHER, Edward 14:425
CALLAHAN, Edward 14:96
  William 14:637
CALLAR, Carles 3:386
CAL(L)ENDAR (CAL(L)ENDER), --- 7:60
  Robert 5:614, 628, 660, 669, 684,
  701; 9:201, 269, 275, 302-303,
  673; 10:101, 718, 736-737, 739,
  768 (See CELLANDER)
  William 7:148-150, 391, 394-395,
  397-398, 637, 760
CALLING, Geo. 1:83
CALOIN, Stephen 8:616 (See CALVIN)
CALUSON, Laurence 3:86
CALVERT, Benedict 3:484
  Charles (Col.) 3:119, 180,
  212-213, 222, 224-225, 234
CALVIL, Thomas 4:698
CALVIN, Stephen 8:156, 176, 180,
  192, 196, 201, 209; 9:737
CALWELL, Samuel 10:400-402,
  405-406, 408, 415-416, 418-420,
  425-426, 429, 434-438, 440-441,
  445-446, 449, 452, 455, 457-459,
  462-468, 471-472, 478-481, 483,
  487-488, 491, 498-499, 503, 509,
  514, 518, 525, 529, 532, 550,
  687-688, 690, 710
CAM(M)ERON, Allen 10:444, 470, 595
CAM(P)BELL, Joseph 14:98, 433
CAMBDEN, --- (Lord) 10:157-159, 161
CAMBERS, --- (Mr.) 5:640
  John 11:340
CAMERER, Ludwig 4:59
CAMINCHODON 5:318
CAMMEL, Joseph 5:692-693 (See
  CAMPBELL)
CAMP, George 14:297, 304, 426
  John 13:676; 14:95, 425
  Joseph 14:295, 302, 433
CAMPBELL 3:369
CAMPBELL (CAMPBEL, CAMPBLE,
  CAMPLE), --- 7:504
--- (Capt.) 16:535
--- (Col.) 9:251
--- (Lt.) 12:545
--- (Maj.) 9:34
--- (Mr.) 12:534
--- (Widow) 13:555
Alexander 11:650
Archibald 11:474, 556, 563, 570,
  579; 14:611, 628
Arthur 11:514, 516-517
Charles 11:618; 12:372; 13:361;
  14:33; 15:172-173, 191, 353,
  396, 620; 16:367
David 10:230-232
Duncan 1:570; 10:377-378, 385-389,
  455, 462, 466, 468, 476, 481,
  618, 639-640
Forguard 10:581
Francis 6:699-700; 8:99, 128;
  9:201, 514; 15:122; 16:214

CAMPBELL (CAMPBEL, CAMPBLE,
  CAMPLE), George 11:45, 190, 195;
  12:137, 507, 573; 13:85, 87,
  112, 253; 14:110, 200, 266, 447,
  492; 16:443, 462
Isabella 13:254
James 5:444, 469; 6:675;
  8:290-291; 12:8, 684; 13:563,
  643, 716; 14:100, 124, 128-129,
  431-432, 434, 541; 16:155
John 6:481; 8:235; 9:414, 428,
  436, 470; 10:141; 11:223, 230,
  335, 610-613; 13:744; 14:30,
  541; 16:515
Joseph 5:692 (See CAMMEL); 13:638
Mary 11:577; 12:430-431
McClarey 13:769
Mich'l. 13:14
Michael 15:430
Patrick 14:237; 15:301
Peter 11:611, 745; 12:325,
  430-431; 13:52
Robert 10:765; 11:65; 12:166;
  13:555; 14:63, 85, 89, 422, 436;
  16:225, 495
Samuel 14:81, 99, 431
Thomas 11:418, 469, 740; 12:17,
  65, 74, 357, 572; 13:558, 714,
  777; 14:86, 125, 129, 214, 374,
  438, 609; 15:37, 141, 301, 592;
  16:32, 176, 215, 533
William 5:691-692, 694;
  11:610-612; 12:385, 493; 14:214;
  16:24
CANA-JA-CHANAH 5:438
CANACARADUCHQUA 5:686
CANACHQUAIESON 5:541-542
CANACHQUASY 5:166
CANACHQUAYESON 5:686
CANADAGAIA 6:74
CANADAGAYON 5:686
CANADAGEH 6:125
CANADAY, Arthur 10:707
CANADEHNIA 6:37-37
CANADIES, Moses 6:443, 551
CANADYORA 6:291
CANAJACHREESERA 5:686
CANAN, John 16:225, 528
CANASATEGO 7:432
CANASQUAGENERAT 3:598
CANASSATEGO 4:564, 566, 577-578,
  580, 660-664, 698-699, 702, 723,
  726-727, 731-732, 736-737, 778
CANASSETEGO (CANASSATEGO,
  CANASETEGO) 5:22, 24, 408, 467,
  474-476, 480, 485, 526, 542
CANATCHIOWANCY 5:685
CANATOWA 3:80
CANAWANGO 8:264
CANAWATO 6:126
CANBY, Joseph 11:514, 516-517
  Thomas 4:313; 11:514, 516-517;
  13:521; 15:613, 624
CANDLER, David 11:371
CANDOR, Joseph 5:247
CANDY, Jacob 15:196
CANE, --- (Capt.) 7:510
  Samuel 14:310
CANES, Wm. 1:118
CANFIELD, Samuel 9:571
CANHOLL, Edmund 1:57
CANIADAROGON 5:84
CANIGAATT 8:293
CANIUCKODON 5:317

CANN, John **1**:61, 96-97, 99-110,
116-117, 119, 121, 125-130,
132-133, 135, 137-140, 145-146,
148-149, 161-164, 169, 170-171,
173-174, 178-181, 189-190, 194,
197-199, 209-210, 212, 214-220,
222, 238-240, 258, 299, 320,
323-327, 330, 335-338, 340,
344-345, 369, 375, 384, 387,
390-391, 399, 404, 434-435, 437,
451
CANNATELLAN **3**:45
CANNAWATOE **3**:271
CANNEWAUNGH **8**:293
CANNON, --- (Mr.) **13**:512
 James **10**:653-660, 662, 664-666,
668, 670-672, 675, 678, 680,
682-683, 686-687, 689, 691-692,
694-698, 701, 704, 708, 710-711,
713-714, 716-718, 722-723,
725-278, 730, 735-742, 750, 753,
762, 764, 769; **11**:1-2, 4, 14,
16, 19, 22-30, 32-33, 36-37,
39-40, 42-45, 47-51, 53-55,
57-64, 66-69, 73, 76, 86-87,
92-93, 95, 286, 306, 325-326;
13:116, 121, 346
 Jane **13**:346
 Jeremiah **10**:264
 John **12**:610, 615, 681; **13**:134,
162, 265, 507-508, 584, 748;
14:224; **15**:109, 139, 300-301,
327-328, 331, 337-353, 356-365,
367-380, 483-488, 490-492,
494-506, 508-509, 512-518,
520-525, 527, 530-533, 539-545,
548-549, 600, 602, 604-608,
612-620, 622, 624-629, 632-658;
16:1-3, 32, 130-138, 141-146,
148-149, 151-152, 154-158, 160,
162-166, 168-169, 171-173,
175-178, 315, 428
 Michael **11**:513, 516-517
 Newton **12**:11-12
CANNUGHSKAYA **3**:608
CANON, John **4**:655
 William **3**:472, 476
CANT, Tho. **8**:517
CANTARRAGHENGRAT **3**:271
CANTERBURY, --- (Archbishop of)
8:438, 552, 557
 Bishop of **6**:264
CANTLER, David **12**:145
CANTUAR, Tho. **5**:360
CANTWELL, Edmund **1**:58-65, 72-73,
76-77, 79-82, 105-110, 113-116,
118-121, 139
 Richard **1**:521, 601; **3**:270; **10**:81,
217
CANTYUCKQUA **5**:317
CANUCKRACAYINK **6**:588, 590
CANUSTA, Abraham **5**:644
CANUSTU, --- **5**:685
CANYASE **7**:296-298
CANYENQUILIQUOA **5**:685
CANYINGOE INDIANS **13**:469
CAPACHPITON **6**:649
CAPEHART, George **10**:700
CAPP, Georg. Frederick **3**:452
CAPPER, John **3**:468-469, 472, 476;
4:111, 135
CAPT. JOHN **9**:103, 212-213, 226
CAPTAIN JOHN **7**:507
CAR(E)Y, Nathan **15**:193, 300, 484,
489; **16**:196, 496

CAR(R)OTHERS (CARITHERS, CROTHERS,
SEE CARUTHERS), John **11**:74, 119,
272, 358, 772
CARAWTAWSEY **4**:501
CARBERRY, --- (Capt.) **12**:347;
13:665
 Christopher **16**:281
 Henry **13**:613, 617
CARBERRY (CARBURY), Henry **14**:61,
99, 105-106, 240-241, 423, 611
CARCASS, Conrad **14**:296, 303, 410
CARE, Conrad **6**:760
CARET, James **10**:142
CAREY, Edward **10**:229
 Matthew & Co. **15**:25, 139
CARIOLANUS, --- **10**:358, 362
CARITHERS, John **10**:756
CARITHERS (CARUTHERS), James **9**:201,
673
CARL, Jacob **3**:415
 Simon **4**:72
CARLE, Hans Michal **4**:72
CARLETON, --- (Gen.) **13**:680
 Joseph **13**:315
 Neal **14**:671
CARLIN, Edward **11**:719
CARLISLE, Abraham **11**:482-485, 600,
603-607, 613-614, 745; **12**:38,
688; **13**:5, 6
 Alexander **13**:250, 305; **14**:363,
666; **15**:33; **16**:387
 James **6**:751
CARLZ, Simon **3**:452
CARMECKLE, John **6**:758
CARMICHAEL, --- (Mr.) **15**:632;
16:144
 James **11**:621; **13**:118
 John **10**:724, 726; **11**:373, 377;
15:62; **16**:538
 John F. **15**:498
 Thomas **15**:464
CARNA(G)HAN, James **14**:91, 134, 425,
610
CARNAGAN, John **11**:180
CARNAGHAN, --- (Col.) **13**:491
 --- (Mr.) **13**:385, 427
 James **5**:210; **11**:98
 John **13**:426, 444
CARNAHAN, James **13**:716
 John **5**:602; **12**:182; **13**:157, 372,
415, 419; **14**:457
CARNAHAN(S), James **11**:67, 120, 526
CARNAUGHAN (CARNAHAN, CARNAGHAN),
John **10**:142, 212, 235-236, 273
CARNER, John **14**:81
CARNES, William **16**:215b
CARNEY, --- **13**:338-339
 John **14**:191, 195, 434
CARNIGHAN, James **13**:553
CARNON, John **11**:114
CARNWELL, Francis **1**:186
CARONDOWANA (CARANDOWANA) **3**:295,
334, 337, 435, 572 (See HUNTER)
CARONIO, Stephen **10**:579, 586
CAROTHERS (CARUTHERS), --- **13**:503
 --- (Mr.) **13**:673; **14**:24, 31, 53
 Anthony **16**:1
 James **14**:95, 419, 615
 John **12**:4, 93-94, 100, 721;
13:396, 415, 698, 726, 737;
14:407-408, 438, 445; **15**:90
CARPENTER, --- (Widow) **2**:595
 Ann **13**:319
 Anne **14**:593-594
 Benjamin **11**:418-419
 Benjamin **15**:212, 450

29

CARPENTER, Christian **13**:512
Daniel **11**:96
Emanuel **4**:152, 248, 267, 272, 313,
  483; **5**:3, 378, 600; **8**:562;
  9:172, 419, 673, 680; **10**:73;
  12:134, 508; **13**:292; **14**:556,
  563; **15**:1, 98
Jacob **9**:589, 591; **10**:692, 698;
  12:134, 331, 395, 508; **13**:88
Jasper **10**:645; **11**:149-152, 156,
  159
John **10**:678, 765
Joshua **1**:185, 380, 382, 559;
  2:172, 320, 397, 411; **13**:140
Saml. **1**:95, 99, 112, 123, 146,
  149, 161-163, 185, 210-236, 238,
  246, 252-254, 257, 262, 266-270,
  272-274, 277-279, 282, 284-286,
  290-292, 294-296, 298, 300, 302,
  304-307, 310, 312, 317, 319,
  321, 327, 341, 343, 371, 382,
  416, 418, 421, 426, 454, 469,
  475, 479, 481-486, 488, 491,
  507, 509, 513-521, 524, 526-527,
  531, 536, 539, 541, 546-547,
  553, 555, 559, 561, 563, 565,
  567-568, 571, 573, 575-576, 578,
  581-584, 586-587, 589, 591-593,
  595-596, 601, 611-612; **2**:9,
  11-13, 18-22, 24-27, 29-30,
  32-34, 36-37, 39-40, 43, 45-49,
  51-55, 60-62, 65-71, 74-75,
  78-79, 81, 86-91, 94-98, 101,
  103-104, 111-112, 114-120, 122,
  124-125, 129, 132, 134-136,
  144-145, 152-158, 161, 164-165,
  179, 182, 204, 223, 226, 232,
  236-237, 240-244, 247, 251, 259,
  262, 289, 297, 308-309, 315-316,
  318, 321, 323, 328, 336-337,
  356-357, 364-365, 372-373,
  377-378, 381-383, 391-393,
  396-397, 403-404, 409, 412-414,
  416, 426-429, 432, 434-435, 437,
  439, 441, 443-444, 446, 449,
  451-452, 459, 461, 463, 466,
  486, 494, 502, 506, 516, 518,
  520, 522, 524-526, 528-532,
  534-543, 546, 550-552, 559-565,
  597
Samuel **3**:50
Thomas **11**:91; **15**:577
William **4**:102; **15**:571, 576
CARR, --- (Mr.) **12**:350-351
Benjamin **16**:308
Elizabeth **8**:628
James **11**:286
John **11**:61, 281, 541; **12**:136-137,
  510; **13**:86, 589, 667;
  14:407-408, 439
Mary **11**:770
Thomas **14**:312
William **5**:247
CARRADEN, William **14**:575
CARRAGHAN, Dennis **12**:329
CARRAL, John **16**:480
CARREL (CARROLL), John **14**:227
CARRELL, William **5**:444
CARRINGTON, --- (Lt. Col.) **12**:761
CARROL(L), Dennis **14**:61, 90, 413
CARROLL, Charles **9**:376
John **14**:608
CARRON (CARSON), Benjamin **14**:93,
  427
CARRUP & FULLERTON **10**:314
CARSON (CARSAN), --- (Mr.) **16**:218

CARSON (CARSAN), Andrew **11**:82, 244;
  14:49, 53, 69, 183; **16**:466
Benjamin **14**:64
Daniel **15**:576
Ebenezer **12**:705, 718; **13**:236, 562,
  623; **14**:97, 409
Hamilton **5**:601-602
James **10**:505; **11**:544; **13**:385;
  16:85
John **5**:762; **6**:132, 653, 762-763;
  7:772-773, 775; **8**:71, 99;
  11:261, 739; **12**:8-9, 16, 19,
  166, 278, 318; **14**:259; **16**:444
Joseph **10**:660, 750; **11**:23, 27, 36,
  77, 397, 462, 476, 630, 670,
  673, 696; **12**:256, 507; **13**:52,
  126, 544; **15**:13, 445; **16**:40,
  210, 466
Samuel **8**:59; **11**:750-751; **12**:687;
  13:631; **14**:192, 611
William **11**:244, 286
CART, Joshua **1**:208
Saml. **2**:106, 520
Samll. **1**:564-565
CART (SEE MC CART), John M. **11**:515,
  517-518, 593
CARTER, --- **12**:63-64
--- (Mr.) **10**:696
Asher **13**:562; **14**:91, 410, 422
Christopher **10**:358, 360, 371-372,
  397, 455
Edward **13**:196
Henry **12**:273
James **10**:367, 650, 761; **11**:61,
  111, 273, 297, 311; **13**:679;
  14:95, 424
John **3**:372; **4**:102; **14**:190, 194,
  438
Mary **15**:430
Robert **1**:547-548, 568
Robt. **2**:106
William **2**:66, 410; **3**:106-107, 111;
  15:430
Wm. **1**:82, 141, 191, 195, 211
CARTER & BAKER **11**:494
CARTER (SEE DEHAVEN &) **10**:782
CARTERET, George (Sir) **6**:556
CARTIE, John **16**:333
CARTLIDGE, Edmund **3**:146, 148,
  150-152, 154-157, 162, 167, 170,
  186, 191-192, 263, 459, 507
CARTLIDGE (CARTLE(D)GE), John **3**:15,
  43, 45, 48, 50, 78, 80-81, 86,
  92-93, 114, 120, 123, 125, 130,
  134, 137, 146, 148, 150-157,
  162, 165, 167, 170, 186,
  189-192, 198
CARTWRIGHT, George **6**:263
Philip **14**:294, 301, 417
CARTWRIGHT (CORTWRIGHT), Elisha
  14:311, 495
CARUNTODON **5**:685
CARUTHER, William **11**:65
CARUTHERS (CAROTHERS), James **7**:637;
  12:776; **13**:679
John **11**:444, 489, 491, 497, 506,
  520, 524, 538; **13**:696
CARVEL, Marlon **11**:642
CARVER, Jno. **1**:521
Nathan **11**:494
Nicolas **3**:368
Richard **3**:158, 177-178
CARY, Joseph **10**:736
Miles **1**:394
CASDROP (CASDORP), --- (Maj.)
  13:661

CHAMBERLAIN(E), Hugh 15:442, 481,
485
CHAMBERLAINE, Charles 12:669
James 12:393; 13:28; 14:592
CHAMBERLANE, Richard 12:535
CHAMBERLEN, Hugh 1:29
CHAMBERLIN, Jacob 4:224
James 10:715
John 11:219
CHAMBERS, --- 9:584
--- (Mr.) 7:497
A. Gaasbesk 6:277
Benjamin 1:74, 86, 111, 152,
166-167, 189-190, 298, 330,
341-342, 478, 581; 5:210, 436,
441, 443; 6:131, 675-676;
12:355; 14:61, 89, 237, 425;
16:102
Benjamin, Jr. 15:120
David 11:231, 614; 14:429
James 11:180, 732; 13:710; 14:83,
91, 194, 208, 415, 440, 538;
15:120, 517
John 5:210; 6:57, 66-68, 72-73,
75, 82, 93, 100, 109-110; 12:8,
64, 120, 298, 391, 570; 13:702;
15:537; 16:65
Joseph 5:84, 87; 11:371
Maxwell 12:134, 301, 508; 13:514;
14:510, 520, 581
Robert 5:210, 436, 443; 6:131;
12:594
Rowland 14:581
Stephen 11:97, 105, 633, 726;
12:137; 13:722; 14:11, 16, 163,
213, 609; 15:636
Thomas 13:215
William 10:449, 729; 11:113, 583
CHAMERS, Stephen 10:756
CHAMNEY 3:486, 490
CHAMPAIGN, Charles 14:455
CHAMPAIGNE, Stephen 13:81
CHAMPION, Billy 9:426, 428, 430
CHANCE, Alexander 5:194
William 9:624
CHANCELLOR, William 16:456
CHANDLER, Eli 15:570
James 15:114
John 6:57, 65, 67-68, 73, 82
Joseph (John) 14:307-308
Thomas B. (Rev.) 10:359
CHAPMAN, --- (Capt.) 10:20
--- (Col.) 7:381
Abraham 3:241; 4:313, 363-364,
406, 523, 752; 5:3, 388, 573;
12:32; 13:543
Abram 11:213, 514, 516-517
Amos 11:514, 516-517
Benjamin 6:638; 7:266; 10:266
David 11:514, 516-517
George 11:154
James 10:474, 496, 516, 730;
13:691
John 3:587; 5:55, 120, 573, 577,
611; 6:305; 7:437; 8:577;
11:708; 15:30, 104, 406
Joseph 4:669, 748, 782; 15:644;
16:286
Nathan 8:566
Russ (Rup.) 6:548, 594
Samuel 11:514, 516-517; 12:400
William 13:543; 16:191, 490
CHAPMANS, William 15:296
CHARACHER (CARAGHER), Alexander
14:205, 438, 446
CHARLES 8:176

CHARLES, --- (Mr.) 9:174
George 15:122
King 9:126
Prince of Lorain 4:677
Robert 3:257, 506-507, 540, 544;
4:18-19, 75, 89; 8:501-502,
512-513, 554-555, 610; 9:10, 48,
50-51
Thomas 14:31, 486
CHARLES I, King 4:38; 7:276; 10:104
CHARLES II, King 2:56, 61, 243,
263, 267, 344, 369, 380, 619;
3:41, 63, 216; 6:207, 271, 448,
556; 7:276, 404; 8:409, 557;
10:122, 174; 14:513
CHARLES THE SECOND 1:17, 32, 42,
48, 132, 309, 403, 410, 473,
534, 537, 613
CHARLES THE SIXTH, Emperor 4:690
CHARLESTON 2:100
CHARLETON, John 5:444
CHARLEVOIX, --- (Father) 5:751, 758
CHARLTON, Arthur 4:102-103
Charles 14:191, 195, 414
Edward 4:101, 103
Henry, Jr. 4:102-103
Henry, Sr. 4:102-103
John, Jr. 4:101, 103
John, Sr. 4:101, 103, 228,
230-231, 251-252
Thomas, Jr. 4:102-103
Thomas, Sr. 4:101, 103
CHARTEER, Martin 2:533 (See
CHARTIER(E))
CHARTIER, --- 5:349, 352
P. 6:678
Peter 5:1-2, 24, 167, 311, 533
CHARTIER(E), Martin 2:182, 390, 403
(See CHARTEER)
CHARTIER(S), Peter 4:656, 757, 759,
780-781
CHARTIERE, Martin 3:22
Peter 3:459, 463
CHARTIR, Peter 8:475
CHASE, George 12:645
CHASTENOY(E), --- (Monsieur)
5:71-72, 78, 122, 131, 201
CHATHAM, John 10:339, 353, 740
CHATTAM, John 13:398
CHEAVER, Peter 3:501-503
CHEBRIS, Charles 14:638
CHEEKAQUETON 4:641
CHEEQUITTAGH 3:601, 603; 4:340
CHEESEMAN, Thomas 13:564
CHEF, Nicolas 5:556-557
CHEN(E)Y, Thomas 11:244, 321, 330,
360, 479, 504, 507
CHENEY, Thomas 12:298, 349; 13:546,
724; 14:226, 228, 238, 248, 264,
510, 555, 619, 647, 660
CHEQUITTAGH 2:15
CHERIGEA 6:493
CHERQUAVA, Hosea 5:201
CHERQUITTAGH 4:338
CHERRY, Ralph 14:146
Thomas 14:214
CHESNEY, Thomas 16:492
William 6:458; 11:330, 479, 504;
12:64, 688; 14:459, 462
CHESNUT, John 15:451
CHESTNUT, Sarah 12:197
CHESTON, Daniel 4:289, 291, 296
CHETWYND, G. 10:91
J. 3:74
CHEVALIER, James 16:446, 530
Jno. 10:591

CHEVALIER, John 9:440; 11:513,
516-517
Peter 9:672; 10:591
Peter, Jr. 8:22, 24, 573-574, 583
CHEVITT, --- (Dr.) 12:221
CHEW, --- (Mr.) 15:648
Benjamin 6:277, 670, 672, 680,
702, 714, 729, 742, 751, 769,
771, 773, 776, 778; 7:10, 18,
59, 64, 70, 74, 78, 83, 87, 93,
96, 110, 118, 137, 148, 151,
168, 172, 202, 204-207, 216,
222, 228, 230, 241, 246-247,
249, 251, 255-257, 264-267,
295-296, 338, 344, 346, 349,
354, 356, 364, 367, 370, 383,
391, 393, 396-397, 400-401, 403,
407, 409-410, 412-413, 416, 429,
433-434, 437, 441, 443, 459,
463-465, 468, 484, 495, 497,
500, 517-518, 522, 558, 565,
622, 635, 637, 649, 652, 656,
660, 663, 665, 671, 679-680,
687, 692, 694, 716, 723, 729,
732, 734, 739, 750, 753, 757,
759, 776, 780-781; 8:1, 11, 19,
21, 24, 26, 29-31, 40, 58,
63-64, 66, 70, 80, 86, 100, 125,
146, 149, 151, 153, 155-156,
161-162, 165, 167, 171-175, 211,
223, 229-231, 242, 259, 297,
299, 301, 315, 319, 323, 329,
337-339, 342, 347, 349, 353,
355, 357-358, 360-362, 372, 399,
402, 407, 409, 412, 414, 436,
463, 472, 480, 482, 496, 505,
516, 520, 573, 588, 592, 602,
605, 618-619, 629-630, 632, 637,
665-666, 671, 673-674, 703, 713,
715, 719, 721, 723, 725, 729,
780; 9:1-2, 4-5, 9, 12, 15, 17,
20, 24, 30-31, 36, 44, 52,
57-58, 71, 88, 93, 100-101, 116,
119, 123, 125, 128, 132, 146,
148-149, 151-152, 172-173, 178,
180, 182, 192, 198, 200-202,
204-206, 236, 238, 240, 243-244,
248-249, 267, 281-283, 285, 290,
293, 295, 297, 302, 308-309,
314-317, 325, 327, 333-334, 336,
340, 347, 350, 354, 356, 359,
362, 365, 375, 378, 385-386,
388-389, 391-392, 394, 397,
399-400, 402, 404, 412, 426-427,
430, 432, 438, 446, 449-451,
459, 465, 467, 490, 492,
510-511, 513-514, 543, 545, 551,
556, 561-563, 565, 567, 569,
576-577, 581, 583, 589, 594,
602, 604, 610, 623-624, 626-627,
642-643, 645, 648, 650-651,
653-655, 658, 660, 663, 671,
674, 677, 680, 688, 693-694,
698-699, 703, 705, 707-708, 715,
718-721, 724, 730-731, 733, 735,
739, 745-746, 748-750, 752, 754,
756, 758-760, 767, 776-778;
10:7-8, 11, 18, 20-22, 24-25,
27, 34-35, 39-40, 43, 45, 50,
52, 55-56, 60-61, 65, 67, 69,
71-73, 87, 90, 93, 96, 98,
101-102, 110,112, 117-118, 121,
125, 138-140, 144, 155, 162,
173, 180, 195, 198, 201, 206,
210-211, 213, 219, 225, 227,
230, 232-234, 237, 239-240,->

CHEW, Benjamin (continued) 10:245,
247, 251, 254, 256, 259, 261,
263, 265-266, 270; 11:264-267;
12:745; 13:435; 14:463, 502,
513, 624; 16:146, 184-185
John 10:9, 217
Richard 10:694; 11:28
Samuel 3:592-593; 10:9, 108, 217
William 10:477
CHEYNEY, Thomas 16:31
CHICALAMY 4:432, 434, 443 (See
SHEKALLAMY)
CHICKASALARY, Jack 8:458
CHICKINGQUIKAMON 8:594
CHIGGAGE, Robert 9:730
CHILD, James 8:573-574, 583; 13:97
John 1:374
CHILDS, James 13:272
CHILLAWAY, Job 8:484-485, 489-490
CHILLOWAY, Job 9:77-78, 85, 754
CHILTON, John 10:422, 448
CHINGAS 5:685; 6:781 (See SHINGAS)
CHOLMONDALY, --- (Earl of) 8:438,
552, 557
CHOLMONDELEY, --- (Earl of) 4:254,
298, 483-485; 5:618
CHOLMONDELY, --- (Capt.) 6:490
CHORLEY, Joseph 1:514
CHOWGHARISA 3:500
CHRESTIEN, Jean Francis 4:72
CHRIESMERG, Wilhelm 3:452
CHRISMAN, Felix 14:438
CHRIST, Conrad 12:608
Henry 8:780; 9:172, 419, 440, 673;
11:195, 340; 12:610, 646, 692,
708, 780; 14:170-171, 617;
15:463; 16:144
Jan. 7:220
John 9:334; 16:143, 174, 443-444
CHRISTAMAN, Jacob 4:73
CHRISTEE, --- (Lt.) 10:730
CHRISTEIN, Gotlieb 14:140
CHRISTIAN 8:84
CHRISTIAN, --- 7:169, 220, 587
Felix 14:297, 304
Hendrick 3:452
Rudolph 3:455
CHRISTIANS, Cornelius 1:390
CHRISTIE (CHRISTEY, CHRYSTIE), ---
(Capt.) 7:714; 13:193, 610, 612,
664-665, 764
David (Dr.) 16:95
James 10:448, 507; 12:774; 13:372,
554, 697, 709, 772; 14:24, 32,
41, 86, 417, 419, 433, 440, 445,
454; 15:368, 375, 526; 16:345
John 10:397, 448, 488; 12:774;
13:57, 709, 717, 753, 766, 778;
14:294, 301, 407, 409; 16:50,
355
Robert 14:123, 126, 429
CHRISTINE, James 13:663
CHRISTIS, --- (Capt.) 13:658
CHRISTLER, Johan Jacob 4:59
CHRISTMAS 8:58
CHRISTWELL, Thomas 13:520
CHRISTY, William 10:168, 227;
11:494
CHRISWELL, William 14:462
CHUBB, Voyall 5:258-260, 265
CHURCH, Edward 3:69
Gideon 14:223
John 13:167
Samuel 16:164
Thomas 10:447; 13:597; 14:49, 132,
608

33

34

CLUNIE, James 14:548; 15:172, 223,
570; 16:498-499
John 16:195
CLUNN, John (Joseph) 12:199,
203-204, 206-207, 224
CLYDE, John 15:4
CLYFFORD, Thomas 1:224
CLYMER (CLYMAR), --- (Capt.) 5:284
--- (Col.) 12:109, 124
--- (Mr.) 11:198, 202, 204;
13:291, 746
Christopher 3:519
Daniel 11:216; 12:128, 323-324,
348, 709; 13:393, 415, 720, 735,
737; 15:135
George 10:46, 262, 305, 373-378,
380-382, 384, 387-390, 395-396,
398-401, 403-408, 410-412,
414-417, 419-420, 422-439,
441-443, 445-446, 449, 451-452,
455-457, 461-463, 465-471,
473-478, 480-481, 483-484,
486-491, 493-496, 498-500, 502,
504, 507, 509, 511-515, 519-524,
526-527, 529, 536, 539, 542-546,
548-550, 552-559, 561-563,
566-567, 570, 572-575, 578, 580,
582-583, 585, 589, 593-595,
597-605, 607-608, 610-611,
614-617, 619, 621, 623, 625-627,
629, 631-633, 635-637, 639-640,
642, 644, 647, 651-652, 678;
11:118, 633, 685; 12:137, 160,
196, 559; 13:168, 491; 14:29,
171, 184, 506, 555, 644, 656;
15:5, 98, 105, 135, 307, 398,
552, 583, 636, 639, 658; 16:185,
353
Henry 12:187
William 3:386; 5:516
CO(O)MB, Thomas (Rev.) 11:284, 288,
296, 300, 525, 527
CO(U)LTER, Thomas 16:36, 77, 361
CO(W)PERTHWAITE, Joseph 15:59,
98-99, 328
CO(W)PLAND, Caleb 4:279, 312, 482
COAKLEY (CHOAKLEY), Robert 14:124,
127, 427
COAL, Simon 11:120
COART, --- (Rev.) 6:668
COATAM, --- (Capt.) 5:267, 282
COATES, --- (Col.) 13:641, 661
--- (Mr.) 12:156
Isaac 10:541, 544, 671, 657;
11:24, 244
Jno. (Dr.) 11:2, 63
John 4:101, 108
John (Dr.) 12:142
Lindsey 16:122
Samuel 16:522
William 3:573; 5:209; 10:100, 212,
270; 11:31, 68, 83, 101, 201,
207, 209-210, 213-214, 221, 226,
246, 257, 259, 261, 275, 319,
386, 391, 419, 640; 12:51, 131,
136, 164, 177, 220, 298, 473,
534, 567, 612-613, 709-710;
13:103, 503
Willm. 2:561
COATS, Enoch 5:60
Lindsay 10:46
Warwick 11:297, 706
William 13:759; 14:230, 250;
15:13, 99, 209, 373-374, 520;
16:179, 482
COBB, Thomas 12:29, 31-32

COBEA, John 13:556; 14:100
COBEA(S), John 11:424, 432
COBEY, John 10:457
COBHAM, Robert 14:298, 305, 412
COBOURN(E) (CABOURN, COBURN), John
10:513, 516, 539, 567, 598, 602,
644, 658, 673, 682, 723
COBOURNE, Thomas 11:590
COBURN, --- (Capt.) 9:508
James 16:184
John 11:31; 14:65
COBURNE, James 14:659
John 15:206; 16:112
COCH, Jurgh 3:285
COCHAWITCHAKE 5:531
COCHRAN, B. 16:11
David 5:78, 95; 11:680-681; 14:365
Edward 12:378
George 14:436
James 5:210; 11:81
John 14:292, 299, 412
Jos. 10:761
Robert 15:40
Sarah 13:302
Stephen 11:15, 424, 455, 500, 633;
13:140
Thomas 15:448
William 11:379; 13:397, 674
COCHREN, William 14:212, 229
COCK, Hans 9:508
Jno. 1:95
John 2:63
Lac(e)y 1:147, 162, 167, 334, 377,
391, 393, 395, 397, 434-435,
437, 441, 447, 452, 460
Lace 1:187
Lass(i)e (Lassey) 1:57-65, 71-72,
74-76, 78-82, 84, 86-87, 91-95,
334-335, 423, 570
Peter 1:93
COCK(E), Lawrence 1:320, 340,
365-368, 370-375, 378, 381-383,
389, 396, 398-399, 401, 404,
407-409, 422-426, 428, 436, 444,
446-448, 450-451, 458-459, 462,
467-468, 472
COCKADAU, --- 9:229
COCKENDORF, John 14:609
COCKLY, Timothy 15:31
COCKQUACQUKEHETON 8:189
COCKS, Robert 12:507
COEB(O)URNE, Thomas 1:208
COECIL, Charles 12:343
COEUR, Jean 6:12
COFFEE, Mary 4:251
COFFEN, Stephen 6:913
COFFIE, James 11:42
COFFIN, Treistram 12:525
COFFMAN, Christian 14:312
John 11:105; 14:453
COGH, Hans Erick 3:369
COGLE, John 4:313
COGLINE, --- (Mr.) 9:756
COHACHGUEY 3:425
COHEN, Benjamin 6:666
Isaac 11:704
Moses 13:142
Solomon Meyers 13:254
Solomon Myers 13:548
COHER, Nicholas 14:296, 303, 429
COHEREN, Edward 12:294
COIL, Thomas 11:162, 166
COILE, Henry 15:129
COILS, Alexander 12:598
COKE, --- (Lord) 6:618, 626
Colin 11:149

36

COKESBURY, Eve **15**:40
COL(L)INET, Louis **14**:240, 447, 449
COLDEN, --- (Dr.) **3**:204
--- (Mr.) **8**:590
Alexander **5**:647
Cadwallader (Gov.) **9**:110-111, 113,
  119-122, 130, 137, 629-631,
  655-656
COLDER, James **4**:211
COLDWELL, --- (Mr.) **13**:104
COLE, Edward **6**:608, 611
Ezra **12**:1
Henry **6**:758
John **4**:276
Philip **10**:744, 746; **11**:81, 83
Robert **1**:375, 383; **15**:571
Sabian **1**:202
William **15**:449; **16**:118
COLEBROOK(E), Robert **10**:388, 476
COLEHENDURFER, Andreas **3**:457
COLEMAN, --- **16**:270
--- (Mr.) **13**:744; **14**:29
David **12**:337
John **11**:154; **13**:777; **14**:84, 417
Joseph **3**:227, 230
Robert **13**:393, 722, 724, 737;
  14:259, 268; **15**:570; **16**:31
Saml. **2**:90
Thomas **16**:500
William **5**:388, 572; **7**:769; **8**:19,
  24, 77, 335, 342, 349, 355,
  360-361, 481, 506, 591; **9**:172,
  286, 334, 387, 393, 398; **10**:750
COLEOFFER, Peter **14**:97, 419
COLESBERRY, Henry **5**:210
COLESTON, --- (Mr.) **10**:422
COLEY, Robert **11**:513, 516-517
COLGAN, Barnabas **14**:190, 194, 412
John **14**:609
Richard **14**:95, 424
COLIDAY, William **14**:110
COLIER, Joseph **10**:480, 542
COLL, Dilman **3**:367
COLLADAY, William **13**:721; **15**:10
COLLET, Jeremiah **1**:95, 374
COLLET(T), Jeremiah **2**:103, 236
COLLHAGEHERAD **3**:163
COLLIDAY, William **11**:770; **16**:53,
  90, 215, 394
COLLIER, James **11**:751; **14**:380,
  407-408
Joseph **11**:181, 578-579; **12**:355;
  13:624, 716; **14**:15, 125, 434,
  438; **16**:186
Richard **10**:450, 470, 480; **14**:300,
  609
COLLINGS, Robert **11**:3
Susanna **12**:712
COLLINS, --- **13**:739
--- (Mr.) **10**:630
Ann **1**:512
Baltus (Battus) **14**:131, 133, 412
Francis **16**:382
James **13**:511; **15**:139, 155, 484
John **3**:199; **14**:191, 195, 438;
  15:246
M. **11**:648
Mary **16**:229
Ralph **14**:170
Robert **10**:425-426; **14**:600
Stephen **11**:656; **12**:751; **13**:532;
  16:66
Tho. **1**:576-577
Thomas **9**:199, 286, 333; **13**:578;
  14:102, 608
William **14**:189, 190, 192, 194, 430

COLLISON, John **3**:38
COLLON, Hugh **13**:389
COLLOSSER, Peter **13**:573
COLMERE, Daniel **3**:455
COLSTON, John **11**:610-611
COLT, Arnold **16**:308, 496
COLTMAN, Robert **13**:713; **15**:192
COLVILL, --- (Lord) **7**:772, 775;
  9:299
COLVIN, John **15**:31
William **9**:508
COMBES, Edward **12**:372
COMBESS, Thomas **16**:190
COMELY, Henry **1**:92; **15**:478
Jacob **15**:478
Joseph **11**:610-612
COMER, Jean **4**:72
COML(E)Y, Jacob **11**:5
COMLEY, Jonathan **12**:447
COMMEL, Mary **11**:166-169
COMPASS, Joseph **8**:750
Philip **8**:211
COMPTON, Mary **12**:2
William **11**:494; **13**:53; **14**:571
COMPTY, John **12**:196
COMSTACK, --- **9**:584
CON, D. W. **9**:122
CON(N)OLLY, John **10**:140-142, 145,
  149, 157, 161, 165-171, 176,
  193, 197, 227-228, 234, 444,
  470, 472, 476, 482, 533
CONACHQUASEY **5**:685
CONAGARATUCHQUA **6**:291
CONAJARCA **5**:521, 531, 538
CONDON, Peter **8**:728
CONDOR, Elizabeth **12**:67
CONDY, Benjamin **10**:730
CONE, Michael **6**:171-172
CONEGHTOGHERTY **7**:60
CONELLY, --- (Lt.) **11**:104
--- (Mrs.) **10**:742, 781
John **16**:465
CONESTOGO INDIANS **4**:585; **13**:467
CONESTOGOE **3**:168, 194
CONGLER, Jno. **11**:165
CONKLE, Henry **16**:335
CONN, Gabriel **9**:508
CONNADAGAUGHIEA **7**:507
CONNAR(R)OE, Thomas **15**:228, 233
CONNARD, Edward **13**:688
E[d]ward **13**:687
Henry **13**:687-688
CONNARROE, Thomas **14**:474, 479
CONNEL, James **14**:556
CONNELL, Sergeant **12**:681
William **10**:743
Zachariah **14**:310
CONNELLY, --- (Capt.) **11**:114;
  15:438
Isaac **13**:98
John **12**:487; **13**:161, 163
Thomas **12**:506
CONNELLY (CONNOLLY), Andrew **14**:133,
  438
Robert **14**:610, 655
CONNELLY (CONNOLY), Patrick **14**:94,
  415
CONNELY, --- (Mrs.) **11**:51
CONNER, John **14**:83, 415
Michael **10**:723
Morgan O. **14**:413 (see O'CONNER)
Sarah **14**:470
Thomas **16**:212b
CONNER (CONNOR), Charles **14**:192,
  435
CONNIACK **8**:218

CONNO(O)DAGHTOH 2:15
CONNODAGHTON (CONNODAGHTAN) 3:601, 603
CONNOL(L)Y, Robert 11:48, 70, 94
CONNOLLY, Andrew 13:710
 John 11:196, 200
 Patrick 13:679
 Robert 10:450
CONNOLY, --- (Mrs.) 10:648, 696
CONNOODAGHTAH 2:17
CONNOODAGHTOH (CONCODACHTO) 4:338, 340, 589
CONNOR (CONNER), Andrew 12:393
 Bryan 15:445
 Cornelius 2:583
 John 10:674; 11:134; 12:754; 13:80, 149, 725, 777
 Katherine (Catherine) 4:47, 209, 224 (See SMITH)
 Mary 13:104
 Matthew 14:295, 302, 421
 Michael 15:49, 51, 93, 149, 410, 426, 445
 Morgan 11:772; 13:562
 Roger 5:327
 Timothy 15:23, 468
 William 14:50, 262-263
CONNOSOORA 3:271
CONOHARRIOKU 8:700
CONOLLY, --- (Capt.) 11:65
CONOSSOORAH 4:80
CONOY, Sam 9:66, 77
CONOY INDIANS 8:730
CONRAD, --- (Lt.) 8:386
 Edward 13:727
 Frederick 14:230; 15:192; 16:311, 384
 George 10:746
 Hans Leond. 3:452
 Henry 13:515, 727
 John 11:458
 Matthias 13:187, 384
 Nicholas 12:445
 Peter 13:777; 14:610; 15:67, 74
CONRADS, Conrad 2:493
 John 2:493
 John, Sr. 2:493
 Matthis 2:493
CONSOLVES, Emanuel 11:65
CONSONTHA 5:685
CONSTABLE, William 12:495-496, 504; 13:545
CONTARONQUE 8:750
CONTEE, Hans 3:368
CONTRECOEUR, --- (Capt.) 6:29-30, 224-225
CONTUGHQUA 5:538
CONTZAT, John 11:206
CONWAY, George 10:465
 Henry Seymour 9:297-299, 308-313, 341, 346-347
CONWELL, William 9:272; 10:81, 217
CONYERS, Samuel 10:563
CONYHOCHEVATOQUIN 8:750
CONYNGHAM, --- 13:297; 14:109, 111
CONYNGHAM, NESBITT & CO. 11:5, 11
CONYNHAM, --- (Mr.) 7:151-152
COOBLE, Hans 3:287
COOCH, Thomas 9:203, 626; 10:81, 217
COOGLER, Adam 13:710; 14:97, 425
 John 12:301, 308, 384-385
 Susanna 12:301, 308
COOK, --- (Capt.) 2:506, 557
 --- (Maj.) 11:329
 Aaron 4:59

COOK, Benjamin 4:602, 748, 782
 Charles 3:74; 12:259, 293
 Dorothy 12:662
 Edward 10:724, 726, 737; 12:372, 406; 13:150, 337, 547; 14:135, 587; 15:120, 173; 16:50
 Elizabeth 13:94
 Fran. 1:341
 Henry 12:450
 Jabez 9:584
 Jacob 12:372, 429, 467, 508, 556; 13:121, 722; 15:91, 129, 244; 16:334
 John 7:621; 10:56, 101, 211; 16:334
 John (alias White Mingo) 9:470
 Jon. 1:322
 Joseph 16:460
 Moses 16:434
 Peden 14:176
 Philip 15:119, 357
 Richard 9:715, 717
 William 10:59, 101, 212, 741, 754, 756; 11:2, 39, 73, 81, 84, 91, 95, 97, 112, 126, 131-132, 180, 270; 13:92, 112, 398, 415; 14:558; 15:93, 170, 311; 16:398, 495
COOK(E), Arthur 1:153, 156, 164, 169-170, 173-181, 183, 185-187, 189-198, 200-208, 211-226, 228-229, 238-240, 242-252, 256-257, 259, 261, 289, 319-320, 322-327, 329-338, 340-344, 370, 378, 505, 573, 607, 609
 Edward 11:220-221, 736
 Francis 2:23, 109, 283, 397, 410
 William 12:138, 306
COOK, POLLOCK & LOCKRY 16:541
COOKCRAFT, William 6:608, 611
COOKE, --- 15:76
 Edward 13:167-168
 Jacob 13:88, 112; 14:45
 Philip 14:459
 William 13:354
COOKS, Jacob 10:684
COOKSON, Thomas 4:313, 483, 656, 658, 675, 678; 5:3, 247, 318, 377-378, 600
COOL, Johan Ulrich 3:516
COOLEY, Preserved 14:495
COOLIN, Annakey 1:95
COOMB, --- (Maj.) 11:123
COOMBE, John 13:122
 Joseph 5:454
 Sarah 13:122
 Thomas 9:197; 13:105
 Thomas (Rev.) 13:122
COOMBES, Thomas 14:506
COOMBS, Andrew 5:454
 Thomas 8:22, 24
COON, Anne 8:629
 Christian 12:332
 Michael 10:54
COONEY, John 14:613
COOPER, Calvin 7:249; 8:562; 9:172, 673
 Charles 10:749, 768; 13:698, 756; 14:87, 427
 Danl. 2:113
 George 13:47, 159, 629; 15:46, 426
 Isaac 13:552
 James 10:199
 Jane 16:156 (See Jane HAMILTON)
 Jeremiah 13:687-688
 Jno. 9:509

COOPER, John **11**:163, 168; **14**:199
Mary **11**:703
Robert **16**:200
Samuel **11**:104
William **3**:277, 279; **12**:31,
272-273; **13**:53, 58, 168; **14**:41,
62, 134, 422; **15**:33
COOPMAN, Johannes **3**:328
COOR, Henry **14**:506
COPE, --- **6**:490
Oliver **1**:499
COPENHAVE(R) (COPPENHAVEN), ---
(Capt.) **10**:690-692
COPENHAVER, Michael **3**:452
Wolfe **3**:452
COPLER, Barney **14**:131, 134, 434
COPLIN, John **8**:575
COPP, Michael **15**:100
COPPEL, Nicholas **15**:499
COPPER, John **11**:150
Norris **10**:591
COPPERSMITH, Casper **4**:60
COPPERTHAWTE (COWPERTHWAITE),
Joseph **12**:170, 208
COPPERTHWAITE, Joseph **11**:10, 28,
58, 88, 423, 606, 619, 775
COPPLE, Michael **12**:563
COPPOCK (COYPOCK), Barth. **1**:169,
213-227, 234-235, 238-239,
242-243, 247, 249-251, 258,
261-262, 267-270, 272, 275, 277,
282, 284-286, 290-292, 294,
296-298, 300, 302, 304-305, 307,
310, 312, 317-326, 335-338, 340,
342-343, 517
COPSON, John **4**:231
COQUECASH **4**:340
COQUETAKEGHTON **8**:618
COQUIL, Stephen **13**:14
CORBER, Nicolas **3**:432
CORBET(T), Roger **1**:454, 503
CORBETT, Thomas **5**:243
CORBIN, Margaret **12**:34
CORBITT, Alexander **12**:744, 754
CORCOCKSAARA **8**:750
CORD, Joseph **3**:254, 259, 270
COREN, Isaac **12**:55, 255, 332, 334,
438, 626
CORGEE, Thomas **11**:128, 602
CORKING, Simon **8**:566
CORKINS, John **8**:566
CORL, William **14**:611
CORLEAR, --- **5**:508, 510
CORN(E)Y, S. L. **10**:428
CORNAGHAN, John **13**:443
CORNALL, John **15**:24
CORNAY (DE CORNAY), --- (Monsieur)
12:368-369
CORNBURY, --- (Lord) **2**:78-79, 91,
100, 113, 115, 136, 138, 411,
421; **3**:120
CORNEL, William **11**:372
CORNELIUS, --- **5**:686
Peter **3**:515
CORNELIUS (INDIAN) **9**:414, 428,
436, 470
CORNELL, --- (Mr.) **7**:36
CORNER, John **14**:98, 425
CORNISH, Andrew **3**:256, 309, 345,
356, 358, 394, 521, 531
John **12**:51; **13**:250; **14**:191, 195;
16:164
CORNLY, Elinor **12**:374
Joseph **12**:374
CORNMAN & BARGE **10**:754

CORNPLANTER, The **16**:501, 506, 508,
510-511, 513
CORNWALL, Franc. **1**:213
CORNWALLIS, --- (Lord) **4**:484-485;
13:94, 98, 143
CORR, Thomas, Jr. **12**:601
CORRAN, John **15**:31
CORRIS, William **11**:181
CORSE, Jno. **2**:51-53
CORSEY, --- (Col.) **11**:301
CORTES, Joannes **3**:288
CORTNEY, Jno. **1**:84
CORTRECHT, Henry **5**:470
CORTWRIGHT, Abraham **12**:313
Francis **14**:656
CORYELL, John **14**:79
COSARD, Lees **1**:81
COSENS, Samuel **3**:367
COSNAY (CASNAY), John Baptist
5:122, 131, 168
COSSINGER, George **13**:191
COST, George **5**:472, 478
Jacob **6**:171
COSTIGAN, Francis **12**:696
COSWENTANNEA **5**:734
COTNAM, George **5**:269
COTTALINNEA **8**:724
COTTER, Patrick **16**:547
COTTINGER, Garret **13**:444
COTTON, Henry **11**:340
Rachel **14**:239
COTTRELL, Steph. **9**:630, 765
Stephen **10**:104
COTTRINGER, John **9**:596
COUCHER, Christopher **11**:340
COUGER, Johan Georg. **3**:452
COUGHLETON, William **16**:334
COUGHLIN, James **7**:559
COULSTONE, David **12**:453
COULTAS, --- (Capt.) **9**:126
James **3**:367; **5**:107, 131, 175;
6:638; **7**:266, 361, 446; **8**:442,
575; **9**:205
John **3**:327
COULTELRN, John **15**:454
COULTER, Nathaniel **10**:683
Thomas **10**:78, 163; **11**:195, 608;
13:730; **14**:602
William **15**:31
COULTMAN (COULTMAR), Robert **14**:64,
90, 425
COULTY, --- (Mr.) **14**:68
COULVER, Ephraim **7**:357
COUNESTRAHO **5**:538
COUNTRYMAN, Jacob **16**:79
COUPAR (COUPER), Robert **11**:513,
516-517
COUPLAND, Christian **14**:296, 303,
420
COUPLAND (COWPLAND), David **11**:339,
729
COUR(T)NEY, Hercules (Herculeus,
Herculus) **10**:523, 619, 742, 775,
782
COURSEY, Henry **4**:717
COURTENAY, Charles **6**:224
COURTER, Herman **14**:451, 488-489
COURTNEY, Francis **14**:498-499
Hercules **11**:10, 67, 96, 124, 126,
162, 166
William **15**:175, 390; **16**:104 (See
William HOLTON)
COUSENS, Samuel **5**:536
COUSER, George **12**:187
COUTTS, Hercules **2**:97, 103, 244
James **2**:97, 103, 129, 425

COUTTY, Samuel **15**:384, 440
COVALT, Bethuel **15**:278
COWACHSORA **8**:750
COWAN, Charles **14**:293, 300, 422
 Edward **11**:82
 John **5**:116-117, 443
 William **11**:119; **12**:626; **15**:613,
 618
COWDEN, --- (Col.) **11**:340
 James **10**:699, 772; **12**:508
COWDEN (SEE HEPBURN &) **16**:483-484
COWDON, James **14**:453
COWEL(L), Ebenezer **12**:20, 24, 30,
 48, 66, 91, 111
COWELL, --- (Dr.) **12**:547
 Ebenezer **11**:133, 409, 488, 519,
 525, 567, 649, 693, 749, 769
 John **13**:140, 718
 John (Dr.) **13**:573; **14**:434
COWEY, John **14**:293, 300, 410
COWHART, --- **6**:490
COWLE, John **6**:171
COWOCKSLAIRA **8**:750
COWPER, John **10**:321, 416
 Nicholas **12**:601
 Wm. **4**:357-358
COWPERTHWAITE, Joseph **10**:440, 467,
 484, 491, 497-498, 549-550, 634,
 640, 707, 756; **13**:118-120, 127,
 153, 192, 720, 722; **14**:230, 555;
 16:57, 211
COWPLAND, Caleb **7**:389; **8**:77
 Jonathan **10**:759; **11**:678; **14**:518
COWPLAND (COUPLAND), Caleb **5**:3,
 107, 203, 303, 387, 566, 603
COX, --- (Capt.) **7**:289
 --- (Col.) **11**:542, 549, 586
 --- (Dr.) **2**:390
 --- (Lt. Col.) **13**:685
 --- (Widow) **7**:242
 Charles **3**:547
 Daniel **4**:270
 Isaac **10**:375, 471, 722-723, 755
 John **5**:106-110; **7**:231, 242-243;
 10:572, 702, 715, 717
 John, Jr. **9**:335
 Martin **13**:594
 Mary **11**:586
 Paul **16**:320
 Richard **7**:242
 William **7**:601
COX(E), --- (Dr.) **10**:496, 575, 580
 John **11**:54, 98, 294, 666; **12**:19,
 40, 423, 616
 Martin **14**:96, 423
 Paul **11**:122, 182-183, 194, 217,
 232, 245, 286-287
 William **8**:24, 231, 575-576
COXE, --- **12**:284
 --- (Col.) **13**:686
 --- (Widow) **12**:284
 Andrew **13**:189
 Benjamin **14**:80, 87, 414
 Church **11**:453; **14**:485
 Cornelius **12**:411; **14**:259
 Daniel **11**:495
 Isaac **13**:531
 John **13**:744; **14**:52, 61, 138, 366
 Joseph **13**:273
 Pau. **12**:557
 Sarah **12**:390; **13**:272, 551
 Tench **11**:494; **15**:5, 86, 135, 425;
 16:10, 33, 232, 238
 William **9**:205, 673; **10**:162;
 12:614; **13**:764; **14**:506; **15**:597
COXE & FRAZIER **15**:78

COXILL, Elizabeth **13**:342
COXWELL, Elizabeth **13**:553
COY (SEE MEAD &) **10**:305
COYLE, Edward **14**:189, 193
 James **11**:621; **15**:188, 526
 John **14**:217
 Miles **5**:594
 Samuel **16**:461
COYLE (SEE KYLE), William
 11:267-268
COZENS, Elizabeth **13**:286
CRABB, Mary **13**:587
 William **14**:259, 266, 605
CRABLE, Hans Erick **3**:287
 Michel **3**:287
CRACKIN, John **14**:296, 303, 436
CRAEMEN, Hans Jerig **3**:284
CRAFFT, Frederick **7**:399
CRAFT, James **11**:773; **12**:33
 Joseph Thorney **14**:347
 Nicholas **5**:61
CRAGAN, Thomas **11**:167
CRAGE, John **1**:390
CRAGGS, --- (Secretary) **3**:70, 75
CRAIG, --- **7**:15, 17
 --- (Col.) **12**:36
 --- (Maj.) **14**:551
 --- (Mr.) **10**:528; **13**:752-753;
 15:143-145
 Alexander **15**:85
 Hugh **11**:32
 Isaac **13**:223, 233, 714, 756;
 14:27, 84, 291, 437, 532
 James **10**:564, 574, 594, 599, 626,
 726, 744; **13**:234, 306, 636;
 14:96, 190, 194, 423, 437;
 15:323-324, 558, 562; **16**:211,
 330, 336, 491
 James, Jr. **13**:31
 Jerard **14**:614
 John **7**:242; **12**:88-89, 275,
 331-332, 355, 576, 609; **13**:38,
 57, 393-394, 407, 415, 557, 582,
 712, 722, 737; **14**:102, 126, 290,
 348, 417, 422, 459, 609; **15**:37,
 55, 132, 140, 290, 390, 583,
 618, 621-622; **16**:215b, 295, 408
 Robert **10**:421, 681, 686; **11**:329,
 340, 467, 544; **14**:455
 Samuel **11**:563; **12**:13; **13**:553;
 14:83, 85, 94, 415, 422-423, 433
 Sarah **16**:480
 Susanna **11**:695
 Thomas **7**:769; **9**:206, 308; **10**:447;
 11:179-180, 732; **12**:372, 405,
 498, 774; **13**:617, 713, 739, 747,
 777; **14**:28, 62, 82, 99, 155,
 166, 202, 204, 229, 302,
 429-430, 437; **16**:61
 Wiliam **14**:232, 248, 660
 William **5**:209, 573, 597; **10**:450;
 11:582; **15**:522, 579, 583, 618,
 621-622; **16**:32, 411
CRAIG(E), John **10**:450, 605
 Thomas **5**:3, 388, 573
CRAIG(H) (CRAIGG), James **11**:223,
 291-292, 513, 516-517, 739, 751
CRAIGHEAD, George **10**:81, 217
CRAIGIE, James **3**:368
CRAIN, Robert **14**:485
CRAISS, --- (Maj.) **13**:456
CRAMER, --- **13**:29
 Jacob **10**:643; **12**:493
 Johan Matthias **3**:417
CRAMPTON, James **7**:154
CRANBACH, Leonhart **4**:59

CRANE, --- 12:255
  Ambrose 11:181
  Josiah 14:64, 300
  Richard 16:119
CRANKLOOK, Ulrick 3:452
CRAPP, Jno. 1:512
CRAPPER, Levin 9:203; 10:81, 217
  Zadok 10:9, 217
CRATHO, John 3:235
CRATZ, Andreas 4:60
CRATZER, Joseph 4:72
CRAVEN, Charles 7:23, 29
  James 12:13; 13:322
CRAWFORD, --- (Adj.) 11:418-419
  --- (Col.) 16:43, 227, 234, 283
  --- (Ens.) 8:386
  --- (Lt.) 13:741
  --- (Mr.) 9:413
  Alexander 11:665
  Andrew 12:627; 13:668; 14:83, 415
  Christopher 11:57, 82, 104-105,
    223, 744
  David 2:102-103; 11:77
  Edward 11:563; 13:573, 717; 14:83,
    202, 204, 370, 436; 16:32, 61,
    221b, 369, 444, 495-497, 516,
    522
  Edward, Sr. 16:496
  George 15:64
  Henry 14:297, 304, 426
  Hugh 5:437-438, 450, 521, 568,
    570-571, 760; 6:160, 762, 779;
    7:507, 509
  James 9:508; 10:586, 670, 672,
    684, 687, 741, 776; 11:106, 155,
    180; 12:137-138, 185, 513, 552;
    13:92; 14:252-253, 652; 16:71,
    496
  John 5:247; 11:330, 340, 479, 504;
    12:287; 13:203, 717; 16:496
  Joseph 14:295, 302
  Josiah 12:353, 486; 14:15
  Josias 9:508
  Robert 11:218
  Samuel 5:210
  Sarah 13:278
  William 5:247; 9:673, 730; 10:78,
    142, 165, 167-168, 172, 228,
    234-235, 449; 11:150, 158-159,
    161; 13:94; 14:181, 310, 417;
    15:1, 310
CRAWFORD(S), John 14:125, 129, 189,
    192, 310, 428, 438, 475, 535,
    558
CRAWL, Christian 3:618
  Christn. 4:67
CRAWLEY & CA. 15:440
CRAY, Alexander 11:731
  Daniel 6:241
CRAYBILL, John 16:500
CRAYMER, Conrad 6:648
  Jacob 13:612
CRAYMUR, Jacob 14:91, 417
CRAYTON, John 13:624; 14:134, 431
CREAMER, --- 13:32
  Leonard 10:698
  Philip 11:596
CREE, David 16:461
CREEF, Sebastian 3:284
CREEPLE, Jacob 3:368
CREETOR, Moret 3:367
CREIGH, Jno. 11:64, 229, 694
  John 12:3, 519; 14:449
CREINER, Martin 3:386
CRES(S)AP, --- (Capt.) 5:218,
    438-440

CRESSAP, Thomas 3:471-472, 476,
    551; 4:58, 62-63, 67-68, 105,
    108-111, 116-118, 121-123, 126,
    128-134, 137-139, 142, 146, 156,
    164, 168, 170, 177-178, 194-195,
    216, 255-256, 260, 719
CRESSAP (CRESSIP), Daniel 8:754
CRESSAP (CRESSUP), --- (Col.) 6:36,
    400
CREWSON, Henry 10:100
CRIBER, Philip 3:456
CRIBS, Peter 10:170
CRICHT, Jocham Michael 3:323
CRICKLEY, Michael 11:515-516, 518
CRIMBLE, --- 6:490
CRIMSHIER, John Dutton 13:15
CRINDALL, Samuel 14:666
CRIPEN, Thomas 10:781
CRIPPIN, Mary Ann 12:133
CRISINGER, Johan Jocob 3:516
CRISLY, --- 9:104
CRISNER, Johan George 3:410
CRISON, Isaac 3:332
CRISPIN (CHRISPIN, CRESPIN), Sylas
    1:298
  William 11:33, 40, 94, 135, 142,
    230, 245, 248, 257, 263,
    266-267, 272, 280, 290, 300,
    308, 312, 387, 405, 408,
    440-441, 448-449, 465, 469-470,
    475, 508, 528, 546, 549, 560,
    572, 576, 591, 594, 615, 640,
    650, 675, 685, 692, 694, 704,
    717, 719, 728, 742, 750,
    777-778; 12:10, 15, 26, 44-45,
    65, 86, 106, 111, 134, 159, 180,
    194, 204, 226, 244, 444, 450,
    477-478, 554; 13:239; 14:320,
    364, 453, 462, 467; 15:246, 425
CRISSAP, --- (Capt.) 4:103
CRIST, Henry 10:765-767
  Jacob 3:432
  Johannes 3:328
  John Martin 3:368
CRISTIS, James 8:629
CRISTMAN, Daniel 3:386
CRITZMER, Godfrey 12:627
CROASDELL, Ezra 2:397 (See
    CROSDALE)
  Willm. 2:397
CROCKET (CROCKAT), David 3:284,
    331, 453
CROCKSON, Dennis 12:28
CROFFTS, Benjamin 11:60
CROFTS, Benjamin 12:175
CROGHAN, --- (Col.) 10:141
  Andrew 5:692, 703
  George 4:7; 5:72, 119, 122, 139,
    150, 166-167, 213-214, 287, 290,
    294, 298, 314, 318, 327,
    348-349, 352, 356, 358, 378,
    387, 408, 431, 433-436, 438,
    440-441, 443, 461, 481, 483,
    485, 488, 495-496, 498, 515,
    518, 521-525, 528-530, 532-535,
    539, 540, 547, 550, 568-571,
    614-615, 622, 657, 661, 665,
    668, 675, 682, 692-693, 695,
    703, 707-708, 730-731, 735, 750,
    756-757; 6:21, 56, 140-141, 145,
    147-156, 160-161, 169, 176,
    180-181, 188-190, 218-219, 226,
    318, 323-324, 369, 371-372,
    374-375, 381, 397-399, 435, 460,
    470, 484-485, 642-643, 699,
    743-744, 762, 779-784; ->

CROGHAN, George (continued) 7:1, 3,
  5, 64, 81, 261, 354-356, 378,
  382-385, 391, 403-404, 434-436,
  462, 465-466, 473, 475-476,
  478-482, 484-490, 503, 505-507,
  513-518, 523-524, 527-528,
  532-536, 543, 545-546, 548-549,
  551, 557, 580, 587, 598,
  600-601, 605, 607-608, 624,
  629-630, 632, 634, 648-650, 652,
  654-663, 665, 667, 671-672, 675,
  679-684, 686, 688-694, 698, 714,
  724-725, 728, 730-731; 8:97,
  169, 175, 179, 200-201, 208,
  218-219, 263-264, 301, 320, 378,
  382-387, 390-391, 394, 429,
  431-433, 690, 700, 702, 726,
  731, 736, 738, 757, 769; 9:30,
  34, 218, 249-250, 263-265, 278,
  318, 322-323, 421, 427, 432-435,
  476-477, 482, 490, 492-496, 501,
  507-508, 514, 516, 518, 520,
  522-523, 525, 529, 533, 536-539,
  709; 11:515, 517-518
CROGHEN, William 14:456
CROHAN, Dennis 12:58, 65
  Margaret 12:58, 65
CROKER, Ambrose 13:325
  Joseph 8:134
CROLL, Christian 3:613
  Johan Christ 3:367
  Michael 11:644; 12:407; 14:629
  Ulrick 3:367
CROLLEY (COOLEY), Preserved 14:311,
  320
CROMZINE, Stephen 11:43
CRONAN, Daniel 16:187
CRONE, Henry 14:615
CRONER, Frederick 16:391, 432
CRONEY, Judith 15:652
CRONY, John 11:130
CROOK, John 6:277
CROOKS, Thomas 13:122, 135
CROP, Daniel 3:369
CROPP, Andreas 3:368
  Christian 3:368
  Christian, Jr. 3:368
  Jacob 3:368
CROPT, John 1:203-204
CROREBIT, Christian 3:290
CROSBY, David 16:372, 424
  John 3:108, 256, 381; 4:279, 312,
    482; 5:3; 9:628; 12:372, 393,
    420, 429, 446, 461, 514; 14:586;
    16:100, 160
  John, Jr. 10:56
CROSCOST, Philip 3:385
CROSDALE, Ezra 2:260, 316 (See
  CROASDELL)
CROSIER, Mathias 7:267
CROSLEY, Jesse 13:715
CROSMAN, Nicholas 3:290
CROSON, Henry 5:209
CROSS, Cornelia 16:101
  Daniel 12:188; 14:49
  James 12:667
  John 4:102
  Patrick 13:640; 14:96, 419
CROSSAN, Samuel, Jr. 15:222
  Thomas 15:605; 16:18
CROSSER, Hannah 16:404
  Robert 16:404
CROSSLEY, George 14:642
  Jesse 13:556; 14:94, 427
  Robert 15:463
CROSSLY, Rich. 1:166

CROSSMAN, Samuel 16:18, 372, 383
CROSTON, --- (Mr.) 7:550
CROTT, Herman 4:60
CROTZ, Casper 14:429
CROU, Nicolas 3:288
CROUCH, James 11:100
  Thomas 11:780; 12:3
CROUSE, Michael 5:327
CROUSILLAT & OLIVER 16:121
CROW, --- 6:491
  Frederick 15:310
  George 12:323
  John 5:506
CROW(E)S, George 10:693, 695-696,
  698, 720
CROWDER, --- 13:29, 32
  George 14:227-228
  George (alias KIDD) 13:135
CROWDERS, George 13:183
CROWEL, Johan Michael 4:59
CROWLEY, James 9:746
CROWLY, David 14:613
CROWSE, Johannes 3:288
CROWSER, Matthew 14:608
CROZER, John 12:393, 429
CRUCEILLIUS, Adolph 13:764
CRUCELLIUS, Adolph 14:408, 439
CRUCKSHANK, Andrew 15:178
  Jane 15:178
CRUIKSHANK, Alexr. 1:556
  Eliz. (See HALL, Eliz.) 1:377,
    556-558
  Hester 1:556-557
  Thomas 1:556-558
CRUIKSHANKS, Charles 9:673
  John 11:367
CRUMURIN, Hans. Mich. 3:452
CRUSAN, Conrad 14:611
CRUSEILLIUS, Adolph 13:758
CRUSEL, Joseph 11:472
CRUSIS (CRUSIUS), Andrew 15:316,
  319
CRYDEN, John 12:615
CRYDER, --- (Capt.) 13:83
  Michael 13:115, 302; 15:301
CRYDER (CRIDER), David 12:333, 576
CRYLBERGER, Hans George 3:517
CUCHAR, Johan Peter 3:456
CUCHDACHER 5:686
CUFF, (Negro) 16:101
CUFI, Philip Leonti 3:457
CUHSHAWMEHWY 8:189
CULBER(T)SON, John 11:83, 624, 633
  Robert 11:61, 120, 455, 734
CULBERSON, John 13:87
  Robert 10:699-700, 712
  Samuel 10:702
CULBERTSON, --- (Mr.) 10:573;
    13:110, 198; 14:320
  Alexander 6:533; 7:77
  Andrew 11:398; 12:43
  Anna 15:428
  Jno. 9:205
  John 5:186, 210; 7:417; 8:573;
    12:131, 512; 13:112, 612; 15:62,
    131, 182, 326, 451; 16:200, 224
  Robert 12:372, 453; 14:39
  Sam. 13:612
  Samuel 11:229, 424; 14:409, 439,
    610
CULIN, Daniel 10:265
CULLEN, James 13:561
CULLOCH, M. 11:286
CULP, Henry 14:140
CULVER, --- (Mr.) 6:757
CUMBERLAND, --- (Duke of) 5:50-51

42

CUMINGS, Enoch **3**:259, 270
CUMMING, William **5**:186
CUMMINGS, James **14**:176
   John **11**:57; **13**:168; **16**:215
   Robert **5**:247, 325-326
   Thomas **5**:3, 387, 572
   William **12**:627
CUMMINS, --- (Lt.) **13**:423
   James **11**:424; **14**:39
   John **12**:623; **15**:109
   Thomas **13**:448
CUNARD, Henry **14**:230
CUNDALL, Wm. **3**:142
CUNDRUM, Martin **12**:601
   Philip **12**:601
CUNINGHAM, Allen **11**:339
   Peter **12**:36
CUNJAQUOA **5**:542
CUNKELL, Baltzer **3**:457
CUNNARD, Edward **14**:208
   Robert **16**:107
CUNNARSE, Thomas **14**:546
CUNNAWAY, Johan Christopher **3**:517
CUNNINGHAM, --- **13**:755
   --- (Mr.) **13**:1, 3-6, 8, 11-12, 14-
     7, 19-25, 27-28, 30-32, 100-104,
     106, 109-111, 114, 116-117,
     119-121, 123, 125, 127-128,
     131-133, 135-140, 143, 145,
     147-148, 241, 243-244, 250-254,
     256-257, 262-266, 268-269, 272,
     274-279, 281, 283-284, 286,
     288-292, 512, 523
   --- (Widow) **11**:166
   Allen **12**:31, 512-513; **13**:87
   David **14**:537
   George **16**:461
   Hugh **10**:691; **11**:32; **14**:118
   James **4**:757; **9**:449-451;
     10:683-684; **11**:330, 367; **12**:134,
     301, 592-595, 597-599, 601,
     603-607, 609-611, 614-616, 618,
     620, 623-624, 628, 630-633,
     636-637, 639, 642, 644-646, 648,
     650-655, 657-658, 660-664, 667,
     669, 672, 674, 676, 678-679,
     681, 683, 685-686, 688-690, 693,
     695, 697, 759-761, 764, 766-768,
     771, 773-774, 776-778, 780-783;
     13:15, 33, 88, 99, 112, 147,
     290-291, 473, 477-481, 484-486,
     490-491, 493-494, 496-501, 505,
     507-508, 510-519, 521, 523-524,
     526-530, 532, 536-538, 540-541,
     546-549, 556, 558-559, 562-564;
     14:447, 633; **15**:405; **16**:325, 351
   John **5**:186; **11**:513, 516-517;
     14:131, 133, 144, 438
   Joseph **12**:63-64; **13**:569; **14**:301,
     433
   Mary **16**:417
   Morris **10**:687
   Robert **13**:601; **14**:93, 419, 615
   Samuel **10**:738; **11**:59, 317, 320,
     551, 696; **12**:125, 554; **13**:406
   Thomas **14**:294, 301, 486
   William **5**:247; **16**:62
CUNNINGHAM (CANYINGHAM), Redmond
   8:24, 59
CUNNINGS, James **16**:185
CUNRAD, Robert **11**:494
CUNTZ, Hans Jorg **3**:452
   Jacob **4**:60
   Johan **3**:389
CUPPAIDGE, George **10**:574

CURGE (CORGEE, CURGEE), Thomas
   10:714, 725, 749
CURGEE, Thomas **13**:306
CURGILL, John **11**:675
CURKEE, John **10**:52
CURLAN, William **11**:515, 517-518
CURNER, Johan Philip **3**:386
CURR(E)Y (CURRIE), Robert **11**:152,
   451, 494, 502, 601, 603
CURRALL, Mary **14**:108
CURRANT, Barny **5**:440
CURREY, Robert **16**:122
CURRIE, George **8**:573
   James **11**:74
   John **12**:464
   Ross **10**:449
   William (Dr.) **10**:734
CURRY, --- (Capt.) **9**:34 (See OURRY)
   --- (Lt. Col.) **11**:49
   James **14**:371
   Mark **6**:648
   Nicholas **10**:735
   Ross **11**:513, 516-517
   Samuel **12**:569
CURSON, Robert **3**:455
CURTIS, James **9**:620
   Jehu **5**:89-90, 92, 418; **6**:135
   John **1**:48, 83, 87, 158, 161-162,
     164-165, 197-198, 206-207,
     268-270, 272, 275, 277, 282,
     284, 290-292, 298, 300, 320,
     322-327, 329-333, 336-339, 451,
     509, 516, 518-521, 525, 547
   Richd. **1**:322, 337
   Samuel **8**:756, 769-770; **9**:44, 66,
     77
   Tho. **1**:513, 515
CURTIS(S), John **9**:44-45, 66, 68-69,
   77, 85-86, 328-329, 331, 620
CURTIUS, John **8**:565-566
CURWEN, John **16**:11
CURWIN, George **10**:302-303, 305,
   409; **11**:692
CURWIN (CURWEN), John **15**:448, 494,
   527
CURZON & GOVERNIEUR **12**:416
CUSEHUAH, Isai **3**:453
CUSHWA, John **14**:114
CUSICK, Ann **16**:254
CUSSANS, Mary **12**:75, 81
CUSTALOGA (CUSTALOGO) **9**:216,
   219-224, 226-227, 251-253,
   259-260, 264
CUSTARD, John **12**:194; **16**:42
CUSTELOGO **8**:313
CUSTOLOGO **5**:660
CUT FINGER, Peter **7**:67
CUTFINGER, Peter **8**:392
CUTHBERT, Anthony **12**:146; **15**:13,
   430, 439; **16**:118, 167, 170, 293,
   299
   John **5**:186
   Margaret **12**:61
   Thomas **10**:462, 562, 593; **12**:149;
     13:240; **15**:68
   Thomas, Sr. **11**:17, 139, 601, 603,
     758, 767
CUTHBERTSON, Samuel **12**:166, 171,
   518, 633
CUTLER, John **3**:56, 69
CUTTIGHEGAN **8**:312
CUTTING, Jno. **10**:555
CUYANQUERRYCOEA **9**:89
CUYLER, Cornelius **5**:553-554,
   557-558
   Cornelius (Cornelis) **6**:61, 276

CUYLER, Jane **13**:522
 Joha. **3**:199
CUZZENS, Samuel **5**:532
 William **7**:500
CUZZINS, William **5**:175
CYPHER, Jacob **11**:514, 516-517
 Michael **10**:694
 Peter **12**:333

D VAIVVE, --- (Monsieur) **12**:470
D'ABREN, --- (Monsieur) **8**:18
D'ESTAING, --- (Count) **11**:553, 692,
 714, 779; **12**:114, 120, 162, 167
D'HAES, Johanes **1**:222-224, 335-338,
 344 (See HAES)
 John **1**:225, 272, 275, 277, 279,
 292, 294, 297, 302-307, 310,
 320, 323-324, 340
D'HAWES, Johanes **1**:335-336
D'PLESSIE, --- **1**:202
D'RUSSEY, --- (Capt.) **12**:470
D(E)ALE, Samuel **12**:137, 164
D(O)UG(H)LASS, Ephraim **16**:26, 32,
 163, 209, 214b, 418, 422, 447
DA(U)NT, Knowles (Knolles)
 4:109-110
DABIS, Caleb **13**:691
DADDER, Philip **16**:283
DAGLEY, James **13**:756
DAGWORTHY, --- (Capt.) **6**:643
 John **10**:217, 352
 John (Capt.) **7**:601-603, 629,
 632-633
DAHAUFF (DEHUFF), Abraham **10**:539,
 714, 765-767
DAHLBERRY, Frederick **15**:465
DAILEY, Daniel **13**:368
 Francis **15**:119
 Peter **15**:310; **16**:37
DAILY, --- (Capt.) **8**:125
DAILY (DAYLY), John **14**:194, 433
DALBEY, Gifford **12**:524
DALBO, Willm. **2**:509
DALE, Andrew **16**:334-335
 Petr. **2**:10
 Samuel **11**:633; **14**:250, 256; **15**:91,
 107, 115
DALLAM, Robert **11**:93, 118
DALLAP, William **11**:304
DALLAS, A. D. **16**:75
DALLEY, Gifford **13**:544
DALSTON, Isaac **9**:769
DALTON, Patrick **15**:471; **16**:382
DALZELL, George **12**:429
DAMPIER, --- (Capt.) **2**:99
DAMPSEY, Patrick **14**:614
DANAE, --- (Mr.) **11**:404
DANALUQUESHON **6**:158
DANBACH, Jacob **3**:328
DANEY, Daniel **10**:683
DANFORTH, Samuel **5**:297
DANGERFIELD, --- (Lt.) **8**:386
DANI, Tho. **1**:84
DANIEL **7**:713; **8**:87, 89, 92-93,
 130, 148-149, 174, 415
DANIEL, --- **6**:749
 George **12**:188
 John **12**:187
DANIEL (SLAVE) **10**:93
DANIELL, Francis **1**:371
DANKS, Thomas **12**:201
DANLER, Hans **3**:454

DANNER, Christian **3**:516
DANNERS, Michael **13**:44
DANUY, Jean Louis **3**:458
DAPPLIN, --- **6**:61
DAR(E)ING, Wm. **1**:132, 134, 144
DARBEER, Pieter **3**:453
DARBY, Daniel **13**:544
 John **1**:48, 188
DARCK, Saml1. **1**:601
DARCUS (DARKESS), Andrew **12**:85,
 364, 568, 779
DARE, Tho. **1**:92
DARFEN, Christian **4**:72
DARK, Saml1. **2**:112, 397
DARK(E), Saml1. **1**:48, 87, 614, 621
DARLING, Thomas **6**:259
 William **12**:576; **14**:608
DARLINGTON, Abraham **3**:289, 370, 387
 Robert **13**:564; **14**:87, 134, 435,
 437
 William **5**:186
DARNALL, John **5**:594
DARRAGH, James **14**:608
 John **12**:188
DARROCH, Robert **13**:356, 630
 Thomas **11**:56
 William **13**:630
DARTER, Edwd. **1**:95
DARTMOUTH **9**:343
DARTMOUTH, --- (Earl of) **10**:102,
 200, 219-222, 240, 242, 244-247,
 250
 Ld. **2**:403
DARVALL, Wm. **1**:83, 104, 106,
 113-118, 123-124, 132-133, 135,
 138-139, 158, 169-170, 173,
 177-184, 202-206, 222-226,
 229-232, 243, 246-247, 249,
 251-252, 254, 439-440
DASHONG, Frederick **11**:772
DASHWOOD, Francis (Sir) **9**:49
DATWEILLAR, Melchoir **4**:73
DAUBERT, Christian **14**:194, 301, 438
DAUGHERTY, Daniel **16**:480
 David **16**:520
DAVENPORT, Humphrey **1**:143-144
 Jonas **3**:285
 Joseph **10**:448
 Josiah **8**:776-778
DAVEY, Morris **13**:515
DAVI(E)S, John **5**:108, 203, 301, 303
 Walter **9**:242
DAVID **8**:132
DAVID, --- **11**:628
 Caleb **11**:301; **16**:30-31, 61, 166,
 272, 380
 Edward **12**:656
 Evan **4**:268
 John **3**:225
 Lewis **4**:272
 Lues **1**:438
 Philip **5**:760
 William **4**:271
DAVID (DOCHSHEWEHMINT) **9**:280
DAVID (the MOHOCK) **7**:34, 46,
 48-49, 109, 774
DAVIDSON, --- **10**:531; **12**:575
 Alexander **13**:627
 Francis **13**:643; **14**:129, 431
 Hugh **14**:212; **15**:546; **16**:168, 461
 James **12**:438; **13**:632; **14**:92, 101,
 394, 417, 419
 James (Dr.) **13**:557, 714
 James (Rev.) **11**:374, 403, 509

44

DERR, John 16:295
DERR (DEER), Matthias 14:191, 195, 413
DERRACK, William 11:155
DERRAUGH, Charles 14:66
DERRICK, Godfrey 15:364
DERRING, Christopher 14:652; 16:460
DERRY, John 10:572, 575
 Michael 14:295, 302, 427
DERST, John Paul 3:467
DERVALL, Wm. 1:164, 168, 171
DERWOOD, Elizabeth 11:703
DESCORBIERES, Ambrose 14:4
DESHLER (DASHLER, DECHLER), ---
 13:367
 Charles 12:460
 David 11:53, 212, 365, 422, 450, 501, 512, 547; 12:44, 303, 306, 310, 364, 376, 411, 438, 460, 486, 596; 13:109, 366, 441, 701; 14:278
DESHONG, Peter 11:482, 484-485
 William 16:478
DESLER, Charles 11:437
DESTLIERRE, Legardeur 6:16-17
DETEMER, Michael 3:328
DETERER, Adam 11:380
DETHEES, --- (Monsieur) 1:122
DETRICK, Jacob 14:85, 418
 Michael 13:718
DETZELL, George 13:562; 14:301, 425
DEVAN, Barnabas 6:142
DEVEENEY, James 14:131,134, 423
DEVENE (DEVONE, DEVENEY), Hugh 14:296, 303, 429
DEVENNY, Samuel 5:327
DEVER, James 10:43
DEVINE, Bernard 14:298, 304, 418
 Magdelen 11:710
DEVINGER, Kilian 12:484
DEVOIR, Cornelius 16:239
DEVOLT, John 14:189, 192, 410
DEVONSHIRE, --- (Duke of) 4:298, 484-485; 7:277
DEWAATYHUNCK 8:661
DEWALL, G. 14:106
DEWALT, Francis 13:368
DEWART, Lewis 1:16
 William 12:513
DEWEES, Philip 5:489
 Samuel 11:340, 591, 765
 Thomas 10:268, 359-360, 402-403, 408, 424, 429, 455-456, 503, 524, 568, 618-619, 677
 William 7:769; 8:575; 9:205, 672; 10:210-212, 260, 267, 270, 668, 673; 11:51, 58, 201, 273; 12:139, 507
DEWICK, Cassimer 13:383
DEWIT, Eze. 9:509
DEWPREE, Andrew 1:82
DEWSBERRY, James 16:162
DEXTER, Enos 4:468
DEYNEN, Johannes 3:467
DIALOG, John 11:682
DICK, Archibald 12:306
 John 9:751-753, 755, 770-771
 Matthias 4:60
DICKENS, Edward 12:242
DICKENSON, John 11:4, 92
 Philemon 11:92
DICKENSON (DICKINSON), Benjamin (Capt.) 5:71, 74-75, 78
DICKERT, Jacob 11:89
DICKESON, Brittingham 11:125
DICKEY, Elizabeth 15:380

DICKEY, Henry 15:523
 John 11:77
 Moses 6:673
 Robert 15:480; 16:215, 521
 William 5:444, 469
DICKIE, Moses 5:186
DICKINSON, --- (Gen.) 12:454
 --- (Mr.) 13:411
 Cadwalader 11:605
 James 13:622; 14:129, 431, 454, 456, 653-654
 John 10:280, 282-283, 298, 307, 314-315, 330, 333-334, 336, 338, 340, 344, 351, 362, 367, 374, 443, 483-484, 486, 548, 607, 754; 13:391, 409, 413-416, 426, 435, 439, 441, 472-473, 476, 483, 490, 518, 521, 533, 538, 542, 561, 616, 629-630, 644-645, 654, 663, 666, 683, 690-691, 728, 733, 737, 495, 498, 500-501, 503-516, 518-519, 521-524, 526-532, 534, 536-538, 540-541, 543-552, 554, 556, 558-559, 561-567, 570-572, 574-579, 589-590, 592, 594-595, 597-601, 605-607, 609-611, 613-615, 617-623, 625-633, 637-638, 641-642, 644-647, 666, 668, 673-675, 677-678, 681, 683-684, 686-687, 690-707, 711, 719, 721, 7 24-729, 731-744, 746, 748, 750-754, 760-766, 768-766; 14:1-6, 8, 10-11, 14, 17, 22, 24, 29-31, 35, 40-61, 65-66, 73-80, 103, 106-122, 130, 135-138, 141, 149-186, 188, 196-203, 205-207, 209-211, 213-217, 220, 224, 228-229, 231, 233-254, 256-270, 274-277, 279-291, 307, 316-317, 323-326, 342-345, 347-348, 350, 356-363, 365, 367-369, 376-388, 393-396, 398-402, 406, 441-446, 449-451, 453, 455-462, 464-470, 483-484, 486-501, 503-506, 508-519, 521-522, 524, 526-537, 539-541, 543-553; 15:107
 Jonathan 3:14-18, 25, 27-33, 37-39, 43-45, 47, 50, 52, 55, 57-58, 62, 64, 67-69, 75, 81, 82, 90, 92, 102, 105, 107-109, 113-115, 120-123, 125, 130, 139-141, 143-145, 147, 156, 321; 11:602, 605; 12:102, 155, 548; 13:61, 478
 Jonathan (John) 2:23-24, 539-542, 545-546, 549-553, 555-557, 560-562, 566-567, 571-573, 575-578, 582-583, 590, 594-597, 603-607, 609-611, 613, 615, 629
 Samuel 6:136
 Stafford 12:2, 21
DICKS, George 13:638; 14:132, 411, 517, 571
 Joseph 16:194
 Peter 5:108, 203, 303; 7:291-293
DICKSON, Helena 13:535
 James 4:228, 230; 16:413
 John 14:293
 Mary 9:745-746
 William 9:745-746
DIDDY, Jerry 12:333
 John 14:297, 304, 428
DIDIER, Henry 11:608, 718
DIEBELLBISSIN, Hans George 3:415

49

DOLL, Casper **14**:447
 Christian **11**:340
 Conrad **5**:318
 Hans Jacob **3**:385
DOLLAND, George **14**:299, 439
DOLLAR, Hance **3**:38
DOLLINGER, George **6**:704; **10**:703
DOLLMAN, Mathias **12**:187
DOLONY, Joseph **13**:212
DOLSTON, Isaac **11**:611-612
 Isaac, Jr. **11**:611-612
 Matthew **11**:611-612
DOLT, Johan Philip **3**:270
DOLTON, George **14**:192, 429
DOLTORS, George **14**:189
DOM, Michael **4**:59
DOMINICK, David **10**:716
DOMM, Joseph **3**:390
DONAL(D)SON, John **1**:323, 369, 458,
 460, 472, 475, 479-480, 482-485,
 488, 491, 498, 502, 504, 541,
 547, 552-553, 569-570, 578, 580,
 595-596, 601, 611-612
DONALD, John **5**:210
DONALDSON, --- (Col.) **13**:385
 Arthur **7**:717; **10**:260, 267, 513,
 525, 535, 648, 651, 676, 704,
 718, 721, 725; **11**:15, 44, 109,
 559-560, 564, 620, 692, 702;
 14:75, 78, 104, 119-120, 153,
 199, 212, 241-242, 500
 Jno. **2**:34, 50
 John **12**:482; **14**:61, 68, 73, 150;
 15:432, 617; **16**:45, 64, 105,
 110, 113, 173, 216, 235, 241,
 252, 299, 301, 370, 393, 443,
 462, 478, 493, 516, 544
 Joseph **10**:163, 735-736; **11**:101,
 234, 340; **14**:504, 632
DONALDSON (DONALLSON), Andrew
 5:444, 469
DONAT, John **16**:24
DONAUGHOO, Patrick **13**:586; **14**:432
DONAVAN, James **13**:709
DONGAN (DUNGAN), Thomas **3**:101, 133,
 205, 273, 600
DONIVAN, George **14**:459
DONLEY, Moses **12**:32
DONNAHUE, John **15**:463
DONNAHY, Cornelius **9**:631-632
DONNALDSON, Hu. **8**:576
DONNEL(L), Nathaniel **11**:244, 286
DONNELL, John **14**:301
 Nathaniel **10**:524
DONNELLY, Francis **13**:567; **14**:93,
 428
 John **12**:76, 102, 718-719
DONOP, James M. **14**:294
DONOVAN, John **13**:755
DONYLEQUESHONEY **6**:160
DORAN, Brian **13**:153
 Bryan **5**:603-604; **13**:272
 Bryian **13**:183
 Henry **14**:327
 James **16**:23
 Jorance **10**:720
 William **6**:648
DORAS, Patrick **12**:188
DORCER, Andrew **14**:91
DOREST, Casper **3**:367
DORLAND, Abraham **14**:407-408, 438
 George **14**:63
DORMAN, Ludowick **13**:598
 Ludwick **14**:89, 411
 William **14**:62, 85, 427

DORMOND (DERMOND), Richard **11**:23,
 121
DOROUGH, Henry **13**:180-181
DORREY, --- (Capt.) **10**:550
DORRINGTON, Wm. **1**:84
DORSAT, C. P. S. **4**:471
DORSET, --- (Duke of) **5**:618; **6**:411
 John **13**:504, 506-507, 527-528, 571
DORSEY, Benedict **8**:234
 Catharine **13**:240
 John **11**:601, 603
 Leonard **16**:316
 Matthew **15**:119
 Robert **11**:282
 Thomas **10**:405-406, 416, 436, 464,
 471, 499; **11**:266, 270, 274,
 276-277, 287, 300, 305, 312,
 368, 374, 376-378, 380, 391-392,
 396, 406, 408, 424, 437, 444,
 447, 450-453, 463, 475, 488,
 493, 509, 511, 521, 543, 553
DORSINS, Jane **7**:344
DORVIL, Joseph **14**:49
DOTT, Henry **14**:492
DOTTERER, Henry **16**:498
DOTY, Samuel **13**:456, 669, 715;
 14:87, 414
 Theodorus **14**:117
DOUCET, Jean **7**:240
 Pierre **7**:240
DOUD, Michael **14**:614
DOUGHARTY, John **6**:144
DOUGHERTY (DAUGHERTY, DOCHERTY,
 DOGHARTY, DOUGHTERY), --- **12**:575
 --- (Capt.) **11**:678
 --- (Mr.) **13**:123, 132, 257, 354,
 760-761
 Ann **8**:728
 Bernard **9**:386, 673, 730; **10**:8, 78,
 101, 163, 212, 265, 271, 280,
 341-342, 346-347, 351-357,
 360-362, 365, 367, 371, 373-378,
 380-382, 384-385, 387-390, 398,
 400, 403-406, 409, 419, 427,
 434, 495, 501-502, 511-512, 519,
 524, 526, 531, 593, 599-600,
 604; **11**:17, 556-557, 581, 628,
 630, 633; **12**:72, 120, 123, 546;
 13:101, 112, 128, 133-134, 198,
 265, 310, 359, 374, 376-377,
 446, 591, 594, 598, 615, 730,
 741, 742-748, 750-751, 754,
 760-763, 766, 768-766; **14**:1-6,
 11, 15-16, 23-24, 86, 175-177,
 179-181, 183-186, 188, 196-203,
 205-207, 209-211, 213-217,
 227-229, 231-233, 239, 243, 413,
 482-484, 486-488, 493-498,
 501-503, 505, 507-513, 516,
 518-522, 524, 526-534, 545-553,
 557-558, 560-567; **15**:84-85, 88,
 90-96; **16**:32, 520
 Cornelius **9**:5
 Daniel **11**:107; **14**:293, 300, 412
 Edward **5**:120
 George **12**:715; **14**:294, 301, 429;
 16:170
 Henry **7**:500; **10**:287, 296, 327,
 335, 375, 379, 442, 445, 606,
 616-617, 619, 702; **11**:80, 223;
 12:383, 483; **16**:334
 James **13**:631; **14**:96
 John **5**:247, 597, 662; **11**:578;
 13:596; **14**:88, 426; **15**:40
 John, Jr. **10**:86
 Michael **15**:310

DOUGHERTY (DAUGHERTY, DOCHERTY, DOGHARTY, DOUGHTERY), Mordecai 11:511
Peggy 8:750
Philip 12:464; 14:536
William 12:162
DOUGLAS, Andrew 4:483
Robert 10:358
Thomas 11:219; 13:456
DOUGLASS, Charles 14:62
Ephraim 13:456, 681, 702, 705, 742; 14:54, 169, 454, 525, 567; 15:121-122, 584
George 9:172, 673; 11:579, 703; 12:618
James 11:81; 16:319
John 8:562; 10:340, 653, 715, 719; 11:2; 12:2, 75; 13:38; 15:499; 16:16
Joseph 15:6, 49, 132
Phoebe 15:424
Thomas 13:713; 14:89, 178, 436, 621
William 13:624, 778; 14:128, 300, 438
DOUGLASS (SEE HOLWEE &) 10:340
DOUNGAN, --- (Gov.) 1:114
DOUSE, John 13:636; 14:97, 420
DOUTER, Thoma 9:508
DOUWES, Inse 14:47-48
DOVE, Robert 11:513, 516-517
DOVENBERGER, Jacob 14:131-132, 439
DOVER, --- (Sergeant) 7:408
Andrew 10:450; 13:557; 14:181, 431
John 10:450; 12:402, 404, 407
DOW, Alexander 14:83, 417
Andrew 13:554
Elijah 11:4, 26
DOWDLE, John 9:545
Rose 15:386
DOWDY, John 7:192
DOWEL, William 8:172
DOWELL, --- (Capt.) 5:332
DOWERS, William 12:519
DOWN, Thomas 9:508
DOWN(E)Y, James 5:444, 469
DOWNAR, Richard 4:256
DOWNARD, James 4:102, 107
William 4:102, 107, 111
DOWNEY, John 14:157, 364
DOWNING, --- (Capt.) 13:189
John 13:360
DOWNY, John 11:248-251, 286
DOWSETT, Peter 15:131
DOYLE, --- (Capt.) 11:158
Charles 14:433
Felix 5:444
John 13:251, 715; 14:295, 302
Judith 12:361
Patrick 14:297, 304, 426
Peter 13:557; 14:303, 431
Samuel 16:396-397, 464, 483-484, 508, 547
Thomas 13:717; 14:178, 533; 15:437; 16:263
William 9:285, 333, 398
DOZ, Andrew 10:462; 12:301-303, 305, 309, 375-376, 392, 397; 13:584
DOZE, Andree 1:451-452
DRAIS, Daniel 13:764
DRAKE, Joseph 9:755
Oliver 12:70
Peter 16:259
Samuel 11:65
DRANK, Peter 14:124, 128, 437

DRANTMAN, Hans Jorig 4:73
DRAPER, --- (Maj.) 9:711
Alexander 1:77, 84, 87
John 10:106, 545, 547, 551, 595-596, 606
Samuel 10:271
DRAPPER, Nehemiah 9:203
DRASBARB, Colas 4:72
DRASON, Matthew 7:202
DRAUGH, Rudolph 3:385
DRAYER, Jacob 16:8
DRAYTON, --- (Mr.) 11:540, 755
DREHER, Christopher 3:569
George 3:569
DRELL, Johannes 3:413
DREUCHABRO(A)D, Andrew 14:81, 100, 434
DREWRY, William 10:94
DRIBELBIS, Martin 16:373
DRICEBACK (DRIESBACK), Simon 11:177, 365
DRIEBLER, Joh. Jacob 3:458
DRIER (DRYER), Jacob 15:159, 164-165, 213, 219, 311, 320, 348, 501, 611, 624, 627, 629-631
DRIES, Andries 3:520
Cornelius 3:520
Johan Adam 3:520
Peter 3:520
DRIESBACH, Adam 15:290
Jost 11:45
Simon 13:723; 14:18, 203, 213
DRINKER, --- (Mrs.) 11:468, 473
Henry 11:283, 288, 295, 309, 460, 472; 13:84; 14:537; 15:425
John 10:486-487, 497; 11:602, 605, 668; 13:30, 131; 14:506
DRINKER (SEE JAMES &) 10:711; 11:119
DRINNEN, Arthur 16:533
DRISCALL, --- (Mr.) 6:142
DRISCOLL, Daniel 14:610
DRISDELL, Alexander 12:450
DRITT, Jacob 11:61; 14:129, 421
DRIVER, Hopkins 13:553, 573; 14:89, 437
DROCHSEL, Peter 3:516
DROGAN, Patrick 12:56
DROMGOOLE, --- (Capt.) 15:238
DRUM, Charles 12:598
Conrad 12:631
DRUMMOND, --- (Lord) 10:445
--- (Lt.) 12:356
And. & Co. 9:50
Henry 9:48, 51
James 15:143
DRUMOND, --- (Dr.) 11:268
DRURY, Sarah 9:192
William 7:717; 10:671
DRYSTREET, Henry 1:95
DU BROY, Jon. (Capt.) 2:90, 96
DU CASSE, Dominique 10:261-262
DU CHAMBOU, --- (Monsieur) 6:447
DU PONCEAU, --- (Mr.) 13:739
DU PONCEAUS, Peter Stephen 14:258
DUANE, --- (Mr.) 12:370
DUARTE, John Goucia 12:64
DUBBS, Henrich 4:60
DUBO, Abraham 3:467
DUBOIS, Abraham 12:136, 510, 646, 747; 13:86, 392, 720; 15:429
Gilbert 13:447
DUBRIC, Jacob 3:50
DUBROIS, Jno. 1:397, 435
DUBS, Hans Jost 4:72
DUBUESON, --- (Lt. Col.) 13:51

DUCHE, --- (Mrs.) **11**:759, 762
Andrew **13**:25-26; **15**:482
Anthony **12**:196, 247, 441, 731;
  13:146
Elizabeth **12**:17-18, 36, 309
Jacob **8**:575; **9**:205, 672; **10**:46
Jacob (Rev.) **11**:759, 762, 764;
  12:578
Jacob, Jr. **13**:26
T. S. **12**:18
DUCHE(E), Jacob **7**:648-649, 669,
  714, 769
DUCHEMON, --- (Mr.) **11**:140
DUCK, Elizabeth **13**:389
Jacob **11**:745
DUCKET(T), Tho. **1**:92, 95, 168, 209,
  322-327, 329-338, 342-343, 607
DUCKETT, Robert **3**:276
DUCKINSON, John **13**:576
DUCKSON, John **14**:300
DUDERMAN, Philip **3**:519
DUDLEY, Gideon **15**:489, 603
Joseph **15**:489, 547, 603
DUER, --- (Mr.) **11**:346, 540
DUFF, --- (Mr.) **10**:339; **11**:163
Daniel **14**:108
James **14**:81, 101, 438
John **12**:187
Thomas **9**:57, 199, 286, 623, 688,
778
DUFF(E)Y, Patrick **14**:87, 418, 430
DUFFELL, Isaac **15**:486
DUFFEY, --- (Capt.) **12**:67; **13**:456
James **15**:183
Patrick **13**:573
DUFFIELD, --- (Dr.) **10**:362, 388,
  409, 412, 545, 549, 553, 614,
  689, 695, 717, 749; **11**:38;
  13:199
--- (Lt.) **13**:189
Benja. **2**:34, 65
Benjamin (Dr.) **15**:346, 365, 369,
  407; **16**:210, 222b
Edward **9**:781; **10**:47, 54, 267, 409;
  16:361
Isaac **15**:119
John **12**:139; **14**:81, 101, 129, 414,
  436, 506; **15**:149, 155, 426, 468
John (Dr.) **13**:157, 643
Ratchford **11**:139
S. (Dr.) **13**:170
Samuel (Dr.) **13**:555; **14**:100, 431
William **11**:366, 498; **16**:32
DUFFIELD & DELANEY **11**:13, 38
DUFFIELD & DELANY **13**:297
DUFFY, James **6**:136
Terence **14**:292, 299, 412
DUGAN, Christopher **14**:452
Henry **13**:474
James **11**:181; **15**:475; **16**:402
Michael **16**:500
DUGBY (DAGLEY), James **14**:91, 421
DUGUID, John **10**:449
DUHL, Martin **14**:61, 408, 439
DUKE OF YORK **2**:39, 56
DUKEY, Mary **15**:503
DULANY, Daniel **3**:612, 614;
  4:115-116, 118, 120-121, 124,
  130, 135-137, 140, 142-144, 146,
  206
DULIKE, Johannes Van **3**:569
DULL, Abraham **12**:333
Casper **10**:219
Christian **10**:680; **11**:21; **15**:100,
  294; **16**:490, 501
George **9**:713

DULT, Jacob **13**:758
DUMAS, --- (Monsieur) **7**:99
DUMBARTON, --- (Lord) **1**:246
DUMBOLB, Abraham **4**:100
Erns Fredrich **4**:100
DUMLAP, Robert **12**:343
DUMOIS, Richard **10**:671
DUN, --- (Mr.) **10**:398
DUN (SEE ROBINS, DUN & HAIL) **11**:29
DUNAHOW, Hugh **12**:536-537
DUNAVON (DUNAVAN), James **14**:424
John **14**:85, 95, 418
DUNBAR, James **16**:211b
Robert **11**:761
Thomas **7**:23, 29, 37, 39-40
Thomas (Col.) **6**:200, 311, 395,
  477, 480, 482-484, 486, 488-490,
  492, 495, 498-500, 502, 510-517,
  519-522, 535, 547-550, 558, 561,
  563-566, 586, 593-596, 600,
  602-604, 730, 733
William **13**:174
DUNCAN, --- (Mr.) **13**:125-126, 234,
  348, 673
Benjamin **13**:59
Daniel **15**:122, 196
David **12**:170, 208, 260, 624, 633,
  653-654, 656, 672, 700, 704;
  13:286, 353, 541-542; **14**:521;
  16:400, 504-505
Edmund **13**:447
James **13**:611, 712; **14**:83, 269,
  364, 417, 446; **15**:9, 93, 126,
  222, 399; **16**:340, 400, 489
John **14**:179
Margaret **12**:283
Matthew **10**:447
Mich'l. (Matthew) **12**:12
Samuel **11**:114
Stephen **11**:54, 229, 633, 691, 739;
  12:296, 518, 526; **13**:112, 133,
  396, 415; **16**:380, 487
Stephne **14**:236, 449
Stewart **11**:100
Thomas **10**:705
DUNCANNON, --- **5**:243
DUNDAS, James **12**:525
Thomas **11**:4; **15**:383, 458
DUNDAS(S), James **11**:6, 19, 34, 139,
  263, 270, 277, 285, 309, 428,
  607, 658, 753, 766
DUNFORD, William **5**:210
DUNGAN, --- (Col.) **10**:178; **13**:467
--- (Gov.) **13**:464, 466, 468
Garrat **11**:179, 281
Garret **15**:48
Thomas **11**:58-59, 244; **13**:465, 717,
  731, 759; **14**:64, 85, 418
William **12**:381
DUNGAN (DONGAN), Thomas (Gov.)
  6:255, 264, 290, 557
DUNGWORTH, Richard **1**:500-501
DUNKEL, Johannes **3**:385
DUNKEN, James **10**:684
DUNKIN, Ann **12**:346
Robert **12**:346
DUNLAP, --- (Mr.) **13**:446
Andrew **5**:444
Arthur **5**:444
Colm **3**:385
James **9**:732; **10**:632, 634, 637,
  639, 680, 713, 752, 768; **12**:30,
  519; **13**:134, 396, 547
John **10**:636, 747, 765; **11**:17, 33,
  46, 264, 281, 409, 426, 432,
  440-441, 483, 495, 521, 615,->

EAST, Thomas 1:367
 W. 1:123
EASTB(O)URNE, Robert 10:633, 761,
 763, 769, 780-781
EASTBO(U)RN(E), Jno. 2:183, 209
EASTBURN, Benjamin 3:573; 5:751,
 760; 7:400; 8:250-252, 260
 Esther 16:427
 Robert 11:51
EASTBURN(E), Benjamin 4:280, 313,
 503
EASTBURNE, Ester 13:337
 Jonathan 16:427
EASTON, Dennis 11:513, 516-517
EASTWOOD, Simon 10:384
EATON, David 13:604
 Henry 13:778; 14:83, 414
EAYRES, --- (Capt.) 11:191
EB(E)NER, Casper 14:96, 423
EBBY, Henrick 3:432
EBENER, Hans George 3:458
EBENOR, Caspar 13:676
EBERHARD, Godfried 4:100
EBERHARD (EBERHART), Philip 14:88,
 423
EBERLY, George 10:503
 John 11:380
EBERMAN, Conrad 3:458
EBERT, Cath. 11:679
 Catherine 12:78
 George 7:620-621
 Gobliep 16:156
 Hans Georg. 3:415
 Hans Michael 3:415
 John 7:620
EBORT, Johan Michael 3:456
EBURN, Wm. 2:605
ECHARD, John 9:557
ECHGOHSON 8:750
ECHLEWICH, Thos. 2:494
ECKERT, Henrich 3:466
ECKFIELD, Elizabeth 14:570
ECKFORD, Philip 3:417
ECKGOHESON (ECKGHOSON) 8:750
ECKHARDDT, William 13:172
ECKHART (ECKART, ECKHARD),
 Valentine 11:404, 423; 12:131,
 308, 466, 594, 721-722; 13:372,
 462, 570; 14:170-171, 442;
 15:11, 295; 16:418
 William 12:570; 13:35, 46; 15:378
ECKHART (ECKERT), John 14:226, 321
ECKL(E)Y (ECKLE), John 1:119, 121,
 127, 146-147, 208-210, 212-228,
 266, 268, 279-282, 293, 312,
 317, 319-322
ECKLEY, Joseph 15:534
ECKNISERA 5:317
ECKOANG 8:435-436
ED(D)IE, John 14:194, 234, 557, 609
EDDY, Alexander 13:38
 Charles 11:284, 289, 296, 309,
 460, 472; 12:28; 15:329-330
 David 16:515
 John 10:477; 12:390
 Mary 13:121, 516
EDELMAN, David 3:519
 Philip Jacob 3:519
EDEN, Robert (Gov.) 10:241-242, 247
EDES & GILLS 11:648
EDESMAN, Joannes 3:328
EDG(S)WORTH (EDGEWORTH), Bridget
 15:16, 216, 290, 299
 John 15:246, 262, 290
EDGAR, --- (Mr.) 5:108, 655; 13:403
 Charles 7:394

EDGAR, David 13:777; 14:436
 James 11:336, 344, 346, 364-372,
 374-375, 383-389, 408-412,
 414-415, 417-419, 421-423, 426,
 428, 430, 432-438, 440-445,
 447-449, 457-459, 461-466,
 468-469, 471, 479, 481, 486-490,
 492-493, 495, 497, 499, 501-503,
 506, 508, 522, 524-530, 541-544,
 547-548, 550-552, 554, 556-567,
 569, 571-574, 576-591; 13:38,
 134, 562, 740; 14:8, 99, 156,
 177, 213, 437; 15:552
 Robert 9:89
 Samuel 13:637; 14:126, 439
EDGE, James 10:555
EDGECUMBE, --- (Lord) 7:277; 10:103
EDGERTON, Edward 14:130, 436
EDGSWORTH, John 14:254
EDIDLE, Elias 11:37
EDIE, John 13:669; 15:102, 297, 579
 Samuel 9:201, 731, 778; 10:56,
 101, 163; 11:633; 14:208;
 15:102, 297, 303-306, 308-309,
 313-317, 320-328, 331, 337-353,
 394-401, 403-412, 414-415,
 417-430, 432-436, 438-449,
 451-460, 538-541, 543-545,
 548-551, 554, 556-564, 566-569,
 571-584, 586-590, 592, 594-600,
 602-608, 610-620, 622-623;
 16:54-57, 59, 62-65, 67-68,
 70-78, 80, 82-91, 93-94, 96-104,
 152-158, 160, 162-166, 168-169,
 171-173, 175-178, 180-183,
 187-194, 196-202, 205, 209-211,
 214-216, 218-220, 222-224,
 209b-212b, 214b-222b, 224b,
 225-227, 229-233, 235-244,
 315-316, 318, 320-324, 326-327,
 329, 331-332, 336, 339-341,
 344-350, 352-356, 358-360,
 362-366, 368-373, 376-384,
 386-390, 392-393, 441-442,
 445-447, 449-459, 461-465, 477,
 479-484
EDIN(G)BURGH, John 11:151, 165
EDLER, Johan Hendrick 3:457
EDMESTON, --- 6:490
EDMINSON, Jno. 1:114
EDMINSTON, Samuel 14:102, 440-441,
 444
EDMISTON, Samuel 7:717; 16:166,
 168, 224, 390, 444, 538, 543
 Samuel (Dr.) 13:263, 593
EDMISTON (EDMONSTON), Samuel 15:8,
 388, 584
EDMONDS, William 8:11, 98, 304
EDMONDS (EDMUNDS), William 7:119,
 163-167, 169, 174-175, 177, 204,
 207, 217, 222, 249, 756, 772-774
EDMONSTON, Charles 9:515
EDMUNDS, Robert 1:547-548
EDMUNDS (EDMONDS), William 10:280,
 331, 333-336, 341, 344, 346
EDNRESS, Zachariah 13:759
EDWARD, Evan 13:709
EDWARDS, --- (Mr.) 6:174, 260, 268
 Alexander 9:205, 672; 10:46
 Charles 11:612, 625
 David 8:436; 14:47
 Enoch 14:629; 15:8; 16:133
 Evan 10:448; 12:705; 13:713;
 14:134, 418
 Henry 14:481; 15:246
 James 5:325

EDWARDS, John 3:542, 587; 5:325; 10:679
  Joseph 11:514, 516-517
  Joshua 12:504-506
  Lewis 7:500
  Marshall 10:473, 477, 657; 11:66, 266, 391, 448; 13:579
  Rachel 12:2
  Simon 5:226
  Susanna 13:279
  Thomas 3:345, 356, 359, 380, 394, 521-523; 4:152, 267, 272, 483, 588; 5:3, 378, 600; 11:335, 350, 423; 12:134, 142, 443, 508; 13:393, 722-724; 14:233, 267-268
  William 11:149
EDWARDS (See ROBERTS, William), --- 15:413, 442
EDWIN, John 8:99
EFFINGER, Henry 11:515-517
EFFINGHAM, --- (Lord) 3:133; 13:465
EGA (SEE ROSS &) 10:722; 11:16, 48
EGAN, John 12:82, 188
EGAR, --- (Mr.) 11:219
  Robert 7:154
EGBERTSON, James 5:194
EGE, George 10:623
EGE(E), George 12:131, 508
EGELBERGER, Fred 3:329
EGG, Joseph 13:103, 123, 184; 15:391, 441
  Rudolph 3:593
EGGER, Leonard 15:499
EGGERSON, James 11:122
EGHKOOHUNT 8:152
EGLING, Johan Adam 3:413
EGNAR, John 11:358
EGO-HO-HOUN (EWGOHOHOWEN) 8:159, 176, 196, 208-210
EGOLF, Jacob 14:284
EGRE(E)MONT, --- (Earl of) 8:677-681, 685-686, 688, 703, 710; 9:12-16, 38-39, 49, 150
EGY, George 13:393
EHRE, John 12:374
  Manuel 14:230
EHRMAN, John 13:3, 723
EIBE, Jacob Michael 3:516
EICHELBERGER, Adam 14:557
  Bernard (Barnet) 10:451, 477
  Frederick 12:374
  George 9:548, 624, 689
  Jacob 11:371, 443; 12:27, 374, 421-422
  Michael 11:143
EICHOLTZ, Adam 16:366
EIKELBERGER (EIKLEBURGER), Martin 9:201, 543, 731
EIN, Johan George 3:452
EISELMAN, Benedict 3:452
EISEMAN, Hans Casper 3:515
  Hans Wolf 3:515
EISEN, Carel 3:458
EISENHOWER, Jacob, Jr. 15:454
EKENBILL, Henrick 3:385
EKESON, Thomas 14:156
EL(L)IOTT, Daniel 15:512, 598, 602, 606
EL(L)WOOD, John 11:72, 514, 516-517, 624, 631, 653, 745
ELDER, --- (Col.) 12:3, 91; 13:141
  --- (Mr.) 15:58
  --- (Rev.) 9:101
  David 11:524
  George 14:375
  James 11:51

ELDER, John 15:176
  John (Rev.) 7:507, 509
  John, Jr. 14:441, 453
  Joshua 11:331, 412; 13:196, 690; 15:432, 441; 16:67, 374, 376-377, 385
  Robert 11:85, 113; 14:380, 453; 15:290
  William 16:141
ELDER(S), John 6:649-650, 653-654, 673, 704-705
ELDERKIN, --- (Mr.) 6:259
ELDERTON, Cornelius 13:153, 183, 272
  Judith 13:175
ELDRICKENS 8:565
ELDRIDGE, James 4:182
  Jeremiah 11:75
ELDRIGE, George 12:29
ELEY, Ulrick 3:369
ELFRETH, Henry 1:587; 2:9-10 (See ELTRETH)
  Jeremiah 1:367
ELFRICTH, Jeremiah 12:710
ELFRITH, R. 2:19
ELICKS, Andreas 3:287
ELIOT, Ed. 8:552; 9:343
ELIOTT, John 15:44
ELIZABETH (MULATTO) 10:172
ELKMAN, Johannes 3:284
ELLARD, Benjamin 4:225
ELLER, Charles 12:607
ELLI(C)OTT, Andrew 16:23, 161, 216, 220, 375
ELLICOT, Andrew 10:445
ELLICOTT, Andrew 14:655; 15:38, 114, 175, 356, 458, 489, 561, 615, 631
  Benjamin 15:561
  Joseph 9:547, 623, 588
  Nathaniel 12:510; 13:86
ELLIGOOD, William 10:217
ELLINGSWORTH, Wm. 1:83
ELLIOT, --- (Mr.) 10:166, 203
  Christopher 10:774
  Elizabeth 14:598, 620
  Fleming 10:268-269
  James 9:386
ELLIOTT, --- (Mr.) 12:285; 14:539
  --- (Mrs.) 11:515, 517-518
  Andrew 11:611-612, 718, 746; 12:353, 746; 13:297, 759; 14:454, 464, 594; 15:172, 202, 212, 230, 340
  Benjamin 14:244, 567; 15:139, 300-301, 330; 16:46, 174, 220b, 241-244, 251-252, 254-264, 267-274, 276, 278-280, 284, 414, 416-429, 432-435, 439, 441-442, 445-447, 449-459, 461-464, 479-480, 524-528, 534, 537-540, 543, 545-546
  Daniel 15:512, 598, 602, 606; 16:21-22
  Elizabeth 13:561; 15:429
  James 14:636, 649; 15:408, 427, 487, 537, 551, 610; 16:3, 18, 50, 61, 82, 95, 415
  John 12:106; 14:401; 15:201, 207, 437
  John, Jr. 12:106
  Johnston 10:735; 16:496
  Joseph 10:335-336
  Matthew 11:515, 517-518

ELLIOTT, Robert **11**:83, 608; **14**:568, 621-622, 632, 635; **15**:150, 205, 372
William **9**:732; **15**:352; **16**:315
ELLIS, --- (Col.) **11**:42
Elizabeth **15**:532
Ellis **1**:438
Evan(s) **4**:247, 309, 352
Humphrey **2**:111, 203
Humphrie **1**:438
John **10**:457
Richard **14**:297, 304, 411, 656
Robert **3**:464; **4**:269; **5**:3, 210, 388; **14**:608
Rould **1**:614
Rowland **2**:109, 111, 159, 203, 276-277, 597; **3**:28
Thomas **1**:206, 208, 210
W. **5**:243
ELLISON, --- (Col.) **6**:294, 299
ELLONAGOA PYANGEACHA **5**:685
ELLRICK, John **13**:141
ELLSWORTH, --- (Mr.) **12**:349, 351, 360, 370
ELLUCHE, John **13**:164
ELMOR, Anne **15**:508
ELMSLIE, John **10**:701, 726
ELMSLIE (EMSLIE), John **11**:18, 60, 92, 130
ELMUTH, Frederick **14**:647
ELPHINSTONE, John **14**:506
ELRIDGE, James **3**:620
ELSON, Richard **14**:214
ELSWORTH, --- (Mr.) **13**:603, 606, 656
Andrew **15**:125
ELTON, Robert **15**:35
ELTRETH, Henry **2**:54 (See ELFRETH)
ELVES, --- (Mrs.) **6**:174
ELWES, Henry **4**:568; **12**:300
ELWOOD, John **12**:48
ELY, Isaac **11**:750; **12**:139, 489
Peter **15**:412
Samuel **9**:571; **11**:195; **14**:226; **16**:319, 538, 542
EMBLYN, --- (Mrs.) **8**:148
EMERSON, Jonathan **9**:645
EMERT, Johan Geo. Fred. **3**:457
Michael **3**:456
EMERY, George **13**:18
Peter **16**:268
EMES, Worsley **10**:742; **13**:253, 713; **14**:93, 420
EMHARD, Henry **11**:248
EMICH, Johannes **3**:467
EMIGER, Hans Leonhardt **3**:516
EMITT, Wm. **1**:82
EMLEN, Caleb **11**:284, 289
George **12**:430, 775; **15**:173
Samuel **11**:41, 283-284, 288; **12**:177
EMLER, Erick Marcus **3**:458
EMLIN, Joseph **11**:114
EMMART, Henry **13**:399
EMMERICK, Adam **14**:383
EMMERSON, --- **4**:389
John **4**:105-106
Jonathan **10**:9, 217
EMMES, John **10**:620
Mary **12**:674
EMMET (EMMITT), Abraham, Jr. **3**:256, 381
EMMICK, John **12**:406, 429
EMMIT, John **5**:210
EMMIT (EMMET), Abraham **4**:312, 482; **5**:3, 378
EMMONS, --- (Lt.) **12**:207

EMORY (EMERY), Elizabeth **15**:214, 486, 508
EMPSON, Ebenezer **3**:254
Richd. **2**:426
EMPSON (EMPSOM), Cornelius **1**:151-152, 183, 218, 311, 320, 340, 374, 418, 426, 490, 503, 507, 518-519, 522, 524, 583-584, 589
EMSON, Cornelius **1**:134
EN(N)IS, James **7**:119, 164-165, 773-774
ENASQUANA **8**:723
ENCHIQUEEN, --- (Lord) **1**:247
ENDERTON, Ann **11**:579
ENDRES, Zacharias **13**:759
ENDT, Johan Valentine **3**:518
John Daniel **3**:518
ENGELAR, Uldrick **3**:331
ENGELER, Adam **3**:331
ENGELL, Jacob **2**:493
Paul **2**:493
ENGERT, Philip **3**:238
ENGLAND, George **14**:290
Joseph **1**:547, 601; **3**:254, 270; **5**:382, 384, 386
Philip **1**:80, 126, 368, 380-381, 387, 390, 437
Samuel **5**:376, 382-384, 386
Thomas **10**:88
ENGLANDT, Christopher **3**:454
ENGLE, --- (Mr.) **13**:229, 230
Andrew **10**:757
Archibald **13**:191
Jacob **11**:21; **12**:298, 445; **14**:230, 250
Paul **12**:281
Sarah **11**:703
ENGLEMAN, Andrew **12**:506
ENGLETON, John **16**:461
ENGLIS, Silas **12**:238
ENGLISH, --- (Maj.) **1**:188-189
Benjamin **13**:96
David **12**:198, 376; **14**:597; **16**:214
Francis **7**:618 (See INGLISS)
James **7**:34, 649; **12**:272; **13**:641; **14**:133, 422; **16**:334
John **6**:143, 162
ENNIS, --- (Col.) **6**:369
James **10**:280; **11**:50, 75, 137; **12**:10
Richard **10**:425
Thomas **11**:67
ENOCH, --- **6**:650
Henry **14**:214
ENSLOW, Abraham **15**:310
ENSMENGER, John **12**:267
ENSOR, George **12**:28, 317
ENTRIKEN (ENTRICAN), William **14**:294, 301, 438
ENYEART, William **16**:210, 527-528
EODGER, John (Dr.) **13**:718
EOMUS **13**:465
EPISCAHA **8**:31
EPLER, Adam **14**:410
EPLY, Christian **3**:457
Hans David **3**:457
EPOWEYOWALLUND (ESSOWEYOWALLUND) **7**:677, 681
EPPLE, Andrew **11**:124; **13**:246, 274, 506
Henry **10**:450; **13**:245
EPRIGHT, Jacob **14**:124, 127
ERB, --- (Lt.) **13**:697
Christian **4**:60
Hans Rudolf **4**:73

ERB, Jacob 15:298; 16:61, 216
  Lawrence 13:316; 14:247; 16:215b,
    536
ERCHELBERGER, George 11:698, 700,
    744
ERCKENBRECHT, Hans Geo. 3:458
ERDMAN, Johan Jacob 3:432
ERENST, Martin 3:458
ERLEWYN, Andreas 3:410
ERM, Frederick 3:453
ERNFIGHTER (ERNFICHTER, EMFIGHTER),
    David 13:596; 14:91
  Jacob 13:555; 14:192, 420, 428
ERSKIN, Jonas 1:113
ERSKINE, William 12:527
  William & Co. 10:626
ERVINS, James 13:263
ERWIG, Johannes 3:453
ERWIN (ERWINE, IRWIN), --- 13:190
  --- (Capt.) 13:191
  --- (Col.) 11:301
  --- (Mr.) 11:60
  Arthur 11:49; 12:343, 577; 14:238,
    250, 255, 657
  Elizabeth (Jane) 9:282
  George 11:52, 340
  Jacob 14:294, 301
  James 12:428
  John 14:45, 192, 437, 439
  Joseph 9:779; 10:59; 12:73, 540;
    14:559
  Matthew 11:32
  Robert 10:54, 297, 315, 328,
    330-331, 580; 11:35, 41, 53-54,
    61, 77, 95, 138, 267; 16:450,
    476
  Samuel 11:244
ERWING, Joseph 11:18
ESEL, Reinhold 3:458
ESHAKANATA 8:159
ESHELMAN, Jacob 3:368
ESHLEMAN, Johannes 3:415
ESHLER, Margaret 12:531
ESLEMAN, Christian 3:517
  Peter 3:517
ESLER, Adam 13:617, 619; 14:532
  Susanna 16:320
ESLING, Rudolph 14:64, 90, 429
ESPING, Philip 3:570
ESPY (ESPEY, ESPIE), --- (Mr.)
    10:141; 13:284
  David 11:121, 620, 628, 630, 646,
    718, 736; 12:561, 575; 13:168,
    729; 14:9, 23, 154, 170, 196,
    213; 15:51; 16:32, 84, 407, 444,
    446, 448, 517, 541
ESRAS, --- 6:614
ESS-CANESH 9:103
ESSENPENAICK 13:465
ESSEPENAIKE 3:321
ESSEXAMARTHATTE 13:463
ESSICK, George, Sr. 16:43, 49
ESSICKS, Anne 14:465
ESSIG, Hans Michel 4:72
  Jacob 14:262
  Jorig Abraham 4:72
  Rudolph 4:72
ESSLER, Aaron 14:293, 300
  Jacob 14:176
ESSOWEYOUALUND (alias Daniel)
    8:87, 89
ESTERLY, George 11:112
ESTEVAN, Blas Marroquin 5:201
ESTHER, Johannes 3:457
ETHERINGTON, George 10:332-333
  Robert 10:734

ETTER, Peter 5:175
ETTING, Elijah 10:729
EUER, Robt. 1:87, 95
EUGER, John Mather 3:288
EUSLOW, Henry 9:509
  Jno. 9:509
EUSTACE, --- (Maj.) 13:223, 233
EUSTON, --- (Lt.) 13:189
EVALD, Lutwig 3:518
EVALT, Samuel 16:204
EVAN, Abigail 8:750
  Owen 3:257, 491; 5:388, 572
  Philip 15:391
EVANS, --- 6:302
  --- (Col.) 6:220, 529; 11:60, 80
  --- (Gov.) 6:721
  --- (Maj.) 10:690
  --- (Mr.) 8:15; 10:766; 11:306;
    12:740; 13:734; 14:171; 15:70,
    121; 16:479
  Abel 10:54; 11:494
  Benjamin 13:97
  Cadwallader (Dr.) 15:379, 389
  Caleb 3:225, 231
  Daniel 10:372, 666, 668; 13:497
  David 1:541, 549-550, 554, 563,
    578; 3:69, 108, 155, 254, 269,
    321, 614; 4:85, 247, 309, 352;
    7:717; 16:49, 516, 534
  Edward 3:472, 476; 4:68; 11:767;
    12:298; 13:6, 63, 171; 14:495,
    553
  Elizabeth 11:154
  Evan 3:225, 231; 9:673; 11:44, 50,
    65, 279, 293, 328, 339, 634;
    12:512, 526; 13:87, 112, 392,
    415, 722, 737; 14:555, 564-568,
    570-571, 573-574, 589-593,
    595-604, 606, 616-635, 637-643,
    646-652, 660-661, 663-665,
    667-670; 15:136-163, 169, 184,
    186-190, 192-195, 277-280, 282,
    313-317, 320-328, 331, 337,
    339-342, 380-391, 394-396, 401,
    406-412
  Frederick 16:254
  George 7:769; 8:575; 11:35;
    12:373, 510; 13:288, 297
  Griffith 13:646, 694, 707, 769;
    14:35, 55, 110, 131, 134, 160,
    197, 411, 454, 456, 654; 15:128,
    139, 179, 220, 244, 356, 358
  Hannah 12:101
  Hugh 3:524, 590, 619; 4:495, 504
  Israel 11:494
  Jabez 5:626-627, 643, 663-664
  Jacob 5:626-627, 663-664
  James 9:205; 13:641; 14:101, 417
  Jane 12:258
  Joel 11:513, 516-517, 745; 12:617;
    13:495; 15:442
  John 1:209; 3:276; 9:203, 595,
    626; 10:81, 217, 450; 11:138,
    173-175, 177-178, 181, 186-188,
    190-191, 193-198, 200, 202-203,
    205-207, 210-214, 225-226,
    228-230, 232-238, 249-253, 255,
    257-265, 267-268, 270-271, 600,
    603, 694; 13:176, 526, 722;
    14:41, 43, 47, 168, 302, 537,
    648
  John (Gov.) 2:68, 115-125,
    128-129, 132, 134-136, 138,
    140-141, 144-148, 150-161,
    163-174, 177-187, 191, 194, 198,
    200, 204-205, 209-210, ->

58

EVANS, John (Gov.) (continued)
2:214-218, 236-237, 239-244,
247-248, 251-253, 255, 258-259,
261-262, 266, 276, 280-281, 284,
289, 297-299, 308-309, 315-316,
318, 320-321, 323, 328, 336-337,
343, 356-357, 361-365, 372-373,
376, 378-379, 383, 385-386, 391,
393-397, 399, 403-404, 406-407,
409, 412-416, 423, 426-428,
435-436, 464, 494-495, 504, 508,
529, 548
Jonathan 9:781; 10:47, 88
Joseph 4:259; 11:610-611
Joshua 10:712; 13:495; 15:399, 442
Lewis 6:118; 9:633-634
Mark 3:613; 4:33, 57-58, 152
Nath. 1:95
Nathan 4:268
Owen 4:312, 482, 628, 762
Peter 2:205-206, 238, 362, 391,
397, 473, 507, 569-570;
3:338-339; 4:172; 9:205; 10:585;
11:215, 424; 14:282
Robert 10:555-556; 11:81
Rowland 5:388, 572; 7:769; 8:575;
9:589, 591; 13:526; 14:537;
16:230
Samuel 7:192, 474, 693, 725; 8:31,
132; 14:555; 15:140
Thomas 7:507; 8:403, 405, 415
William 4:504; 10:573, 591, 738,
741; 11:1, 123, 302, 328, 330,
339, 479, 494, 504, 542,
610-611, 729; 12:370-372, 411,
435, 440, 463-464, 478, 660;
13:97, 547, 584; 14:15
EVANS & MATLACK 11:659
EVANS (EVENS, EVINS), Daniel 11:15,
29, 45, 58, 122, 142, 368, 709
EVANS (EWENS), Griffith 16:16, 50,
216-217
EVANS (SEE TOWERS &) 16:289
EVANS (SEE WORRALL, ALLISON &)
16:432, 486, 490-491
EVARET, Edwd. 1:157
EVE, Ann 12:391
Oswald 9:293; 11:494; 14:495, 545
Oswell (Oswold, Oswald) 10:283,
301, 306, 341, 375, 398, 412,
417, 426, 458, 502, 504
EVE(S), John 12:402, 668
Oswald 12:175, 668
EVELAND, Nicolauz 3:454
EVELYH, J. 5:245
EVENRIDER, Peter 14:274
EVERAT, John 5:612
EVERHARD, Frederick 14:528
Philip 13:669
EVERITT, Abner 13:757; 14:87, 427
EVERITT (EVERETT), Jacob 14:222-223
EVERLEY, Michael 13:632
EVERLY, Michael 12:353, 483;
13:714; 14:92, 419
EVERMAN, Johannes 3:454
EVERSON, George 15:452; 16:45
EVES, James 9:337; 10:218
Oswald 5:113
EVIE, Andreas 3:328
EWENECUMEE 9:229
EWER, David 1:438
Robt. 1:236, 370, 382
EWICK, Nicolas 3:453
EWICKUNWEE 9:232
EWIN, Samuel 11:219
EWIN (EWEN), James 10:450, 704

EWING, --- 6:559-569; 11:388
--- (Gen.) 11:78, 691; 13:125,
198, 221, 228
--- (Mr.) 13:98, 100-104, 106,
109-111, 114, 116-117, 120-121,
123, 127, 177, 179-180, 182,
184-186, 188, 195, 197-198, 201,
203, 205-208, 210-211, 214-216,
218-219, 222-223, 231, 233-235,
315, 317-319, 323-325, 328-332,
334-343, 345, 347-348, 350-357,
388, 390, 394-395, 397-399,
402-404, 406-407, 409-410,
412-413, 571, 678
--- (Rev. Dr.) 11:267
David 13:709; 14:193
Edward 14:609
George 11:265
James 10:209; 11:196, 623, 676,
693-694, 698, 700; 13:93, 96,
112, 124, 225, 227, 234, 355,
413-414, 416-417, 495, 498-501,
503-519, 521-524, 526-532, 534,
536-538, 540-541, 543-549, 567,
570-572, 574-590, 592, 594-595,
597-603, 605-607, 609-611,
613-615, 617, 633-635, 637-642,
645-647, 666-668, 670-675,
677-679, 681, 684, 686-687,
691-697, 719, 721, 724-727, 729,
731-732, 734-748, 750, 753;
14:5-6, 8-11, 15-16, 18, 23-43,
58-60, 66-68, 70-72, 105,
108-122, 130, 135-153, 170-172,
174-185, 200-203, 205-207,
209-211, 213-219, 224-228, 234,
485
Jane 9:235-236
Jasper 16:120, 122, 396, 398,
494-495
John 11:330; 12:213, 704; 13:79;
16:460, 535
John (Dr.) 14:316-317, 402, 443,
454; 15:2
John (Rev. Dr.) 13:271, 685, 753
Patrick 11:251, 265; 14:208, 259
William 14:191, 195
EYCHELBERGER, Martin 10:163
EYER, John 3:332
EYERS, --- (Capt.) 3:29
Rd. 11:6
EYLER, Casper 15:407
EYRE, --- (Col.) 13:661
--- (Mr.) 13:104
Benjamin 11:12, 28, 103, 529, 673,
756, 776
Benjamin G. 13:100, 564
Emanuel 16:480
Jehu(e) 12:263-264
Manuel 12:39; 13:46; 14:242, 248,
250
Mary 16:374, 419
Richard 11:126, 543, 549-550
William (Capt.) 6:608, 611
EYRE (EYER), John 11:32, 564, 572,
756
EYRE(S), Benjamin G. 12:75-76, 205,
266, 293, 317-318, 413; 15:12,
99, 346-347
Emanuel 11:122, 182-183, 232, 640,
670
EYRES, Emanuel 10:283, 290-291,
296, 335, 750
Richard 10:352, 379, 511, 514;
14:298, 305, 429
Robert 10:339

FEGAN (FAGAN), Lawrence **11:**513,
516-517, 714
FEGELEY, Barnard **3:**518
Henrich **3:**518
Matthias **3:**518
FEGELIN, Hans Peter **4:**60
FEGEN, Hugh **12:**645
FEGLEY, Jacob **3:**515
FEIDER, Michael **3:**413
FEIT, Debolt **4:**100
FELIX, Peter **13:**635; **14:**414
FELL, Amos **13:**139
Benjamin **11:**179, 217, 372, 378;
12:136, 510
George **10:**100, 211, 270
Jesse **14:**555; **16:**196, 496, 499
John **13:**439, 542
Joseph **2:**520
Thomas **11:**199, 650; **14:**306, 435
William **11:**513, 516-517
FELLKER, Godfrey **15:**439
FELLMAN, Jacob **4:**59
FELTER, Hans Erick **3:**288
FELTIN, Christian **15:**40
Philip **15:**40
FELTMAN, William **13:**579; **14:**103,
423
FELTON, Robt. **1:**84-85
FELTZER, Henry **14:**293, 299, 412
FENCE, Richard **11:**340
FENNELL, Daniel **16:**163
FENTON, Joseph **14:**655
Joseph (Dr.) **15:**42
Joseph, Jr. **10:**471
Robt. **1:**88
Thomas **3:**257
FENWICK, James **3:**387
Tho. **1:**578, 580, 595-596, 601,
612, 615, 621-623; **2:**136
FERGUSON, --- **14:**67, 559
Biddy **16:**310
Catherine **12:**391
Charles **10:**702
Eliza (Mrs.) **11:**522, 629
Elizabeth **12:**351-352, 365-366, 386
Henry Hugh **11:**482, 484-485, 745
John **16:**187 (See John TAYLOR)
Josiah **14:**215
Mary **12:**387
Samuel **7:**717
Thomas **11:**363; **14:**532
William **10:**742; **12:**573, 718;
13:669, 714, 757; **14:**89-90, 191,
195, 427, 609; **15:**19, 381, 394,
430, 437; **16:**95, 263, 281
FERGUSON (FURGUSON), Thomas **12:**147,
544
FERKLE, Peter **13:**635; **14:**83, 421
FERMAN, Charles **11:**373
FERMIER, Sieur **13:**481
FERNANDEZ, Juan **15:**148
FERNE, Joshua **15:**478
FERRALL, Patrick **12:**714
FERRAUGH, Michael **14:**296, 303, 427
FERREE, Isaac **10:**101, 211, 270
Joel **10:**290
John **10:**101, 211, 270, 681, 686,
690, 692, 698-699, 704; **11:**306
Joseph **10:**637, 660, 665, 685, 700,
713, 720-721, 724, 728, 732-733,
738, 752, 784; **11:**12, 124;
12:378; **15:**422
Michael **11:**358
FERRIS, --- (Capt.) **10:**308, 312
Owen **13:**308, 554
FERRIS (FARRIS), John **12:**368, 392

FERUSER, Philip **3:**284
FESSELER, Henrich **3:**516
FETTEE, Richard **3:**367
FETTER, Casper **12:**447
Jacob **3:**367
Jerig **3:**369
William **10:**600
FETTERS, Casper **10:**473, 477; **11:**244
FETZEN, Henry **15:**470
FEW, Ann **9:**564, 580
Joseph **14:**475
FEYSEG, Joannes **3:**290
FEZWATER, George **3:**50, 77, 107,
111, 239
FIANS, William **16:**121, 131
FICHER, Thomas **11:**373
FICK, --- (Lt.) **12:**334
FIELD, --- (Maj.) **9:**214
Benjamin **3:**520
John **14:**32, 647
Nathan **15:**606
Nehemiah **1:**340, 371, 517, 568;
2:136, 181, 183
William **5:**226
FIELD(S), William **14:**80, 88, 411
FIELDIN, William **15:**361
FIELDING, Abraham **12:**85
George **14:**650 (See John STANLY)
John **14:**383 (See STANLY)
Thomas **5:**413
FIELDS, Daniel **11:**611-612
George **11:**611-612
Gilbert **11:**611-612
FIELL, Hans Michael **3:**284
FIERSLER, Philip Mich. **3:**369
FIFAR, Vandel **3:**452
FIFER, John Brown **13:**758
FIFLER, Felix **3:**455
FIGEL (FIGAL), John **15:**54, 60
FIGH, John **14:**62, 126, 611
FIGHT, Christian **16:**184
FIKEL, Michael **3:**570
FIKUS, Valentine **3:**367
FILBERT, Peter **13:**720; **14:**232, 554;
15:98-99
FILBY, John **12:**716
FILCHERBEIT, Wm. **9:**343
FILDON, John **12:**7
FILINGER, Andreas **3:**454
FILKISYNGER, Hans **3:**284
FILLER, Godfreyt **3:**323
FILLERAPPAMOND **13:**463
FILSON, George **14:**615
FINAVER, Joseph **11:**107-108
FINCHER, Benjamin **12:**665-666
Francis **1:**108-110
John **9:**43-44
Joshua **3:**260, 289
FINDLAY, William **12:**519
FINDLEY (FINLEY), James **14:**54;
15:472
John **5:**436, 441, 443, 570
Joseph **11:**181
Samuel **14:**15; **16:**480
Susanna **13:**337
William **14:**170; **15:**281, 318, 552,
636; **16:**215, 216b-220b, 222b,
224b, 225-227, 229-230, 233,
235-236, 240-242, 244, 251-252,
255-264, 267-269, 271-274,
278-293, 295-298, 301-313,
365-366, 368-371, 374-386,
418-429, 432-437, 439, 441-442,
445-447, 449-459, 461-466,
518-528, 545

61

FINGLADI(E) (FINLADE), Traverse
  11:157, 160, 162, 164
FINK, John 12:29
 Michael 14:293, 300, 422
FINLA, Andrew 5:210
FINLAY, --- (Lt.) 11:126
 George 16:298
FINLEY, --- 12:507; 14:346
 --- (Capt.) 11:56
 --- (Rev. Mr.) 13:481
 Andrew 13:730; 14:611
 Archibald 5:209
 James 13:520
 James (Rev.) 13:500, 617
 John 10:449; 11:375, 599; 12:513;
  13:716, 759; 14:193, 521, 607
 Joseph 10:765; 13:611, 715
 Joseph L. 16:385
 Joseph S. 14:438
 Josiah L. 14:193
 Michael 10:770
 Samuel 11:367, 609
 William 11:367; 12:166; 13:730;
  14:8, 18, 179, 213
FINLEY (FINLAY), --- (Mr.) 15:121,
532
FINNEY, --- (Capt.) 15:337
 --- (Dr.) 10:109
 --- (Lt.) 10:573
 David 5:248; 9:203, 626, 707;
  10:81, 109, 217, 276
 James 5:247
 John 2:68-69, 75, 98, 135, 178,
  180, 297-298; 5:89-90, 92, 234;
  9:337, 600; 13:14
 Walker 13:758
 Walter 13:62, 668, 709, 717, 747;
  14:84, 100, 177, 433, 437, 458,
  462, 533; 16:96
 William 5:193; 12:350
FINNEY (FINNEIS, FINNES), Saml.
  2:37, 48, 52, 61, 63, 65-71,
  86-87, 89-91, 93-98, 101-104,
  107-109, 111-112, 114-117,
  120-122, 124-125, 128-129, 134,
  141, 147-149, 151-152, 154,
  156-157, 159-161, 163-164,
  167-169, 180, 184-187, 194, 198,
  200-201, 206, 219, 237, 239,
  241, 243, 248, 258, 262, 343,
  363, 365, 391, 394, 396, 403,
  412, 416, 439, 441, 451, 463,
  466, 468, 478, 490, 510, 513,
  525-526, 532, 539, 549
FINWICK, James 3:416
FIRE POKER (The) 7:64
FIRKMAN, Michl. 3:386
FIRRUMSLER, Mathias 3:332
FISCH, John Henry 15:447
 William 13:14
FISCHER, David 3:455
FISCUP (FISCUS), Abraham 14:452,
547
 Garret 14:452, 547
FISH, John 5:489
 Thomas 14:506
FISHBACK, Hans Jacob 3:570
FISHBOURN(E), William 3:50,
  225-231, 233-234, 236, 238,
  240-252, 256-259, 264, 266-267,
  270-271, 276, 278-283, 287-294,
  302-303, 307-309, 315-316, 327,
  332-333, 336, 338, 340, 343-347,
  351, 354-355, 358-359, 364, 366,
  369-372, 375-376, 379-381, 384,
  386-389, 395-396, 400, 537, 542

FISHBOURNE, Benjamin 11:468; 13:715
FISHBURN, Benjamin 10:733
 Ralph 2:103
 Wm. 2:630
FISHEIR, Ulrich 3:432
FISHEL, John 13:432
FISHER, --- (Mr.) 14:77
 Catherine 11:780
 Christian 14:382
 Coleman 11:494
 Fenwick 9:338-339, 655
 Finwick 10:9, 217
 Henry 10:337-339, 470, 526-527,
  534, 537, 593, 620, 753, 755;
  11:9, 184, 240, 574; 12:120;
  13:302
 Henry (alias Weaver) 9:548-549
 J. Francis 1:11
 Jabez 8:403
 Jacob 6:443
 James 11:513, 516-617; 12:468;
  13:529, 544; 15:469
 James Coleman 15:324
 Jeremiah 11:37, 91; 15:267, 524,
  562, 635; 16:103, 136
 Jno. 1:95, 536
 Johan 3:410
 Johan Henrich 3:515
 Johan Michael 3:390
 Johan Wilhelm 3:515
 John 13:496; 14:384 (See STEVENS)
 Joseph 1:87, 298, 371, 607-610;
  2:65, 597; 3:417
 Joseph Coleman 12:195
 Joshua 3:465, 524, 575
 Joshua & Son 11:31, 283, 288, 296
 Joshua & Sons 10:439, 449, 451,
  453-454, 460, 486-487, 570
 Ludwick 11:695
 Margarett 1:227-228
 Miers 14:79, 105, 111; 15:201,
  207, 399, 437, 459, 481, 485,
  499; 16:55, 108-109, 130, 153,
  232, 238
 Myers (Miers) 11:283, 288, 296,
  309, 460, 472
 Samuel 5:210; 10:486-487, 497;
  11:283, 288, 296, 309, 460, 472,
  729, 735; 12:221, 463; 13:615;
  14:79, 105, 111, 299, 435;
  15:516
 Samuel R. 13:13
 Tho. 2:136, 426
 Thomas 1:227, 517, 601;
  10:486-488, 497, 682; 11:219,
  283, 288, 296, 309, 460, 472;
  12:177; 14:79, 105, 111, 256
 Timothy 11:157
 William 7:391, 760-761; 8:59;
  11:494; 12:187; 13:28
 Willm. 2:426
 Wm. 1:568
 Yost 9:557
FISHER & ROBERTS 14:492, 570
FISHER (SKAYANAS) 7:68
FISHORST, Henry 11:772
FISS, Jacob 14:610
FITCH, --- 8:565-566
 --- (Gov.) 6:255, 259, 261-262,
  267, 606
 Eleazer (Maj.) 6:608, 611
 Gebish 8:566
 Thomas (Gov.) 7:23, 124; 8:564,
  571, 600, 620, 623, 627-628
FITCHE, Thomas 5:771, 773
FITCHWATER, Thomas 1:65, 87, 186

62

FITLER, George 14:159
FITTERMAN, George 10:660
FITZ, Christian 12:222
FITZER, Jacob 16:163
FITZGERALD, Edward 3:591
 James 12:657
 Maurice 16:216b
 Robert 10:758; 11:44, 69, 87
 Thomas 11:85; 13:729
FITZIMMONS, James 14:27
 John 16:335
 Nicholas 12:720; 13:555; 14:100,
 433
 Patrick 14:308
 Thomas 12:582; 13:511, 555, 721,
 769; 14:68, 231, 555; 15:5, 98,
 281, 386, 432, 544, 604, 617,
 636, 639, 657-658
FITZPATRICK, James 11:511, 582,
 584-585, 600, 616-617
FITZRANDOLPH, Edward 5:194
FITZSIMMONS, Nicholas 10:506, 531;
 11:576; 13:631
 Patrick 16:461
 Thomas 10:567, 592, 596, 616;
 11:28, 45, 182-183, 191, 194,
 629, 645, 683, 702; 13:239, 370;
 16:2, 119, 127, 353
FITZWALTER, --- (Earl of) 5:618
FITZWATER, George 3:491, 547;
 4:312, 482, 762
 Thomas 1:48, 69, 228, 322
FIX, Samuel 13:507
FIZER, Nichel 3:385
FLACK, Joseph 12:380-381
 Samuel 12:380-381
FLAHARTY, Susanna 14:191, 195
FLAHEAD (FLAKEAD), Thomas 14:124,
 129, 432
FLAHERTY, John 11:748
FLAKE, George 16:289
 George, Jr. 15:457
FLANAG(H)AN, John 12:687, 730, 735,
 779
FLANAGAN, Timothy 13:756; 14:91,
 416
FLANAGHAN, Patrick 13:462
FLANGAN (FLAUGHAN, FLANAGHAN), John
 14:190, 193, 439
 Patrick 14:609
FLAUGHERTY, William 14:461
FLAVAHAN, Thomas 13:544
FLE(T)CHER, Robert 3:158, 177, 257
FLECK, Adam 14:51
FLEESON, --- (Mr.) 7:385
 Plunket 8:22, 24; 10:499; 11:121,
 194, 215, 601, 603, 648, 665,
 678, 681; 13:20, 52, 181, 269,
 403, 753; 14:135, 149, 455, 511,
 548-549; 15:568
 Plunket(t) 12:204, 339, 404, 546
FLEGER, Hans Georg. 3:410
FLEISER, Jacob 3:432
FLEM(M)ING, Hugh 14:298, 413
 John 10:738, 776
 Robert 14:83, 369, 411
FLEMING, Alexander 9:702; 10:116
 Archibald 11:53
 Charles 12:378
 David 16:461
 Henry 14:81, 99, 427
 James 16:461
 John 11:17, 114; 12:131, 459
 Richard 13:642
 Robert 11:367; 13:708; 16:396
FLEMMIN, Low 12:28

FLEMMING, William 15:503
FLETCHER, --- (Col.) 2:351-352;
 8:76
 Benjamin 1:49, 345, 352-353, 357,
 364-375, 379-380, 383-384, 387,
 390-391, 393, 398-399, 401-402,
 404, 407-411, 414, 416, 422,
 424-426, 428, 442-444, 446, 453,
 458-470, 474, 480-481, 484-487,
 490-492, 494, 497, 503-504, 506,
 520
 James 10:505
 Joseph 13:597; 14:83, 438
 Nathan 12:87
 Thomas 3:542, 586; 4:258, 312,
 762; 5:388, 572; 13:757; 14:89,
 422
FLETZER, Ann Elizabeth 12:178
 George 12:178
FLEURE, Johannis 3:517
 Joseph 3:517
FLEURY, Abraham 16:166
 Pierre 3:458
FLEXER, Hans Philip 4:72
FLICHRER, Ulrich 3:516
FLICKART, David 12:209
FLICKINGER, Joannes 3:368
FLIDE, Samuel 12:680
FLINN, James 14:609
FLINT, Royal 12:227
FLOCK (FLACK), Matthias 13:669;
 14:127, 435
FLOHAVAN, John 13:45
FLOOD, Mary 12:149, 196
FLORA, John 15:310
 Robert 15:310
FLORENTINE, Ann 12:781
FLOWER, --- (Col.) 13:521
 Benjamin 12:232, 439; 15:559;
 16:278, 285
 Enoch 1:87, 91, 95
 Henry 1:588; 2:9
 John 13:510; 14:475
 Richard 13:510
 Samuel 5:3, 185, 387, 572; 7:417;
 8:573; 9:205
 William 5:113-114
FLOWERS, Benjamin 10:681; 11:235,
 278, 306, 313, 497, 735, 739,
 771-772
 Mary 14:294, 301, 429
 Philip 14:294, 301, 429
FLOYD, --- (Mr.) 11:677
 James 11:159-160; 12:74
 John 13:521
 Mary 14:520; 16:61
 William 14:636
FLOYER, --- (Capt.) 6:491
FLUERY, Francis 12:35, 37, 39, 86
FO(R)STER, Thomas 6:131-132, 648,
 653, 657, 667
 William 8:156, 179
FOESBROOK(E), John 14:189, 193, 414
FOGG, Daniel 15:462
FOGGON, William Brown 13:356
FOGHT, Andrew 14:383
FOGOE, David 4:96-97
FOHRER, Lewis 11:91
 Ludwig 10:550; 11:136; 13:23
FOIBER, Abraham 3:413
FOKT, Johan Matthias 4:59
 Johan Valentine 4:59
FOLKE, Daniel 16:484
FOLLET, Benjamin 9:584
FOLLIETT, Thomas 12:651
FOLLWELL, John 12:405

FOLWELL, John 10:778; 11:372
  Thomas 11:372; 12:136, 598
FONTLEROY, Moore 13:712
FOOKS, Paul 10:729; 11:48, 177,
  200; 13:735-736
FOOS, Conrad 13:88; 14:176
FOOT, --- (Maj.) 6:608, 611
  David 11:77
FOOTMAN, --- 15:592
  Richard 11:641, 710; 15:650;
  16:36, 40, 196, 311, 340
FOR(R)EST, Andrew 14:87, 91, 414,
  428, 537
  Malcolm 14:99, 430
FORAINEY, James 14:609
FORALT, Jon. 1:253-254
FORANTGER, Henry 14:612
FORBES, --- (Mr.) 12:293
  Alexander 5:77
  James 11:469, 573
  John (Gen.) 8:27, 59, 61, 63,
  78-79, 83-84, 97, 100, 110-111,
  124, 146, 167, 169, 187, 212,
  217, 223-225, 227-229, 234,
  236-238, 240-241, 263-264,
  269-270, 283-285, 292, 296-298,
  309, 315-317, 373-374, 388, 624
  William 10:537; 12:170, 208, 620;
  14:506
FORCETT, Walter 1:185
FORD, Benjamin 13:96-97; 14:63, 86,
  422
  Charles 14:292, 299, 416
  David 10:353
  Dennis 15:187, 640
  James 11:151
  John 3:50-51; 14:81, 99, 434
  Philip 2:455; 8:781; 9:199, 285,
  302, 333, 551
  Samuel 10:99; 11:565-566
  Thomas 9:515
  William 3:389; 13:337
FORDE (SEE READ &) 16:345
FORDENBAUGH, Philip 16:329
FORDER, Jane 13:329-330
FOREMAN, Charles 14:289
FOREPAUGH, George 15:77; 16:483
FORESTER, William 10:377
FORGESON, Robert 11:729
FORKER, Michael 14:382
FORMAN, --- (Gen.) 11:185
  Charles 11:220
  Ezekiel 13:528
  George 1:374-376, 378-379, 384,
  401, 404, 407, 409, 416-417,
  422-428, 434, 442-444, 446, 450,
  453, 455, 458-460, 462-470
  John 12:182
  Margaret 13:528
FORNWAL, Jacob 7:303
FORRER, Joannes 3:290
FORREST, --- (Adm.) 8:714
  --- (Col.) 13:571
  --- (Lt. Col.) 13:456
  Andrew 10:450; 13:582; 16:408
  James 10:713, 775
  John 10:453
  Malcolm 13:636
  Sarah 13:97
  Thomas 10:514, 517-518, 520,
  546-547, 730, 742-743; 11:25,
  201; 12:746; 13:97, 130, 136,
  175, 283, 323, 326, 331, 336,
  500, 505, 507, 544, 563; 14:85,
  190, 194, 416, 546; 15:3;
  16:213b

FORREST, Walter 1:389
FORRESTER, --- 12:534
  --- (Mr.) 7:272
  Alexandr. 2:120
  Garret 13:345
  Gerald 13:545
  Gerrald 13:324
FORRESTER (ALIAS BILES), Jemima
  12:397
FORRY, Michael 13:393
FORST, David 13:346, 441
  Hendrich 3:594
FORSTER, Alexander 13:389
  Basilion 13:330
  Bazel(l)ion 15:397, 437, 440
  Cato 15:386, 420
  James 4:468
  John 3:620; 11:335; 12:513; 14:15,
  256
  Joseph 12:25; 14:157
  Moses 8:242
  Thomas 9:335-336; 14:80, 89, 259
FORSYTH, Andrew 11:602
  John 5:318; 14:376, 585, 589-590;
  16:214, 223
  Nathaniel 13:480
  Robert 7:187; 12:522
FORSYTHE, John 15:264
  Peter 15:409
FORTESCUE, --- 10:563-564
FORTINEAUX, Jean Henrix 3:385
FORTUNE, George 7:500
FORTUNE (NEGRO) 16:480
FOS(S)TER, Thomas 5:247, 378, 600
FOSMAN, Alexander 16:195
FOSS, Nicholas 3:413
FOSTER, --- (Dr.) 2:628
  Allen 2:34
  Anne 14:279
  David 10:462
  Hans 3:285
  John 1:568; 2:83; 4:182;
  11:272-273; 12:137-138;
  13:735-736, 739; 14:163, 465
  Jonathan 14:124, 128, 433
  Thomas 8:562; 9:131, 172; 10:746;
  14:433; 15:216
FOTHERELL, Patrick 14:407-408, 439
FOTZE, James 16:461
FOUKE, Richard 9:701
FOULK, --- (Capt.) 7:15-17, 164
  Cadwallader 4:312
  Judah 8:172
FOULKE, --- (Mr.) 15:267, 306
  Adam 10:538, 542; 12:123
  Amos 14:537; 16:230
  George 15:66
  John (Dr.) 15:93
  Judah 9:688, 777; 10:56, 111;
  13:759
  Mary 13:599
  Samuel 13:720
  Stephen 11:357-358
  Thom 10:162
  Thomas 11:136
  William 14:259
FOUNDER, Conrad 10:172
FOUNTLEROY, --- (Maj.) 12:774
FOUQUIERE (FAUQUIERE), Francis
  (Gov.) 8:224, 779
FOURY, Leonard 3:390
FOUST, Johan Peter 3:516
  Johan Philip 3:516
FOUTTS, Christian 11:745
FOUTZ, Christian 11:315
FOUX, Merick 3:288

FRANKLIN, Benjamin (continued)
 15:352-353, 356, 358, 360, 363,
 394, 410-412, 443, 465, 503,
 514-515, 529, 535, 557-558, 563,
 575; **16**:68, 341, 344-345, 358,
 360-361
 Benjamin (Dr.) **11**:232, 385
 John **14**:486, 644; **15**:35, 67,
 78-79, 162, 279-280, 290-291,
 300, 304, 385-386, 394, 408,
 427, 497, 499, 533, 537, 551,
 571, 575, 578, 610, 640; **16**:4,
 17-18, 21, 50, 61, 82, 95, 102
 Rosewell **15**:547
 Thomas **11**:606; **12**:351; **13**:539
 William **5**:135; **6**: 123, 127, 378,
 398, 408; **7**:150, 293; **13**:470
FRANKLYN, Michael **3**:414
 William **4**:274
FRANKS, --- (Col.) **16**:513
 --- (Mr.) **10**:500
 Conrad **14**:63, 194, 439
 D. S. **11**:680-681, 683
 Daniel **14**:233, 253
 David **8**:576; **11**:679; **12**:195, 199,
 206, 499, 502, 505, 509; **14**:451
 David Solebury **12**:141, 296,
 495-496, 547
 Isaac **15**:457-458; **16**:1
 John **8**:140
FRANS, Frans Baltzar **3**:288
FRANTZ, Christian **3**:431
 Christian, Jr. **3**:431
FRASER, --- **6**:641
 John **3**:76-77; **5**:614-615, 660, 731
 (See FRAZIER, John); **7**:381
FRATER & SOROR **10**:358, 362
FRAY, Johannes **3**:454
FRAZ(I)ER, John **5**:482 (See FRASER)
 Persifor **14**:133, 238, 440, 463
FRAZER, George **4**:99
 John **9**:539-541, 730; **10**:8, 78
FRAZIER, --- (Col.) **13**:486
 --- (Gen.) **13**:289
 --- (Lt.) **9**:250-251, 497
 --- (Mr.) **13**:485; **14**:61
 Daniel **13**:565
 Hugh **11**:105
 Percifer **13**:87, 112, 289; **16**:443
 Percifor **13**:392, 415, 676
 Percifor (Persifor, Percifer)
 15:4, 38, 179
 Persifor **12**:301-302, 306, 334
 Robert **9**:711; **16**:318
 William **5**:248
FRAZIER, COXE & **15**:78
FREAME, Thomas, Jr. **4**:347, 468
FRED, Jacob **14**:301
FREDEHER, Isaac (alias Jacob
 WALTER) **15**:145
FREDERICK, Jacob **7**:717; **14**:63, 93,
 295, 302, 413
 Johan Georg. **3**:456
 Michael **16**:131
 Noah **7**:303
 William **14**:71
FREDLER, Hans Michl. **3**:285
FREDRICK, John **3**:620; **4**:182
FREE, Jacob **5**:186
FREEBY, --- (Lt.) **6**:490
FREEK, Christian **13**:624
FREELAND, --- (Ens.) **15**:1
 George **8**:200, 217
FREEMAN, Abraham **3**:413
 Benjamin **13**:266; **15**:207
 Justice **16**:422

FREEMAN, Mary **13**:527
 Moses **3**:332, 370
 Samuel John **13**:504
 Thomas **4**:432, 443; **13**:419
 Wm. **1**:458, 583
FREES, John **14**:494
FREEZE, John **11**:608
FREH, Henrich **4**:73
 Jacob **4**:73
 Lorentz **4**:73
 Nicolas **4**:73
FREIDRICH, Jorig Mich. **4**:60
FRELAND, Wm. **1**:320, 322, 340
FRENCH, --- (Maj.) **11**:12
 Arch'd. **10**:303
 Arthur **14**:43; **16**:112, 120, 211
 Christopher **10**:302-306, 313
 David **3**:338
 John **2**:386, 448, 467, 469,
 511-513, 529, 531-532, 537;
 3:13, 18-19, 21, 32-33, 37, 43,
 58, 60, 65, 67, 71, 75, 77,
 80-82, 90, 93, 96, 121-123, 125,
 138, 145-149, 153, 155-156, 163,
 165, 167, 170, 178-179, 181-182,
 184-186, 192, 199, 204, 235-236,
 241, 243, 252-254, 268, 338-339
 Margaret **7**:172, 283, 621
 Mary **11**:584
 Robert **2**:31, 77-78, 83, 362, 426;
 9:338; **11**:766, 770-771
 Robt. **1**:589, 601-602, 610, 612,
 614, 616, 620
 Thomas **3**:254, 260
 Thos. **2**:494
FRENCH MARGARET **8**:487, 499, 586
FRESHORN, Hans George **3**:457
FRETCH, Christian **14**:426
FRETWELL, Ralph **1**:124, 155, 186;
 5:551-552
FREW, John **5**:210
FREY, Andreas **3**:515
 Conrad **3**:569
 Hans George **3**:454
 Hans Peter **3**:515
 Henry **7**:460
 Jacob **3**:593
 Johan Jacob **3**:454
 Johannes **3**:415
 Joshua **6**:6
FRICHMAN, Michael **15**:85
FRICK, Conrad **3**:452
 Philip **13**:233
FRICKROTT, Hans Adam **3**:516
FRIE, --- (Capt.) **14**:361
FRIECHELL, Elias Lewis **12**:470
FRIEDEL, Peter **3**:569
FRIEDLE, Hans Georg. **3**:415
FRIEDLER, Lodwig **3**:453
FRIEDLY, Michael **3**:520
FRIEDRICH, Zacharias **3**:597
FRIEND, George **11**:214
 John **14**:244
FRIES, Hans Welchier **3**:515
 John **14**:583
FRIGGS, --- **9**:509
FRILT (FRITT), Henry **14**:94, 429
FRISMAN, Casper **3**:385
FRITH, Peter **3**:432
FRITLEY, Jacob **16**:391
FRITS, Jacob **10**:709
FRITT, Henry **13**:573
FRITZ, Catherine **12**:150
 Jacob **3**:285
 John **12**:576
 Philip **13**:186, 447

FRITZRANDOLPH, Edward 12:86
FRIZBY, William 13:552
FROMBERGER, John 11:26; 12:348;
  13:26, 29, 54, 366; 14:109,
  114-115
FRONT, William 8:383
FRONTINIAC, --- (Count) 1:453-454
FROOM, Coarse 3:329
FROSON, --- 6:524
FROTHINGHAM, Ebenezer 15:660
FRUIT, Robert 11:367; 14:443
FRY, --- (Col.) 6:29
  Christopher 3:368
  Conraad 3:457
  George 6:648; 11:394; 16:12
  Hans Uldrick 3:368
  Jacob 14:611
  Johan Lenhart 6:125
  Joseph 14:8; 16:445, 486
  Joshua (Col.) 5:747, 751, 761
  Lawrence 14:63, 93, 413
  Michael 14:63, 93, 413
FRYAR, Cutfrith 6:648
FRYE, Tobias 3:284
FRYER, Thomas 10:43
FRYLINGHAUSAN, Peter Casper 14:529
FRYMOST, John 11:134
FUCHS, Johan Frantz 3:455
  Johannes 4:60
FULKNER, Daniel 2:430 (See FALKNER)
FULLART, Jost 7:477
FULLER, --- 8:576; 13:673
  --- (Mr.) 12:84; 15:159
  Benjamin 11:648; 13:64, 625, 707,
  742; 14:451, 652
  John 1:236
FULLERT, Henry 10:100, 270; 11:212,
  260
FULLERTON, --- (Ens.) 12:88-89
  --- (Maj.) 10:670, 672
  George 16:185
  H. (Dr.) 13:710; 14:127, 437
  Humphrey 13:266
  Humphrey (Dr.) 15:413
  John 11:33; 12:421; 13:424
  Mary (Mrs.) 15:185
  Patrick 11:181, 545, 549
  Richard 12:355, 550, 717; 13:635,
  716; 14:81, 100, 432
  William 11:297, 705; 12:647
FULLERTON & MORAN 10:686
FULLERTON (SEE CARROUP &) 10:314
FULSOM, --- (Gen.) 11:404
FULTON, James 7:155; 10:749;
  11:115; 13:191, 228
  John 10:611; 11:633; 12:131
  Robert 9:126-127
  William 11:33; 16:539-540
FULTZ, Frederick 15:424; 16:333
  Hendrick 3:288
FUNCK, Henry 13:74
FUND, Anthony 13:753
FUNK, Fredirch 3:520
  George 13:134, 730; 15:600-601;
  16:32, 212
  Henry 11:72, 269; 13:102
  Jacob 3:332; 10:450
  John 14:306, 436; 15:44
FUNSTON, James 12:468
  John 12:468
FURBY (FURBEE), Caleb 10:56, 101,
  211
FUREMAN, John 15:616
FURFEY (FURFY), Hugh 15:586, 614;
  16:30, 91
FURKHILL, Johan Georg. 3:457

FURLEY, Benjamin 2:432
FURMAN, --- (Capt.) 10:375, 379,
  398
  David 12:362
  Moore 11:471; 12:394, 435
FURNACE, Abraham 14:611
FURNER, Edward 11:611-612
  Morris 11:611-612
FURNESSE, John 2:122-123
FURNEY, Adam 5:409
FURNIS, John 13:327
FURREY, --- (Capt.) 11:105
FURSUER, Andrew 11:515, 517-518
FUTCHER, Wm. 1:48, 84
FUTHEY, James 11:462
  Samuel 11:455, 462, 474
FUZ (FUSS), William 6:493-494

GAB(B)LE, Isaac 14:80, 84, 608
GABEL, Peter 14:94, 410
GABELL, Peter 13:636
  Pieter 3:453
GABERTZ, Michael 3:413
GABRIEL, George 6:645-647, 649-650,
  655, 657, 661, 669; 7:154;
  9:414, 417-419, 453
GACHADOW (GACHRADODOW) 4:720, 722
GACHRADODA 6:112-113
GADDESDEN, --- (Col.) 10:435
GADDIS, John 14:54
  Thomas 14:310
GAERME, Thomas 3:507
GAETSHALCK, Jacob 2:493
GAFFERY, Cornelieus 7:558
GAGE, --- (Gen.) 4:7
  --- (Lt. Col.) 6:490
  Thomas 6:548, 594
  Thomas (Gen.) 9:90, 92-93,
  104-105, 110-111, 118-120,
  123-125, 127, 129, 133, 137,
  170-171, 177, 196, 238-239, 249,
  257-258, 262, 266-269, 272-275,
  277, 281, 292, 297, 299-301,
  303, 307, 317-319, 321-323,
  402-407, 422-423, 428, 431, 443,
  454, 457, 459, 531, 581-582,
  585-586, 592, 663-665, 685-686,
  718; 10:17-18, 20, 68-69, 146,
  200, 302-304, 332-333, 378, 389
GAGER, Daniel 12:519
GALAGHER, Alexander 11:130
  Peter 11:122
GALBRAITH (GALBREATH, GALBREITH,
  GILBRAITH), --- (Col.) 12:64
  Andrew 3:359; 4:69, 152, 313, 483;
  5:3; 14:124, 128, 609
  Bartram 12:480
  Bertram 8:676; 10:666, 674,
  681-682, 684, 686, 690-692,
  694-695, 718; 11:83, 95-97, 212,
  214, 241, 257, 259-301, 313,
  328-329, 340, 365, 442, 496,
  538, 574, 578, 597, 744, 776;
  14:478, 485; 16:178, 182, 209b,
  260, 274, 308, 529
  James 4:86, 309, 602, 669; 5:3,
  247, 348, 378, 431, 435, 441,
  443, 600, 614; 6:131-132, 150,
  667, 669; 7:59, 736, 754-756,
  773; 11:11, 47, 145-146, 205,
  208

GORDON (GORTON), Daniel 10:363,
  376-377, 723
GORE, --- 9:584
  Daniel 9:712
  Elijah 9:711-712
  John 14:223
  Nathaniel 9:711
  Obadiah 9:571; 15:212
  Silas 9:711
  Simeon 14:614
  Simon 11:236; 15:363, 530, 576-577
GORELEY, Mary Ann 11:772
GORGAES, John 2:493
GORGAS, --- (Lt.) 13:189
  Jacob 12:277; 16:426
GORMAN, Henry 14:69
  Joseph 14:610-611
  Lawrence 13:631; 14:95, 425
GORME, Henry 4:500
GORRECHT, Elizabeth 16:367
GORRELL, James 5:418
  Robert 13:679; 14:98, 420
GOSCH, John Henry 4:250
GOSLIN, William 11:281
GOSLING, John 11:514, 516-517
GOSNER, Peter 14:87, 435
GOSNOLD, Mary 12:24
GOSS, Charles 1:515
  Lewis 12:138
  Peter 1:439
GOSSLINE, William 16:515
GOSSNER, Peter 10:457
GOTCHELL, Elisha 3:50, 345, 356
  (See GATCHEL)
GOTSCHUE, --- (Capt.) 12:19
GOTTIGH, Christopher 12:513
GOTZ, Frederick 3:518
GOUCHER, Thomas 10:496, 615;
  11:605; 14:583
GOUDRYON, Jean 14:240
GOUDY, Hugh 14:313
  Samuel 10:713, 776
  William 12:188
GOUDYS (GOWDY), Samuel 11:88, 93,
  138
GOUERLY, Thomas 10:765
GOUGER, --- (Mr.) 10:459, 484
GOUGH, Wililam 16:184
GOULD, James 2:240; 3:80
  John 14:295, 302
GOURLA, John 11:477
GOURLY, Thomas 11:465
GOVERNIEUR (SEE CURZON &) 12:416
GOVETT, Joseph 10:283
  William 10:282, 359, 441, 500,
  509, 578, 651-652; 11:461;
  12:219, 225; 13:721; 14:625;
  16:185
GOWAN(S), Hugh 14:96, 420
GOWANS, Hugh 13:643
GOWDY, Samuel 12:376
GOWER, Earl 8:40, 320-321, 517
GR(O)EME, Thomas (Dr.) 5:100, 108,
  112, 121-122, 136, 244, 294,
  344, 410, 700
GRAAF, Christian 3:332
  Hans 4:248, 267
  Hans Geo. 3:452
  Jerich Palk 3:453
  Johan Wilhelm 3:570
  Matthias 11:223
  Michael 3:458
  Sebastian 4:73
GRAAF(F), Hans (Hance) 3:394,
  521-523, 620
GRABLE, Michael 12:552

GRACE, George 12:333, 576; 16:318,
  333
  John 16:465
  Robert 5:186
  Robt. 2:405
GRACE (NEGRO) 13:154
GRADY, David 15:187, 640; 16:413
  Patrick 1:83
GRAE, Velde 3:328
GRAEFF, Jacob 14:264
GRAEME, Thomas 3:247-250, 293-294,
  400, 429, 544
GRAF, Hans Georg 4:73
GRAFF, --- (Mr.) 6:757
  Abraham 5:601-602
  Andrew 11:82, 85; 13:722; 15:98,
  173; 16:408
  Catharine 11:113; 12:639
  Geoprge 16:118, 192-193, 493-494,
  499
  George 3:331; 11:592; 13:78-79,
  584; 14:233, 274, 278, 445, 532,
  620; 15:570, 572
  Hans 4:182, 272
  Jacob 12:61; 13:184
  John 13:246; 15:205, 363
  Sebastian 10:705
GRAFFTS, Bastian 4:173-174
  George 4:173-174
GRAFTON, --- (Duke of) 9:341,
  346-347
  Richard 3:254, 269
GRAGDON, --- (Col.) 5:267
GRAGG (GREGG), Robert 14:92, 420
GRAHAM, Archd. 4:468
  Charles 11:162, 164, 166, 168-169
  Daniel 14:293, 300, 410
  Edward 11:143; 12:333; 13:568;
  14:95, 412
  Francis 5:194
  George 10:709, 758; 14:296, 303,
  429
  Henry 10:231
  Henry Hale 8:573; 9:205, 627, 673;
  10:358; 11:254; 16:214, 217-218,
  242
  James 5:186, 247; 13:464
  John 5:454; 14:91, 415, 424
  Michael 15:140
  Richard 14:606
  Samuel 12:198; 15:296
  William 3:370; 4:495, 503; 10:451,
  693, 748; 11:286; 13:64, 193,
  395; 14:396, 400, 501; 15:55;
  16:498, 512
GRAHAMS, Michl. 6:649
  Noble 14:310
GRAINGER, Nicho's. 2:426
GRAIRTEUS, Johannes 3:455
GRAM(P)TON, John 1:218, 224, 253,
  260
GRAME (GREEME, GRAEME, GROEME),
  Tho. 4:145, 232, 244, 293, 295,
  306, 348-349, 469, 496-497,
  515-517, 524-531, 640, 674
GRAMMER, Jesse 12:333, 576
GRANDONDAWE 8:383, 386
GRANDSON, John 13:26
GRANOW, Lewis 11:225
GRANT, --- (Capt.) 9:214, 269-274,
  276; 12:356
  Alexander 16:510
  Charles 4:482; 5:3, 387, 572
  Elizabeth 9:735
  George 3:63; 10:765; 11:473-474
  Isaac 15:576-577

GRANT, Isabella 12:336, 338
 James 8:267, 269
 John 11:418-419, 423; 14:365, 620
 Lewis 10:484, 497, 741, 777;
　11:10, 18, 108; 13:250, 268,
　544, 585
 Marmaduke 12:329
 Patrick 13:53
 Samuel 13:441
 Thomas 12:311; 13:398; 14:445,
　558; 15:118, 170, 310; 16:231
 William 7:202; 11:45
GRANTHAM, --- (Earl of) 5:66
 --- (Lord) 9:761
 John 1:258, 260
GRANTHUM, --- 1:259
 --- (Duke of) 4:298, 483-485
GRANTON, John 1:218
GRANTSHIER, Anthony 14:116
GRANTUM, John 1:258-260
GRANVILLE, --- (Earl of) 5:424
 P. 8:517
GRANWAY, Joseph 10:464
GRASSHOLD, Christian 5:218-221
GRATZ, --- (Mr.) 10:473
 George 13:251
 Jacob, Sr. 13:396
 Michael 13:246
 Palatine 3:290
GRAUEL, John 15:472
GRAUL, --- (Capt.) 16:535
 John 14:459
GRAUNT, Wm. 1:323
GRAVES, Samuel 12:544
 Thomas 1:396-397, 435
GRAW, Leonard 3:385
GRAY, --- (Capt.) 13:428
 --- (Lt.) 6:491, 502
 --- (Mr.) 13:369; 15:472
 Anderson J. 12:411
 Archibald 9:282
 G. 13:509
 George 5:99; 9:334; 10:215, 266,
　280-281, 283-292, 296-302,
　304-307, 314-315, 322-323,
　327-328, 330-331, 334-336,
　353-355, 357, 360, 362-363, 365,
　367, 371, 373-374, 378, 380-382,
　390, 395, 398-399, 401-402, 443,
　445-446, 448, 452, 455, 465-466,
　469-472, 474, 476-478, 480,
　483-484, 486, 490, 502, 537,
　542, 454, 548, 551-552, 560-563,
　568, 578, 588, 594, 602, 615,
　617, 619-621, 623, 627-629,
　632-633, 636-640, 642-643,
　648-652, 677, 679, 683, 687,
　689, 692-693, 696, 698-700, 702,
　704-705, 709-714, 716-718,
　720-722, 724-727, 733, 376-379,
　742, 744, 748, 750, 752-753,
　758-759, 761-766, 769-770, 772,
　775, 777, 781-784; 11:1-2, 4-5,
　9-12, 15, 33, 77, 97, 99,
　111-112, 113-115, 117, 122,
　124-128, 134-137, 141, 143, 145,
　181; 12:507, 534, 690, 710;
　13:85, 112, 304, 391, 415, 646,
　721, 737
 George, Jr. 5:175, 209
 Hannah 13:622
 Isaac 13:391, 415, 721, 737;
　14:555; 15:98
 James 11:155
 John 3:457; 8:781; 9:57, 286
 Neigal 10:728

GRAY, Neigel (Neigle) 11:180
 Robert 11:180
 Sam 1:82, 140-141, 168, 188, 321,
　323
 Samuel 9:571; 11:469
 Thomas 9:333
 William 11:66, 74, 89, 98, 108,
　423, 448; 12:769, 773-774, 776;
　13:31, 268, 622; 14:133, 148,
　151, 295, 302, 409, 426, 444,
　447; 16:231, 355, 422
GRAY (GREY), George 14:555
GRAYDON, --- (Col.) 5:325
 Alexander 4:389-390; 5:193, 209,
　264, 388, 573; 7:437; 8:58, 577;
　10:447; 12:745; 13:568; 14:126,
　376-377, 431; 16:61, 169, 176,
　541
 Caleb 9:30; 10:43
GRAYHAM, Henry 16:428
GRAYTON (GRAYDON), Alexander
　15:542, 588, 599, 603, 621, 656,
　658
GREAFF, Andrew 13:393
GREAME (GREEME, GROEME), Thomas
　(Dr.) 6:170, 173, 174, 319
GREAT ARROW 5:538
GREAVES, Samuel 12:91
GREBLE, Andrew 15:178
GREEN, --- (Gen.) 13:107
 --- (Maj. Gen.) 11:703
 Ashbel(1) (Rev.) 16:497, 519
 Bednall 4:274
 Edward 13:519
 George 1:80
 Henry 13:456
 Isaac 11:494; 12:778
 Isaac, Jr. 13:4
 James 9:578, 580; 13:14, 29, 32,
　116, 120
 John 13:562; 14:101, 420; 16:307
 John (alias HURRIN & WILSON)
　10:129
 Joseph 13:358, 741, 771; 14:465,
　539
 Jospeh 11:393, 424, 583
 Martha 11:703
 Mary 11:250
 Michael 12:715
 Patrick 14:76
 Pyramus 5:113, 233-234, 262
 Thomas 3:394, 522; 5:414; 11:212,
　610-612; 13:673; 14:108, 144;
　16:369
 Timothy 9:673; 10:691-692, 713,
　715, 718, 739; 14:348; 16:274
 William 4:274; 5:325; 10:405, 432;
　13:62, 245, 594; 15:68, 440;
　16:307, 491
 Wm. 1:390
GREEN (SEE KNIGHT &) 10:523
GREEN(E), Edwd. 1:127, 133, 135,
　137-139, 149-151, 157-160,
　167-171, 173-176, 182, 188-193,
　211
 Nathaniel 12:229, 248, 300, 305,
　326, 328, 395-396, 428, 482
 Thomas 4:248, 267, 684, 748, 782
 Timothy 11:23, 73, 78-79, 110
GREENAWALT, Jacob 16:518
 Philip 11:417, 479, 504; 13:642
GREENAWAY, Joseph 5:112
 William 13:118, 595; 14:298, 305,
　429
GREENE, --- (Gen.) 13:343
 --- (Gov.) 12:444

74

GREENE, George **10**:671, 679
 Jno. **1**:94
 William (Gov.) **7**:559
GREENLEAF, Isaac **8**:750
GREENLEE, William **4**:102
GREENMYER, --- (Capt.) **16**:364
GREENTREE, Alexander **10**:600
GREENVILLE, George **11**:151
 J. **6**:61
GREENWALT, Philip **10**:776; **12**:508;
 13:621
GREENWAY, --- (Capt.) **3**:51
 --- (Mr.) **13**:594
 Joseph **10**:522, 694
 Robert **5**:106
 William **10**:525, 554, 566, 740;
 11:223, 607; **13**:64, 593
GREER, David **10**:768; **11**:473;
 12:513; **13**:93, 397
 George **14**:416
 Henry **13**:624, 715
 James **13**:591; **14**:295, 302, 410,
 427
 John **9**:235; **13**:635; **14**:215, 410
 Joseph **11**:473; **12**:101, 350, 434;
 13:436, 630
 Matthew **11**:43, 372
 Phillis **13**:326-327
GREESEMAN, Dirick **3**:368
 Johannes Dirick **3**:368
GREGEMIER, Henry **16**:204
GREGG, Amos **16**:1-7, 9-17, 19-29,
 31, 33-35, 37, 39-44, 46-47, 52,
 54-57, 59-60, 62-68, 70-75, 78,
 82-85, 88-91, 93-94, 96-99,
 102-116, 118-120, 122-127,
 129-133, 135-138, 141-146,
 148-149, 151-160, 163-166,
 168-170, 172-173, 175-178,
 180-183, 187-188, 190-194,
 196-201, 211, 214-216, 218-220,
 222-224, 209b-212b, 214b-224b,
 225-227, 229-233, 235-244,
 251-252, 254-264, 267-274,
 278-291, 293, 295-307, 309-313,
 315-316, 318, 320-324, 326-327,
 329-332, 336-337, 339-341,
 344-350, 352-360, 363-366,
 368-373, 375-384, 386, 388-390,
 392-396, 399-405, 408-429, 432,
 434-436, 439, 441-442, 446-447,
 449-452, 454, 463, 489-494,
 496-501, 507, 509-528, 540, 543,
 545
 Amos (Dr.) **15**:83, 272, 567,
 571-572, 577-584, 586-588,
 595-597, 599-600, 602-604,
 606-607, 612-616, 618-620,
 622-623, 625-629, 632, 641-646,
 651-658
 Andrew **5**:247
 James **11**:281; **11**:281; **14**:364,
 393-394, 516
 John **8**:781; **9**:57, 199; **11**:181;
 13:275; **16**:333
 Matthew **11**:398, 755; **12**:453
 Michael **14**:611
 Robert **10**:449; **11**:181; **13**:604
 Thomas **16**:407
GREGORY, Benjamin **14**:243, 454
 David **11**:513, 516-517
 James **11**:257; **12**:4, 93-94
 Thomas **16**:110, 478
 William **16**:244
GREGSON, James **11**:513, 516-517
GREMES, Lawrence **11**:501

GRENAUGH, Ruth **15**:258
GRENOW, Lewis **15**:118
GRENVILLE, J. **5**:712
GRESHAM, Ambrose **11**:163, 167
GRESLER, George **12**:733
GRESSEL, --- (Col.) **12**:145
GRESSWOLD, Jos. **10**:711
GRESWOLD, Joseph **12**:27-28, 83
GREUTTER, Abraham **3**:518
GREW, --- (Mr.) **5**:758, 761
 Margaret **12**:343
 Michael **14**:62, 88, 428
GREY, James **5**:551
 John **1**:203; **5**:570; **7**:548-549
 Jonathan **11**:282
 Joseph **14**:581
 Tho. **2**:111, 160, 205-206, 241,
 395-397
 William **13**:320
GRI(E)SWOLD, Joseph **12**:450,
 566-567, 587, 617
GRIB, Jacob **3**:519
GRICE, Francis **11**:42; **14**:555
 Jon'n. **11**:63
GRIER, --- (Maj.) **12**:774
 David **10**:451; **13**:723, 745; **14**:234,
 558; **15**:656, 658
 George **13**:708
 J. **11**:732
 James **13**:592, 717, 757; **14**:85, 99
 John **10**:451; **12**:631; **14**:36, 189,
 192
GRIER (GREER), William **14**:295, 302,
 430
GRIER (GUITER, GREER), Henry **14**:87,
 95, 413, 424, 427
GRIEVES, George **13**:373
GRIFF(E)Y, John **14**:63, 93, 203, 413
GRIFFI, Samuel **3**:456
GRIFFIN, --- (Col.) **11**:235
 --- (Mr.) **12**:250
 Cyrus **13**:474
 John **11**:235; **15**:173
 Sellwood **12**:619
GRIFFING, Sarah **13**:279
GRIFFIT(T)S, Thomas **3**:389, 413,
 416, 491, 529-531, 534-542, 544,
 571, 573-574, 585, 591, 598-599,
 604, 607, 609, 612, 614-615, 617
GRIFFITH, --- (Mrs.) **12**:501
 Benjamin **5**:388
 Evan **11**:483-485; **12**:522
 Gidean **5**:55
 Gideon **4**:782
 Griffith **4**:270
 John **16**:180
 Levi **10**:450; **13**:717, 763
 Rebecca **12**:522
 Thomas **3**:410
 Timothy **5**:248
GRIFFITHS, Benjamin **13**:554; **14**:101,
 431
 Daniel **14**:138, 149
 David **16**:8
 Griffith **5**:209
 Levi **13**:615; **14**:15, 82, 417
 Thomas **4**:17, 19-21, 23, 32-33,
 39-41, 47, 49, 51, 53, 56, 60,
 63, 66, 71-73, 80, 82, 85-87,
 90, 95-97, 100, 104, 106, 109,
 112-113, 119-120, 124, 129, 136,
 140, 143-144, 147, 149-153, 155,
 158-159, 165, 167, 174-175, 181,
 186, 190, 195-196, 198, 201-203,
 205, 208-209, 224, 226-227,
 232-233, 235, 238, 241, ->

GRIFFITHS, Thomas (continued)
  4:243-245, 247-250, 253,
  256-257, 259-260, 262-264,
  273-274, 277, 280, 283, 285,
  288-290, 292-297, 301-307,
  309-314, 317-319, 321, 329-331,
  333-334, 336, 341, 343, 347-348,
  350, 352-356, 359, 364-365, 371,
  376, 380, 384-385, 387, 391-392,
  395, 398, 402, 413, 420-422,
  439, 431-432, 435, 448, 459,
  461, 469-470, 478-483, 496,
  498-499, 501-503, 506, 524, 640
William 7:293-294
GRIFFITTS, Isaac 5:464, 550,
  561-562
William 8:666-667
GRIFFITZ, Thos. 2:410
GRIFFY, Jonas 9:470
GRIGER, Casper 3:385
GRIGGS, Philip 15:519
GRIGSON, --- (Mr.) 10:684
GRILL, Godfriedt 4:60
GRIM, Henry 15:561
Johannes Conrad 4:59
GRIMES, Anne (Mrs.) 11:599
Christopher 13:382
James 14:311, 495
Thomas 7:34
William 13:427
GRIMSHAW, Edmund 12:300
Jane 12:300
GRIN, Johan Egidius 3:332
GRINDER, George Ja. 13:757
George Jacob 14:100, 418
Jacob 13:757
GRINNTEN, Ellenar 1:259
GRINTEEM, --- 1:260
GRISCOM, Sarah 1:522
GRISCOM(E), Andrew 1:93, 95, 522
GRISEL, Edward 12:334
GRISIMER, Velde 3:385
GRISPIN, William 13:450
GRISSBACH, Michael 9:282
GRISSIL (GRISSEL), Edward 11:514,
  516-517
GRIST, Barbara 14:466
John 3:137-138
GRISTOCK, William 14:126, 435
GRISWOLD, Matthew 10:120
GRITER, Friedrich 4:72
Hans Jacob 4:72
Martin 4:72
GRIZZLE, Edward 12:419
GROEME, Thomas (Dr.) 7:6, 70
GROENENDICK, Peter 1:81, 160, 191
GROENENDUCK, Peter 6:122
GROFF, George 12:506, 554; 15:297
GRONDT, Hans Jorg 3:519
GRONENDICK(E), Peter 1:77, 82, 160,
  191
GRONENDICKS, Peter 1:90
GRONENDIK(E), Peter 1:157, 192,
  224, 286
GRONES, Thomas 1:77, 84
GRONO, --- (Col.) 11:772-773
GRONOW, --- (Mr.) 11:571, 760
Lewis 12:298, 600
GROOM, Henry 16:310
Johan Georg. 3:519
GROP, Johan Eorl 3:517
GROSCUP, Paul 14:226, 279; 16:436
GROSHER, Adam 11:106
GROSS, Andreas 4:59
Henry 13:366
Johan Peter 3:570

GROSS, John 10:448
Michael 3:455
Philip 14:604
GROSSCUP, Paul 15:439, 454, 482
GROSSENGEISE, Conrad 14:415
GROSSQUILL, John 14:131, 134
GROTZ, George 13:47
Jacob, Sr. 13:89, 724
GROUSE, Adam 11:160-163, 165
GROUST, Johan Jacob 3:410
GROVE, Christian 13:442
Jacob 13:442
Thomas Cotterell 9:390, 392
GROVE(S), Michael 11:7, 33, 139;
  12:493
Peter 12:493, 680
GROVER, George 13:448, 537
Mary 13:605; 14:43
Timothy 13:605; 14:43
GROVES, --- (Mr.) 10:331
Icabod 11:21
Mark 13:457
Michael 15:77
Peter 11:45
Thomas 1:367, 585
GROVUL, Johan Michl. 3:516
GROWDEN (GROWDON), J. 3:541;
  4:20-21, 36-38, 40-41
Jos. 1:108-109, 169, 196-200,
  202-208, 211-212, 214-220,
  222-226, 228-229, 238, 267-270,
  272-275, 277-279, 284-286, 290,
  292-293, 320, 322, 324, 331,
  335, 343, 370, 399, 413, 415,
  418, 478-479, 483, 485-486, 488,
  491, 509, 513-514, 516, 518,
  521, 523-524, 526-529, 536, 539,
  541, 547-548, 552-555, 578, 582,
  595-601, 604-606, 610-612,
  614-615, 619, 624
Joseph 2:30-31, 34, 36, 39, 60,
  74-75, 77-78, 80, 82, 84-85,
  109-110, 146, 153, 164, 179,
  181, 185, 206, 224, 239, 250,
  254, 406-408, 412-414, 416,
  427-429, 432, 434-435, 437, 439,
  441, 443, 446-449, 451-452, 479,
  482-484, 486, 490-491, 503, 506,
  508-511, 513, 520-522, 524-527,
  530, 532-533, 537-539, 542,
  544-546, 549-550, 553, 555, 568,
  571, 579-580, 582, 584-587,
  589-592, 594-597, 599, 608
Lawrance 9:172, 201-202, 205, 316,
  663
Lawrence 3:590-591; 4:313, 482;
  5:3, 65-68, 70-71, 110, 264-265,
  268, 345, 370-372, 559-560, 566;
  6:360-361, 459, 666; 7:83, 87,
  91, 96, 265-266, 389, 464, 637;
  8:86, 100, 174-175, 211, 333,
  336, 481-482, 506, 591; 12:77,
  191-192, 751
Sarah 12:77, 191, 193
GROWNOW, Lewis 13:282
GROWSE, Adam 12:188
GRUB, Amer 11:11
Curtis 10:781
Jacob 15:499
Peter 10:696-697, 705, 709,
  711-712, 767
GRUBB, --- (Col.) 10:346
  --- (Mr.) 10:373
Adam 12:187; 14:487; 15:96;
  16:218b
Ann(e) 9:564, 568, 580

GRUBB, Curtis 9:564, 566-567, 580;
  11:334, 498, 525-526, 528;
  13:393, 678
Daniel 11:83, 123; 13:603
John 1:369, 547-548, 552, 589, 614
Peter 13:393, 724
Peter, Jr. 11:17, 333, 335, 350
Thomas 5:194
GRUBB(S), Nathaniel 4:495, 503
GRUBE, Bernard A. (Rev.) 12:346
Bernard Adam 6:749
GRUBER, Edward 15:14
Everhart 9:673
Hans Jacob 3:517
Hans Peter 3:542
Henrich 3:458
John Adam 12:448
GRUGG, Conrad 16:334
GRUMBACHER, Hans 3:517
GRUMBL(E)Y, Jacob 14:80, 98, 421
GRUNG, Peter 4:468
GRUVER, John 11:137
GUARD, Jeremiah 14:310
Robt. 2:20
GUDGEON, Andrew 9:508
GUERNEY, --- (Mr.) 13:263
GUESSE, Tho's. 9:509
GUEST, --- 6:488 (See GIST)
Alec. 1:167
Christopher 5:537, 693, 703, 708
Henry 13:638; 14:86, 424
John 2:25-30, 34, 36-37, 39-40,
  45, 48-49, 51-55, 61-63, 65-71,
  74, 78, 81, 86-87, 89-91, 93,
  95-98, 101-104, 107-109,
  111-112, 114-120, 136-138,
  140-141, 146-148, 150-156,
  159-161, 163, 178-180, 184, 201,
  204, 209-210, 212, 214-215,
  218-224, 227, 229, 232, 234-235,
  237, 241, 255, 258, 262, 276,
  298-299, 301, 308-309, 315-316,
  318, 320-321, 365, 372-373, 383,
  386, 391; 6:529
Justice 4:63, 67
Wm. 1:48, 89, 127, 218, 221,
  589-590
GUFFEE, James 16:445
GUIER, George 14:94
GUIGER, Henry 13:310
GUILE, Manuel 15:148
GUILER, Henry 14:86
GUILLIM, Danll. 1:166
GUILLION, Jane 14:383
GUIN, Thomas 1:394 (See Wynne)
GUION, Thomas 12:142-143, 151, 153
GUION (GUYON), Lewis 10:712, 750,
  780; 11:65, 84
GUITER, Henry 13:669
GUIZE, William 13:142
GULDIN, John 12:519
GULLMAN, Philip 4:72
GULYPPENNAA 3:316
GUMBER, Johannes 3:466
GUMBLY, Benjn. 1:518
GUMP, Johan George 3:454
GUNDY, Ephraim 11:152
GUNKELL, Michael 13:283
GUNKLE, Michael 14:635; 15:434
GUNNEHATOROOJA 3:149
GUNNERSON, Mary 12:81
GUNT, Hans Georg. 3:415
Jacob 3:415
GUNTHER, George 11:38
John 16:315
GURK, Joannes 3:332

GURNEY, --- (Col.) 13:739
--- (Mr.) 13:104
Francis 10:436, 577, 714, 717-718,
  720-721, 723-733, 735-742, 744,
  747-750, 752-756, 758-760,
  762-766, 768-775, 777-784;
  11:1-9, 12-17, 19-20, 22-23, 27,
  29, 31-33, 36-43, 45, 47-51, 54,
  57-62, 64, 66-69, 72-73, 75,
  112, 134, 180, 197; 13:100, 316,
  384, 481, 517, 739; 14:107, 162,
  176, 241, 403, 453, 462, 529;
  15:322, 338-339, 374, 538, 558;
  16:212, 251
Henry 11:525
GUSLAR, George Bickham 14:71
GUSTOCK, William 13:573
GUTHREY, John 11:220
Robert 14:365
GUTHRIE, George 13:712
James 13:517; 16:27, 224, 466, 521
John 12:31; 13:332; 14:63, 134,
  422
William 12:367; 14:374, 376; 15:85
GUTREY, James 16:215
GUTT, Hendrick 3:385
Jacob 3:432
GUTTAMAACK 8:594
GUY, Henry 16:227
James 11:112
Jonathan 15:290
Sarah 13:398
William 11:501
GUYER, --- (Capt.) 11:65
Adam 11:244
Casper 11:565; 12:237
Elizh. 12:237
Gasper 10:671, 677
George 10:765
GUYWSUDAY (GUYUSUDAY) 8:383, 386
GWIN, Priscilla 13:381
William 11:166
GYBERTZ, Frederick 3:414
GYER, Andrew 10:666
GYGER, Johannes 3:459
Michael 3:414

HAAG, Hans Michal 3:456
HAAK, Hans Dirik 3:328
HAAKE, John 3:367
HAALING, Michel 4:73
HAAS (HAOS), George 11:91, 104
Nicholas 12:608
Peter 4:100
HABACKER, John 15:119
HABARAKER, Johan 3:284
HABERLING, Johannes 3:456
HABERSTICK, Michael 11:438, 443
HACHLEIN, Peter 15:298
HACHMAN, Jacob 3:415
HACK, --- (Dr.) 8:271
HACKER, William 4:135
HACKERT, Frans 4:59
HACKET, --- 13:29, 32
HACKETT, John 10:476
Richard 13:14; 14:314
HACKMANN, Rudolph 4:59
HADDEN, Adam 1:565
Samll. 1:564-565
Samuel 13:751
HADGE, Hugh 13:63
HADLEY, Simon 3:254, 270

HAERKERMAN, C. D. G. 12:503
HAES, Johanas (Johannes D.) 1:127,
  214 (See D'HAES)
HAFFA, Henry 11:596, 598;
  12:131-133, 508
HAFFNER, George 11:181
HAFNER, George 10:765
HAGA, Jacob 16:426
HAGAMAN, John 16:391
HAGAN, Hugh 15:613
  John 11:16
HAGE, James 10:563-564
HAGE (HOGE), Andrew 14:102, 439
HAGEMAN, Ulrick 3:248
HAGEN, Hugh 16:101
HAGENBUCK, Henry 11:128
HAGENMULLER, Christian Ernest 3:417
HAGERTY, James 15:469
HAGEY, John 16:284
HAGGY, Hans 3:284
HAGI, Hans Georg. 3:458
HAGNER, --- (Col.) 12:160
  Frederick 11:669; 12:298
  Philip 13:343
HAGUE, Francis 4:352
  John 15:626
HAHN, --- (Mr.) 13:207
  Michael 11:41, 308, 371, 443, 736;
    13:93, 112, 397, 415, 584;
    14:201, 211, 234
HAIG, --- (Capt.) 5:304, 346-347
HAIGE(E), Wm. 1:47, 57-68, 70-73,
  142
HAIGUE, Wm. 1:74-75, 89-91, 93-94,
  105-106, 114-119, 122-124, 147
HAIL (SEE ROBINS, DUN &) 11:29
HAILER, Frederick 13:36
HAILLMAN, Andreas 4:60
HAILMAN, Johan Peter 3:432
  Johannes 3:456
HAILS (SEE ROBINS, DUN &) 10:727
HAIN(E)S, John 11:229, 572
HAINES, --- 12:275-276
  Caleb 11:514, 516-517
  Casper Wm. 13:358
  Charles 1:182
  Daniel 14:320
  Elinor 12:579
  George 13:218
  Joseph 3:543
  Reuben 10:646; 11:559; 12:651,
    727; 13:293; 14:230
HAINS, Daniel 9:584
HAL, Egram 3:390
HAL(E)Y, John 14:407, 409, 439
HAL(L)IFAX, --- (Lord Dunk.) 6:61,
  305-306, 308, 333-334, 510, 730
HALBERT, --- 8:612
  Henry 9:286
HALBURN, Casper 11:380
HALBURT, Rhuben 9:584
HALDER, Reynd. 3:368
HALDIMAN, --- (Gen.) 10:141
HALDIMAN (HALDEMAN, HALDYMAN),
  William 8:59, 64-65, 71, 76, 505
HALDYMAN, --- (Col.) 7:737
HALE, Alexander 15:83, 371, 394;
  16:216
  John 10:661-694
  Samuel 15:482
  Thomas 11:277, 528, 767; 12:11,
    104, 189, 196, 202, 222, 238,
    247, 256, 260-261, 263, 265-266,
    268, 281, 283, 299-300, 317,
    320, 323-324, 326; 13:243, 366,
    584

HALE, Warwick 15:482
HALE & LAWTON 11:765; 12:354
HALE (SEE DUNN &) 11:68, 117
HALES, Edwd. (Sir) 1:246
  John 11:513, 516-517
  Robert 3:71
  Sarah 3:189
HALEY, John 11:220, 240, 306
  Mary 13:526
  Patrick 14:359
HALFNIDE, --- 4:274
HALFPENNY, James 13:679; 14:91, 415
  Mark 14:107
  Thomas 12:343
HALIFAX, --- (Earl of) 4:7
  --- (Lord) 5:515, 605, 618
  Dunk 5:712; 8:517, 552, 557
  Dunk (Earl of) 9:113-114
HALKET, --- 7:37
  --- (Maj.) 8:124
  Francis 6:489-490, 494, 502
HALKET(T) (HACKET), Peter (Sir)
  6:200, 311, 395, 481-483, 488,
  490, 494, 499-502, 519, 549,
  559, 600, 636
HALL, --- (Col.) 11:151-157
  --- (Mr.) 6:322, 327; 11:264;
    13:399
  Alexander 10:450, 460
  Benjamin 10:718; 15:516
  Charles 11:599; 13:128; 14:143;
    15:344
  David 8:439-440; 9:203, 671, 698;
    10:5, 7, 49, 81, 108, 218, 267;
    11:31, 166; 13:568; 14:132, 430
  Edwd. 4:62, 67
  Eliz. 1:556, 558 (See CRUIKSHANK)
  Elwood 14:310
  Ezekiel 13:544
  Hugh 1:477
  Jacob 1:194, 371; 5:193; 8:575;
    9:205, 672; 11:118
  James 5:121; 11:85; 13:632;
    14:409, 440
  Jesse 15:119
  John 3:28, 31, 56, 108, 140, 254,
    332, 387, 416, 465, 520, 575;
    5:247; 9:633; 10:461; 11:154,
    244; 13:38, 52; 15:73
  Mary 13:29, 32, 116, 121, 127,
    135, 285
  Peter 4:500, 602
  Richard 1:558; 14:264; 16:43
  Robt. 1:48, 87, 162
  Solomon 3:218
  Stephen 15:344-345
  Tho. 1:576
  Thomas 16:121
  Walter 11:214; 12:631
  William 11:426; 12:170, 208;
    14:310, 461; 16:330, 336
HALL & ALLEN 11:52, 79
HALL & SELLERS 10:54, 267, 471;
  11:31, 654; 12:197; 15:366, 392
HALL(I)WELL, Richd. 1:369, 452,
  482, 491, 495, 509, 515,
  518-521, 525-526, 529, 541,
  546-548, 550-553, 559-561, 563,
  578, 589, 591, 593, 595-596,
  1:611-612, 614, 616, 620 (See
  HALLYWELL and HALWELL)
HALL, SCHULL & 15:390
HALLER, --- (Col.) 11:13, 64
  Henry 9:398; 10:681, 705, 713,
  755, 771; 12:12, 47-48, 250,
  436, 646, 703, 780; 15:62, 180

HALLER, Jacob **16**:323
 Peter **3**:516
HALLER (HULLER), Henry **11**:146, 340,
 428, 479, 504, 550, 583, 771
HALLETT, Jonah **13**:712
HALLIARD, Jno. **1**:59, 62
HALLIDAY, William **12**:372, 561
HALLIDAY (HOLLIDAY), William
 11:379, 392, 697
HALLIFAX, Dunk **7**:275, 387, 634,
 637, 648, 739
HALLIFIELD, Saml. **2**:153
HALLING, --- (Dr.) **13**:199
 S. (Dr.) **13**:170
 Solomon **14**:82, 102, 440
HALLIWELL, Thomas **2**:520
HALLIWELL (HALLEWELL), Richd. **2**:31,
 34, 50, 52, 62, 79, 83, 92
HALLOCK, William **10**:745
HALLOWAY, Elijah **9**:584
HALLOWELL, Jesse **16**:287
HALLSTED, Charles **15**:348
HALLYMAN, Tho. **1**:182
HALLYWELL, Richard **1**:458, 475,
 479-481, 483-486
HALTER, Bridge **16**:61
 Jacob **13**:778
HALTON, James **14**:419
HALTSBEILDER, Stephen **3**:328
HALWELL, Richd. **1**:601, 616, 619,
 622
HALYFAX, --- (Earl of) **3**:71
HALZARFALL, Erasmus **3**:415
HAM, Ester **13**:437
 Hans Jerick **3**:386
 James **12**:244, 341
HAMAKER, Adam **16**:266, 362
HAMBLE, --- (Mrs.) **13**:282
HAMBLETON, Wm. **1**:182
HAMBRIGHT, --- (Mr.) **8**:774
 Abraham **12**:626
 John **11**:336, 342-344, 346-347,
 349-351, 364-370, 372-373,
 375-379, 381-389, 391-396,
 398-399, 402-403, 405-412,
 414-415, 417-419, 421-423,
 425-426, 428, 430, 432-438,
 440-445, 447, 490-493, 495,
 501-503, 506, 508, 512, 518-520,
 524-531, 533-534, 591, 596,
 598-600, 606-609, 612-617,
 651-652, 655-660, 663-668,
 672-679, 682-684, 691-693, 695,
 697-698, 701, 705-709, 713-724,
 727-728, 735, 738, 740-741,
 743-745, 747-749, 751-753;
 12:43-46, 48, 50, 62, 66, 68-71,
 73-74, 76-77, 79-80, 83-85,
 86-88, 90, 92-94, 100-102, 104,
 106-107, 112, 127-128, 130,
 132-133, 136, 139, 141, 144-145,
 147-148, 150, 153-154, 158-164,
 166-167, 169, 171-172, 174,
 176-177, 179, 181-182, 185-186,
 191-195, 198, 202-203, 205, 207,
 209, 212, 215-219, 221, 223-226,
 228-233, 235, 237, 240-242,
 245-246, 249-251, 257, 260,
 262-263, 265, 267-274, 276, 280,
 285, 287, 289, 296-299, 301-302,
 305, 307, 309, 311-313, 315,
 318-320, 322-324, 326-328, 330,
 333-335, 337-338, 373, 375-376,
 378-379, 384, 387, 389, 391-395,
 397, 399-402, 404-407, 409-410,
 414-415, 417, 419-420, ->

HAMBRIGHT, John (continued)
 12:422-426, 428-429, 431,
 434-438, 440, 442-444, 446,
 448-452, 454-456, 466, 469, 473,
 477-479, 481-483, 485, 488,
 493-495, 497-498, 510, 751
HAMBRITH, John **5**:186
HAMELL, John **13**:23
HAMER, John **13**:501
 Moses **14**:610
 Rachel **13**:501
HAMERSLY, Robert **14**:500
HAMILTON, --- **6**:491; **12**:727
 --- (Capt.) **7**:230-231, 633
 --- (Col.) **13**:603, 607, 656
 --- (Dr.) **15**:571, 578
 --- (Maj.) **13**:777
 --- (Mr.) **13**:606
 A. **13**:659
 Alexander **13**:608; **16**:189, 206,
 212, 244
 Andrew **2**:32, 48, 62-63, 66-67,
 70-71, 74-75, 77-78, 81, 84, 86,
 89, 92, 94, 96, 98, 105, 109,
 114, 121, 130, 138, 153, 239,
 348, 354, 370; **3**:29, 106-107,
 109-110, 113, 115, 130, 138,
 144-145, 147, 156-158, 160,
 162-163, 166-167, 170-172, 175,
 177-178, 180, 189-193, 199, 204,
 212, 214, 229, 237, 266, 271,
 293, 318, 324, 371, 388-389,
 407-408, 417, 421, 429, 434,
 466, 494, 543-546, 554, 557-560,
 563, 576, 582-583, 597, 611,
 615-617; **4**:28, 35, 46, 53, 95,
 97, 119, 129, 136, 153, 161,
 168, 186, 203, 218-219, 221,
 236, 239, 241, 250, 260, 273,
 280, 293, 295, 311, 322, 331,
 333, 349, 393, 429; **5**:106, 132;
 6:720
 Andrew, Jr. **3**:548, 554, 563
 Charles **16**:392
 Gavin, Sr. **13**:307
 Hance **7**:77
 Hance (Hans) **5**:411, 468, 551
 Hans **4**:228, 230-231; **6**:675
 Henry **9**:76
 Hugh **5**:193; **12**:231
 James **3**:615; **4**:312, 482; **5**:1, 4,
 28-31, 33-35, 43, 49, 51-52,
 239, 343, 362-372, 374-381, 384,
 387-388, 391, 394-398, 403, 405,
 410-413, 416, 418, 421-426, 428,
 430-431, 437, 440, 451, 455-458,
 460-468, 470, 480, 484, 486,
 488, 494-496, 498-499, 502,
 505-506, 508, 512-513, 516, 518,
 522, 525, 527-528, 530, 532-534,
 543, 545-546, 548, 550-551, 553,
 558-562, 564-568, 570-573,
 575-583, 586, 589, 595-599,
 601-607, 609, 612, 618, 620-622,
 625-626, 628, 630, 632, 634,
 638-643, 646-647, 654-659,
 661-662, 665, 687, 689, 696,
 698, 700, 704-706, 708-710,
 712-713, 717-719, 722, 730,
 735-736, 746, 755, 757, 765,
 767-768, 770-771, 773, 777; **6**:1,
 3-5, 7, 9, 13, 16, 21, 23-28,
 31-32, 38-39, 44, 48, 50, 54,
 56-57, 111, 130-133, 140-141,
 143-145, 147-148, 150, 160,
 165-166, 176, 187, 192, ->

HAMILTON, James (continued)
  6:207-209, 240, 255, 259, 261,
  308, 336, 421-422, 459, 492,
  506-509, 518, 618, 662, 666,
  670, 676, 702, 715, 718, 745,
  755, 761, 763, 765, 770,
  779-781, 783; 7:1, 3, 5, 7,
  46-47, 50, 64, 70, 79, 91, 110,
  118, 120, 122, 201, 220, 222,
  230, 236, 238, 241, 246-247,
  249, 251-252, 255, 264-266, 268,
  280, 290, 349, 354, 356, 361,
  382, 393-394, 396-397, 401, 407,
  409, 412, 416, 441, 464-465,
  517-518, 527-528, 534, 543, 546,
  622, 635, 637, 649, 652, 656,
  660, 663, 665, 671, 679-680,
  687, 692, 694, 714, 716-717,
  720, 723, 727, 729, 739-741,
  750; 8:245, 256, 259-261,
  409-415, 422-423, 427, 435-436,
  438, 447-450, 456, 460, 463,
  467, 472, 482-484, 487, 490,
  492, 494-497, 500-501, 505-507,
  509-510, 513-514, 516, 520, 522,
  524, 559-560, 563-564, 567-568,
  570, 572-574, 576-583, 586-588,
  592, 594, 600, 602, 604-605,
  609, 612, 614, 618, 622,
  625-627, 629-630, 632, 637, 641,
  643-644, 652-653, 655, 659,
  662-667, 670-675, 677, 683,
  690-692, 694, 697-698, 700, 703,
  706-707, 709, 711-715, 719, 721,
  723, 725, 729, 733-734, 737,
  741, 750, 752, 757, 759, 766,
  772, 775, 777-780; 9:1-2, 5-6,
  9, 12-13, 15-20, 22, 24-31, 33,
  36-37, 39-44, 52, 55-63, 66,
  70-71, 73-74, 77, 91, 100,
  115-116, 123, 125, 146, 148-152,
  163, 167, 172, 175, 178, 180,
  182-183, 186, 201-202, 205, 330,
  412, 450, 459, 547-548, 563,
  603-604, 631-633, 635, 663, 698,
  704, 733-735, 737, 739, 742-743,
  745-748, 750, 752, 754, 756,
  759-760, 766-767, 773, 776-778,
  780, 782; 10:1, 3-4, 45, 90,
  125, 129-130, 138, 158-160, 172,
  177-179, 232-233, 259-260, 379,
  765; 11:63, 269, 303, 426, 469,
  478; 12:705, 708; 13:709, 713;
  14:87-89, 107, 191, 195, 266,
  411, 414, 423, 441, 449, 608,
  611, 655; 15:44, 91; 16:385,
  444, 521
John 10:296, 329-330, 335, 343,
  408, 427, 468, 606, 665, 702;
  11:137, 340; 15:513, 598;
  16:223b, 283-284
Mary 11:770; 12:632
Robert 9:515; 10:7; 12:3; 15:242
Samuel 15:35
Thomas 7:267; 10:757; 15:310, 570
W. C. (G.) 7:387, 739
W. G. 8:552
William 4:782; 8:562; 9:172;
  11:328; 12:495, 499, 502-503,
  520, 534, 549, 632, 681; 13:559,
  698; 15:14, 615, 618, 641, 645
HAMILTON (ALIAS COOPER), Jane
  16:156
HAMLETT, --- (Mr.) 12:389
HAMMA, James 12:513
HAMMER, Hans Michael 3:520

HAMMER, Rinard 3:369
HAMMERLY, Isaac 14:659
HAMMERSLY, Jane 14:263
HAMMILL, William 12:568
HAMMON, Benjamin 11:446
  Thomas 3:385
HAMMOND, David 13:717, 758; 14:98,
  430
  George 14:538, 662
  James 14:567; 15:109, 121
  John 4:231
  Thomas 9:513-514
  William 4:67-69; 11:613
HAMPILL, Edward 4:135
HAMPTON, --- (Col.) 10:754, 763
  Ann 13:304
  Jonathan 7:164-165
HAN, Lutwig 3:410
  William 12:392
HAN(D)COCK, John 11:70, 197, 228,
  231
HAN(D)LEY, Marmaduke 14:86, 416
HANAH, Isaac 11:73
HANAS, --- 8:132
HANAWER, Johannes 3:454
HANBURY, --- (Mr.) 6:4
HANCE, --- (Capt.) 11:106
HANCOCK, Henry 12:592
  John 10:401, 415, 438, 457, 463,
  564-565, 591, 603, 621, 628,
  635, 685; 14:587
  John (Gov.) 15:435, 443
HAND, --- (Col.) 11:62, 108, 152
  --- (Gen.) 12:138, 284, 364, 427
  David 11:259
  Edward 11:119, 152, 158, 179-180,
  261; 13:712, 756; 14:23, 25, 52,
  90, 139, 162, 165, 172, 180,
  200, 437, 556; 15:656, 658
  James 11:79
  John 12:368
  Matthew 10:704, 708; 14:456
  Nathan 12:507
HANDEL, Adam 13:569; 14:85, 427
HANDLYN, John 10:471, 532
HANDROP, Henry 7:717
HANDS(C)HUE, --- (Mr.) 7:398
HANDWERK, John 15:454
HANDWREK, John 12:734
HANELY, Patrick 15:564
HANES (HAINS), Peter 15:613, 625
HANEY, Simeon 14:383
  Thomas 10:706; 13:368; 14:618
HANG, Rudolph 4:72
HANILTON, Andrew 1:469, 498, 502,
  524, 570
HANINGS, Ludwig 16:428
HANKEY, Jacob 11:64
HANKS, William 13:543
HANLEN, James 15:476
HANLON, Edward 11:482, 484-485
  Jno. 10:668
HANLY, Marmaduke 13:755
HANNA, --- (Col.) 16:121
  --- (Maj.) 13:188-189, 191, 228
  James 12:589; 13:139-140, 431;
  15:441; 16:443, 455
  John 9:730; 15:406
  Robert 10:78, 106, 142, 166,
  227-228, 235, 597
  Samuel 16:24
  Stephen 10:765
  William 13:591; 14:97, 424
HANNAH, John 14:599; 15:2
  Robert 14:179
HANNEWALD, Johannes 4:59

HANNON, William **16**:333
HANNOTEAU, Joseph (Don) **5**:283
HANNUM (HANNUMS), --- (Col.)
  13:112, 485
--- (Mr.) **13**:365, 537, 732
James **12**:401; **13**:333
John **8**:573; **9**:205, 657, 673;
  11:83, 479, 504, 507, 596;
  12:372, 401, 451, 477, 539, 647;
  13:87, 105-106, 264, 445, 508,
  722, 724, 737; **14**:53, 171, 184,
  238, 555, 644; **15**:534; **16**:192
HANNUMA, John **13**:112
HANS, Jacob **3**:452; **10**:543, 554
John **2**:246
HANS JACOB **8**:84, 149, 151
HANSARD, --- **6**:490
--- (Mrs.) **6**:522
HANSE, Hend **3**:199
HANSMINGER, Peter **3**:515
HANSON, John **13**:105, 138, 147, 154,
  173, 185
Thomas **9**:645; **10**:9, 217, 283, 479,
  499, 730; **12**:21
Timothy **3**:254
HANSSEGER (HAUSSIGER), Nicholas
  10:446, 460
HANTWERG, Hans Jorig **4**:60
HANUKHUNGO **6**:125
HAPPEL, Jacob **14**:659
HAR(R)ISON, James **1**:47, 57-75, 77,
  79-82, 86-89, 92-94, 96-97,
  99-110, 118-120, 124, 129,
  153-154, 156, 164, 187
HARAGAN, John **13**:755
HARBACH, John **11**:219
HARBE(R)SON, Benjamin **11**:32-33;
  12:709, 781
HARBERSON, George **12**:187
HARBERT, Arthur **15**:119
HARBESON, --- (Mr.) **11**:667
 Benjamin **13**:36, 81, 141, 164, 170,
  204, 209, 250-251, 320, 346
HARBESTON, Jno. **11**:66
HARBISON (HARBESON), Benjamin
  10:462, 612, 641, 702, 704, 783
HARD-CASTLE, William **14**:506
HARDENBERG, Abraham **15**:340
HARDER, John **14**:311
HARDIE, Robert **10**:560, 601, 716;
  11:718; **14**:298, 305, 432, 637
HARDIGE, N. **4**:358
HARDIN, Jno. **1**:87
John **14**:311-312
HARDING, --- (Capt.) **12**:7, 148
 Elisha **14**:223
 George **12**:149, 196, 238, 458
 John **1**:48; **12**:136
 Mary **12**:242, 741
 Nathaniel **1**:502
 Robert **7**:447-448
 Thomas **16**:522, 531
 Timothy **3**:50
HARDMAN, Peter **11**:17
HARDWERK, John **14**:274
 Peter **14**:274
HARDWICK, C. **5**:360
HARDY (HARDIE), --- (Capt.)
  3:53-54; **12**:85
--- (Gov.) **8**:217, 669
 Charles (Sir) **7**:9, 23, 29, 35-36,
  41-42, 44-45, 97-98, 100, 103,
  105, 107-108, 112-113, 115-117,
  120, 122-123, 125, 127, 142-143,
  183, 194-195, 197, 221-223, 270,
  307, 339, 447, 495-497, 501,->

HARDY (HARDIE), Charles (Sir)
  (continued) **7**:560, 580-581, 596,
  608
 Charles (Sir-Gov.) **6**:623, 680
 George **12**:38
 Peter **11**:515-516, 518
 Samuel **14**:162
 Thomas **13**:615; **14**:432
 William **11**:286
HARDY (HARDING), George **11**:753-754,
  760-761, 764
HARE, --- (Capt.) **10**:780
 Jacob **11**:610-612; **12**:340
 Matthew **16**:8
 Michael **11**:610-612; **13**:474; **15**:372
 Philip **12**:680
HARE, ROBERT & CO. **11**:137
HARFIELD, Will. **12**:5
HARGEY, John **14**:293, 300, 412
HARGIS, Abraham **10**:708; **13**:619
HARGON, John **14**:410
HARGRAVE, Charles **3**:458
HARGUES, Abraham **11**:23
HARIAN, Ezekial **3**:382
HARKINS, Daniel **15**:288
 Isaac **14**:97
 James **14**:420
 John **13**:439, 542
 Margaret **15**:288
HARLAN, Moses **4**:108
HARLAN(D), Ezekeil (Ezekiel) **3**:43,
  217, 219
HARLAND, Michael **3**:227
HARLE, Ralph **4**:59
HARLEN, George **1**:521
HARLIN, Ezekial **3**:246 (See
  HARLAN(D))
HARMAN, --- **1**:109
 Casparus **1**:48
 Casper **3**:385
 Ephraim **2**:42
 Henry **1**:83
 Josiah **13**:669
 Thomas **16**:20
HARMAR (HARMAN, HARMER), James
  11:732
 Joseph **14**:447
 Josiah **10**:405-406, 418, 425, 434,
  445, 459, 464, 467, 472, 483,
  487, 491, 525; **11**:179-180;
  12:705; **13**:671, 709, 715, 757;
  14:71, 177, 182, 185, 193, 199,
  215, 237, 311, 356, 373, 437,
  470, 473, 480, 513, 516, 533,
  535, 549, 559, 579, 662; **15**:6,
  13, 19, 337-338, 379, 381,
  394-395, 437, 473, 496, 498,
  529; **16**:41, 258, 263, 503
 Wm. **1**:536
HARMEL, Johan Henrick **3**:410
HARMONY, Nicholas **9**:340
HARMS, John H. **15**:378
HARNDITS, Samuel **3**:454
HARNING, William **13**:454
HAROLD, Samuel **12**:12
HAROSS, Jacob Wilhelm **3**:607
HARP, Peter **3**:429-430
HARPER, --- (Capt.) **10**:115
 Andrew **12**:302
 George **14**:506
 James **15**:95
 John **1**:500-502; **10**:480; **13**:580,
  680, 714, 722-723, 757;
  14:86-87, 134, 238, 422, 427,
  435; **15**:98-99
 Robert **12**:668

81

HARPER, Wm. **2**:151
HARPLE, George **16**:212b
HARRAGAN, John **14**:91
HARRAWAY, William **5**:194
HARREL, James **14**:401
HARRIET (HARRIOTT), Andrew **14**:191,
   195, 431
HARRING, --- (Mr.) **15**:108
HARRINGTON, --- **5**:361
--- (Earl of) **6**:356
--- (Lord) **3**:525; **4**:298, 484-485
John **14**:62, 86, 427
Lewis **11**:88
Thomas **13**:624; **14**:432
HARRIOTT, Saml. **2**:112
HARRIS, --- **9**:509
--- (Mr.) **12**:486, 534
Benjamin **14**:313
David **11**:301, 305; **12**:42, 75
Elijah **14**:223
Esther **4**:655
Hannah **15**:112, 114
Henry **5**:3
Hugh **15**:32
J. **5**:197; **12**:544, 633, 740, 748,
   754; **13**:60
James **14**:441-442; **15**:191, 353,
   384; **16**:46, 171, 211b
John **1**:246; **3**:503-504, 620;
   4:181-182, 278, 283, 285, 631;
   5:139, 150, 247, 325, 614-615,
   760, 762; **6**:35, 132, 150, 176,
   184, 226, 341, 444, 457-459,
   468, 494-495, 551, 613, 645-646,
   650, 653-657, 660-661, 667,
   669-670, 673, 675, 753-754, 762,
   771, 780, 783; **7**:33-34, 48, 57,
   244, 358, 479, 485, 506-507,
   509, 597; **8**:754, 757, 768-769,
   771-772; **9**:235, 438, 464, 672;
   10:752, 754; **11**:31, 87, 97, 105,
   366, 469, 633, 691, 730, 738,
   760; **12**:166, 188, 358, 362, 518,
   636, 680; **13**:757; **14**:27, 193,
   236, 250, 415; **15**:9; **16**:160,
   211b
Lydia **15**:399, 442
Martha **15**:399, 442
Robert **5**:378; **13**:710; **14**:125, 485,
   519, 610, 616
Robert (Dr.) **10**:492, 525, 599,
   604, 644, 700, 713, 721, 724,
   752, 772; **11**:30, 50, 88, 140;
   12:144, 153; **13**:714; **15**:379,
   382, 468
Roland **10**:670
Samuel **10**:271; **11**:87, 651, 657;
   12:559; **15**:397
Tho. **1**:311, 325, 329, 478
Thomas **5**:247; **6**:418, 669; **10**:113;
   12:188
William **6**:649; **11**:181, 347;
   12:131, 164, 185, 512, 525, 534;
   13:193; **15**:399, 442
HARRISON, --- **6**:490
--- (Capt.) **7**:400, 474; **8**:31-32,
   51
--- (Dr.) **10**:447
--- (Gov.) **13**:334, 637, 639, 674,
   685-686; **14**:38
Benjamin **10**:235
Colo. **3**:204, 208
Edwd. **4**:468
Elizabeth **12**:478
Francis **1**:169-171, 173, 176-184,
   189-191, 320

HARRISON, Henry **8**:19, 575-576;
   9:205; **14**:295, 302, 426
Humphrey **10**:89
James **3**:60; **12**:138
Jno. **1**:132, 140, 145-146
John **11**:199, 251, 393; **13**:327;
   14:298, 305, 417; **15**:571, 576
Joseph **15**:198
Lawrence **9**:508-509
Mary **16**:432
Richard **3**:257, 491, 524; **4**:312,
   482, 495, 504, 762; **9**:509
Saml1. **1**:550
Thomas (Dr.) **13**:591
HARROD, Ashur **9**:584
William, Sr. **15**:310
HARROLL, Thomas **16**:333
HARRY, Samuel **4**:505
the Indian **2**:15, 26, 71, 155, 244,
   387, 469, 533, 537, 553, 555,
   565-566, 607
HARRY (INDIAN) **9**:103
HARRY (NEGRO), --- **11**:263-264
HARSEL, Jacob **15**:451
HARSTICK, John Frederick **14**:480
HART, --- **6**:490
--- (Col.) **10**:551; **13**:83
--- (Dr.) **7**:164-165
--- (Gov.) **3**:37, 60
--- (Maj.) **13**:189
--- (Mr.) **13**:744
--- (Mrs.) **6**:522
Ann **13**:538
Charmless **11**:494
Coll. **2**:575
D. **11**:766
Eleanor **11**:117
Ephraim **16**:376
James **5**:89, 93, 117-118, 247;
   13:687
John **1**:48, 109-110; **3**:260, 416,
   465, 468-469, 472-473, 476, 520,
   615; **4**:85, 135, 247, 309,
   352-353, 500, 601, 669, 748,
   782; **5**:345, 411, 573; **8**:124,
   135, 137, 163; **10**:671, 697;
   11:92, 120, 128, 159-160, 251,
   258, 494; **12**:47, 157, 187, 554,
   610; **13**:8, 22, 51, 95, 117, 674,
   708; **14**:95, 424, 545; **15**:570
Joseph **5**:209, 464, 550; **7**:437;
   8:577; **9**:235, 635, 672; **10**:162,
   452; **11**:19, 21, 90, 122, 128,
   187, 213, 249-252, 255-265,
   267-268, 270, 280, 282-283,
   285-287, 290-291, 293-295, 297,
   300, 302-304, 306, 308, 311-312,
   317-319, 328, 341-342, 349-352,
   357-361, 376-380, 387-396,
   398-399, 406-412, 425-426, 428,
   430, 432-438, 440-445, 447-453,
   455, 457-459, 461-466, 468-469,
   471-472, 474-479, 481, 486-490,
   492-493, 495, 497-499, 501-503,
   506, 508-512, 522, 525-526, 531,
   533-535, 537, 539-544, 546-548,
   550, 554, 556-563, 566-567, 569,
   571-574, 582-590, 592-596,
   598-600, 606-609, 612-617, 620,
   622-626, 628-637, 644-653,
   655-661, 663-667, 672-680,
   682-685, 691, 693-699, 701-710,
   713-724, 726-728, 732-733, 735,
   738, 740-741, 743-745, 747-749,
   751-762, 764-767, 769, 771, 773,
   775-776, 778-779, 781, 783;->

84

HAYES, Henry **3:**256, 345, 356, 381; **4:**312, 482; **10:**56, 100; **12:**131, 164, 512
James **12:**137, 513; **13:**92
Jane **3:**32
John **12:**5, 31, 384, 440; **13:**584
Jonathan **3:**40
Margaret **13:**340
Richard **4:**279, 312
Richd. **2:**297, 596
William **8:**212
HAYHURST, William **2:**239
HAYL, George **3:**459
Hans George **3:**459
HAYLY, Jon **1:**320, 340
HAYNES, --- (Mr.) **6:**491
Christopher **13:**218
George **12:**29-30, 185-186, 465
John **12:**30, 85
HAYS, --- (Capt.) **7:**15-17
Abraham **10:**629
Christ'r. **11:**373, 445, 716, 726
Christopher **14:**346; **16:**297
David **12:**559
Jo. **7:**768
Joe **9:**89
John **4:**53; **10:**756; **11:**673; **13:**704
Samuel **11:**179-180, 444
Thomas **13:**400
William **10:**673
HAYSER, Matthias **3:**452
HAYSTOE, Jacob **3:**328
HAYWARD, Henry **1:**578
John **3:**230
Nicholas **1:**538-539
HAYWIGH, Pieter **3:**467
HAYWOOD, Joseph **2:**102
HAZARD, Ebenezer **13:**122, 354, 420
HAZELHURST, Isaac **11:**197; **16:**40
HAZELWOOD (HAZLEWOOD), --- (Capt.) **13:**96
--- (Commodore) **13:**16-17, 44, 63
--- (Mr.) **13:**445, 725
Hamilton **10:**727
John **10:**437, 535, 540, 550, 553, 557, 567, 575, 592, 602, 611, 629, 659, 661, 678, 699, 703, 708, 726, 734, 744, 781, 783; **11:**14, 26, 72, 74, 96, 119, 135, 192, 232, 237, 277, 293, 361, 471, 529, 541, 557, 566, 577, 585, 596, 607, 659, 724; **12:**57, 397, 406, 423, 440, 450, 456, 473-474, 486, 585, 612, 680, 748; **13:**183, 410, 444; **14:**55, 73, 107, 241, 403, 407-408, 438, 475; **15:**454; **16:**224
Thomas **10:**659, 668; **11:**643, 733; **14:**559
HAZEN, --- **13:**555, 568, 598, 611, 624, 635, 756; **14:**123, 126, 129-130, 134, 193, 300, 303, 306, 425, 436
--- (Col.) **11:**320; **13:**364
--- (Gen.) **13:**165, 615, 712
HAZEN (HASEN), Moses **12:**65, 215, 252, 254-255, 262, 278, 500, 712-713
HAZLEHURST, Isaac **10:**775; **12:**688
HAZLEHURST, ISAAC & CO. **15:**368
HAZLET, --- (Capt.) **13:**191, 229
Wililam **14:**260, 321
William **13:**140
HE(E)STON, Edward **12:**70, 131, 164
HE(P)BURN & COWDEN **16:**483-484
HEAD, John **3:**390; **13:**84

HEADLER, Michael **14:**191
HEADY, Jno. **2:**456
HEAGEY, Henry **14:**190, 194
HEALIE, John **1:**614
HEALY, Jno. **2:**129
John **1:**589, 590, 616, 617, 622
HEANY, Patrick **6:**669
HEAP, George **5:**411, 464
John **12:**166
HEARD, John **13:**712
Richard **4:**250, 253
HEARR, Wm. **1:**559
HEATH, --- (Col.) **5:**297
Andrew **13:**139
Daniel Charles **13:**547
James **3:**560
Jno. **1:**576
Robert **2:**65
HEATHCOTE, George **1:**367, 450, 585
HEATHER, Tho. **1:**101, 104
HEATLY, John **2:**31
HEATON, James **2:**407, 508
John **15:**310
Robert, Jr. **2:**239
Robt. **1:**547-548, 614, 621
HEBURN, William **12:**513
HECK, George **16:**478
Johan Yost **3:**519
Lutwig **3:**410
HECKARD, John **12:**342
HECKENDORN, Daniel **4:**72
Hans **4:**73
Jacob **4:**72
HEDERICK, --- (Capt.) **11:**105
HEDOCKER, Johan Michl. **3:**456
HEDRICK, Adolph William **11:**2, 91
HEER, Benjamin **14:**50
HEESTER, John **11:**736
HEFFER, Andrew **16:**163
HEGEMAN, Christian **11:**281
HEGER, Jonadan **4:**60
HEGGEN, Gaetshalk Vander **2:**493
Vander **2:**493
HEIBNER, George **3:**569
Melchior **3:**568
HEIKY, Charles **14:**293, 299
HEILER, Conrad **12:**597
HEILIGAS, Frederick **3:**284
HEIMER, Charles **12:**506
HEIN, Hans **3:**285
Paul **3:**285
HEINBURGHER (HEINBERGHER), Thomas **10:**493, 561, 593
HEINEKEN, --- (Monsieur) **14:**451
HEINER, Casper **13:**520
Henry **13:**195
John **13:**195
HEINS, John **16:**523
Joseph **4:**313
HEIRONIMOUS, Peter **4:**60
HEISER, Andrew **10:**42
HEISLER, Jacob **14:**63, 88, 612
HEISTAND, Johan **3:**415
HEISTER, Daniel, Jr. **13:**74, 281
Gabriel **11:**64, 301, 471; **12:**131, 486
Joseph **12:**508; **13:**88
HEISTER (HEESTER, HESTER), Daniel **11:**195, 330, 340, 479, 504, 538, 633; **12:**131, 164, 507
HEISTER (HIESTER), Joseph **14:**232, 554
HEIT, Johannes **3:**593
HELDMAN, John **14:**616
HELER, Rudolph **3:**328
HELFURT, John **3:**432

HELICK, Philip 13:526
HELLAR, John 9:5; 13:758
HELLER, Jacob 4:268; 13:680
  John 14:87, 420
  Michael 10:100
  Simon 10:219
  William 14:300, 422
HELLIAR, John 1:92
HELLICK, Philip 11:432
HELLINGER, Christian 15:66
HELLSTEDT, Charles 15:433
HELM, George 13:594; 14:608
  John 10:448; 13:553, 633; 14:130,
    423; 15:322
HELME, Arthur 13:497, 500
HELMONT, Hezekias 1:122-123
HELSON, William 14:84
HELSTED, Charles 14:276
HELTZEL, Nicholas 3:524
HEMBELL, William 10:103-105
HEMBERGER, Hans Bartel 3:386
HEMES, --- (Lt.) 11:167-169
HEMING, Lewis 14:310
HEMLER, Andreas 3:453
HEMLY, --- (Ens.) 12:546
HEMMELBRIGHT (HIMMELWRIGHT), John
    14:192, 416
HEMMELWRIGHT, John 13:668
HEMMING, Hugh 14:305
HEMPHILL, James 13:768
  Thomas 10:741, 744
HEMPLIN, Thomas 12:46
HEMROD, Simon 11:101, 367
HENBURY, Elizth. 2:11
HENCKELS, Pieter 3:607
HENDENREID, William Frederick 9:173
  (See AUTENREIT)
HENDERSHAT, Jacob 11:121
HENDERSHIT, Jacob 12:147
HENDERSON, --- (Capt.) 11:118;
    12:88-89; 13:456
  --- (Lt.) 12:355, 550
  Alex'd. 11:223, 468
  Alexander 10:315, 352-353, 379,
    411-412, 428, 511, 514, 740
  Andrew 12:357, 427; 13:202, 569,
    717; 15:283, 370, 407, 546,
    623-624; 16:32, 174, 225, 434,
    444, 528
  Angews 14:76, 110, 127, 178, 223,
    237, 320, 414, 454, 458, 462
  Arthur 7:618-619
  David 13:76
  Gustavus 13:153
  Gustavus H. (Dr.) 13:557; 14:98,
    410
  Jacob 4:102, 107-109
  John 10:756; 11:153, 513, 516-517,
    745; 12:619; 13:185, 429, 756;
    14:98, 454, 532, 551; 15:143;
    16:344
  Margaret 13:756
  Matthew 9:732; 11:4, 15, 56;
    12:110, 519, 554; 13:583;
    14:612; 15:121; 16:214
  Peter 10:666, 681
  Thomas 13:457; 14:458
  William 11:39, 112, 114, 418-419;
    12:332, 570; 13:183, 187, 561,
    591, 714; 14:102, 292, 299, 427,
    429-430; 15:140, 545; 16:147,
    402
HENDIRCKS, James 12:9, 247
HENDRICK, --- 6:76, 79, 81, 97,
    113-115, 117-118, 124, 127,
    182-183, 243, 249-252, ->

HENDRICK, --- (continued)
  6:268-269, 274, 276-279, 281,
    286-291, 474; 7:23, 95
  Christopher 3:385
  George 15:462
  Tobias 7:34
  Turgen 3:410
HENDRICK THE SACHIM 5:625
HENDRICKS, Abraham 14:257
  David 5:570, 626-627, 663
  Evert 1:105
  Hendrick 2:493
  Henry 4:75
  James 3:45, 429, 472; 4:655-656
  John 3:543, 548, 550, 555, 561,
    612-613; 4:63, 66-67, 74, 150,
    190, 194
  Lawrence 2:493
  Rebecca 3:472
  Tobias 3:256, 345, 356, 358, 472;
    4:152, 313; 5:210, 551, 597;
    6:151; 8:475
  Wm. 2:493
HENDRICKSON, Albertus 1:95
  Getro. 1:96
  Isaac 11:255
  Jacob 1:96
  James 3:80
  Jeremiah 11:514, 516-517
  John 2:237
  Yeshro 1:93
HENDRIE, Evan 1:438
HENDRY, James 12:421
  Thomas (Dr.) 10:763
HENEBERGER, John 3:432
HENEY, --- (Capt.) 14:181
  Robert 15:453
HENLEY, Frederick 7:303
HENLY, --- (Mr.) 7:272
  Henry 12:357, 427, 573; 13:717;
    14:93, 412
HENNARD, Jonathan 14:342
HENNEL, Jacob 3:519
HENNES(S)EY, John 10:354-355,
    520-521, 531, 762, 781
HENNESLY, James 16:101
HENNESSY, John 14:81, 413
HENNING, Daniel Andrew 12:726
  Herrenonimus 10:703
HENNINGER, Hans Michael 3:415
HENRICH, Jacob 3:516, 567
  Valentine 3:569
HENRICK, Jerig 3:413
HENRIQUE, Jacobus 3:188
HENRY, --- (Capt.) 11:82
  --- (Col.) 13:619, 661
  --- (Mr.) 12:360
  Adam 8:490
  Elizabeth 16:186
  George 11:194, 203, 215, 297, 477,
    641, 643-644, 649, 654, 656,
    662, 669-670, 685, 691, 718-720,
    724, 730, 747-748, 752-753, 765,
    779; 12:38-39, 158, 161, 173,
    194, 279, 296, 323, 360; 13:66,
    409; 14:61, 197, 211; 15:145
  Hugh 11:513, 516-517
  James 15:457, 478; 16:91, 182
  John 11:211; 13:324, 727; 16:443
  John, Jr. 10:450; 12:501
  P. (Gov.) 12:16, 21
  Patrick 10:340; 11:725; 14:467,
    645, 651
  Philip 13:604; 14:93, 420, 613
  Samuel 11:181; 15:413; 16:364-365
  the Eighth 2:278

86

HILL, Richard (continued)
  2:472-473, 477-479, 482-486,
  489-491, 494, 502-503, 506, 508,
  510-511, 513, 516-518, 531-534,
  537, 540-543, 545-546, 553,
  555-557, 560-562, 566-567, 571,
  573, 575, 577, 584-585, 587-588,
  590, 596-597, 599, 601, 603-607,
  610-611, 613, 616, 629; 3:14-19,
  21, 25, 28-31, 33, 37-39, 58,
  63-64, 67-68, 71, 75, 81-82, 90,
  98, 102, 105, 107-109, 111,
  113-115, 120-123, 125, 130, 134,
  137,139-141, 143-145, 147,
  156-158, 160-163, 165-167,
  170-172, 175, 177-178, 180, 187,
  189-193, 196, 199, 204-205, 212,
  214, 221-222, 225-229, 231,
  233-236, 238, 240-246, 250-254,
  256-259, 261, 263-264, 266-267,
  269-271, 276, 278-284, 287-291,
  298, 303, 315-316, 322, 325-328,
  333, 337-338, 343-347, 354-355,
  359, 361, 364, 381, 398, 400;
  6:529; 13:321-323, 327, 503;
  14:359, 464, 558; 15:399, 442,
  486
 Richard (Dr.) 7:728
 Richard, Jr. 7:728-729, 739-740
 Tho. 1:83
 Thomas 5:686-687; 13:588
 William 3:189, 193, 283; 4:443,
  447, 464
 Wm. 1:321
HILL & MARRET 10:779
HILL & MARROT (MARRIOTT) 11:24,
 765
HILL(S), John 16:165, 227
HILLARD, Charles 3:254
HILLARY, Samll. 2:605
HILLBACK, Frederick 16:503
HILLBOURN, Joseph 13:276
HILLEGAS (HILLIGAS), Adam 3:432
 Michael 6:175-176; 10:53, 215,
  266, 268, 281, 300, 334, 344,
  354, 361, 374, 379, 381-382,
  384-385, 388, 395, 401, 404,
  415, 417, 434, 436, 438, 453,
  457-458, 462-463, 474, 477, 480,
  482, 485, 487, 489, 491, 493,
  500, 502, 513, 516, 520, 525,
  527, 529-530, 533, 537-539, 542,
  545, 549, 551, 554, 557,
  560-561, 569, 571, 580, 583-584,
  589, 593, 595, 599, 601,
  603-604, 606-607, 617, 620, 625,
  631-632, 634-636, 638, 642,
  647-653, 656-657, 679, 703, 712,
  735, 738-739, 745, 755, 771;
  11:7, 12, 18, 37, 65, 316,
  580-581, 748; 12:72, 300, 351,
  423, 444, 551, 689, 693; 13:504,
  571, 759; 14:75-76, 451, 625;
  15:107
 Peter 11:644
 Samuel 13:504, 571
HILLIARD, --- (Widow) 1:173
 Chas. 9:203
 Jno. 1:57-58, 60-73, 79-82, 84,
  101, 103-106, 173
HILLIGAS, John 16:299
 Leopold 3:386
HILLINGS, John 11:37
HILLMAN, Benjamin 14:311, 320, 495
 Cornelius 11:766
 Daniel 15:123

HILLMAN, Michael 16:377
HILLSBOROUGH, --- (Earl of) 9:80,
 341, 346-347, 545-547, 551-555,
 636-637, 639-640, 645, 706-709,
 760-761, 772
HILLYER, David 13:669
HILPATRICK, John 15:1
HILSHELWOOD, Archibald 12:24
HILT, John 14:613-614
HILTON, --- (Capt.) 11:129
HILTZHEIMER (HILTSIMER), Jacob
 10:560, 583; 11:261; 13:81;
 15:98, 105
HILTZIMER, Jacob 14:230
HIMEBURG, Thomas 11:389
HINDE, George 7:187
HINDERSON, Edward 11:55
HINDMAN, --- (Capt.) 11:109
 James 10:662
HINDS, --- (Capt.) 13:189
 Samuel 14:471
HINES, John (alias John WILLIAMS)
 9:173
 Samuel 15:294-295, 564-565; 16:191
HINING, --- (Capt.) 8:516
HINKER, Leon'd. 3:332
HINKLE, John 11:219
 Philip 11:36
HINKSON, John 10:199
 Thomas 16:194, 231
HINMAN, Jacob 11:31
 Richard 3:259, 270
HINSLEY, --- (Capt.) 5:263
HIRNSHALL, Theelman 4:72
HIRONS, Mark 5:248
 Symond 1:340
 William 5:248
HIRTY, Andrew 13:20
HISLE, Valentine Perhart 3:369
HISTANT, Jacob 3:290
 Jno. 3:290
HITCHCOCK, Eleanor 11:620
 Eleanor (Mrs.) 15:566
 John 11:152-153, 620; 14:599
 Mary 13:100
HITE, Peter 3:520
HITHQUOQUEAN 1:447, 449
HJUBLEY, Adam 13:613
HLDMAN, Tho. 1:548
HO(D)GE, Jonathan 12:164, 166, 279,
 518
 William 7:291-292
HOAK (HOKE), Andrew 15:260, 263
HOAR(E), Jona. (Maj.) 6:608, 611
HOARSNET 3:316
HOBACKER, George 13:28
HOBBERT, William 16:479
HOBBY, Jonathan 9:727, 729
HOBLON, I. 1:550
HOBSON, --- (Capt.) 7:103
 John 8:562; 11:211, 237, 328
 Samuel (Capt.) 6:490, 594, 777
HOBZINGER, Jacob 13:708
HOCKAGOY, Samuel 13:620
HOCKERMAN, Christopher 14:408, 436
HOCKLEN, John 14:143
HOCKLEY, --- (Mr.) 6:401, 681, 744;
 7:463, 468
 Benjamin 15:442, 481, 485
 James 15:100, 605; 16:122, 240
 Richard 8:77, 335, 408, 456-457,
  475; 9:102, 178-179; 13:695
 Thomas 9:673; 10:502, 613, 650,
  679, 682-683, 685-687, 689,
  695-697, 741
 William 12:458

89

HOCKOGOY, Samuel 14:101, 436
HODEECHERICH 5:212
HODEMAN, Hugh 10:496
HODGDON, Samuel 13:614; 16:446
HODGE, Andrew 10:496; 11:39, 661
Andrew, Jr. 13:543
Henry 4:468
Hugh 11:24, 32; 13:64
Hugh (Dr.) 10:478
Margaret 13:272
William 5:197; 12:222; 13:640
HODGE (SEE BAYARD &) 10:477
HODGES, --- 2:179
Benjamin 3:50-51
Christopher 1:376-377
HODGESON, Jno. 3:287
HODGSON, Samuel 13:547; 14:530, 551
HODGSON (HODGETON), Samuel 15:9,
240, 277
HODGSON, PICKERING & 14:501
HODSON, Joseph 5:248
HOE(W), --- (Lord) 8:146-147
HOF(F)MAN, Charles 14:95, 423
HOFF, Hans Jacob 3:515
Isaac 11:281
Johan 3:389
Johannes Peter 3:288
Sybilla 13:282
HOFFART, Jerig 3:369
HOFFER, Gideon 3:467
HOFFMAGLE, Peter 10:700
HOFFMAN, --- (Widow) 13:561
Baltzar 3:569
Baltzar, Jr. 3:569
Charles 13:561
Christian 3:458
Cornelius 13:636; 14:83, 416
Daniel 15:230
Frederick 13:111
George 3:569
Hans George 3:385
Hans Henrich 3:570
Hans Jerig 3:290
Hans Peter 3:516
Henrick 3:288
Jacob 3:520; 15:230
Johan Georg. 3:456
Johan Jacob 3:288
Johan Philip 3:458
Johannes 3:385
John 15:286
Mans Lenord 3:288
Michael 12:8, 355
Nicholas 13:557; 14:90, 429
Porcas 3:287
Valentine 15:455, 561; 16:411
HOFFNAGLE, Peter 11:76, 82, 89, 195
HOFMAN, Rachel 14:95
HOFNAM, Hans Jurg 3:517
HOFSTEDLER, Jacob 4:59
HOG(G), --- (Capt.) 6:436, 452,
460, 467, 493, 499-500
HOG(G)BEAN, Richd. 1:203, 207
HOGAN, Francis (Dr.) 13:140
John 7:561-562
Richd. 2:108
HOGE, --- (Mr.) 12:486, 544
Andrew 13:556
Daniel 13:439
David 9:548, 624, 691; 13:531
James 14:354
John 14:62, 95, 245, 247, 419,
441, 445, 544, 597; 15:85, 589;
16:36, 44, 218, 280, 440, 536,
538

HOGE, Jonathan 9:487-488, 732;
11:173-175, 177-178, 181-182,
184, 186-188, 190-191, 193-195,
198, 200, 202-203, 205-214,
216-217, 219-223, 225-226,
228-238, 241-243, 245-253,
255-265, 267-268, 270-278, 280,
282-283, 285-287, 290-291,
293-295, 297, 300, 302-307,
314-322, 325, 328, 341, 357-366,
449-453, 455, 457-459, 461-466,
468-469, 471-472, 474-477,
486-493, 495, 497, 501-503, 506,
508-512, 522, 526, 531, 533-535,
537, 539-541, 546-548, 550-554,
556-562, 564-567, 569, 571-574,
576-595, 633, 726; 13:396, 415;
14:236, 246, 248-250, 252-270,
274, 276-279, 281, 283-285,
287-291, 307-309, 315-318,
321-327, 342, 344-348, 356-365,
367-369, 371-376, 378-387,
393-396, 398-402, 404-406,
441-448, 478-484, 486-489,
491-496, 498, 512-514, 516-522,
524, 526-554, 556-558, 560-567,
569-571, 573, 577-582, 584-593,
595-603, 606-607, 622, 642-643,
646-657, 659-672; 15:1-3, 6-8,
21-29, 31-32, 35-47, 58-81,
84-88, 90, 92-97, 101-116,
120-121, 128-179, 187-190,
192-195, 197-204, 206-209,
211-230, 232-237, 247-267,
269-280, 282-285, 287-289,
291-292, 582; 16:460
HOGELAND, Benjamin 11:105
William 16:147
HOGG, --- (Lt.) 7:261-262
George 1:503
John 4:483, 631, 655; 5:3;
11:267-268; 15:91
Jonathan 9:201, 673
Robert 14:260
HOGLAND, Richard 10:78, 163
HOGLE, Tobias 3:453
HOHHLER, Peter 12:8
HOI, Hans Ulrich 3:455
HOILL, Hans Wendell 3:432
HOKE, Conrad 15:565
HOL(L)INGSWORTH, Valentine 1:48,
87, 127, 601, 607
HOL(L)MAN, Anthony 14:134, 422
HOL(L)WELL, Richd. 1:323, 339
HOL(T)ZINGER, Jacob 14:129, 436
HOLBOURN, --- (Adm.) 8:26
HOLBURN, Thomas Corbyn 10:358
HOLBURNE, --- (Mr.) 7:560
HOLCOMB, Jacob 2:520
HOLDEN, Jeremiah 11:103
HOLDER, Charles 13:756; 14:93, 421
George 11:483-485; 12:11-12
Jacob 11:483-485
John 11:483-485
HOLDERNESSE, --- (Earl of) 5:689,
690, 700, 709, 713, 717-721,
747-748, 753-754, 756, 764-765;
6:18, 167, 177, 185, 191, 233,
449, 507-509; 7:277, 340; 8:40,
320-321
HOLDERSINGER, Rosina 7:343, 388-389
HOLDMAN, Michael 14:10
HOLDSTOCK, Joseph 12:133
HOLDSWORTH, Elizabeth 11:772
James 11:772

HOLEGATE, Matthew **13**:415; **15**:12,
17, 422
HOLEPEEKA (KOLAPEEKA, HOLAPECKA)
7:187, 189
HOLGATE, --- (Col.) **12**:61-62
--- (Mr.) **14**:171
Matthew **12**:507; **13**:85, 112, 391,
721, 737
HOLIDAY, Thomas **8**:42
HOLINA, Tho. **1**:166
HOLKER, --- (Mr.) **11**:692, 699, 714,
779; **13**:8, 54, 144; **14**:405
--- (Sieur) **13**:59
John **12**:30, 32, 35, 37, 46-47, 54,
56, 59-61, 63, 66, 68-69, 71,
74, 80, 85-86, 90, 94, 100, 109,
152, 183, 191, 197, 233, 262,
275, 296, 368, 402, 419-420,
470, 488, 634; **13**:242
HOLLAN, John (alias Moody) **15**:431
HOLLAND, Edward **5**:646
Henry **5**:181
Hitchen **5**:622-623, 640-641; **6**:9,
34, 411
Joanna **16**:547
John **3**:144
Nathaniel **8**:99, 129, 499-500, 773
Thomas **10**:449, 453, 484, 515
William **10**:217
HOLLANDBACK, John **16**:496
HOLLAPETER, Mathias **16**:62
HOLLEDAY (HOLLYDAY), --- (Lt.)
7:557, 599
HOLLENBACK, John **15**:221
Matthew (Matthias) **15**:143, 212,
237, 285-286, 295, 380, 423, 519
Matthias **16**:11-12, 317
HOLLENSWORTH, Valentine **1**:205
HOLLER, Henry **16**:122
HOLLIDAY, John **14**:63, 125, 411,
602; **15**:26
Robt. **9**:203, 339
Samuel **11**:339; **16**:363
Thomas **5**:601; **11**:89
William **11**:637; **12**:123; **14**:395;
15:353
HOLLIDAY (HOLLYDAY), James **3**:554,
563
HOLLIN(G)SHEAD, William **12**:129,
156, 164, 316, 358
HOLLIN(G)SWORTH, Levi **14**:75, 78,
104, 119-120, 153, 199, 212,
241-242, 500-501, 551, 574, 616
HOLLINGER, Jacob **4**:60
HOLLINGSHEAD, William **11**:640, 665,
766
HOLLINGSWORTH, Christopher **15**:59
Hen. **1**:218
Henry **2**:71, 122; **12**:18
John **1**:145
Levi **10**:563, 565, 591, 632; **11**:5,
16, 193, 767; **12**:16, 18, 203;
13:282; **15**:75, 106
Samuel **3**:345, 356, 381; **4**:313
Thomas **1**:499
Zebulon **11**:10
HOLLINSHEAD, Samuel **12**:4
HOLLMAN, Anthony **13**:620
HOLLOCK, Jacob **10**:81
HOLLY, --- **8**:566
HOLMAN, Martin **10**:712
Michael **10**:703, 705; **13**:18
HOLMES (HOLME), --- (Lt.) **11**:166
Alexander **12**:453
Andrew **15**:216
Catherine **12**:590

HOLMES (HOLME) James **10**:678, 765;
11:69; **14**:133, 439
James (Dr.) **11**:158
John **9**:201, 286, 333, 399, 441,
450-451, 453, 461, 463, 465,
490, 628, 673, 732; **10**:51;
11:30, 229, 691; **13**:135, 183,
320; **14**:293, 300, 422; **15**:86;
16:145
Jon. **1**:320, 334, 476
Jonathan **5**:210
Joseph **11**:462, 472; **14**:372
Samuel **10**:487, 776; **11**:67, 115
Thomas **1**:47, 57-60, 62-73, 75-82,
84, 86-94, 96-97, 99-133, 135,
137-138, 140-149, 151-168,
187-188, 194, 199, 201, 264;
8:248; **13**:326, 497-498
William **12**:166, 519; **13**:133;
15:576
HOLSIKGER, Rudolph **3**:415
HOLSTED, Richard **14**:223
HOLSTEIN, Frederick **5**:193
Hendrick **3**:369
Mathias **5**:193
Peter **10**:690
Samuel **10**:690
HOLSTEINDER, Joh. Leon'd. **3**:332
HOLSTEINER, Simon Peter **3**:452
HOLSTELLER, David **3**:455
HOLSTEN, Mathias **9**:241
HOLSTENIER, Geo. Michl. **3**:452
HOLSTONE, John **11**:581
HOLT, --- (Chief Justice) **8**:286
Evan **13**:612; **14**:93, 419
John **12**:479
Michael **10**:581
Rives **3**:260, 289, 332, 371; **4**:394
Rs. **5**:111
Ryves **6**:136; **9**:203
Saml1. **1**:452
Samuel **2**:241, 410
Sarah **12**:479
HOLTHAUSEN, Casper **3**:410
HOLTOMEN, Christopher **8**:728
HOLTON, --- (Mr.) **11**:540, 677
Arthur **1**:576
Francis **10**:681-682, 684
William (Alias COURTNEY) **16**:104
HOLTSPAN, Andrew **3**:284
HOLTZINGER, Ingleholt **11**:483-485
Jacob **3**:417
HOLTZMAN, Henry **12**:601
HOLZINGER, Conrad **12**:277
HOME, William **11**:39, 345-346,
348-349, 482, 484, 604, 613, 745
HOMES, --- (Mr.) **10**:528, 637
HOMMONY, Big **5**:290
HOMWHYOWA (Wolf King) **8**:135
HONANSCHELL, Johan Adam **4**:60
HONDERSON, William **14**:102
HONEST, Michael **3**:328
HONEY, George **11**:661; **15**:188, 378
George, Jr. **13**:172, 181, 193, 205
HONEYMAN, --- (Lt.) **11**:647, 753
David **14**:357
William **12**:14, 51, 114-115, 260,
279, 372, 397, 421-422, 448,
466, 492, 527, 555, 588, 603,
633, 675, 693; **13**:556, 709, 713;
14:43, 85, 100, 427, 437
HONEYWOOD, --- (Lt.) **12**:267
HONI, Nicolaus **3**:455
HONIG, Conraad **3**:452
John George **3**:456
HONNET(S), Jno. **1**:583

HONNETS, Martha 1:583
HONNETTER, Valentine 15:454
HONON, Daniell 1:443
HOOBER, John 16:495
HOOD, --- (Capt.) 6:451
 Andrew 13:201
 Jacob 12:326
 James 11:602; 13:305
 Jno. 1:601
 John 2:397; 11:139; 13:63, 254,
  305, 306, 346, 506; 15:518
 Mary 11:695
 Nathaniel 14:81, 98, 422
 Thomas 13:557; 14:92, 425
 Walter 16:291
 Zachariah 10:90
HOODT, Casper 2:493
 John 13:515
HOOEL, Ludwig 3:467
HOOFFNAGLE, Michael 13:157
HOOFMAN, William 13:233
HOOFNAGLE, --- (Mr.) 10:140
 George 10:668
 Michael 10:448; 11:252-253, 432,
  469, 475; 12:632
HOOGH, Jacob 3:328
HOOGNUNK, Leonrd. 3:385
HOOK, Chester 10:540
 Christian 3:519; 11:482, 484-485;
 13:695
 Marcus 10:540; 14:464, 479
HOOKEN, Henry 16:191, 490
HOOKER, Timothy 12:34
HOOKES, William 15:484
HOOP(E)S, Adam 6:318, 369, 466,
 673-674
 Joshua 2:34, 106, 260, 318,
  321-322, 480 (See HOPPS)
HOOP(P)S, Joshua 1:503, 517, 521,
 601
HOOPE, Robert 10:451
HOOPER, --- (Col.) 12:2
 --- (Mr.) 12:250
 A. 13:327
 Henry 6:457
 Phillis 13:327
 R. S. 11:425
 Robert L. 11:207, 418-419, 453;
  12:411
 Robert Lettes 14:125
 Robert Lettis 9:238, 242
 Robert Lettis, Jr. 13:596
HOOPES, Joshua 1:169
HOOPS, --- (Mr.) 7:619
 Adam 5:468; 7:231, 242, 244;
  9:201, 583, 672
HOORLE, Johannes 3:452
HOOSTE, Dorst. 3:417
HOOTER, Michael 9:508
HOOTON, Benjamin 8:750
 Elizt. 1:476-477, 479, 515
 John 12:187
 Tho. 1:92, 112, 209-210, 332
HOOVER, Henry 10:604; 16:306
 Jacob 6:482
 John 15:541
 Martin 12:552
 Michael 6:482
HOPE, Philip 13:569; 14:97, 419
 T. 10:612
 Thomas 5:210
HOPHACK, John Jacob 3:368
HOPKINS, --- 15:430
 David 13:712
 E. (Commodore) 10:564-565
 James 11:237, 241-242; 12:1, 43

HOPKINS, John 12:301; 13:514;
  14:509, 559
 John Estangh 11:719-720
 Richard 12:260; 16:228
 Sarah 12:387
 Stephen 6:58, 67, 71, 83, 92-93,
  96, 100, 606; 7:168
 Thomas 10:423, 433, 435; 14:653
 William 4:499
HOPKINSON, Francis 10:693; 11:260,
  773-774; 12:17-18, 49-50, 81,
  102, 197, 267, 307, 309, 347,
  567, 573-574, 578-584; 13:35,
  64, 183, 329, 381, 451, 532,
  600, 692, 776; 14:53, 142, 212,
  310, 314, 385, 486, 540, 602,
  660; 15:2, 45, 79, 86, 133-134,
  185, 191, 199, 234, 282, 290,
  352, 398, 400, 411, 474, 487,
  517, 520, 536, 626; 16:26, 53,
  159, 361, 511
 Thomas 4:151; 5:65-68, 70-74,
  76-80, 82-83, 89-90, 93-96,
  100-101, 104-105, 108-114,
  117-118, 120-121, 123, 127, 130,
  132, 134, 136, 140, 143; 5:148,
  152, 154, 158-160, 163, 168-170,
  173-175, 181-184, 186, 193-194,
  198, 203, 205, 208, 215,
  220-221, 223, 228-229, 232, 235,
  238, 245-246, 248-249, 252, 256,
  258-260, 264-265, 268-270,
  273-274, 277, 280, 282, 284,
  289, 297-300, 306-307, 311-312,
  316, 318-319, 326, 328, 330,
  332, 338-339, 343, 345-347, 359,
  362-363, 365, 367-372, 376-380,
  388, 391, 394, 437, 451, 456,
  460-461, 464, 467-468, 470, 484,
  488-492, 494, 502, 506, 512-513,
  516, 525, 527
HOPPER, Isaac 10:289
 Joshua 10:289
 Levi 10:289
HOPPS, Jos. 2:308 (See HOOPES)
HOPSEN, Moses 16:49
HOPSON, --- (Col.) 7:168
 P. 5:228
HOPWOOD, John 11:156
HORGAN, John 14:556
HORLACHER, George 11:133
HORLACKER, Joan Carlo 3:288
HORLOCHER, Hans Georg. 3:520
HORLOGER, Hans Michl. 3:414
HORN, Andreas 3:455
 Hartman 14:235
 John 14:568
 Ralph 14:620
 Stephen 10:498
HORN(E), Edward 3:298, 301
HORNBERGER, Jacob 3:466
 Johan Carl 3:386
 Stephen 11:340
HORNE, George 14:66
 John 12:284
HORNER, David 14:208
 Hugh 12:343-345; 15:43
 Jack 15:143
 Jacob 11:212
 Joseph 12:344
 Levi 10:720
 Matthew 14:294, 301, 438
 Thomas 11:65
HORNETS, --- (Capt.) 9:508
HORNHETH, Jeremiah 14:127, 437
HORNHETHE, Jeremiah 13:562

HOWELL, Samuel (cont'd) 10:577-578,
580, 585, 589-590, 592, 594-596,
600-602, 604-605, 607-608,
610-612, 614-617, 620-621, 623,
626-629, 633, 635-637, 640,
642-643, 647, 649-652, 656, 695;
11:118, 538; 12:507
Samuel, Jr. 10:522
Thomas 5:203
William 15:68
Wm. 1:48, 87, 264, 320, 335, 438,
478
HOWELL & DOUGLASS 10:340
HOWER, Jacob 3:288
HOWEROFT, Thomas 14:290
HOWES, George 11:74
HOWICKYOMA 3:310
HOWSTON, Anthony 2:494
Wm. 2:127, 494-495 (See HOUSTON)
HOX, Jos. 10:47
HRLLEGAS, --- (Mr.) 9:440
HUBBARD, J. 6:612
T. 6:310, 317; 7:111
HUBBS, Henry 15:60
HUBER, Hans 3:455
Hendrich 3:593
Henry 10:493, 665, 667, 732-733;
11:49, 91
John 12:134, 301; 13:461, 514;
14:509
William 4:72
HUBERT, Christian 3:415; 15:620
Daniel 3:415
Thomas, Jr. 5:325
HUBLER, Abraham 6:755
Adam 10:219
Frantz 9:44
HUBLEY (HUBLY), --- 13:515
--- (Capt.) 16:109
--- (Col.) 13:71, 141
--- (Mr.) 14:24, 31; 15:135, 306
Adam 10:281; 11:35, 97, 180, 436,
770, 778; 12:628, 702, 765, 768,
775; 13:18, 27, 82, 275, 351,
514, 580, 722, 732, 735, 737,
746; 14:430, 509, 556, 558;
15:321, 323-324; 16:92, 155,
235, 303, 386, 541
Bernard 12:659; 13:573; 14:127,
430; 16:237
Frederick 16:31
George 10:634; 13:777; 14:306, 436
John 10:669-672, 675, 677-678,
680-683, 686-687, 689, 691-702,
704-705, 707-708, 710-711,
720-722, 724-726, 728, 730-731,
736; 11:14, 16-20, 22-28, 30,
32-34, 36-37, 39-45, 47, 73,
75-79, 81, 83, 85, 86-88, 90,
92-95, 97, 99-105, 107-109, 111,
113-115, 118-121, 143, 177-178,
181-188, 190-191, 193, 195-198,
237, 241, 251-253, 271, 274,
364, 402, 442, 459, 556-557,
582, 585, 736, 738, 754; 12:32,
53, 65, 84, 231, 255, 301, 444;
13:146, 542, 613, 701, 703-704;
14:69, 127, 157, 159, 236, 478,
583; 16:62, 183, 216b-217b, 355
Joseph 10:447; 13:777; 14:264,
436; 15:542, 553, 588, 599, 603,
621; 16:169
Michael 5:318; 11:93, 211,
252-253, 271, 405, 506; 12:306;
14:157, 259, 618; 15:412, 499
HUBNER, George 10:733

HUBNER, Hans 3:569
HUCHART, Jacob 5:611; 6:305
HUCK, Christian 14:292; 15:180, 638
HUDDLE (HUDDELL), John 11:26, 107,
773; 12:33-34
Joseph 11:707; 12:34; 14:506
HUDSON, Frances 15:618
George 4:269; 16:461
Hannah 12:120
John 8:149-151, 156-157; 11:59;
16:461
John V. 15:613, 618-620
William 2:335; 13:586; 14:96, 423;
16:386, 461
Wm. 1:371
HUEHART, Jacob 5:577
HUES, Jno. 1:561
HUFFNAGLE, Michael 12:75, 487;
13:158, 288, 594, 598, 603, 700,
731, 754, 766, 774; 14:175, 202,
287, 289-290, 457, 471-472, 517,
607; 15:175; 16:162-163, 466
Philip 15:13, 161
HUFTY, John 11:100
HUGG, --- (Capt.) 11:156
Jno. 1:477
Joseph 10:328
HUGGINS, Elizabeth 14:550, 551
William 14:550-551
HUGGINS (HUGGAMS), Thomas 14:189,
193, 431
HUGH, Evan 4:268
Michael 10:78
Moreland 14:421
HUGHES, --- (Capt.) 13:428
Alexander 13:720
Barney 6:131, 669
Ellis 9:651, 666-667; 10:43;
16:224
Evan 3:225, 230-231
Francis 15:208
George 5:209; 15:396
Greenbury 12:312
Henry 14:33, 36, 67-68
Hugh 3:225, 231; 4:269; 12:316;
14:82, 102, 424
James 13:598; 14:130, 422
Job 9:651, 670
John 5:193; 6:241, 702, 775; 7:46,
50, 64, 79, 153-154, 201, 207,
249, 313, 370, 380, 469,
617-618, 656-657, 662, 666,
671-672, 697, 708, 729, 734,
736, 754, 756, 760-761, 773;
8:19, 41, 69, 84, 114, 134-135,
163, 170, 175, 211, 269-270,
467, 575, 655; 9:300; 11:578;
12:355, 441; 13:99, 160, 168,
176, 302, 308, 533-534, 539,
557, 593, 692; 14:34, 88, 146,
214, 258, 322-324, 426, 532,
567, 608-609; 15:191
Kitty 12:101
Mathew 5:3, 209, 388, 573
Matthew 4:244, 313, 482; 15:476
Matthews 2:520, 543
Sarah 11:679
Thomas 4:229, 231; 12:665-666;
13:39
Uriah 11:610-612
HUGHS, Francis 3:112
HUGLEY, Jacob 16:6
HUKEY, Charles 14:416
HULET, William 14:614
HULINE, John 16:271
HULING, Marcus 3:304

94

HULING(S), Thomas 16:178, 182, 209b, 260, 274, 308
HULINGS, --- (Mr.) 10:296
John 10:447; 11:32; 14:610
Marcus 11:84
Michael 9:293, 366
Samuel 15:608, 611-612; 16:285
HULL, Cornelius 9:571
Susanna 13:384
HULSCAMP, Garret 10:428
HUMBERGE, Thomas 11:546
HUMBERGER, Hans Leond. 3:517
Hendrich 3:517
Thomas 10:720, 724
HUMBLE, Frederick 11:77
HUME, Robert 10:408, 488, 589
HUMMEL, George 15:499
Thomas 4:59
Valentine 15:570
HUMMELL, Valentine 16:195, 498
HUMPHERIS, Allex. 1:160
Jno. 1:127
Plant 1:160
HUMPHREY, --- 4:108
--- (Mr.) 5:122
Benjamin 4:505
Edward 4:505
Isaac 13:515
Jacob 13:676, 715
John 12:89; 14:64, 91, 433
Walter 1:63
HUMPHREYS, --- (Col.) 11:456; 13:281
Ann 11:263-264
Ashton 12:753
Assheton 13:167, 302, 445
Benjamin 12:572; 15:424, 442
Charles 9:491; 10:281, 374; 14:238
Clement 10:396
Daniel 14:609; 15:395, 518, 642; 16:257
David 4:312
Jacob 14:76, 90, 421
James 7:501; 9:678; 10:46, 215; 11:269, 306, 494, 525; 12:120
James (younger) 11:494
John 13:456, 715
Jonathan 11:263-264
Joseph 15:390
Joshua 11:544; 12:592; 14:474
Lewis 15:142
Mary 12:120
Owen 10:564
Richard 11:321; 12:525
Samuel 3:524
Whitehead 15:11, 269
William 9:205
HUMPHRIS, Benjamin 2:277
HUMPTON (HAMPTON), --- (Brig. Gen.) 13:731
--- (Col.) 12:575; 13:449, 492, 542, 614, 664
Richard 10:767, 769, 777-778, 780, 783; 11:1-2, 5-6, 16, 22, 28, 32-33, 37, 40, 54, 65, 68, 91-92, 106, 108, 119, 124, 133-134, 180, 270, 563, 744, 748, 753, 761, 765; 12:320-321, 718; 13:80, 155-156, 180, 187, 198, 205, 247, 281, 305, 330, 347, 419, 494, 555, 711, 716; 14:62, 94, 429, 431, 605, 644; 15:357
HUNGARIUS, Gabrael 14:614
HUNN, --- (Capt.) 11:251
John 5:248; 10:626

HUNOUS, John 16:104
HUNSINER, Johannes 3:455
HUNSUCKER, Hartman 3:413
HUNT, --- 7:336
--- (Mr.) 8:586
Edward 3:109-110
Elijah 14:394
James 1:561
John 11:283-284, 288-290, 296, 309, 460, 472; 12:85; 14:494
Martha 3:244
Roger 5:186
HUNT & LOWREY 10:313
HUNTER, --- 7:231
--- (Capt.) 9:584, 587
--- (Col.) 6:394, 408, 429, 445-446; 11:480, 491; 13:428
--- (Gov.) 3:21, 30, 59-60, 62, 68, 87
--- (Lt.) 12:569
--- (Mr.) 7:447; 11:264, 758
Alexander 5:209; 11:81, 94, 132; 14:445
Coll. 2:532, 534, 537-538, 557, 566, 624
Daniel 11:51, 56, 73, 78, 94, 110, 276-277, 358, 531, 598, 633, 654, 765; 12:133, 508; 13:88; 15:305, 482
Edwd. 1:122-123
Ephraim 13:693
George 11:360; 13:710; 14:83, 414; 15:429, 442
James 5:186; 9:205; 10:450; 11:110, 269, 306, 426, 490-491, 494, 525, 601, 603; 12:146, 257; 13:64, 81, 306; 16:354
John 5:55; 8:342-343, 351, 353, 362, 398, 402, 535, 538, 553, 557-558, 694; 14:81, 99, 414; 15:572; 16:301
Jonathan 11:360
Joseph 9:57
Mary 10:668; 11:139
Nicholas 15:437
Patrick 13:431
Robert 3:295, 334; 12:146; 13:46
Robert, Jr. 16:162, 215, 311
Samuel 6:762-763; 9:30, 680; 10:43, 59, 101, 212, 271, 274, 280, 341-342, 346-348, 374, 486, 490, 524, 593, 600, 602; 11:73-74, 76, 80-81, 187, 218, 312, 368, 393, 490-491, 503, 508, 510, 528, 646, 719, 749, 765; 12:46, 50, 63, 72, 100, 234, 229-230, 307-308, 379, 461, 490, 591, 623, 662, 743; 13:104, 132, 137, 150, 292, 313, 356-357, 520, 684; 14:115
William 12:338; 13:343, 621; 15:429, 442; 16:529
HUNTER, QUARRIER & 15:77
HUNTHO, Tohomady 5:431, 435
HUNTINGDON, Hezekiah 8:566
Samuel 12:21, 60, 116, 145, 149, 200-201, 227, 229-230, 232, 236, 238-239, 248, 250, 286, 293, 328, 359, 363, 382, 395-396, 462, 516-517, 520, 522, 543, 546, 562, 569, 671, 713-714, 736, 742, 778, 783
HUNTINGTON, --- (Lord) 1:246
Samuel 10:565; 13:7
Samuel (Gov.) 15:385, 393-394, 575
HUNTSIDER, Jacob 3:519

HUNTSMAN, John **11**:494
HURLBUT, Christopher **16**:126
HURLEY, Daniel **5**:602-603
  John **14**:189, 193, 413
HURLOCKER, Michael **9**:704
HURRIN, John (alias WILSON & GREEN)
  10:129
HURST, --- (Baron) **13**:137, 240
 Baron **14**:52
 Charles **12**:72, 258-259; **15**:136,
  379, 382, 399, 442, 481, 485
 Thomas **2**:102
 Timothy **11**:494; **15**:88, 235, 399,
  413, 481, 485
HURST, BARON & **15**:28
HURTZELL, George **3**:385
 Lutwig **3**:385
HUSBAND, Harman (Herman) **11**:363,
 394
 Joseph **11**:426-427
HUSON, Anne **3**:109-110
HUSSEY, John **1**:503
HUSTANNECKO **7**:529-530
HUSTON, --- (Capt.) **5**:105
 Alexander **11**:92, 114
 David **11**:79
 Hugh **13**:596; **14**:192, 435
 James **5**:209; **14**:296, 302, 434
 John **12**:187; **14**:441, 567; **15**:121
 Joseph **11**:220
 Thomas **5**:454; **12**:733; **13**:640
 William **10**:679, 715; **13**:665
HUTCHCHAON **7**:220
HUTCHESON, Cornelius **11**:566
HUTCHI(N)SON, Cornelius **14**:292,
 299, 410
HUTCHINS, --- (Lt.) **8**:386
 Benjamin **3**:38
 Robt. **1**:122
 Thomas **9**:515; **13**:685; **14**:236,
  316-317, 402, 442, 454
 Zachariah **12**:49
HUTCHINSON, --- (Col.) **11**:170
 --- (Dr.) **13**:492
 Francis **13**:432
 Isaac **11**:610-612
 James **12**:2, 65, 106, 227, 267,
  278, 323, 367, 403, 430,
  444-445, 473, 506, 509, 526,
  547, 627, 654
 James (Dr.) **11**:294, 543, 641, 765;
  13:12-13, 57, 76; **14**:71, 624,
  653, 655; **15**:316, 340, 356, 381,
  596, 640; **16**:82
 John **12**:496-497; **13**:568
 Marmaduke **11**:610-612
 Matthias **15**:131
 Richard **13**:586; **14**:97, 424
 Robt. **1**:145
 Thomas **5**:8, 297; **6**:65, 67-68, 82,
  91, 93; **11**:610-612
HUTCHINSON (HUTCHINTON), John
 14:294, 301, 415, 426, 614
HUTCHISON, James (Dr.) **13**:247
HUTE, John Michael **6**:758-759
HUTER, Christian **3**:454
HUTHERS, James **14**:482
HUTSMAN, Jonathan **14**:47
HUTTON, George **11**:20
 James **14**:94, 428
 Jonathan **12**:598
 Joseph **9**:201
 Mary **10**:664
HUWES, Josiah **16**:184
HYAT(T), John **4**:294, 500, 601, 669
HYD(E), Thomas **5**:626-627, 663-664

HYDE, --- (Lord) **10**:103
 Elizabeth **13**:61
 James **8**:156
 John **15**:489, 603
 Joseph **15**:508
HYDE, ROBERT N. & CO. **11**:197
HYDER, John **8**:260
HYDLER, --- (Lt.) **8**:386
HYLIER, David **14**:614
HYMER, Daniel **14**:90, 413
HYNDSHAW, James **8**:612, 614, 625
HYNES, Elizabeth **13**:381
HYNSON, Nathaniel **3**:60

I. ANNOTTOWE **13**:463
IBEL, Nathll. **1**:317
ICHELBURY, Frederick **12**:280
 Jacob **12**:280
IDQUAHON **13**:463
IDQUOQUEQWON **13**:463
IHRIE, Conrad **15**:100
 Conrad, Jr. **13**:395, 723;
  14:556-557, 608
ILAY, --- (Earl of) **3**:70, 75; **4**:298
ILER, Philip **14**:131-132, 429
ILLER, Conrad **3**:369
ILLIG, Hans Rudolph **3**:458
ILLINGSWORTH, Francis **10**:715
IMBERMAN, Hans **4**:72
IMBLE, Jacob **3**:381
IMLAY, William **11**:284, 289, 295-296
IMMEL(L), Michael **11**:357
 William **11**:315
IN HOFFEE, Evert **2**:494
 Gerhard **2**:494
 Herman **2**:494
 Peter **2**:494
INBERT, Andrews **1**:81
INCE, James **10**:398
INDIAN HARRY **2**:15, 26, 155, 244,
 387, 469, 533, 537, 553, 555,
 565, 607
INDIAN HENRY **3**:603
INDIAN PETER **3**:321
INDIAN PETERS **9**:507
INDIAN SAM **3**:321
INDIAN SAMUEL **7**:477
INDIAN SIGNERS OF TREATY **6**:127-128
INDIANS, Cornplanter et.al. **16**:506,
 508, 513
 Six Nations **16**:358, 362
INDIE, Nicolas **4**:72
INGELO, Richard **1**:47, 131, 133,
 144, 149, 154
INGELS, George **15**:322
INGERSOL, --- (Mr.) **15**:177
INGERSOLL, --- (Mr.) **13**:188,
 194-197; **14**:529
 Jared **11**:291, 737; **12**:371, 440,
  517, 573, 581, 583; **13**:296;
  14:33; **16**:215, 209b, 220b, 226,
  443
INGHAM, Jonathan **8**:577; **9**:672;
 10:162
INGLES, Edmund **11**:162
 George **11**:11, 144
INGLESON, Samuel **12**:188
INGLIS, George **13**:271
 James **11**:513, 516-517
 John **4**:97; **7**:62; **8**:323, 576;
  13:759-760
 Samuel **13**:271

ISAAC, Richard 15:38
ISAAC (NEGRO) 14:33
ISBY, Peter 15:168
ISEET, Margaret 13:501
ISERLO, Casper 12:760
 Peter 12:772
ISGOE, Peter 1:60
ISHELMAN, Hendrick 3:328
ISLER, George 16:399
ISRAEL, Israel 15:240, 623; 16:12
ITHELL, John 1:209
IVERSON, John 4:280
IVORY, Patrick 11:753

JACK 2:11
JACK, Andrew 14:153, 179
 James 5:210; 9:286, 333, 399
 Matthew 12:540; 13:158, 419;
  14:180, 615; 15:271
 Patrick 10:711, 713, 715, 717;
  16:30, 91
 Son of Shick Calamy 4:685
 Thomas 14:609
 William 12:182, 540; 13:158, 419,
  730; 14:287, 563; 16:163, 292
JACK (SLAVE) 12:134, 450
JACK(S), John 11:70, 114
JACKELL, Abraham 3:569
 Baltzar 3:569
 Baltzer 3:569
 Caspar 3:569
 Christopher 3:569
 Goerge 3:569
 Hans Henrich 3:569
 Jeremias 3:569
 Matthias 3:569
JACKNACHDORUS 6:551
JACKS, --- (Mr.) 13:58, 673
 James 12:134, 156, 164, 486, 508;
  13:88, 112, 393, 415, 681;
  14:65, 361; 16:443, 495
 John 9:564
JACKSON, --- 12:255
 --- (Capt.) 6:171; 12:774
 --- (Dr.) 13:71
 --- (Mr.) 9:763-764
 David 11:27, 109, 135; 13:584,
  597; 14:90, 435, 442, 549, 581;
  16:91, 333
 David (Dr.) 12:146, 458, 497,
  705-708; 13:557, 599
 George 10:344
 Isaac 13:699
 James 11:426-427; 14:189, 193,
  414, 609; 15:373
 Jeremiah 11:772; 12:534; 13:22,
  714; 14:89, 429-430
 John 10:100; 12:496-497; 13:56,
  333
 Joseph 4:469, 500, 601; 13:601;
  14:92, 420
 Margaret 15:531
 Matthew 11:605
 Nathan 15:571, 576
 Richard 9:48, 50-51
 Robert 14:312
 Samuel 9:688; 11:284, 289; 12:342,
  676
 William 8:525, 728; 11:426-427;
  13:315; 16:286
JACKY, Abraham 4:72
JACOB 8:614, 616; 9:104, 413, 424

JACOB, --- 6:291, 749
 Hans 4:72
 Stephen 4:72
JACOB (YOUNG) 7:381
JACOB(S), --- (Capt.) 7:77, 232,
  242, 259-261, 381
 Barnet (Barent) 16:23, 92, 97, 383
JACOBI, Leonard 12:527, 631; 13:81,
  343, 539
JACOBIE, Leonard 13:171
JACOBS, --- (Capt.) 6:781; 9:208,
  212
 Albert 1:168
 Benjamin 10:67; 11:188, 197, 230;
  13:759
 John 3:254, 259, 270, 333, 371;
  11:49-50, 70; 14:204, 218;
  15:526
 Jos. 14:192, 435
 Joseph 13:643
 Nicholas 12:712
 Richard 10:715
 Samuel 9:305-306, 344-345, 350
JACOBS (INDIAN) 7:230
JACOBSON, Hendrick 1:93
 John 14:314
JACOBY, Leonard 14:47-48, 555
JACQUET, Peter 5:210
JAGER, Peter 3:569
JAGO, John 14:233, 253
JAGREA 6:194, 198-200, 206, 504,
  522-523, 566, 682, 685 (See
  ZIGAREA); 7:1, 3, 6, 33-34, 47,
  64, 105, 107, 109, 118, 137,
  142, 144, 151, 174; 8:257, 261
JAKY, Johan Jorig 4:59
JAMES, --- (Capt.) 12:419
 --- (Duke of York) 6:556; 7:404
 Aaron 4:283, 285-286
 Abel 7:394, 638, 646, 648; 8:19,
  244; 10:53, 266, 381; 11:283,
  288, 494; 12:300; 15:260
 Able (Abel) 9:293, 366
 Benjamin 11:514, 516-517
 David 4:503
 Duke of York 1:17, 42, 48,
  132-133, 322; 2:56
 Edwd. 1:583-584
 Evan 13:746
 George 10:511
 Hugh 11:157
 Jacob 10:762; 11:483-485; 12:314
 James 4:312; 5:325
 James, Jr. 3:254, 270, 345, 356,
  381
 John 1:64, 68, 87, 342-344;
  11:283, 288, 342
 King 2:313
 King of England 1:132-133, 142,
  281, 303
 Mary 12:218
 Mesach 6:674
 Mordecai 5:572
 Owen, Jr. 13:249
 Phillip 1:267
 Richard 4:470
 Samuel 4:495, 503
 Thomas 5:248, 550, 597, 662;
  7:164-165; 9:203, 626; 10:81,
  217; 12:368
 Thos. 2:576
 William 5:454; 8:492; 10:741
JAMES & DRINKER 10:711; 11:119
JAMES (NEGRO) 12:502
JAMES (the Indian) 8:148
JAMES I, King 6:16, 101

JAMES II, King **3**:561; **8**:410
JAMESON, --- (Capt.) **7**:294
 David **9**:201, 731; **10**:163; **11**:219;
  12:27, 201
 Jno. **11**:123
 John **9**:235, 672; **10**:162, 684, 764;
  12:73; **14**:615
 Richard **14**:419
JAMILTON, James **13**:698
JAMISON, David **1**:404-405, 407-409,
 415-416, 424; **9**:543
 Hannah **13**:278
 James **16**:461
 John **5**:444, 469; **7**:437; **12**:508
 Richard **13**:604
JANDAHASS **8**:156
JANE, T. Y. **14**:224
JANGEPAPAWEY **7**:677
JANIFER, --- (Mr.) **12**:131-132
JANIVER, Francis **5**:248
JANNEY, Abel **3**:69; **9**:285
 Thomas **1**:96-97, 99-110, 116-117,
  124-130, 133, 135, 137-138, 140,
  148-149, 151, 164, 169-171, 173,
  175-183, 185-186, 190-191,
  193-195, 320; **5**:388, 573; **7**:437;
  8:577
JANNY, Abel **8**:234
JANNY (JENNY), Thomas **14**:129, 181,
 439
JANSEN, Claus **2**:494
 Conrad **2**:494
 Der(r)ick **3**:257, 491, 618
 Dirk, Jr. **2**:493
 Jan. **3**:619
 John **2**:494
 Peter **2**:494
 Wm. **2**:494
JANSON, Deuck **4**:312
JANSSEN, Derick **4**:58
JANUARY, Joseph **7**:717
 Thomas **3**:270
JANVIER, Thomas **8**:79, 84
JAQUIES, Joseph **12**:393
JAUNCY, Elinor **12**:391
JAVERT, John **2**:493
JAWERT, Johannes **2**:430-431
JAY, John **11**:648, 697, 723, 725,
 742, 478, 753, 766, 775; **12**:32,
 43, 49; **14**:165, 356, 363, 399,
 405, 480, 521, 560, 564; **15**:78,
 463, 465; **16**:48, 361
JAYNES, Thomas **12**:261
JEANES, Joseph **13**:499
JEANS, Daniel **13**:204
 Jacob **16**:287
JECASSO (Tho's. HICKMAN) **9**:212
JEFF(E)RIES, Emmor (Emor) **15**:99,
 566
JEFFERIES, Joseph **11**:693
 Margaret **16**:225-226
 William **13**:635
JEFFERIS, Samuel **13**:411
JEFFERSON, --- (Mr.) **15**:463
 Thomas **12**:224, 250, 444; **16**:315,
  319, 347, 358, 360, 374, 381,
  384, 392, 398, 401-402, 408-409,
  415, 428, 433, 456
JEFFERYS, Jos. **11**:398
JEFFREYS, Samuel **11**:513, 516-517
JEFFRIES, Jacob **11**:151
 Samuel **12**:505
JEFFRYS, --- (Ens.) **7**:313
JEFFS, Mary **1**:137, 319, 320
 Robt. **1**:199, 201-202, 204

JEGLER, John Charles (alias
 SEIGLER) **7**:343-344, 388-389, 398
JEM (NEGRO) **12**:502
JEMISON, John **8**:577
JEMMISAN, James **15**:332
JEMMISON, --- (Dr.) **7**:77
 Robert **5**:247
 Samuel **5**:210
JEMMY **8**:614, 616-617
JEMMY (DELAWARE) **7**:382
JEMMYSON (JEMMISON), John **5**:3, 573
JEN(N)INGS, Edmund (Edmond)
 4:115-116, 118, 120-121, 124,
 130, 135-137, 140, 142-146,
 212-213, 698
JENKASARONE **7**:507
JENKIN(S), John **15**:35, 42, 67,
 78-79, 280, 465, 489
 Mary **15**:68, 71, 430, 439-440, 478,
  480-481
JENKINGS, Saml. **2**:112
JENKINS, --- **4**:390
 David **3**:542, 586; **11**:334; **16**:154,
  529
 Eleazer **16**:14, 42
 George **10**:457; **11**:57
 Jabez **8**:506
 James **13**:684
 John **9**:571
 Joseph **14**:233, 253
 Josiah **13**:561; **14**:128, 423
 Levi **14**:640
 Mary **13**:174, 295, 323
 Robert **4**:422, 429
 Stephen **2**:520, 543; **16**:5
 Stephens **15**:610
 Thomas **5**:282-283; **13**:14; **16**:384
 Wilkes **15**:489, 603
 William **10**:406, 426, 429, 462,
  467, 503; **11**:62; **14**:223
 Willm. **2**:111, 203
 Wm. **1**:324, 375
JENKINSON, C. **9**:48, 50
 Charles **10**:358, 362
JENKS, John **13**:345
 Joseph **15**:99, 297
JENNER, --- (Widow) **2**:65
 Thomas **1**:396-297, 435
JENNEY, Thomas **10**:449
JENNINGS, --- **3**:51
 Benjamin **9**:509, 584
 Edmund **3**:549
 Edward **3**:260, 289, 370
 Gibbons **4**:102
 Jno. **8**:780
 John **3**:332; **9**:57, 206, 308, 398,
  548, 569, 572-573, 585-586,
  606-607, 609, 623; **10**:156;
  11:365
 Joseph **16**:221b (See GILLINGS)
 Margaret **13**:327
 Michael (Dr.) **11**:54, 106, 124, 767
 Saml1. **1**:221, 370, 378, 505
 Solomon **4**:154-155, 206
 Thomas **9**:713; **15**:474; **16**:335
 William **13**:327; **14**:172
JENNY, Robert (Rev.) **7**:741
 Thomas **13**:757
JENOCHIAADA (JENOCHRYADA) **8**:632,
 638, 652
JENONTOWANOS INDIANS **4**:584 (See
 SINIKERS)
JENYNS, Soame **7**:739; **8**:552; **9**:40,
 80
JEOQUANTA **8**:652
JEPISCAUHUNS **7**:677

JOHNSTON (JOHNSON), James (cont'd)
  14:236, 250, 320, 401, 441-442;
  15:91, 301, 425, 592, 604;
  16:215, 219b, 385, 412, 541-542
John **9**:497; **12**:166; **13**:448, 529,
  536, 542, 569, 578, 636, 709;
  14:83, 125, 127, 412, 429, 432,
  442, 540, 563; **15**:119, 301, 588,
  604, 607; **16**:32, 150, 210, 215,
  219b, 378-379
Joseph **14**:613; **15**:129
Martha **12**:400
Matthew **14**:297, 304, 365; **16**:227
Philip **16**:185
Rachel **13**:778
Richard **12**:623; **13**:121, 203, 584,
  756, 778; **14**:141, 434, 610
Robert **10**:451, 458; **13**:718; **14**:590
Robert (Dr.) **13**:591; **14**:101, 410;
  16:219b, 385, 412
Samuel **9**:201, 283, 714, 731;
  10:163, 690; **13**:38; **14**:293, 300,
  412; **15**:524, 537
Simon **14**:590
Thomas **11**:98, 367; **12**:166; **13**:266;
  14:191, 195, 293, 300, 428, 430,
  442; **15**:35, 129, 487; **16**:478
William **4**:7, 16; **12**:57; **13**:168,
  282, 586; **14**:96, 424
William (Col.) **5**:72, 74, 297-298,
  431, 436, 462-463, 465-466,
  471-472, 475, 480-481, 508, 510,
  518, 548-549, 573-574, 607, 615,
  622, 624-626, 630, 632, 637,
  641-642, 644-646, 702, 774-775,
  777; **6**:9, 13, 57, 64, 67-68, 73,
  75-77, 81-82, 86, 88-89, 93,
  100, 109-110, 116-119, 182-183,
  249, 269-270, 275, 280-287,
  291-293, 313, 366-367, 371, 374,
  412, 431, 436, 462, 468-471,
  473-474, 600, 603, 605-608,
  610-612, 637, 640, 678, 697,
  700-701, 752
William (Sir) **7**:9-11, 14, 19-21,
  35, 41, 43-44, 46, 67, 69, 71,
  81-82, 97, 100-102, 106-109,
  112-114, 116-117, 120, 123-124,
  127-128, 143-145, 147, 154-155,
  157-159, 171, 176, 182, 188-189,
  193-195, 202-203, 206, 222-223,
  225-226, 244, 270, 278-279,
  282-283, 285-287, 298-299, 305,
  308, 322, 326, 331, 351,
  354-356, 360, 377-378, 382-385,
  390, 434-436, 462, 466, 480-481,
  486, 488, 490-492, 506-507, 509,
  515, 519-520, 522-524, 527 ,
  535-539, 541-542, 544-545, 548,
  564, 577-578, 588-589, 607,
  622-626, 628-629, 631, 634,
  641-645, 648, 652, 654-655, 659,
  665, 667-668, 675, 683-685, 688,
  690-691, 698-699, 702, 707-709,
  711, 724, 730, 736, 753-754,
  762, 768; **8**:56, 62, 97, 119,
  141, 145, 153, 162, 165, 167,
  175, 177, 186, 195, 201, 204,
  208, 218, 222, 264, 306,
  380-386, 390, 393, 400, 429,
  432-433, 492-493, 507-508, 564,
  569-570, 595, 618, 622, 624,
  628, 640-645, 647, 649, 652-653,
  656, 699, 702, 707-709, 727,
  732, 755, 757-758, 764, 769,
  780; ->

JOHNSTON (JOHNSON), William (Sir)
  (continued) **9**:8, 46-47, 62-64,
  68, 77, 79, 104-106, 110-113,
  118, 121-122, 129, 131, 137-138,
  170, 189-191, 206-207, 209, 211,
  217-218, 225, 227-228, 233-234,
  239, 249-251, 253-257, 259-263,
  266, 277-279, 305-306, 332, 403,
  407-408, 411-412, 414-415,
  422-425, 428, 431, 433, 437,
  457, 459-460, 466-469, 474, 477,
  482, 490, 492, 494-498, 500,
  506-507, 518-519, 523, 534-535,
  553-554, 568, 582, 592, 603,
  614, 616-617, 646, 690-691,
  695-696, 706, 708-709, 738, 741,
  774-776
Wm. (Sir) **13**:466
JOHNSTONE, Francis **14**:400, 526
John **14**:438
Joseph **13**:669
Samuel **14**:366, 379
William **14**:634
JOHOUNOT, Gabriel **13**:373
JOINER, Mary **14**:630
JOKE, Adam **10**:219
JOLLIBOIS, Jacque **13**:116
JOLLIE, Sarah **11**:96
JOLLY, --- (Maj.) **13**:189
  Charles **9**:393, 672; **10**:29, 31
JONAS **9**:428, 436
JONAS, Owen, Jr. **14**:47-48
JONATHAN **6**:249, 443, 640, 649,
  661, 749
JONATHAN, --- **11**:478
JONATHAN (UNATA) **8**:132, 176
JONATHAN THE DEER **5**:691-692
JONER, Jacob **4**:72
  Jonas **4**:72
JONES, --- **9**:414; **12**:245, 385, 439
  --- (Capt.) **10**:436
  --- (Chevalier) **14**:560
  --- (Dr.) **16**:512
  --- (Ens.) **13**:189
  --- (Lt.) **12**:93
  --- (Mr.) **13**:426
  Abraham **5**:175
  Anne **13**:527
  Benjamin **4**:313, 482; **5**:3; **11**:251;
    14:585
  Blaithwaite **11**:125, 389, 486-487
  Blaitwaite **10**:730
  Blathwaite **15**:24
  Cadwallader **1**:342
  Caleb **13**:527
  Castner **16**:387
  Catharine **13**:413
  Charles **1**:166; **3**:468-470, 472;
    4:58; **13**:515; **16**:163
  Daniel **3**:387; **11**:679; **12**:28
  Daniel (Rev.) **14**:437
  Danll. **1**:123, 320, 339, 451, 607
  David **2**:277; **3**:416, 521; **4**:483;
    5:3, 466; **9**:666; **11**:432, 610;
    13:30
  David (Rev.) **10**:551; **13**:573, 714;
    14:101, 495; **15**:143, 289
  Edward **5**:209, 256; **7**:62;
    11:610-612; **12**:57, 350, 381;
    13:722, 737; **14**:238, 250
  Edwd. **1**:79-80
  Evan **2**:83, 136; **4**:250, 277, 505;
    5:597, 662; **6**:144
  Fra. **1**:527
  Frank **12**:390
  Gib(b)s **11**:49, 195

KACHGUESCONK 3:321
KACHHAWATCHIKY 6:155
KACHLEIN (KACHELINE, KEICHLIN),
  Peter 10:56, 100, 156, 211, 270,
  502, 675
KACHLINE, Charles 13:112
KACHNEGHDACKON (KOCHNEGHDACKON)
  6:120-121, 123
KACHSHWUCHDANIONTY 5:686
KACKANAPAULIN 5:750
KACKLIEN, Peter 15:178
KAGHRADODON 6:122
KAGUNDANOYAGH 2:159
KAHATOODO 8:152
KAHICKDODON 5:686; 6:122
KAHISKEROWANE 4:80
KAHUKTODON 6:524
KAIG, William 13:464
KAIGHN, John 13:251
KAIN, Hugh 11:155
  James 10:49
  Matthew 14:298, 305, 434
  Michael 13:669; 14:96, 419
KAINE, Hugh 4:102, 104
  James 4:102
  John, Jr. 4:102, 104
  John, Sr. 4:102
KAKAUSCUNG 8:294
KAKOWATCHY 3:309, 442, 463, 507
KALATOMA 9:227
KALB, Andrew 14:65
KALE, Lewis 15:369
  Ludowick 13:253
  Ludwick 13:368
  Ludwig 12:522
KALKERSON, Casper (Alias
  KIRKISSELTLE) 16:79
KALKIESER, Jo. Hendrick 3:368
KALKLIESER, Christopher 3:368
KALLENDER, --- (Capt.) 7:600
KALLOCH, Joseph 5:135
KALRICKDODON 6:120-121 (Alias
  Groote Younge)
KAMEY, William 12:187
KAMMERER, Henry 14:571, 580;
  15:322, 569, 648
KAMMERER & GLENTWORTH 14:571
KAMMERER (KEMMERER), Henry 16:147,
  276, 464
KAMMERER, STEEL & GLENTWORTH
  14:571-572
KANACHJAKANYJADY 6:160
KANADAKOYON, Johannes 6:119-121,
  123
KANAWATOE 4:80
KANDT (alias Last Night) 8:176
KANE, John 14:265
  Rawley 7:344
  William 10:424
KANER, Michael 12:570
KANES, Tho. 1:83
KANICKHUNGO 4:80, 82
KANJUCHHA 6:160 (Alias Penn)
KANNANNOWACH 3:152
KANNENQUAS 9:103
KANNYGOODK 3:130
KANUKSUSY 6:588
KANWONHUNT 2:553
KAP, Andreas 3:456
KAPLIN, Mathias 3:329
KAPP, Michael 15:296
KARCHER (KARGHER), Ludwig (Ludwick)
  10:638, 712
KARHAWGUGH-ROANU INDIANS 4:586
KARKER, David 3:520
KARLIN, John 11:127, 358

KARN, Nicholas 11:340
KARNAUGHAN, John 3:533
KAROCHYAKTATTY 6:127 (Alias
  Nicholas Peters)
KARR, Michael 13:758
KARROD, Levi 13:264
KARSE, Johan Jacob 3:518
KASEY, Morris 14:193, 608
KASHWUGHDANIUNTO 6:524
KASTARUGA 8:84
KATARIONIECHA 3:501
KATAWEYKEITA 3:495, 507
KATNER, Georg. Michael 3:524
  John 3:524
KATT, Frederick 12:608
KATTAKE 5:284
KAUFFMAN, Isaac 12:223, 296
KAUNS, Johannes 3:410
KAXHAAYU 4:80
KAYANTARRA 1:435-436
KAYCOWOCKECAR (KAYCOWOCKEWR)
  4:336, 341, 346-347
KAYNHARRO 1:447-448
KAYODAGHSCROONY (Madelina) 7:95-96
KAYSER, Valentine 13:747
KEAGY, Isaac 15:296
KEAN, David 12:1
  J. 10:770
  Jane 14:165
  John 15:41; 16:352, 500
  Philip 13:759
KEANE, Jane 13:588
  Patrick 12:176-177
KEARN, Peter 13:367
KEARNEY, Philip, Jr. 8:576
KEARNS, Robert 14:560, 613
KEARSLEY, David (Dr.) 10:358-359,
  362, 367, 371-372
  John 12:27-28
  John (Dr.) 10:358-360, 372-374,
  378, 380-381, 385, 403, 408-409,
  773; 12:27
  Jus. 4:363-364
  Paul 10:359
KEARSLY, Jno. 3:298, 301
KEARSTUCKER, Martin 3:288
KEAS, John 11:153
KEASE, Philip 14:100, 411
KEATES, Barbara 10:685
KEATING, Ignatius 13:563; 14:92,
  425
  Katherine 14:586
  Luke 10:769; 14:227, 586
  Maurice 14:268
KEATON, Morris 13:345-346
KEBLE, Abraham 10:8, 78, 163
KEBZ, John 11:657
KECHLEIN (KACKLEIN, KACHLEIN,
  KECHLENE), Peter 9:199, 285,
  333, 688, 710-711, 713, 723,
  732, 778
KECHLER, Jacob 13:444
KECHLINE (KEIKLEIN, KECHLEIN),
  Andrew 11:21, 36, 150, 330, 393,
  424, 500
KECHLINE (KICHLEINE), Abraham
  12:136, 510
KECKENSKUNG 8:386
KEEBNER, Abraham 16:167
KEEFER, Abraham 16:481
  John Leond. 3:432
  Valentine 12:601
KEEHLIN, Andrew 10:448
KEEKMLE, John 15:207
KEEKYUSCUNG 8:147
KEEL, Hans Erick 3:287

KING, Robert **4**:698; **10**:741; **11**:85,
97; **16**:396-397, 440, 442
Rut **7**:507, 513
Simon **4**:248, 267, 272
Thom. **4**:102
Thomas **7**:485, 507, 513, 519-521,
533, 536, 539, 543, 597; **8**:176,
191, 196-197, 199, 208-209, 219,
221, 263-264, 270, 595, 646,
734, 741, 743, 748, 752, 754,
757-759, 765-766, 771; **9**:7,
504-505, 775-776
Valentine **11**:165, 169
Walter **1**:87, 387
William **8**:403, 506; **9**:632
KING(S)LEY, Nathan **16**:196, 269
KINGSLAND, Mary **11**:153
KINGSLEY, Nathan **15**:212
KINGSTON, John **16**:282
KININGER, Christian **3**:429
KINK, Christopher **3**:410
KINKALDY, John **15**:5
KINKEAD, James **10**:106, 212; **13**:158
John **13**:634
KINNARD, William **12**:21
KINNEAR, George **15**:274-275
KINNEER, James **7**:23
KINNEY, Abraham **12**:3; **13**:778;
14:94, 415
Michael **14**:294, 301, 423
Stephen **8**:566
Thomas **15**:489, 547, 603
KINNIER, --- (Capt.) **6**:520
KINNIS(S)ON, Edward **4**:279, 287 (See
KENNISON)
KINNOUT, --- (Earl of) **8**:438
KINNSMAN, Robert **8**:566
KINSEL (KENCIL), John **11**:35, 50
KINSER, Nichol. **3**:385
Nicholas **9**:557
KINSEY (KINZEY), Abraham **10**:607
John **4**:197, 204-206, 208-209, 215,
219, 223, 229, 242, 289, 353,
355, 360-361, 366, 368, 375,
388-389, 392, 404-405, 417, 425,
448, 459, 470, 478, 493, 495,
510, 514, 558-559, 573-575, 583,
602, 618, 622, 628, 637, 640,
669, 672, 674, 742, 749,
774-775; **5**:4, 26, 28, 32, 37,
43, 45-46, 49, 54, 56, 58, 64,
73-74, 90, 94, 104, 123, 126,
130, 160, 183, 185, 237-238,
275, 282, 294, 333, 338,
341-342, 344, 368, 373-374, 411,
415, 430; **6**:356, 723; **8**:368
Neil W. **14**:81
Samuel **13**:771; **14**:24, 155, 170,
197, 213; **16**:174, 179
KINSLER, William **16**:428
KINSLEY (KENSLEY), Frazer **10**:572,
575
KINSMAN, Jno. **1**:95
KINTON, Thomas T. K. **5**:524, 532
KINTSELL, Jacob **3**:456
KINTZ, Philip **3**:417
KINTZING, Abraham **12**:331, 591
KINTZINGER, Elizabeth **13**:394
KINTZLER, William **16**:196-197
KIPPELL, Nicholas **15**:499
KIPPING, Joannes **3**:369
KIPPS, Francis **4**:62
KIPSHAVEN, John **1**:48
KIRBACH, Simon **3**:570
KIRBY, Timothy **12**:188
KIRCHENSCHLAEGER, Elinor **12**:77

KIRCHIN, Margaretta Catharine **8**:336
KIRK, --- (Mr.) **10**:573
Alice **3**:167, 189
Ann **12**:387
James **13**:604; **14**:93, 417
John **10**:666, 673
Samuel **3**:254; **7**:313
Timothy **7**:417; **8**:573
KIRK(E), Samuel **5**:617
KIRKBRIDE, Jonathan **12**:744, 754
Jos. **2**:577, 585, 590, 596, 630
Joseph **3**:28, 241, 359-360; **5**:3;
9:235, 673, 704; **10**:162, 665,
675, 711, 715, 730, 758; **11**:19,
37, 206, 208, 214, 217, 227,
236, 245, 257, 260, 266,
275-276, 317, 320, 396, 473, 480
Joseph, Jr. **4**:244, 313, 355, 482
Mahlon **5**:388, 573, 729; **9**:237,
589, 593
Meihlon **7**:291-292
Richard **5**:443
KIRKBRIDGE, --- (Col.) **10**:783
Joseph **11**:194, 281
KIRKBRIGHT, Joseph **2**:456, 458
KIRKER, Johannes **3**:414
KIRKHOF, Christopher **3**:285
KIRKLAND, Moses **10**:567, 661-664,
667, 694, 713; **11**:145
KIRKLEIN, Andrew **10**:471
KIRKPATRICK, Abraham **15**:604, 607
Elinor **13**:471
James **11**:199
KIRKT, Johannes **4**:59
KIRSHMET, Anthony **12**:608
KIRWIN, Peter **3**:330
KISH, Matthias **3**:518
KISHAW, Pala **5**:290
KISHYCOQUILLAS **6**:421-422
KISLE, Hans Ulrick **3**:369
KISLER, Nicholas **14**:114
KISLING, Jacob **11**:11
KISNER, Johan Philip **3**:455
KISSACK, Robert **11**:515-516, 518
KISSAKOCHQUILLA **6**:154
KISSONAUCTHTHA (KISSINAUGHTHA)
9:528, 538
KITCHEN, Philip **15**:419
KITCHEN (KITCHIN), Stephen **11**:586,
609
KITCHENER, Frederick **12**:201
KITE, --- (Lt.) **13**:189
KITSINTAUDER, Christian **3**:368
KITTS, George **10**:651-652
John **12**:451
KITZMILLER, Jacob **5**:582, 586,
596-597
Martin **5**:582-586, 589-595
KLAIN, Velentine **3**:414
KLAKNER, Johan Hendrich **3**:570
KLEAS, Hans Philip **3**:467
KLECKNOR, Frederick **16**:122
KLEIN, --- **7**:620
Christian **7**:493-494
George **7**:119, 460
Hendrick **3**:459
Jacob **3**:459
Johannes **3**:454
John **14**:671
Marcus **3**:516
Philip **3**:594; **13**:432
KLEINFELTER, George **14**:581
KLEINHOFF, John **14**:4
KLEINHOOF, Casper **2**:493
KLEIR, A. **11**:759
KLEM, Gotleb **3**:518

KOOKEN, Joseph 13:603
KOON, Christian 12:740
KOONS, George 14:208
KOPLIN, John 7:769
KOPP, Johan Georg. 3:410
KOPPENHOFFER, Thomas 3:332
KOPPLER, Hans Martin 3:458
KOPPLINGER, Johs. 3:385
  Leond. 3:385
KOQUE(E)ASH 3:601, 603
KOQUEEASH 4:338
KOQYEEASH 2:15
KORBER, Johan Casper 3:515
KORR, Michael 3:331
KOSCIUSZKO, Thaddeus 10:764
KOSER, Jacob 3:570
KOSTER, Johannes 2:241
  John 11:483-485
  Samuel 11:483-485
KOUGH, Adam 16:154
KOWATZ, --- (Col.) 11:531
KOYLE, Zachariah 14:611
KRAFFT, Gottfried 3:414
KRAFT, Michael 13:558
KRALER, Jacob 3:516
KRAM, Henrick 3:415
KRAMER, Andreas 3:455
  Casper 3:457
  Matthias 3:454
  Philip 12:131
KRANS, Wilhelm 3:518
KRAUS, Hans Jacob 3:453
KRAUSE, Charles 16:348
KRAUZE, David 16:498
KRAYMER, Lawrence 14:489
  Peter 14:489
KRAYMER (KRAEMER), Catharine
  14:489, 568
KREAMER, Jacob 12:623, 679
  Philip 11:358, 445; 13:393-394,
   617, 720; 14:554
  Will'm. 13:28
KRECKER, Peter 12:601
KREEMER, Bernard 14:577
  Henrick 3:413
  Philip 12:508; 13:88-89; 15:565;
   16:491
KREIBEL, George 11:269
KREIDER, Conrad 12:431, 438, 446;
  14:457
  Michael 3:432
KREIGER, Hans Michl. 3:456
KREITZER, John 13:709
  Peter 12:601
KREMER, Jacob 13:14
KREMMER, Hans Adam 3:413
KRESLER, Hans Philip 3:466
KREWSON, Derrick 12:619, 673
  Henry 10:211
  John 11:372
KREY, Jno. 2:494
  Willm. 2:494
KREYL, Thomas 3:454
KRICHNER, Johannes 3:516
KRICK, George 9:557
KRIDER (KREIDER), Conrad 11:330,
  479
KRIEBLE, Caspar 3:569
  George 3:569
  Melchior, Jr. 3:569
  Melchoir 3:569
KRINSTON, Hans Ulrick 3:386
KRIST, Jacob 3:519
  Marcus 3:519
KRITTER, Peter 3:456
KRONER, Johan Dietrich 3:459

KRONER, Johan Georg. 3:459
KROPS, Christian 3:515
KROWSE, David 14:556
KRUG, Jacob 13:88; 16:83, 290
  Joseph 12:566
KRUMRINE, Stephen 11:73
KRUSE, --- (Capt.) 14:77, 103
KRYGER, Peter 6:704
KRYHE, Frank 3:414
  John Jacob 3:413
KRYL, Johan Adam 3:454
  Johannes 3:454
KUCHDACHARY 4:80
KUCHER, Christopher 12:134, 164,
  301, 392, 508; 13:88, 275, 393,
  415, 698; 16:1-7, 9-17, 19-22,
  24-29, 31, 34, 37, 40-41, 52-57,
  59-60, 62-68, 70-78, 80, 82-91,
  93-94, 96-116, 118-120, 122-127,
  129-131, 133-138, 141-149,
  151-155, 173, 175-177, 180-183,
  187-188, 190-194, 196-197,
  199-202, 205, 209-212, 214-216,
  218-220, 222-224, 209b-212b,
  214b-215b, 217b-224b, 225-227,
  229-233, 235-236, 238-243,
  251-252, 254-264, 267-274, 276,
  278-291, 293, 295-307, 309-313,
  315-316, 318, 320-324, 326-327,
  329, 331-332, 336, 340-341,
  344-350, 352-354, 357-360,
  362-366, 368-373, 375-384, 386,
  388-390, 392-396, 399-405,
  408-420, 422-429, 432-435, 439,
  441-442, 445-447, 449-459,
  461-465, 477, 479-484, 487-488,
  499
  Christopher (Christian) 15:296,
   309-317, 320-328, 331, 338-353,
   356-359, 367-372, 374-380,
   383-391, 394-401, 403-412,
   414-417, 450-473, 475-477, 480,
   482, 484-488, 490-492, 494-506,
   508-509, 523-527, 530-536,
   538-541, 543-545, 548-551,
   557-564, 566-569, 571-581,
   613-620, 622-623, 625-629,
   632-658
KUEHAR, Bartell 3:619
KUHL, Frederick 10:653-660,
  664-666, 668, 670-672, 675,
  677-678, 680-683, 686-687, 689,
  691-692, 694-702, 704-705,
  707-710, 713-714, 716-718,
  720-729, 732-733, 735-742, 744,
  746-750, 752-756, 758-764, 766,
  768-775, 777-784; 11:1-9, 11,
  13-14, 16-20, 22-27, 29-30,
  32-34, 36-37, 39, 47, 78,
  102-103, 139-142; 14:229, 250,
  508
KUHN, Adam 11:284, 288
  Adam (Dr.) 12:501-502, 504,
   515-517, 650
  Adam Simon 5:600; 8:562; 9:172,
   419, 673; 10:42, 458, 636
  Christian 12:576
  Dewall 14:461
  Frederick 12:650
  Frederick (Dr.) 16:31, 194, 494
  Jacob 11:310; 12:650
  John 12:650
  Ludwig 12:160-161
  Michael 10:734, 770
  Peter 12:650
KUHNS, Mich'l. 11:444

KUHTANAMAKY 7:677
KUKTAMAKA 7:681
KULL, Frederick 11:640
KULLAR, Jurg 3:465
KULM, Frederick 15:570
KULP, Hans Casper 3:369
KUMMERLIN, Hans Jacob 3:515
KUNCKEL, John 14:489
KUNDERS, Dennis 2:493
KUNIUS, Catherine 16:233
KUNN, Johannes 3:385
KUNST, George Pieter 3:455
KUNTZ, Hans Georg. 3:456
 Hans Michael 3:285
 Johan Jacob 3:453
 Jurg Micxhael 3:285
 Lorentz 3:454
KUNTZER, Hans Bern 3:466
KUNTZMAN, August Henrich 3:570
KUR, Christian 3:517
KURIAHTAATY 8:218
KURR, Hans Thomas 4:72
KURTZ, --- (Mr.) 6:657
 Elizabeth 13:548
KUSER, Michael 15:454
KUSICH (KUSICK), John 16:333, 335
KUSMAN, Roolof 3:413
KUSSENAUCHTHA 9:231
KUTAIKUND 8:144
KUTZ, Jacob 3:455
 Peter 14:610
KUYKEN-DAHL (KUYKENDALE), Peter
 8:564, 612-613
KUYN, Ludwig 9:735
KYLE, Charles 10:235
 John 4:483; 5:3, 378, 600; 14:662
 William (See COYLE) 11:267-268
KYLL, John 4:313
KYUNQUEAGOAH 9:103

LA BLANC, Charles 7:240
LA CAZE, James 12:615-616
LA FAYETTE, --- (Gen.) 4:6
 --- (Marquis) 13:479
LA FORCE, --- (Monsieur) 6:22, 142,
 162, 225, 288
LA MAR, Marien 11:179-180
LA MARIE 8:313
LA MISSIONET 5:556
LA RADINE, --- (Col.) 11:776
LA(I)RD, Matthew 6:482
LABAN, Abraham 10:219
LABAR, Abraham 13:613, 723
LABATTE, Ignatius 11:568
LABBOYTEAU, Hannah 13:282
LAC(E)Y, John 11:208, 330, 340,
 372, 396, 398, 411, 447, 452,
 472, 497, 522, 533, 558, 614,
 619, 633, 685; 16:22, 542
LACANNUNTY 6:126
LACAZE, --- (Mr.) 13:596, 598
LACAZE & MALLET 15:657
LACEY, --- (Gen.) 13:73-74, 84, 90,
 110, 123, 189-190, 192, 221,
 225, 228, 243, 358; 14:655
 --- (Mr.) 13:1, 3, 5-6, 8, 11-12,
 14-17, 19-21, 62
 John 10:447; 13:5, 101, 225
 John, Jr. 12:124, 135, 150,
 152-153, 158-159, 161-164,
 166-167, 169, 171-174, 176-177,
 179, 181-182, 185-186, 189, ->

LACEY, John, Jr. (continued)
 12:191-195, 197-198, 200-201,
 205, 207, 209, 217-218, 220-221,
 223-229, 231-233, 235, 237,
 242-246, 248-251, 253, 256,
 258-260, 262-263, 265, 267-272,
 274, 276, 279-281, 283, 285,
 287-289, 292, 296-299, 301-302,
 304-305, 307, 309, 311-313, 315,
 317-320, 322-324, 326-328,
 330-331, 333, 335-342, 347-348,
 350-352, 354, 357-358, 360-364,
 367-368, 370-376, 378-379, 384,
 401-402, 404-407, 409-410, 415,
 417, 419-420, 422-423, 425-426,
 428-430, 434-437, 445-446,
 468-469, 473, 476-477, 479-484,
 486-489, 491, 493-495, 497-499,
 503-504, 506, 508, 510, 514,
 517-518, 520, 522-524, 534, 536,
 538-544, 546-548, 551, 558,
 560-564, 566, 568-570, 572, 575,
 577-578, 582-584, 588, 591-595,
 599-600, 614, 616, 640, 645-646,
 648-650, 661-664, 667, 670, 672,
 674, 676, 678-683, 685-686, 688,
 690, 693, 695-696, 699, 701-702,
 705-708, 711-713, 715, 717-723,
 725, 727-729, 731, 758-761, 764,
 766-768, 771, 773, 776-778, 780,
 782-783; 13:24, 49, 52, 73, 90,
 112, 139, 149, 151, 252, 388
 Thomas 1:437, 440
LACK, Jacob 10:682
LACQUIS, Abraham 8:403, 405
 William 7:105, 107-109, 118, 137,
 145, 182
LACY, --- (Mr./Gen.) 13:22-25,
 30-33, 35, 37-39, 41-43, 51-52,
 62, 65, 90, 94-96, 98-102, 104,
 106, 109-111, 114, 116-117,
 119-121, 123, 125, 127-128,
 131-133, 135-140, 142-143, 145,
 149-150, 219, 222-223, 238-239,
 242-244, 250-254, 345, 347,
 355-360, 362, 384-386, 388
LADD, John 7:468
LADICK, Jacob 16:319
LADLIE (LEDLIE), Andrew (Dr.)
 14:34, 610
LAFERTY, Daniel 6:143
LAFFERTY, Daniel 13:709; 14:130,
 423
 Patrick 13:680; 14:102, 428
LAGEROM, John 3:328
LAHALAPOWHY (KITCHIN) 9:228
LAHBER, Hans Wendel 3:458
LAHMAN (LAYMAN), Henry 14:63, 94
LAHYA 3:15
LAIRD, Hugh 11:229; 14:512; 15:213
 James 11:367
 John 16:427
 Matthew 11:367
 Samuel 9:779; 10:56, 101, 664,
 700; 11:691; 12:647, 703;
 13:396; 14:442, 553; 15:216
LAITCHER, Abraham 10:739
LAJONQUIER(R)E (LEJONQUIER), ---
 (Monsieur) 5:558, 633, 688
LAK, Johan Engelbert 3:414
LAKE, --- 5:113
 William 7:10
LAL(L)OR, --- (Col.) 11:210,
 250-251
LALLY, Francis 12:216
LAMB, Caleb 5:532

LATTIMER, James **9**:203, 626
John **14**:593
Robert **13**:112; **14**:593
William **14**:593
LATTIMORE, Arthur **8**:780; **9**:57;
  10:156
Robert **9**:548; **11**:340; **13**:89, 395,
  415
LAUB, Conard **16**:193-194, 492
LAUBACK, John **13**:18
LAUDENBERGER, John **10**:643
LAUER, --- (Capt.) **10**:709
Christian **13**:393, 720
Hans **3**:518
LAUGHLAN, Jacob **11**:601, 603
LAUGHLIN, Alexander **11**:67, 229;
  14:242
Hugh **14**:362, 571
Jacob **10**:473, 477
Robert **14**:215; **16**:170
LAUMAN, John **14**:204
Lodowick **10**:669
Ludwick **12**:306
Ludwig **11**:521
Stephan **3**:517
LAUR, Christian **9**:440, 561; **12**:131,
  308
Christopher **12**:709
LAURENCE (LAWRENCE), John **12**:338
Jos'a. **3**:614
Moritz **3**:467
Thomas **3**:238-240, 257, 269,
  302-303, 309, 315-316, 327-329,
  333, 337-338, 340, 344, 346-347,
  351, 354-355, 358-359, 365-367,
  370-372, 374-376, 379-384,
  386-387, 390, 393, 399-400, 404,
  406, 411, 413, 418, 422, 426,
  429-430, 433, 435, 437-438, 446,
  459, 463-464, 466-467, 474, 479,
  491, 506, 520-521, 544, 566,
  574, 585, 589, 591, 594-595,
  607, 609, 612, 614; **4**:17, 19-21,
  23, 32, 39, 47, 49, 51, 56, 58,
  60, 63, 72-73, 82, 85, 87, 90,
  95-97, 99, 100, 104, 106, 112,
  129, 136, 140, 143-144, 147,
  149, 151-153, 155, 158-159, 165,
  167, 171, 174-175, 181, 186,
  190, 195-196, 198, 201-203, 205,
  208-209, 224-226, 228, 241,
  243-245, 289-290, 293-297,
  309-310, 312, 314, 317-319, 321,
  331, 336, 341, 353-354, 365,
  371, 376, 380, 387, 390-391,
  394-395, 398, 420-422, 429, 431,
  435, 443, 448, 461, 469-470,
  478-483, 501, 503, 506, 524,
  548, 560, 568-569, 572-573,
  575-578, 583, 586, 618, 620,
  626, 628-629, 652, 669-670, 675,
  677, 685, 687-689, 697, 737,
  743, 754, 756, 761-762, 770-772,
  774-775; **5**:4, 26, 29, 31, 34-35,
  39, 43, 48-49, 52, 55, 58-59,
  61-63, 66-68, 70, 73-74, 76-80,
  82-83, 90, 92-96, 100-101,
  104-106, 108-113, 119-120,
  133-136, 140, 143-145, 147-148,
  152, 154, 156, 158, 162-164,
  167, 171, 173-175, 181, 183,
  185-186, 188, 193-194, 198,
  200-201, 203, 205-206, 208,
  211-212, 215, 221, 223, 228-229,
  232, 235, 238, 245, 248-250,
  252, 256, 258-260, 264-265, ->

LAURENCE (LAWRENCE), Thomas
  (contined) **5**:267-268, 277, 284,
  289, 294, 298-300, 306, 319,
  323, 326, 328, 330, 362-363,
  365, 367, 372, 377, 379-380,
  388, 390-391, 395-396, 398, 403,
  405, 413, 431, 437, 451, 456,
  461, 467, 470, 484, 488-490,
  492, 495, 502, 506, 512-513,
  516, 525, 527-528, 548, 550,
  558-559, 562, 565-566, 572, 575,
  577, 580, 582, 597, 601,
  606-607, 638, 657, 662, 704,
  710, 722, 730, 736; **12**:353, 441,
  450, 537, 617
LAURENS (LAWRENS), Henry **11**:379,
  381, 437, 461, 466, 487, 580,
  648, 737; **12**:60, 422
Joseph **14**:558
LAURY, --- (Mr.) **12**:662
LAUSEL, Christian **3**:515
LAUSSENESS, Johan Frederick **3**:386
LAUTERMILCH, Johann **3**:458
Wendel **3**:414
LAUVERSTEIN, Peter **13**:747
LAVAN, Abraham **11**:451
LAVERING, Wickart **14**:432
LAVID, Alexander **12**:421
LAVINGAIR, Christopher **10**:724, 726
LAW, Albert **14**:303, 410
William **12**:463
LAWACHCANRICKY (LAWACHCAMICKY)
  5:317-318
LAWACHKAMICKY **6**:153
LAWACQUAQUA **5**:290
LAWAGHANNICKO **5**:524
LAWALL, William Henry **13**:89
LAWELL, David **5**:193
LAWER, Christian **14**:232, 250
LAWISSIMO **9**:229
LAWLESS, Eliza **14**:300
LAWOUGHGUA **9**:259
LAWRENCE, --- (Col.) **6**:311
--- (Gov.) **7**:239-241
--- (Mrs.) **13**:131
Charles **10**:536, 554, 593, 620,
  656, 680; **14**:298, 305, 433, 532
Charles (Gov.) **6**:451, 464-465,
  555, 587, 601, 711-713, 751
Christian **16**:388
Elizabeth **12**:773
John **5**:106, 110; **6**:766; **9**:205,
  393, 510, 513, 545, 548, 596,
  601, 632, 666, 678, 682, 734,
  745, 778; **10**:43, 53, 129,
  172-173, 266, 448, 727; **11**:269,
  525, 565-566, 579, 625; **13**:131,
  555; **14**:90, 426, 634; **16**:429,
  524
John, Jr. **12**:152
Staats **12**:144; **13**:131
Thomas **7**:367; **9**:205, 634-635, 672;
  10:358-359, 381, 460, 468, 570;
  11:583
Thomas, Jr. **5**:174
Wendell (Windle) **14**:62, 90, 415
William **10**:114; **12**:458; **15**:478,
  542, 640
Wm. **1**:320, 340
LAWRIE, James **5**:135
LAWRIE (LAURIE), Thomas **4**:289, 347,
  351, 371, 386, 397, 400, 402,
  424-426, 428-429, 468
LAWRIER, Harman **1**:479-480
LAWS, John **10**:264
LAWSEN, Joseph **16**:72

112

LAWSON, --- (Capt.) **5**:342
--- (Col.) **11**:151, 154, 160,
  163-164
James **11**:515-516, 518; **15**:431
Neals (Neels) **1**:151, 154
LAWTON (SEE HALE &) **11**:765; **12**:354
LAY, George Christopher **3**:456
Ludwig **4**:60
Matthias **3**:515
LAYERSWYLER, Jacob **10**:765
LAYLACHTOCHOE **4**:307
LAYLAND, William **13**:566
LAYMAN, Joannes **3**:288
LE BANE, Joseph **16**:184
LE BEOUF, Francis **13**:344
LE BLANC, Andrew **14**:265, 447, 449
Charles **7**:446
Daniel **7**:240
LE BRASIEUR, --- (Monsieur) **12**:470
LE BRUICE, Charles **7**:240
LE CAIN, --- (Gov. Gen.) **6**:10, 12
LE CATEN, --- **6**:225
LE CRAKE, --- (Chevalier) **6**:12
LE FORT, J. **2**:17 (See LE TORT)
LE GEORGE, John **12**:576
LE JOSEPH, --- **6**:225
LE LEOPARD, --- **6**:225
LE MAR, Marien **10**:406, 437, 458,
  464, 480, 487, 498, 525
LE MERCIER, --- (Chevalier) **6**:29-30
LE ROY, --- (Ens.) **13**:680
--- (Monsieur) **8**:714
George **12**:116, 687; **13**:716
LE ROY (LE ROI), --- (Ens.) **14**:30,
  44, 95, 418
LE TELIER, John **13**:547
LE TORT, Ann **1**:396-397, 435-436
James **2**:100, 138, 140, 155, 163,
  170-171, 389, 403, 471, 539,
  554, 562 (See LE FORT); **3**:123,
  181-182, 187-188, 197, 202,
  209-210, 215, 274, 295, 297,
  330, 506, 603
LE TORT(S), James **4**:237, 340,
  562-563, 574
LEA, Thomas **16**:316
LEA (LEE), Isaac **5**:55, 120, 345,
  411, 464
LEACH, Tobias **1**:157, 384 (See
  LEECH)
LEACOCK, John **12**:110; **14**:555;
  15:98, 567, 574; **16**:208, 490
Joseph **15**:328; **16**:312
LEADER, St. John **4**:468
LEADOM, John **13**:674
LEAMAN, Hans **3**:285
LEAMING, Thomas **12**:507; **14**:112,
  259, 364
Thomas, Jr. **12**:195
LEAMON, Michael **13**:602; **14**:96, 425
LEANY, John **14**:146
LEAP, George **3**:519
Johan Conrad **3**:519
LEARCH, Anthony **13**:680
LEARRIN, Andrew **1**:81
LEARY, Christian **11**:100
Daniel **13**:778
Dennis **16**:531, 534-535
John, Jr. **13**:535, 549
Margaret **12**:343
LEARY (LEAHY), Daniel **14**:94, 415
LEAS, William **10**:163; **11**:219, 443
LEATHAM, Robert **11**:744
LEATHERMAN, Conrad **12**:560
Tewalt **3**:285
LEAUGEAY, Jean **10**:683

LEB, Nicholas **13**:708
LEBEEGOOT, Johan **3**:524
Ulrich **3**:524
LEBEGOOD, Hans Jacob **3**:519
LEBERGER, Johan Adam **3**:454
LEBERGHER, Hendrich **3**:457
LEBLANE, Simon **7**:14
LEBO, Henry **12**:601; **16**:494
Jacob **12**:601
Peter **12**:601
LECENE, Jean **3**:455
Paul **3**:455
LECHNER, Hans Leonard **3**:515
LECKKERUM, John **11**:75
LEDER, Frederick **3**:328
LEDERER, Johan Paulus **3**:454
LEDERMAN, Hans Peter **3**:414
LEDILE, Andrew **16**:542
LEDLIE, Andrew **9**:756
Andrew (Dr.) **11**:95
D. Andrew **15**:224-225, 344, 471,
  583
William **9**:623, 688
LEDREE, Joseph **11**:666
LEDTREMAN, Jacob **4**:60
LEE, --- **13**:669
--- (Adj.) **14**:422
--- (Capt.) **12**:52, 210, 245, 255,
  439
--- (Col.) **13**:710, 712, 756, 758;
  14:63, 408
--- (Gen.) **10**:753; **11**:348
--- (Gov.) **12**:400
--- (Lt. Gov.) **12**:638
--- (Maj.) **12**:210, 235, 521
--- (Mr.) **11**:204
Andrew **13**:568; **14**:130, 165, 436
Anthony **4**:762; **5**:388
Apt. **8**:431
Edward **3**:516; **12**:69
Elizabeth **13**:282
Francis **12**:553; **13**:168; **14**:252
George (Sir) **5**:618
James **14**:512, 613-614
John **9**:584; **11**:86, 110, 166-167,
  251; **13**:62, 594; **15**:68, 440;
  16:395
Joseph **9**:584
Joseph Brown **10**:678
Rachel **15**:285
Richard Henry **11**:569-570, 613,
  737; **14**:270-271
Robert **12**:188
Stephen **9**:584
Thomas **4**:698; **5**:423-424, 470;
  9:699; **15**:285
Will. **1**:267
Willm. **2**:108, 163, 397
LEECH, Archibald **14**:312
Benjamin **13**:31
Isaac **3**:289; **4**:85, 98, 309, 352,
  482
Jacob **5**:193, 325
Thomas **4**:363-364, 459, 523; **5**:91,
  416; **7**:249, 635-636, 772, 776,
  783; **8**:9, 37, 39, 52, 54, 66,
  72, 75, 110, 112, 170-171, 335,
  396-397, 443; **11**:56
Tobiah **13**:31
Tobias **1**:158 (See LEACH)
Toby **2**:147-148, 152, 539-541, 543
William **11**:156-157, 160, 162
LEECHE, Francis **10**:116
LEED, Jacob **14**:296, 303, 416
LEELY, Isaac **14**:127
LEEMAN, Peter **3**:290

LEEPE, Orick 3:288
LEEPER, James 12:145
LEEPER (LIEPER), Charles 11:120, 229
LEEPHART, Valentine 16:460
LEES, James 13:449
 William 11:357
LEES (See DAVIDSON &) 15:647; 16:4
LEESTER, Richard 14:103
 Thomas 13:624; 14:425
LEET, Daniel 13:38, 531; 14:245, 577, 620; 15:138; 16:147-148, 439, 448
 David 13:240
 Edward 4:101-102, 104, 106, 108, 147
 William 16:147
LEFEVER, Jacob 16:160
 John 5:577
LEFFERTY, Peter 11:281
LEFFLER, George Lewis 14:234, 557
LEFLER, George Lewis 13:397, 723
LEGA, Edward 12:280
LEGATE, John 10:584
LEGGE, Henry 5:618
LEGGIT, George 5:325
 Thomas 5:325
LEHAY, --- (Capt.) 5:113
LEHMAN, Christian 10:9-10
 Christopher 3:414
 Gottfried 3:417
 Johan Christian 3:417
 Ludwig 3:454
 Samuel 15:384
LEIB, George 14:656
 Michael 14:558, 561; 16:61
 Nicholas 14:127, 439
LEIBERT, John 15:256
 Nicholas 16:544
LEIBY, Elizabeth 15:357
LEIDENPINNER, Joseph 14:306, 436
LEIMBACK, Daniel 16:224, 444
LEIPER, Thomas 13:305, 320; 16:539
LEIPER (LEEPER, LIEPER), Charles 14:236, 478; 15:102, 300, 577-578
LEISLEAR, Jacob 1:332
LEISNER, --- (Mr.) 10:782
LEISURE, John 14:199
LEITHISER, Jacob 16:460
LEIVZ(E)Y, Thomas 9:237, 240
LELAND, Thomas 12:341
LELEGHANAN 13:464
LEM(M)ON, John 5:584, 586, 591-595
LEMAN, Christian 3:385
 Hendirck 1:127
 John 14:8
 Tom 7:774
LEMANE, Phil. 1:106
LEMBOCH, Frederick 11:212, 269
LEMEISTER, Willhem 12:608
LEMES, Christopher 9:481, 483, 506, 508, 673
LEMMON, Thomas 10:43
LEMON, John 16:212
 Patrick 13:154
 Thomas 9:390, 392
LEMONS, John 12:393
LEMONT, Elizabeth 13:353
LEMOYTUNGH (LEMOYTAUGH) 2:15; 4:338, 340, 589
LENASCOKANA 8:723
LENES, Samuel 6:649
LENHART, Godfrey 16:492
LENINGTON, Timothy 15:399
LENMAR, Philip Thomas 1:47

LENNICK, Michael 14:434
LENNOTT, William 11:284
LENNOX, David 13:755; 14:38, 455, 492, 511; 15:74
LENOX, David 10:447; 11:287; 12:537
 Grafton Richmond 4:471
 Hugh 11:43; 13:341
 William, Jr. 11:289, 291-292
LENROYTUNGH (LERNOYTUNG) 3:601, 603
LENSEN, Jno. 2:493
LENSENNS, Hans 3:386
LENTZ, Hans David 3:456
 John 3:432
LEO, Edmund 14:295, 302, 426
 William 14:295
LEOH (LESH), Peter 14:88, 428
LEONARD, Ezekiel 15:98-99, 296, 566; 16:192
 Frederick 14:97, 424
 John 9:584
 Joseph 12:39
 Leonard 13:591
 Lydia 11:530
 Thomas 7:467
 William 9:584; 11:775; 12:187
LEONIX (LENOX), George 14:131-132, 418
LEOP, Christopher 14:8
LEOPER (LOEPER), Charles 11:69, 72
LEPAGHPETUND 7:677, 681
LEPERT, Adam 3:290
LEPFORD, Thomas 13:327
LEPLEY, Mary Anne 16:420
 Michael 15:358
LEPPER, --- (Capt.) 10:693
LERMITTE (LER MITTE), Isaac 10:358, 362
LERYSTEIN, Hans Martin 3:284
LES(E)Y, Samuel 14:615
LESAN, John 5:210
LESCHINSKEY, Sigismund 12:194
LESH, Jacob 10:156
LESHER, --- 11:282
 Frederick 11:74
 George 12:182
 Jacob 3:520
 John 6:760; 12:372, 635; 14:184, 529
 Leonard 16:106, 401
 Margaret 12:635
LESHINCKSY, Siegumnd 13:82
LESK, Peter 13:632
LESLER, George Lewis 13:93
LESLIE, --- (Mr.) 6:383, 394, 408, 415 (See LESSLEY)
 Robert 15:380, 387, 618; 16:180, 220, 488
 William 12:681
LESNET, --- 16:38
LESSLEY, Matthew 6:489 (See LESLIE)
 William 14:612
LESTER, John 3:542, 587
 Leonard 11:10
 Peter 2:108-109
LESTOR (LESTER), John Smith 15:13, 26
LETHERMAN, Peter 14:124, 128
LETORT, Jaques 1:436
LETTS, Ezekiel 10:450
 James 15:372
LEUISTANWALLNOR, Johan 3:515
LEVAN 8:143
LEVAN, --- (Mr.) 13:102-104, 106, 109-111, 114, 116-117, 119-121, 123, 127-128, 132-133, 135, ->

LEVAN, --- (Mr.) (continued)
13:137, 193, 222-223, 228,
234-235, 237, 239-242, 262-266,
268-281, 283-284, 286, 288-296,
298-305, 308, 310-311, 313-319,
323-324, 326, 328-331, 335-343,
345, 347-348, 350-535, 356-360,
362-363, 365-370, 372-374, 376,
378-379, 381-386, 388, 390,
394-395, 397-399, 402-404, 409,
411, 413, 417, 425, 430-432,
435, 437, 439-444, 446, 448-454,
458-460
  Daniel 11:186-187, 358, 500, 526,
532; 13:603, 751; 14:60, 236,
478; 15:357, 383, 458; 16:31,
372, 538
  Daniel, Jr. 13:701
  Isaac 9:778; 12:131; 16:31, 372
  Isaac, Jr. 10:56, 537, 714; 11:358
  Isaac, Sr. 11:358
  Jacob 5:612; 8:562; 9:172, 340
  Sebastian 11:36, 256, 358, 633;
12:164; 13:88, 100, 112, 238,
243, 289, 326, 379-380, 414,
442, 461, 471, 473, 476,
478-482, 484-485, 491, 493, 496,
503, 516, 521-523, 530-531, 534,
538, 540-541, 544-547, 549-552,
554, 559, 561-567, 570-571,
574-576, 578-579, 582-585,
588-589, 591, 594-595, 597-603,
605-607, 609-611, 613-615,
618-623, 625-626, 639, 641-642,
645, 647, 670, 672, 674,
677-678, 681, 684, 686, 691-692,
699, 702, 706-707, 711, 719,
721, 724-725, 747, 775-776;
14:1-6, 24-25, 27-28, 37-38,
41-44, 54-55, 65, 75, 80,
103-105
LEVAR, Dan'l. 3:619
LEVENS, Robert 13:91
LEVERIN, Aaron 10:670
LEVERING, --- (Capt.) 10:765
  Anthony 16:122
  Griffith 13:503
  Jeremiah 12:686
  John 14:611; 15:26
  Nathan 14:181
  Septimus 10:239, 243
  Wickart 13:615
  William 11:6
LEVERS (LOVERS), Robert 9:245, 308;
10:156; 11:2, 187, 191, 212,
228, 260, 307, 309, 330, 401,
478-479, 504, 525, 528, 557,
583, 706; 12:47, 316, 646, 703,
767, 769, 777; 13:21, 44, 74,
102, 150, 193, 310, 402, 526,
617, 701; 14:9, 15, 23, 67,
154-155, 174, 217, 231, 634;
15:248, 279, 298, 460-461;
16:323
LEVERSWELL, Jacob 10:605
LEVI, Nathan 14:610
LEVINGSTON, --- (Mr.) 12:198
LEVINS, --- (Mr.) 13:370
  Jane Mary 13:399
LEVIS, --- (Justice) 12:433
  Joseph 5:193
  Saml. 2:33 (See LEWIS)
  Saml1. 1:320, 607, 614
  Samuel 3:428, 431; 4:283, 285,
287, 406, 628, 752; 5:108, 203,
303; 9:627

LEVIS, Thomas 11:256, 328, 330,
339, 455, 479, 504, 535; 12:245,
257, 298, 651; 13:392; 15:392;
16:190, 303
  William 12:715
LEVY, --- (Miss) 11:676
  Aaron 11:678; 13:684; 16:316
  Asher 12:258
  Benjamin 8:576
  Cornelius 12:256
  Eleazer 12:737
  Hannah 13:511
  Hayman 11:108, 525
LEVY (SEE SIMON &) 11:85
LEWELLEN, --- (Capt.) 13:191
LEWELLYN, David 3:231
LEWELLYN (LEWELLIN), Griffith
4:482, 495, 762
LEWES, Saml1. 1:438
LEWES (LEWIS), --- (Maj.) 7:133
LEWIS, --- 1:435-436
  --- (Capt.) 9:214
  --- (Maj.) 12:747
  --- (Mr.) 11:290; 13:188, 192,
194, 201; 15:481, 544
  Abraham 11:529
  Alexander 11:60
  Ann 8:496
  Curtis 10:115; 11:494, 745; 13:735
  Daniel 2:203
  David 2:106, 111; 5:444
  Ellis 12:577
  Evan 2:397; 3:256
  Ezekiel 14:324
  Francis 10:421; 12:708
  Francis, Jr. 13:549
  Harvey 11:255
  Henry 2:480; 3:615; 11:281
  Henry (Henrie) 1:48, 74, 155, 159,
176, 209, 601
  Isaac 16:334-335
  Jacob 9:657, 703, 781; 10:47, 66,
69-70, 113, 117
  James 1:550; 4:483; 5:325; 13:163
  Jehu 13:777
  John 8:496; 10:113, 498, 585;
12:57; 14:204, 426; 15:246, 255,
285
  Joseph 12:480; 13:582; 14:97, 424
  Lemuel 16:7
  Mordecai 15:423-424
  Nathan 9:701; 10:114; 11:340
  Peter 1:579
  Phenias 3:620
  Robert 10:651, 656, 682, 690, 733;
11:35, 66
  Saml. 2:283, 397 (See LEVIS)
  Saml1. 1:169, 370, 454, 477, 601,
621
  Samuel 16:7
  Thomas 13:173; 14:53, 212, 512,
522, 599, 601, 619, 647, 663
  William 11:124, 137; 12:324, 335,
572, 582, 744; 13:136, 621;
14:463; 15:446; 16:456, 459
  Wrixam 7:267; 10:81, 217
  Wrixman 9:203
LEWIS (SEE SHERMAN &) 11:105
LEWIS XIV, King of France 5:359
LEX (SEE HERPST &) 16:415
LEXINGTON, --- (Lord) 6:264
LEYB, Johannes 3:284
LEYMAN, --- (Maj.) 6:268
LEYNARD, Richard 13:604
LEYRE, William 14:8
LIBEKIP, Paul 3:368

115

LIBENSTEIN, Johan George 3:429
LIBHART, Jacob 4:60
LICHTENIN, Hans 3:454
LICHTNER, Hans Jorig 3:456
LIEBERTZ, Philip 13:741
LIEBY, Friedrich 3:515
LIEPER, Charles 16:32
 Thomas 11:426; 12:256
LIER, Henry 3:290
LIGHBURN, John 10:759, 769
LIGHT, Jacob 12:577; 16:122
 John 13:758; 14:409, 439
 Peter 14:454
LIGHTB(O)URNE, John 11:629, 636
LIGHTBOY, --- (Mr.) 10:563-564
LIGHTFOOT, --- (Ens.) 8:386
 Benjamin 5:597, 612, 662; 6:144;
  8:562; 9:563, 673; 10:54
 Francis 11:669
 Samuel 5:547, 572; 7:417; 8:142,
  573
 Thomas 8:242; 11:269; 12:496-497;
  13:18
LIGHTS, Peter 13:578
LIGONIER, John (Sir) 5:618
LIGORE, John 12:333
LIKENBERGER, Frederick 3:385
LIKENS, Catharine 13:169
LILE, John 13:346
LILITTAS 7:478
LILL(E)Y, Thomas 11:371, 479, 504,
  633
LILLEY, --- (Mr.) 13:125-126
 Thomas 13:93, 112, 397, 415
LILLINGTON, Edward 1:370
LILLY, --- (Mr.) 13:671, 673;
  15:306, 392; 16:205, 212
 Joseph 14:234, 250, 557
 Thomas 12:513; 14:208; 16:444
LILLY (NEGRO) 13:451
LIMBACH (LIMBACK), David 13:638
 Frederick 13:723; 14:174, 185, 261
LIMBACK, Frederick 13:74, 91, 102
LIMBOCH, Frederick 12:298
LIMIS, John 4:101
 Thomas 4:102, 108
 William 4:101
LIN, William 5:454
LINARD (LYNYARD), Richard 14:90,
  422
LINASS, John 4:102
 Thomas 4:102
 William 4:102
LINCE, Denis 1:95
LINCEY, Thomas 1:64
LINCH (LYNCH), John (Patrick)
  12:312, 324, 350-351, 353, 361
LINCOLN, --- (Gen.) 13:323
 --- (Maj. Gen.) 13:164, 432, 460,
  479, 731
 Abraham 13:393, 415, 720, 737;
  14:250, 554; 16:122
 Benjamin 13:254
 Hannaniah 10:741
 Mordecai 3:304, 491
LINCORN, Abraham 14:232
LINDEMOTH, --- (Col.) 11:654
LINDEMUTH, --- (Col.) 12:566, 721
LINDENMUTH, Michael 11:471
LINDER, Michael 4:59
 Simon 3:516
 Simon, Jr. 3:516
LINDERMUTH, Michael 15:249; 16:90,
  187, 373, 428
LINDERSMITH, George 13:679

LINDLEY (LINSLEY), Demus 13:740;
  14:214; 16:227, 294
 Jacob 11:426-427
 Susanna 13:270
 Thomas 3:227, 230; 4:313
LINDON, Hugh 11:513, 516-517
LINDSAY, --- 11:584
 --- (Capt.) 5:548-549
 James 6:241
 John 12:285, 513; 13:87, 112, 392,
  415
 Robt. 1:439
 Samuel 12:665-666; 13:676; 14:87,
  416, 437
LINDSAYS, James 15:129
 Margaret 12:101
LINDSEY, Char. 9:509
 John 15:140
LINDSLEY, Isaac 16:227
LINDT, Mich'l. 11:362
LINDY, Uriah 11:514, 516-517
LINE, George 4:268
LINECHQUE 9:212
LINGAHNOA 13:467
LININGTON, John 11:590
LINK, Jacob 10:746
LINLD, Jacob 13:192, 229
LINLEY, John 13:94
 Joseph 13:94
LINN, Andrew 9:508; 11:398; 12:216,
  388; 14:312
 Felix 16:491
 Matthew 13:389
 William 9:508
 William (Rev.) 10:487
LINNEL, Thomas 7:717
LINNEY, Joseph 12:188
LINNINGTON, John 12:554; 13:6;
  14:488
LINNLATE, Robert 14:613
LINS, Tenniss 1:478
LINSENBEGLER, Paulus 3:452
LINSEY, Benjamin 13:565
 Thomas 15:119
LINTON, David 15:540; 16:125
 John 13:174
LIONS, Solomon 13:271
LIPHART, Henry 4:67
LIPPENONT (LIPPENENT), Jedidiah
  14:298, 305, 434
LIPPS, Henricus 3:455
LIRCH, Anthony 11:760
LISCHER, Jacob 3:457
LISK, Morris (Maurice) 11:510-511,
  583
LISLE, Henry 11:494
 John 11:234, 238, 286, 306, 494
 Robert 11:494
LISLEY, David 3:369
 Jacob 3:368
LISLIE, Maurice 3:91
LISTON, Edmund 5:89, 93, 117-118
LIT(T)LE, John 11:1, 41, 114, 423,
  448
 William 11:598
LITCHFIELD, Henry 13:322, 326-328
 Mary 1:166-167
LITE, Daniel 12:681
LITMAN, Henry 10:668
LITMAN (LITINAN), Henry 11:15, 56
LITTELER, --- (Lt.) 6:490
LITTLE, --- (Capt.) 10:379
 Andrew 10:765
 Christian 15:646
 Christiana 16:486

117

LOGAN, James (continued) 2:239-241,
243-244, 247-248, 251-253, 255,
258, 261-262, 266, 275-276,
278-281, 283-284, 289, 297-299,
308-309, 315-316, 318, 320-321,
323, 328, 336-337, 343-348,
356-357, 361-364, 366, 369-370,
376-379, 383, 385-386, 391-397,
403-404, 406-407, 412-413, 414,
416, 426-429, 432, 434-435, 437,
439, 441-443, 446-449, 451-452,
459, 461, 463, 465-470, 472-473,
477-479, 482, 484-486,
489-491,493-495, 502-503,
506-508, 545-546, 549-553,
555-557, 559, 563, 566-568,
571-573, 575-580, 582-587,
589-591, 594-599, 601, 603-607,
609-611, 613-614, 625, 629, 631;
3:14-19, 21, 25, 27-33, 37-39,
43-45, 50, 52, 55-58, 62-69, 71,
75, 81-82, 85, 90-93, 98-99,
102-103, 105, 107-109, 111,
113-115, 120-123, 125, 130, 134,
138-141, 143-145, 147-148,
155-158, 160-166, 170-172, 175,
178, 180, 187, 189-193, 196,
203, 209, 212, 214, 216, 218,
221-222, 232, 236-245, 251-254,
256-258, 261, 263-264, 266-267,
269, 271, 276, 278-285, 287,
289, 291, 293, 295, 298,
302-303, 305, 307-309, 316,
320-324, 326-327, 329, 331-333,
338, 340, 343-344, 346, 359,
361, 364, 366-367, 369, 374-376,
379-384, 393, 399, 401-404, 406,
409-410, 412-413, 418, 422,
425-426, 430, 433, 435, 437-438,
442, 446, 459, 463-464, 467,
474, 479, 491, 502-503, 524,
528-529, 534-535, 537, 539-540,
542, 544-545, 563, 571, 574,
591-592, 601, 603, 607, 609,
612, 614, 617; 4:17, 20-21, 23,
26, 32-33, 39-41, 47-49, 51, 53,
56, 58, 60, 63-64, 66, 70-73,
75, 79-82, 85-87, 89-90, 95-97,
100, 104, 106, 112-113, 115-117,
119-120, 124, 129-130, 136,
139-141, 143-144, 146-147,
149-153, 155, 157-159, 165-167,
174-175, 181, 186, 190, 194-196,
198, 201-203, 205-206, 208-210,
224-229, 232-233, 235, 238, 241,
243-250, 253-254, 256-260,
262-264, 266, 269, 273-274, 277,
280, 282-285, 288, 306-307,
309-310, 336-337, 340-341, 343,
345, 347-348, 546, 560, 563,
566, 569, 572-580, 582-583,
587-588, 699, 709, 711; 5:84,
147-149, 151; 6:35, 529, 640,
649; 7:49; 9:102; 13:468; 14:528
John 14:188; 15:290, 432-433, 435;
16:187, 210b, 233
Samuel 15:31
Susana 11:666
William 5:67-68, 70-72, 74, 89,
90, 92, 105, 108, 110, 120-121,
124, 127, 132, 136, 139-140,
143, 145, 147-148, 154, 156,
158, 162-163, 167, 188, 193-194,
198, 200, 205, 208, 212, 215,
220-221, 229, 232, 235, 238,
248, 252, 256-260, 264-265, ->

LOGAN, William (continued)
5:269-270, 273-274, 280, 284,
289, 297-300, 306-307, 311-312,
316, 318-319, 328, 338-339, 343,
345, 365, 367, 378-380, 387-388,
390-391, 396, 398, 403, 405,
410-411, 421, 426, 431, 451,
456, 460-461, 464, 467-468, 470,
488-490, 492, 506, 512-513, 516,
525, 527-528, 545, 548, 550,
559-560, 562, 565, 572, 580,
582, 598, 606, 657; 6:57, 132,
144, 188, 193, 204, 220,
360-361, 639, 666, 755, 762,
765, 778, 781, 783; 7:1, 3, 5,
55-56, 58-59, 70, 74, 78, 83,
87, 97, 105, 107, 135, 144-145,
151-152, 163, 204-207, 216, 220,
222, 228, 230, 247, 249, 251,
265-266, 280, 305, 308, 313,
317-319, 321, 326, 328, 332,
336, 338, 344, 354, 361, 383,
393, 396, 407, 429, 441, 459,
462, 464-465, 484, 487-488, 495,
500, 505, 513, 516-518, 522,
527-528, 534, 543, 546, 592,
635, 637, 649, 652, 656,
659-660, 663, 665, 671, 679-680,
687-688, 692, 711, 713; 8:31-32,
40-42, 86-87, 89, 99, 112, 116,
122, 124-125, 128, 146, 148,
173-175, 217-219, 223, 242,
244-245, 333, 360, 362, 372,
402, 405, 409, 412, 415, 422,
463, 467, 472, 721, 723, 725,
729, 750, 757, 772-775; 9:12,
17, 20, 24-25, 30-31, 37, 42,
44, 63, 66, 73, 77, 85, 88, 93,
101-101, 123, 125, 128, 132,
135, 146, 148, 170, 172, 192,
201-202, 204-205, 315, 426-427,
430, 432, 435, 446, 450, 459,
465, 467, 481, 488, 490, 492,
510-512, 514, 547-548, 554, 562,
569, 589, 603-604, 627, 629,
642, 645, 648, 650-651, 653-655,
658, 660, 663, 666, 674,
688-689, 693-694, 699, 704,
719-721, 733, 735, 737, 739,
745-746, 750, 752, 760, 767,
773, 776-778, 780, 782; 10:1,
15, 23-24, 27, 43, 45, 55-56,
61, 90, 99, 110, 180, 206, 210,
213, 224, 227, 230, 232-233,
237, 239, 247, 251, 254, 256,
261, 265, 270
LOGAN, William Portsmouth 12:177
LOGSDON, John 5:593, 596
LOGUE, John 16:51, 93
LOHR, Andreas 3:453
LOHRA, Peter 15:527
LOLLAR, --- (Mr.) 13:448; 15:70,
303, 583
Robert 12:5, 95, 111, 131, 189,
326, 463, 534, 567; 13:102, 503,
618, 625; 16:156, 169, 444, 446
LOLLAR (LOLLER, LOLLUR), Robert
11:330, 434, 475, 488, 633,
639, 759; 14:230, 250, 555
LOMBARB, Casper 4:100
LONARB, Johan Jorig 4:60
LONDON, --- (Earl of) 8:332
LONE, James 14:189, 193, 438
LONES, Griffith 1:206 (See JONES,
Griffith)
LONG, --- 14:581

118

LOWE, Joshua **4**:86, 309, 352-353,
470, 500
William **3**:471-472, 476, 479, 482;
13:14
LOWER, Adam **3**:452
Christian **11**:466; **13**:415
Christian Laver **6**:443
Christian, Jr. **12**:164
Hartman **3**:452
John **11**:340
Michael **12**:626
Peter **11**:46-47
LOWERS, --- (Capt.) **10**:710
LOWMAN, Hans Jerig **3**:290
Ludwig **11**:328, 434, 575
Saml **2**:121
Samuel **3**:253
LOWNE, Caleb **12**:102
LOWNES, Caleb **13**:278
John **13**:334; **14**:323, 326, 347;
16:232
William **14**:33
LOWREY, Alexander **15**:91, 98, 244,
307, 532
John **10**:555
LOWRIE, Jno. **1**:549
LOWRY, --- (Mr.) **11**:434
Alexander **12**:508, 576, 631, 664;
14:447, 556
James **5**:438, 461, 481, 483, 663;
6:143, 431; **7**:154-155, 157-158;
16:277
Lazarus **7**:154-155
Samuel **12**:354
Stephen **11**:116
Thomas **10**:784
William **11**:82
LOWRY (SEE HUNT &) **10**:313
LOWTHER, George **2**:115, 136, 151,
226
LOXLEY, --- (Mr.) **7**:737
Benjamin **6**:770; **10**:285, 342, 407,
428, 438, 441, 447, 520, 555,
573, 580, 591, 622-623, 626,
641, 656, 657, 688, 695,
734-735, 754, 778; **11**:17, 23,
32, 77, 107-108, 131, 601, 603,
766, 770, 782
LUBCHEN, George **3**:570
LUBE, Frederick **14**:611
LUCAS, --- (Capt.) **11**:157, 160
John **14**:311-312
Mary **12**:2
Richard **14**:62, 86, 413
Robt. **1**:48, 87
Thomas **11**:65
LUCK(E)Y, Joseph **14**:260, 321
LUCKEN, Jno. **2**:541
LUCKEY, Joseph **12**:446; **13**:217
LUCKHART, Christopher **16**:387
LUCKY, Joseph **11**:511
LUCQUEST **9**:228
LUD(A)GAR, Peter **1**:241, 243-245
LUDI, Samuel **3**:524
LUDOWICK, John M. **14**:613
LUDWICK, --- (Mr.) **11**:303
Char. **10**:528
Christ'r. **10**:398, 421, 467, 482,
493
George **12**:608
LUDWICK (LUDWIG), Christopher
11:32, 595
John **11**:57, 195
LUDWIG, Christopher **12**:131
Daniel **3**:518; **14**:554; **15**:98, 202;
16:535

LUDWIG, John **13**:393; **14**:170-171;
15:577; **16**:224
Michl **3**:518
LUELLON, Morris **1**:438
LUES, Davis **1**:438
LUFF, Nathaniel **11**:34
LUGEE, Mark **16**:391
LUKE, --- **11**:478
LUKEMBURG, Johan Ekel **3**:385
LUKENS, --- (Mr.) **10**:784; **13**:331,
678
Charles **11**:219
Daniel **10**:593
Derrick **12**:445
J. **13**:322
John **10**:88; **12**:67, 233, 252, 621,
635, 651, 689, 703-704, 714,
722, 727, 779; **13**:50, 65, 123,
130, 146, 148, 295, 321-322,
388, 685, 724, 776; **14**:370, 394,
444, 447, 454, 512, 583, 653;
15:49; **16**:137, 185, 199, 208
Matthew **13**:121
Matthias **14**:235, 459; **16**:69
Peter **10**:738
LUKINS, Nathaneil **1**:439
LUKINS (LUKENS), Charles **10**:212,
271
John **9**:627, 781
LUMBECK, Henry **11**:269
LUMM, John **7**:717
LUMSDALE, Robert **15**:576
LUMSDEN, Robert **11**:112, 544
LUNAN, Alexander **14**:506
LUND(A)Y, Ebenezer **10**:684, 711,
715, 726, 761, 779
LUNDY, Ebenezer **11**:19, 82, 129
LUNEN, --- (Mr.) **7**:132
LUNNING, Philip **13**:14
LUPTON, John **15**:95, 209
Joseph **3**:289, 370
LURCH, William **12**:608
LURNEN, John **2**:493
LUSH, Ely **1**:439
George **10**:301, 333, 365, 382, 441,
542
Jacob **10**:600, 728, 760; **11**:26, 50
LUSH (LUSK), William **14**:86, 427
LUSK, --- (Capt.) **12**:774
Hugh **11**:350
John **11**:78
William **10**:451; **12**:92; **13**:713, 777
LUSS, Conrad **12**:608
LUTET, Jane **12**:343
LUTHER, John **15**:4
LUTRIDGE, --- (Mr.) **6**:61
LUTTERLISH, --- (Col.) **11**:409
LUTTINGTON, Asa **9**:711
LUTUK **8**:337
LUTZ, --- (Col.) **13**:427
Jacob **16**:154, 161, 205
Johan Philip **3**:414
Nicholas **12**:302, 306, 310, 364,
372, 394, 411, 445, 722;
13:58-59, 362, 421, 581, 720;
14:133, 171, 232, 250, 438, 554;
15:294, 565; **16**:192, 211b, 444
LUTZ (LUTE), Jacob **14**:407, 409, 439
LUX & BOWLEY **12**:12
LUX (LUA), George **12**:12
LUZERNE, Dela (Chevalier) **13**:284
LYBERT, Michael **3**:285
LYCON, Andrew **5**:441-443, 445, 448;
7:155

LYD(D)IUS, John **6**:111-112, 117,
183, 248-249, 251, 257, 269,
271-275, 277, 284, 286, 289,
291-293, 473
LYDIE, Jacob **3**:288
LYDINS, --- **10**:178
LYDIUS **5**:72, 74, 774
LYDIUS, Margaret **6**:293
LYELL, William **11**:199
LYINBURGER, Hans **3**:607
Hans, Jr. **3**:607
LYING, Charles **12**:119
LYKIN, Neils **2**:480
LYLE, Robert **9**:206
LYMAN, Daniel **9**:571
James **14**:297, 304, 431
Peter (Maj. Gen.) **6**:608, 611
Phineas **6**:260
LYN, Felix **11**:212
LYNCH, James **11**:145; **14**:312
John **11**:214; **15**:110
Patrick **16**:212b
Terence **12**:342
LYNE, Balzer **3**:288
George **6**:648
James **9**:509
LYNN, Felix **10**:156
John **11**:605
William **13**:575
LYON, Benjamin **11**:578-579
James **11**:367
John **12**:166
Mary **15**:119
Samuel **9**:732; **13**:514, 698
Thomas **14**:115
William **12**:47, 647; **13**:703; **16**:32,
443, 487
LYON(S), Charles **14**:488, 492, 532
Samuel **11**:229, 565-566; **12**:302,
306, 310, 371, 411
William **9**:201, 444, 448, 450, 491,
510-512, 673, 732; **10**:756,
758-766, 768-773; **11**:54, 58,
60-64, 66-69, 72, 75-77, 93-97,
99, 101-102, 104-105, 107-109,
111, 113-115, 117-122, 124-127,
130-143, 145, 178, 221, 244,
694, 697; **14**:75, 264, 407, 409,
440, 477
LYONS, --- (Lt.) **12**:355
Philip **14**:504
Samuel **13**:222, 311, 515; **16**:216
LYPERSBERGER, Jacob **3**:458
LYSLE, William **10**:506
LYT(T)LE, Andrew **12**:334, 437
LYTLE, Aaron **16**:24
Andrew **11**:115; **13**:715, 753, 766,
777; **14**:62, 85, 91, 124, 127,
409, 423, 431, 436-437, 440;
15:383, 458-459
John **16**:189
LYTTLE, --- (Capt.) **13**:764
Andrew **13**:508, 510-511

M'ALISTER, John **13**:395; **14**:81, 243
M'ALLISTER, Richard **13**:723
M'CALL, Joseph **12**:513
M'CALLA, --- (Mr.) **13**:101
Thomas (Dr.) **13**:712
William **13**:67, 165
M'CALLISTER, Abdiel **12**:513
Daniel **14**:219

M'CALMONT, James **15**:286-287, 318,
527
M'CAMMON (MC CAMMON), John **15**:260,
266
M'CANN, Catharine **15**:119
M'CANNAUGHY, David **10**:101, 163
M'CANNY, William **12**:314
M'CAPE, Patrick **16**:305
M'CARKEY, Felix **11**:366
M'CARTE, Dennis **14**:615
M'CARTER, Charles **14**:219
M'CARTHY, Dennis **14**:615
John **14**:615
M'CARTNEY, Laughlin **11**:368
M'CASLAND, Samuel **13**:597
M'CASLIN, James **13**:680
Mark **11**:55
Samuel **13**:680
M'CAUSLAND, Mark **10**:79, 84
M'CAWLEY, Cornelius **11**:195
Robert **13**:273
M'CILTON, Margaret **15**:119
M'CLAIN, Moses **13**:723
M'CLAY, William **13**:92; **16**:243, 390
M'CLEAN (MC CLEAN, MC LEAN),
Alexander **13**:168, 252-254, 334,
519
Archibald **13**:9, 674, 701; **15**:15,
17
James **11**:79, 210, 215, 217, 227,
317, 366, 616-620, 622-626,
628-632, 634-642, 683-685, 691,
693-694, 696-699, 701-705,
707-710, 713-714, 724, 741
John **14**:93-94
Joseph **16**:460
Moses **12**:513, 662
M'CLEERY, William **13**:403, 443
M'CLELLAN (M'CLELLAND), John
13:682, 713; **14**:83, 86, 217,
411, 415, 427, 590, 592, 612
William **15**:297
M'CLENAHAN, Blair **13**:307
M'CLINTOCK, Alexander **13**:777
Sarah **13**:777
M'CLISTER, Francis **13**:306
M'CLOSHEY (MC CLOSKEY), Samuel A.
14:87, 434
M'CLOSKY, Samuel (Dr.) **13**:596
William (Dr.) **13**:758
M'CLUNE, William **11**:367
M'CLURE, James **13**:456, 713
M'COLLOM, Hugh **13**:575
M'COMB, William **13**:135; **15**:121
M'CONNAUGHY, David **13**:723
M'CONNEL, Margaret **13**:442
M'CONNELL, Matthew **13**:273-274, 713
Patrick **13**:214
M'COOMBS, William **14**:597
M'CORD, Isaiah **14**:613-614
Thomas **14**:86, 413
M'CORMICK, Alexander **16**:461
George **13**:443
James **11**:119
M'CORTLEY, Michael **14**:432
M'COSKRY, William **9**:199
M'COWAN, William **14**:418
M'CRACKEN, William **11**:181; **14**:590
M'CUE, Dennis **13**:135
M'CULLOCH, Joseph **11**:544
M'CULLOH, James **13**:482, 513
John **13**:346, 513
M'CULLOUGH, James **13**:221, 308
William **12**:599
M'CULLY (MC CULLY), George **14**:97,
409

M'CULTOM, Allen 11:673
M'CURDY, Daniel 14:217
  John 15:216
  Robert 11:145; 13:713
M'CURE (MC CLURE), Abdiel 14:127,
  435
M'DONALD, --- (Capt.) 10:671
  Alexander 13:183, 272, 430
  Arthur 14:614
  Godfrey 14:613, 615; 16:333
  John 9:521
  Richard 5:210
  Sarah 13:430
M'DORMAN, Patrick 15:119
M'DOWAL, William 15:80
M'DOWELL, --- (Dr.) 13:512
  Andrew 5:186
  Christina 12:343
  Henry 14:278, 362, 473
  James 15:66
  John 11:41; 13:392, 414, 452, 500,
    677
  John (Dr.) 14:80
  Joseph 15:191
  Robert 15:66
  Thomas 14:581
  William 14:132, 440, 471
M'DOWELL (MC DOWELL), --- (Mr.)
  13:409-412-413, 417-419,
    421-426, 430-432, 435, 437,
    439-444, 446, 448-455
  John 13:496-501, 503-515, 524,
    526-527, 530-532, 534, 536-538,
    540-541, 543-546, 615, 617-623,
    626-628, 630-633, 646-647,
    666-668, 670-675, 677, 681,
    683-684, 687, 691-696, 698, 719,
    721, 724-727, 729, 731-732,
    734-736, 738-742, 744, 746-748,
    750, 752-754,760-766, 768-776
M'ELROY, George 13:217
M'ELVAIN, Ferdinand 11:380
M'EURY, --- (Widow) 10:719
M'FALL, Archibald 14:93
M'FARLAND, John 16:165
  Mary 13:360
  William 13:443
M'FARLANE, Andrew 10:142, 169-171
M'FARREN, John, Jr. 13:265
  William 13:89
M'FEE, Cathareine 13:300
M'FETERIDGE, Thomas 10:61
M'GARRITY, Arthur 15:119
M'GARVEY, John 16:303
M'GASLIN, Patrick 14:92, 420
M'GAUGHEY, --- (Mr.) 13:672
  John 16:333
M'GAUGHY, Arthur 13:597
  James 9:549
M'GAW, --- (Col.) 10:600
M'GINNIS, John 15:19
M'GLAUGHLIN, Owen 13:594
M'GOWAN, John 13:712; 14:90, 100,
  413, 417, 430
M'GRADY, --- (Capt.) 13:428
M'GRAW, James 13:725
M'GUIRE, Barnabas 13:596
  Nathaniel 11:676
M'IBER, Elizabeth Bell 15:119
M'ILHATTON, William 13:713
M'ILNOSE, Isaac 14:127, 437
M'ILVAINE, Andrew 15:1
  John 14:88, 423
  Joseph 11:330, 340; 14:488
  Thomas 14:88, 423
M'INTIRE, James 13:597

M'INTIRE, Thomas 13:180
M'INTOSH, --- (Gen.) 14:662
M'KAY (MACKAY), Eneas (Aeneas)
  10:78, 141-142, 149, 166, 169,
  171
M'KEAN, Elizabeth 15:125
  Joseph Borden 15:34, 239, 629, 631
  Thomas 9:204, 626; 12:145, 490,
    578, 614, 783; 13:64, 101, 220,
    231.
M'KEE, James 11:367
  Robert 10:692
  Samuel 13:146
M'KEEVER, Isabella 14:534
M'KELLAR, Edward 14:417
M'KEWN, Margaret 12:346, 349
M'KEY (M'KEE), Alexander 10:78,
  142, 195, 200
M'KIM, John 13:109
  Thomas 9:626
M'KIMM, John 13:315
M'KINLEY, John 14:96, 217, 424, 432
  Peter 14:92, 420
M'KINNEY, Andrew 13:634
  David 12:513, 526
M'KNIGHT, Robert 12:332, 620
M'KONKY, Mary 13:337
M'LAUGHLIN, --- 7:16-17
M'LEAN, Archibald 14:615
  James 14:614
M'LENE, --- (Mr.) 13:125-126, 366
  James 11:424, 434-435, 455-456,
    498; 13:132, 257-258, 396, 726
  Thomas Brown 14:441-442
M'LENE (MC LENE, MC LEAN),
  Alexander 15:19, 608, 635
M'MAHAN, James 11:367
M'MAHON, John 14:615; 15:426
  Matthew 9:678
M'MAKEN, James 5:186
M'MANUS, John 14:88, 423
M'MANUS (MC MANUS), James 15:285,
  365, 429, 500
M'MASTERS, George 16:461
M'MINN, Robert 13:314
M'MULLAN, Hugh 14:614
M'MULLEN, James 11:514, 516-517
  John 16:461
  William 16:165
M'MURDIE (MC MURDY), --- (Rev.)
  12:421, 465
M'MURDY, Robert (Rev.) 13:714
M'NAIR, Andrew 10:54, 267
  Archibald 14:125, 432
  Christiana 13:507
M'PHERSON, --- (Mr.) 13:430, 734
  Robert 9:57, 199, 201; 13:723;
    14:234, 250
M'VEAUGH, --- (Col.) 13:211, 228
M'WARTERS, Thomas 10:699
M'WILLIAMS, Elizabeth 16:489
MAAG, Henry 11:244
MAC DANIEL, Daniel 4:135
MAC KEE, William 15:457
MAC MULLEN, --- 6:491
MAC NEMARA, Thomas 2:457
MAC PHERSON, --- (Maj.) 12:241
  John 10:292
MACCAY, William 15:520
MACCLELLAND (MC CLELLAN), John
  5:444, 469
MACCOLLIN, John 5:444
MACCONNELL (MC CONNELL), Adam 5:444
  Alexander 5:444, 469
  William 5:444, 469
MACCUBIN, --- (Capt.) 11:152

MACE, Jacob **11**:181
MACHAN, John **11**:99
MACHAROCHELLYTHA **7**:220
MACHBANKS, Mary **12**:257
MACHINE-UKA **8**:484
MACHLIN, Jacob **13**:730
John **14**:535
MACHMITAWCHCHINK **7**:220
MACHOLOHA **13**:465
MACK, Alexander **3**:368
Alexander, Junr. **3**:368
Felte **3**:368
Joannes **3**:368
Martin **5**:576
William **16**:377
MACKAY, David **13**:219
James **11**:79
Omas **11**:112
William **13**:620
MACKAY (MAC KEY), William **14**:127,
261, 434
MACKAY (MACKEY), John **11**:375-378,
466, 468-469, 471-472, 474-479,
486-490, 492-493, 495, 497, 499,
501-503, 506, 508-512, 518-520,
524-531, 533-535, 537, 541-544,
546, 548, 550-554, 556-567, 569,
571-574, 576-592, 595-596,
598-600, 606-609, 612-620,
622-626, 628-653, 655-661,
663-667, 672-680, 682-685, 691,
693-694, 696-699, 701-710,
713-724, 726-728, 732-733, 735,
738, 740-741, 743-745, 747-749,
751-762, 764, 766-767, 769, 771,
773, 775-776, 778-779, 781, 783;
12:1, 3-5, 7-11, 13, 15-20,
22-25, 27, 30-35, 37, 39-40,
42-46, 48-51, 54-58, 60, 62-71,
73-74, 76-77, 79-80, 82-88, 104,
106-109, 111-115, 117, 119, 121,
123-125, 127-128, 130, 151
Robert **11**:529, 670, 673
MACKENELLY, Hugh **4**:135
MACKENETT, Charles **11**:273
MACKENEY, Jno. **1**:134
MACKENNESS, Thomas **15**:82, 153
MACKENZIE, James Stuart **10**:103
MACKEY, David **12**:15, 105, 131-132,
150-151; **14**:260; **16**:89
James **10**:273-274; **14**:610
John **5**:75, 79; **16**:229, 316
Mary **16**:316
William **11**:521, 667; **12**:137, 202,
453; **16**:389
MACKINESS, Thomas **12**:27-28, 106,
197, 260
MACKINET(T), John **12**:27-28
MACKINTERFEER, John Jacob **3**:368
MACKLAY, William **10**:725
MACKLIN, Jacob **12**:540
MACKNAMARA, M. **6**:465
MACKRAN, Alexander **4**:135
MACKY, John **5**:252-253, 255-256
Robert **5**:210
MACLALOHA **13**:464
MACLANAJAN, --- (Mr.) **10**:496
MACLAY, --- **11**:566
--- (Mr.) **13**:132, 354, 356, 366,
410, 567; **14**:169, 171
Charles **11**:110
Samuel **10**:262
William **9**:673; **13**:112, 371, 398,
410, 415, 421, 426, 428, 494;
14:182, 186, 205, 441; **16**:1-7,
9-14, 100, 225, 243, 494

MACLAY (MC CLAY), Samuel **16**:319,
338-339, 347, 350, 436
William **10**:43, 47; **12**:305, 411
MACLELLAN, Alexander **9**:515
MACMANAC (MC MANNACK, MC MANAC),
William **3**:468-469, 472, 476
MACMEAN (MC MEANS), John **5**:444, 469
MACNAIR, Ralph **13**:607
MACOMAL **8**:189
MACOTTAWELOMA **5**:685
MACOY, William **15**:326
MACPHERSON, John **13**:13
William **11**:655, 657
MADAN, Samuel **14**:3
MADDEEN, Joseph **13**:758
MADDEN, Edward **14**:295, 302, 410
Joseph **14**:426
Thomas **12**:179
MADDISON, James **12**:213, 704
MADDOCK, Thomas **15**:163
William **11**:514, 516-517; **13**:251
MADDOX, Joshua **4**:482, 762; **5**:388,
572; **7**:769
MADERIA, Christian **16**:536
MADERY, Christian **15**:421
MADINGER, George Sebald **3**:410
MADISON, --- (Mr.) **13**:482
MADOLENE **8**:613
MADTER, Jacob **3**:593
MAFFET, Thomas **13**:392
William **14**:39
MAFFITS, Thomas **13**:112
MAGALAKUTWAY **8**:723
MAGARY, Michael **10**:61
MAGAW (MAGAU), --- (Col.) **16**:543
Robert **10**:443, 464, 470, 479, 490,
518, 754, 768; **11**:34, 124, 154,
156, 179-180; **13**:133, 579;
14:132, 236, 434
William **14**:92, 102, 419, 440
William (Dr.) **13**:563
MAGEE, --- (Capt.) **7**:148
--- (Commissioner) **11**:351
Dudley **14**:426
Henry **11**:611-612
James **14**:294 (See MC GEE)
John **11**:267-268
Peter **11**:432
Robert **11**:115
Thomas **7**:119
MAGEE (MC GEE), Daniel **14**:64, 90,
411
MAGINTY, Alexander **5**:662-664 (See
MC GINTY)
MAGOFFIN, --- (Mr.) **13**:354, 518;
14:188
Joseph **13**:415, 723
MAGUIRE, John **12**:479
Margaret **13**:32
Mathew **13**:562, 713; **14**:84
Matthew **13**:253
Peter **12**:575
MAHAN, John **13**:759
MAHN, Isaac **3**:142
Jurig Bernhardts **3**:454
MAHON, James **12**:187
John **13**:716; **14**:130
Thomas **14**:611
MAHONY **11**:123
MAHQUAHOTONOI **2**:509
MAIGHLING, Dewaldt **3**:618
MAILER, --- (Mr.) **12**:64
MAINS, William **10**:666, 680
MAIRES, Geo. **2**:33
MAIRS, John **16**:122
MA(I)SONVILLE, Alexander **9**:251

MARKOE, Abraham **13**:621
MARKS, Henry **14**:290
 Isaiah **13**:727
 John **11**:458; **14**:62, 124, 128, 299,
  309, 429, 432
 Joseph **8**:576
 Levi **14**:290
MARKY, Hans David **4**:73
 Marcus **4**:73
MARLBOROUGH, --- (Duke of) **9**:629
MARLBRO, --- (Duke of) **3**:71
MARLE, Thomas **11**:31, 33, 62, 134,
 138
MARMIE, Peter **16**:158-159
 Turnbull **14**:521
MARMIE (SEE TURNBULL & CO.)
 16:158-159, 324
MARMIE (SEE TURNBULL &) **15**:444,
 536, 616
MARN, Robert **10**:428, 511
MARNS, John **13**:474
MAROT, Pierre **3**:518
MAROTT, Philip **12**:49
MARPLE, Richard **14**:57
MARR, John **13**:710; **14**:89, 437
 Lawrence **11**:515-516, 518
MARRET (SEE HILL &) **10**:779
MARRIOTT, Samuel **15**:68
MARROQUIN **5**:199-200
MARROT (MARRIOTT) (SEE HILL &)
 11:24, 765
MARSH, --- **14**:587
 --- (Col.) **13**:661
 Benjamin **15**:440, 480
 Frederick **3**:368
 John **13**:136, 175, 507
 Joseph **10**:283, 328; **11**:117, 122,
  124-127, 182-183, 194; **13**:146;
  15:12
 Peter **12**:354
 Robt. **1**:89
 William **3**:43, 522-523
MARSHAL, Abraham **13**:467
 Edward **7**:400
 Hubert **6**:61
MARSHALL, --- **7**:621
 --- (Mr.) **11**:63, 159; **12**:132;
  15:599
 Abraham **10**:645
 Benjamin **10**:422, 705; **11**:88, 754;
  12:196, 356; **13**:589; **14**:34, 128,
  431, 506
 Charles **11**:12; **13**:136, 175, 507;
  14:149, 453
 Christian, Jr. **11**:12
 Christopher **11**:34-35, 39, 41, 47,
  81, 326, 343-344, 346-347,
  349-352; **12**:84; **13**:346; **14**:506
 Christopher, Jr. **14**:149, 453;
  16:51
 David **5**:325; **13**:557, 591, 718;
  14:93, 431
 Edward **8**:250, 254, 260; **13**:468
 George **13**:608; **14**:92, 425
 Humphrey **11**:213, 307
 James **3**:597; **10**:714, 723, 765-767;
  11:180, 220; **12**:681-683, 699,
  704; **13**:144, 150, 245, 546;
  14:15, 165, 214, 245, 247, 255,
  597; **15**:103, 107, 121, 160, 162,
  310, 517; **16**:32, 41, 280, 434,
  440, 444, 461
 John **11**:418-419, 427, 508; **12**:81,
  88-89, 355, 550; **13**:38, 443,
  564, 714, 757; **14**:132, 422;
  15:580

MARSHALL, Joseph **10**:235
 Moses **10**:744
 Vint. **4**:468
 William **10**:363, 367, 376-377;
  11:61, 233, 610-611, 615;
  13:642; **14**:215, 297, 304, 324,
  426; **15**:517
MARSHALLS, --- (Col.) **13**:297
MARSHE, --- **9**:702
 --- (Col.) **13**:98
 Thomas **10**:116
MARSHLAND, Hugh **1**:253
MARSTELLER, --- (Col.) **13**:673
 Philip **12**:46, 52, 57, 117, 203,
  306, 361, 372, 392, 443-444,
  459; **13**:426, 492, 496
MARSTELLER (MARSTILLER), Philip
  11:36, 272, 301, 317, 321, 368,
  388, 412, 417, 448, 493, 749
MARSTILLER, Johan Peter **4**:60
MART, Derrick **4**:60
MARTA, Henrick **3**:386
MARTEN, David **3**:288
 Jacob **3**:288
MARTI, Johannes **3**:607
MARTIN **7**:17
MARTIN, --- **15**:112; **16**:358, 361
 --- (Mr.) **12**:104
 --- (Widow) **13**:759
 Alexander **10**:692, 696-697; **13**:568;
  14:98, 431; **16**:304
 Anne **13**:382, 495
 Anthony **10**:384
 Arthur **14**:306, 435
 Barak (Barrack) **15**:205, 213
 Benjamin **15**:113; **16**:383, 385, 387
 Bernard **5**:115-116
 Caspar **3**:516
 Christian **13**:457
 Daniel **13**:769; **16**:455
 Eberhard **6**:760
 George **1**:144, 158-159, 186, 320,
  339, 431 (See MARTON); **5**:248;
  6:136; **9**:508
 Hans Georg. **3**:467
 Hans Henrick **3**:414
 Henry **10**:505; **11**:199, 694, 771,
  782; **13**:81, 510, 512, 554;
  14:99, 421; **15**:113, 307
 Hugh **11**:220; **13**:556; **14**:257; **15**:85
 Hugh (Dr.) **12**:270
 Ja's., Jr. **13**:777
 Jack **13**:360
 James **5**:209, 573; **7**:769; **9**:390,
  392; **11**:251, 302-303, 363,
  556-557, 581; **12**:372, 647;
  13:198, 624, 710; **14**:97, 133,
  232, 415, 419, 611, 617-618;
  15:126; **16**:212, 220, 222-224,
  209b-212b, 214b-224b, 225-226,
  228-232, 235-236, 238-244,
  251-252, 254-264, 267-268,
  270-274, 276, 278-291, 293,
  295-307, 309-313, 315, 318,
  320-324, 326-327, 329, 331-332,
  340, 344-346, 354-356, 376-384,
  386-390, 392-393, 395-396,
  399-406, 408-409, 419-429,
  432-435, 439, 441-442, 445-447,
  449-459, 461-465, 477, 479-484,
  487-488, 490-491, 497-501, 507,
  509-528, 530-531, 534-535,
  537-540, 543, 545-546
 Jeffrey **1**:452
 Jesse **9**:508

MARTIN, John 1:174; 5:444, 469;
  9:508; 10:40, 53-54, 703, 745;
  11:367; 13:49, 322, 326-327,
  684, 777; 14:157, 217, 237, 368,
  563, 619; 15:301, 347, 487
Jonathan 11:10
Joseph 11:97; 14:81, 99, 436;
  16:491
Miles 12:657, 760, 779; 13:50
Moses 4:269
Murdock 13:566
Peter 13:759; 14:129, 427; 16:426
Richard 3:491
Richd. 1:607
Robert 10:662; 11:34, 218, 368,
  726, 736, 782; 12:46, 53, 82,
  137, 164, 356, 493; 13:716, 741,
  758; 14:99, 116, 120, 319, 414,
  572; 16:15, 316, 516
Samuel 5:247; 9:49
Thomas 11:514, 516-517; 16:357
Walter 1:95; 2:103
William 10:72-73, 77, 563-564;
  12:720; 13:456, 586, 607, 713;
  14:298, 305, 365, 433, 609
MARTINDALE, Margaret 13:330;
  15:409-410
MARTINE 2:389
MARTON, George 1:149 (See MARTIN)
MARTSELLER, Philip 13:371
MARTY, Geo. 1:84
MARVIN, --- 9:584
Samuel 9:584
MARY, Queen 1:49-50, 302-305, 341,
  352, 357, 364, 423, 473, 484,
  492, 538; 2:241, 278, 294, 350
MARY (NEGRO) 13:154
MASEECHEINEN 6:360
MASERACRE, Joshua 12:51-52
MASH, George 12:577
MASKHILL, Lawrence 12:312
MASLAND, Hugh 1:336-337
MASON 14:360 (see also DIXON)
MASON, Abraham 5:175; 10:630, 641,
  668
Colo. 3:211
George 16:328
Isaac 12:182, 540; 13:112,
  742-747, 750-754, 760-766,
  768-776
James 13:112
John 12:779; 13:748; 15:485
Mary 1:154
Richard 10:260, 267; 12:133
Richd. 2:527, 530
Samuel 13:38
Thomas 13:50, 140, 324, 331;
  14:314, 434, 458; 15:430, 442,
  478-479; 16:174
MASON & DIXON 12:635, 661, 704
MASON (& DIXON) 10:150, 161, 183,
  187
MASON (MASSAN), Abraham 11:6, 46,
  59, 66, 76, 90, 112, 132, 310
MASON (MEASON), Isaac 14:1-6, 8-11,
  15-16, 18, 23-43, 122, 130,
  135-155, 252-270, 274, 276-279,
  282-285, 287-291, 307-311,
  313-318, 321-327, 342, 344-348,
  356, 365, 367-369, 371-381,
  449-452, 455-465, 546-554,
  556-558, 560-565, 633-635, 637,
  639-643, 646-647, 649-661,
  663-667
MASSER, John 13:603

MASSEY, Joseph 1:144, 151 (See
  MASSIE)
Sarah 13:523
Wm. 1:537
MASSEY (MASSAY), Samuel 11:127,
  182-183, 194, 330, 479, 504
MASSIE, Joseph 1:142 (See MASSEY)
MASSONNARE, --- (Monsieur) 12:767
MASTER, --- (Capt.) 10:315
--- (Widow) 9:781
Joseph 1:143; 11:624
MASTER(S), Tho. 1:154-157
MASTERS, Sybella 3:18
Thomas 3:18-19, 113-115, 120, 130,
  134, 137-138, 140-141, 147,
  156-158, 162, 165-167, 170-172,
  175, 178, 180, 189, 193, 196,
  209, 212, 214, 216, 232, 573
Thos. 2:23-24, 87, 172, 410, 546,
  562
Vendue 15:153
William 7:249, 313, 370, 380, 499,
  518, 635-636, 656-657, 662, 666,
  671-672, 697, 708, 776; 8:41,
  69, 84, 170; 10:46-47, 88;
  11:34-35, 37, 55, 65, 68, 83,
  104, 157-158, 160-162, 164-165;
  15:452
MASTERSON, --- (Capt.) 5:255-256,
  273, 283, 301
MASTERSUNDTS, Rudolph 3:386
MASTIN, James 11:302
MAT(T)SON, Margaret 1:93, 95-96
MATCH, Jane 15:391, 549
MATERN, Peter 3:458
MATHER, James 10:377
John 4:482, 484-485; 7:417
Joseph 13:545
MATHER(S), James 5:108, 186, 303
John 5:3, 185-186, 387, 572
Joseph 10:100, 680, 684, 782;
  11:66, 145
MATHERILL, Marjery 12:503
MATHERS, Peter 10:674
MATHEW, Chas. 4:468
MATHEWS, --- (Mr.) 12:593
Edmund 6:648
James 11:281
Solomon 10:686
MATHIASON, Mathias 1:105
MATLACK, --- 13:692
--- (Mr.) 13:540
Josiah 16:132
Mary 12:50
T'y. 13:473, 476, 533
T. 13:268
Timonty 13:471
Timothy 10:600, 634, 641-642,
  653-656, 658-660, 662, 664-666,
  672-673, 678, 680, 683, 690,
  705, 709, 712-725, 727-733, 735,
  740, 753-756, 758-762, 769-774,
  777, 779-780, 782-784; 11:1-2,
  4-9, 11-19, 22, 24-26, 29, 32,
  36, 39-40, 45, 47-50, 54-55, 57,
  61, 102, 174, 176, 240, 243,
  299, 353, 370, 429, 439, 447,
  474, 485, 503, 509, 518, 612,
  638, 649, 666, 671, 675, 734,
  747, 764, 768, 778, 784; 12:29,
  122, 126-127, 170-171, 184, 189,
  214, 225, 283, 289, 293, 295,
  320, 350, 371, 384, 386, 388,
  405, 408, 415, 433-434, 464,
  497, 538, 590, 667, 699, 711,
  725; ->

MATLACK, Timothy (continued) **13**:41,
  60, 95, 125, 312, 333, 339, 375,
  378, 401, 435, 537, 539, 558,
  591; **15**:220, 379, 382, 429, 440,
  537; **16**:178, 182, 186, 274, 278,
  319, 338-339, 347, 349-350, 366,
  383-384, 391, 406-407, 429, 436,
  462-463, 512-513, 547
 Titus **10**:528, 560, 577
 White **12**:50; **13**:45
MATLACK (SEE EVANS &) **11**:659
MATLACK(S), Timothy **14**:281, 284,
  286, 604
MATSCH, John Conrad **15**:372
MATSON, Neels **1**:93, 96
MATTEN, Christopher **3**:368
MATTERN, Thomas **3**:453
MATTHES, Stephen **3**:467
MATTHEWMAN, Luke **13**:283
MATTHEWS, --- (Lt.) **8**:386
 Benj. **9**:235, 672
 Benjamin **10**:162
 George **11**:109, 229; **14**:345;
  15:129, 199, 487; **16**:261
 Henry **12**:483; **14**:609
 Hugh **5**:602
 James **3**:50
 John **16**:32
 Margaret **12**:377
 Mary **12**:343
 Peter **14**:466
 Robert **12**:250
 William **13**:283; **14**:461
MATTHIAS, Benjamin **4**:16
MATTHIS, Hans Jacob **3**:516
MATTIES, John **1**:531
MATURIN, G. **9**:119
MAUBL(E)Y (MABLY), William **14**:94,
  190, 194, 414
MAUGHOUGHLIN **13**:465
MAUGRIDGE, William **8**:562; **9**:172,
  340
MAUL, James **10**:489, 523, 723
 John **5**:226
MAULBY, William **13**:620
MAULE (MAWLE), John **5**:267, 324
MAULL (MAULE), Nehemiah **10**:363,
  376-377, 531
MAUPHETT, William **12**:344
MAURER, Jacob **3**:594
MAURICE, Alex'r. **10**:669
 Theodore **9**:203, 626; **10**:81, 217,
  231
MAURITZ, Nicolaus **3**:520
MAUS, --- (Dr.) **12**:693
 Bernhard **3**:518
 Mathew **13**:713
 Matthew **13**:159; **14**:87, 435
 Matthew (Dr.) **13**:620
MAUSE, Matthias **9**:683
MAUSLIN, Abraham **3**:607
MAUTICUS **10**:366
MAVERICKE, S. **6**:263
MAWHORTER, Thomas **15**:100
MAXFIELD, James **1**:160; **15**:199;
  16:516
 William **12**:4
MAXWELL, --- (Gen.) **11**:676
 --- (Mr.) **12**:51
 Alexander **14**:199, 356
 Henry **14**:297, 304, 435
 James **1**:451; **11**:229, 691; **12**:667;
  14:190, 194, 438, 471; **15**:72,
  129, 537; **16**:380
 Jas. **9**:201, 270-273, 276, 444,
  673, 732

MAXWELL, Jno. **1**:560
 John **9**:337, 600; **11**:235; **12**:481
 Patrick **10**:450; **11**:79, 633;
  13:396, 415
 Ruth **11**:584
 Will. **7**:395
 William **5**:3, 210, 378, 436, 443,
  446; **6**:434-435, 437
MAXWELL (MAXFIELD), Elizabeth
  16:380
MAY, A. **11**:106
 Abram **1**:108
 Daniel **14**:234, 449; **15**:420, 474;
  16:194, 492
 Edward **15**:413, 442, 481, 485
 Enoch **14**:611
 George **11**:106
 John **3**:254, 270
 Joseph **1**:544
MAYBERRY, Thomas **16**:335
 William **8**:575; **13**:668
MAYBURY (MAYBERRY), William **14**:132,
  411
MAYCEMO **13**:467
MAYE, Dudley **14**:190, 193
MAYER, Bernhard **3**:386
 Elias **3**:284, 432
 George **12**:601
 Jacob **11**:513, 516-517; **13**:563;
  14:489, 506
 Johannes **4**:59
 John **3**:542
 Vincent **3**:290
MAYES, Edward **2**:122
MAYHKEERICKKISHSHO **13**:465
MAYNE, Benja. **2**:569-570
 Benjamin **3**:394, 400
MAYO, Thomas **6**:673
MAYOS, Edward **2**:127
MC ADAM, Elizabeth **8**:728
 Rebecca **12**:680
MC AFEE, Neal **14**:190, 194, 438
MC AFFEE (MC FEE), Robert
  11:563-564, 616-617
MC ALEAVY (MC ALEWY), William
  11:86, 89
MC ALEVY, William **12**:340
MC ALLA, Daniel **12**:187
MC ALLEN, Martha **10**:706
MC ALLISTER (MC CALLISTER),
  Archibald, Jr. **10**:451
 John **10**:256-258
 Richard **10**:163, 682-683; **11**:219,
  223, 257, 316, 406, 444; **12**:546
MC ALPIN, --- (Lt.) **7**:313
MC ALPINE, James (alias James
  THOMPSON) **15**:397-398, 400, 402,
  417, 424
MC ANNALLY, Matthew **16**:547
MC ANNINCH, John **14**:647
MC ARTHUR, Niel **10**:581
 Thomas **6**:649
MC ASKELL, Murdoc **10**:581
MC AULAY, Cornelius **13**:730; **14**:244
MC AULEY, Cornelius **11**:608; **15**:298
 Frances **13**:439
MC BEAN, Mary **11**:582
MC BEAN (MACBEAN), Angus **10**:531-532
MC BEATH, Andrew **11**:229
MC BRIAR, Andrew **6**:143
MC BRIDE, Peter **13**:612; **14**:432
 Robert **12**:491
MC BRIGHT, James **10**:713
MC CABE, Edward **10**:756
MC CAGGEN, Edward **10**:730
MC CAGNEY, Hugh **12**:188

MC CAHAN, Hugh 13:538
MC CAHON, John 6:648
MC CALEB, Ann 12:613
 Robert 12:613
MC CALESTER, John 14:101
MC CALL, Arch'd. 11:92
 Archibald 8:576; 10:763; 16:224b
 George 3:239, 597; 5:203-204;
  6:235
 Lydia 9:173
 Mark 12:570
 Mathew 12:162
 Matthew 11:375, 599
 Robert 15:572
 Samuel 5:175, 181, 183, 205; 8:571
 Samuel, Jr. 7:10
MC CALLA, Daniel (Rev.) 10:458
 Thomas 12:332, 576, 609
 Thomas H. 14:429
 Timothy 12:343
 William 12:306, 310-311, 363, 372,
  400, 405, 411, 426, 442, 467,
  484; 13:83
MC CALLISTER (MC ALISTER), ---
  (Mr.) 12:412
 Abdiel 13:93; 14:611
 John 12:27, 31, 41, 198, 304, 663
 Richard 9:731; 14:4, 8, 23, 182,
  209, 213, 234, 239-240, 242-250,
  252-265, 449-451, 456-473,
  476-484, 486-489, 491-497,
  500-509, 511-512, 516-521,
  617-625, 628-635, 637-643,
  646-653, 656-657, 659-661,
  663-670; 15:126, 152, 245
MC CALLMENT, James 12:341
MC CALMONT, James 16:167
 John 15:408; 16:46
MC CALPINE, James 16:426
MC CALVERY, James 10:746
MC CALVEY, Thomas 16:267-268
MC CAM, Charles 14:607
MC CAMANT (MC CALMONT), James
  14:236, 250, 563
MC CAMMONT, James 13:520
MC CAMRON, James 14:611
MC CANDLES, James 10:697, 703
MC CANDLESS, James 11:450
MC CANLESS, James 10:738
MC CANNON, John 15:329
MC CANNOUGHY, David 11:219
MC CARACHER, Alexander 14:407-408
MC CARAKEN, Alexander 13:153
MC CARELL, William 5:469
MC CARIHER, Neal 10:43
MC CART, John (See CART) 11:515,
  517-518
MC CART(NE)Y, Thomas 16:120, 211
MC CARTHY, Dennis 13:562
MC CARTIE, Adam 5:444
 Alexander 5:444
MC CARTNEY, Henry 14:64, 300, 416
 John 14:131, 134, 411
 John (Dr.) 12:294-295
 Laughlin 16:322
MC CARTY, James 11:472
 Justin 12:537
 Patrick 13:447
 William 12:332
MC CASHEN, John 13:179
MC CASKEY, William 10:209
MC CASLAND, Patrick 13:638
MC CAULY, Cornelius 12:544
MC CAUNAGHY (MC CONAUGHEY), David
  15:102, 297, 579
MC CAUSLAND, Marcus 13:178-179

MC CAY, --- (Capt.) 11:339
 Dan'l. 9:508
 James 7:395
 Robert 6:466-467
 William 14:242, 485
MC CLAIN, Moses 10:451
MC CLANCE, John 11:576
MC CLANE, Jacob 16:453
 Jenny 6:641
MC CLARE, John 5:443
 Michael 4:247
MC CLARIN, James 11:515-517
MC CLAY (MACLAY), --- (Mr.) 13:693
 John 11:229; 14:568
 John, Jr. 9:732
 Samuel 16:547
 William 9:547; 11:187; 13:698;
  14:29, 40, 45, 53-54, 242, 322,
  374, 385, 393, 485, 514, 518,
  531, 536, 558, 604, 644, 658,
  663; 15:8-9, 103-116, 118,
  142-170, 251-255, 258-267,
  269-279, 306, 308-317, 320-324,
  326, 376-391, 394-401, 403-405,
  508, 513-518, 520-527, 530-536,
  538-542, 544-545, 547-551,
  554-599, 651-658
MC CLEAN, --- 15:116
 --- (Capt.) 9:190
 --- (Lt.) 12:633, 675, 693
 --- (Mr.) 12:181; 13:132, 531,
  541-542
 Alexander 10:142; 13:419, 516,
  530, 532, 541, 702, 732, 763;
  14:54, 153, 263, 346, 667
 Alexaner 13:510
 Andrew 14:63, 192, 438
 Archibald 7:769; 8:575; 9:205,
  672; 10:46, 78; 12:47, 93, 201,
  610, 635, 684, 704; 13:741;
  14:73, 164, 191, 195, 453
 Charles 12:49
 James 3:176; 12:172; 13:407;
  15:103-105, 132, 135, 209
 John 14:93-94
 Jos. 9:508; 10:679
 Joseph 13:112; 14:47, 50
 Moses 13:93, 112, 397, 415, 737;
  14:221; 16:102, 317, 321
 William 10:209; 11:219
MC CLEAN (M'LEAN), David 14:124,
  129, 429
MC CLEAN(E), Joseph 12:131, 164,
  507
MC CLEEN, Allen 12:335, 638
MC CLEERY, Joseph 13:702
 William 13:698; 14:216
MC CLEIRY, William 13:158
MC CLELAN 7:599-600
MC CLELAN, Joseph 11:138
MC CLELAND, James 10:671
 Joseph 10:767
MC CLELEN, John 10:724, 726
MC CLELLAN, --- (Lt.) 11:464
 David 14:557
 James 11:143; 14:402; 16:24
 John 10:212, 273; 12:355; 15:264,
  312, 381
 Joseph 10:645; 11:555; 13:708;
  14:179, 238, 427; 16:419, 492
 Priscilla 15:312
 Samuel 13:562; 14:95, 422, 621
 William 16:193
MC CLELLAN (See DICKEY), Elizabeth
  15:380
MC CLELLAND, --- 10:451

MC CLELLAND, John 13:607, 708;
  14:80, 83, 312; 15:85
  William 14:526, 571
MC CLENACHAN, --- (Mr.) 15:381
  Blair 11:21; 13:558; 16:31, 316,
  320
MC CLENAGHAN (MC CLENACHAN), Blair
  11:231, 614, 714, 720-721, 724,
  730, 735, 741-743, 747, 766,
  775; 12:7, 37, 54, 154, 203,
  477, 559, 580, 582
  Elijah 11:339
  Roger 14:459
MC CLENAGHANS, --- (Mr.) 13:768
MC CLENTOCK, Sarah 14:134, 436
MC CLENTOCK (MC CLINTOCK),
  Alexander 14:134, 436
MC CLEOD, Alexander 10:581
MC CLERRACHAN, Blair 15:636
MC CLESTER, Francis 11:752; 12:238
  James 9:678
MC CLINTOCK, Alexander 10:449
  Daniel 16:538
MC CLOSK(E)Y, John 14:124, 129, 429
  William 14:102, 434
MC CLOUD, --- (Lt.) 6:491
  Thomas 13:524
MC CLUNE, Samuel 11:229
MC CLUNG (M'CLUNG), Matthew 14:233,
  253; 15:105, 435
MC CLURE, --- (Capt.) 13:456
  Abdiel 14:80, 290
  Alex. 6:649
  Christopher 10:717
  David 5:247, 378; 11:229; 14:180,
  242, 485; 15:325, 520
  James 9:583; 12:513; 13:756;
  14:84, 124, 127, 411, 428
  John 5:662; 6:144; 7:267
  Jonathan 14:201, 259; 16:274
  Randall 12:134, 508
  Randell 13:88
  William 6:649; 11:229, 340; 14:223
MC COLLISTER, John 14:415
MC COLLOM, John 5:469
MC COLME, James 1:561-563
MC COMB, Thomas 10:765
  William 11:363; 13:740
MC COMBS, John 12:187
  William 14:245
MC CONAGHY (MC CONNAUGHY, MC
  CONAUGHTY), David 9:286, 333,
  399, 731; 14:234, 250, 557
MC CONAUGHY, --- (Mr.) 6:675
  David 6:241
  Samuel 14:37
MC CONKEY, John 11:90
MC CONN, Mary 15:345
MC CONNEAUGHY (MC CONNAUGHY), James
  10:676-677, 693
MC CONNELL (MC CONEL), Daniel
  11:363
  Elizabeth 15:101
  James 10:676, 679; 12:353; 14:600
  John 11:60; 14:492
  Matthew 12:139; 13:38, 555; 14:84,
  411, 456
  Robert 13:715
  William 9:730; 10:59, 78; 15:103
MC CONOUGHY (MC CONAUGHY), David
  8:719, 729
MC CONOUL, James 10:714
MC CORD, John 16:398
  Mark 14:292, 299, 433
  Thomas 13:636
MC CORKILL, William 15:185

MC CORMAL, --- (Capt.) 11:149
MC CORMICK, Henry 15:292
  Hester 11:154
  Hugh 11:64, 107
  John 5:210
  Patrick 13:669; 14:299, 416
  Thomas 7:344; 16:8, 18, 335
  William 11:42; 14:296, 303, 411
MC CORMIER, Charles 14:576
MC CORTLEY, Michael 13:636
MC CORVEN, William 14:98
MC COSKRY, Samuel A. 14:567;
  16:454, 487
MC COULL, John 5:186
MC COW(A)N, James 12:430
MC COWAN, Archibald 15:11
  Felix 10:42
MC COWELL, D. 14:194
MC COWEN, William 13:573
MC COY, --- (Mrs.) 13:766
  Aeneas 11:2, 49
  Catherine 12:602
  Francis 5:506; 13:368
  Gilbert 12:678; 16:445
  James 10:746
  John 16:223b
  Robert 11:208
  Thomas 11:469
  William 11:266-267; 12:5-6;
  13:622; 14:432; 16:199
MC CRACKEN, Henry 15:339
MC CREA, --- (Mr.) 14:621
  George 14:567
  Gilbert 14:191, 195, 413, 612
  James 14:635
  William 5:194, 248
MC CREERY, John 13:568; 14:89, 418
MC CREIGH, Anthony 14:360
MC CROSKEY, William 16:395
MC CRUM(M), John 15:25, 246, 311
MC CULLAM, John 13:640; 14:195, 417
MC CULLOCH (MC CULLOCK, MC
  CULLOUGH), David 12:146; 16:519
  George 14:485
  James 11:469, 541-542, 546, 573,
  667; 14:610
  John 13:29, 81
  Robert 10:708
  William 11:69, 151, 775
MC CULLOCK, James 14:192
MC CULLOCK (MC CULLOCH), John
  14:305, 418
MC CULLOGH, John 12:10
MC CULLOH, George 13:778
  James 13:778
  Jean 13:523
  John 13:320, 554
MC CULLOM, John 13:716
MC CULLOMS (MC CULLAM), Thomas
  14:179, 501
MC CULLOUGH, --- (Maj.) 13:661
  --- (Mr.) 6:560
  George 5:186
  James 13:768
  Kenneth 11:494
  Patrick 13:38
  Robert 12:188
  Thomas 5:248
  William 14:259, 266, 605
MC CULLY, George 13:569, 717
  Thomas 12:730; 16:214-215
MC CUNE, --- (Capt.) 10:712
  James 14:180, 242
  Thomas 15:330
MC CUNN, Frederick 12:527
MC CURDY, David 15:437

MC CURDY, William **12**:587; **13**:202,
607; **14**:130, 177, 431, 533, 610;
15:8, 13
MC CURDY (M'CURTY), David **16**:95,
263
MC CURRY, Francis **11**:210
MC CUTCHEON, David **10**:616, 731
 Hugh **15**:426
 James **14**:632, 659; **15**:13, 28, 36,
52, 61, 78
MC DADE, --- **12**:331
MC DANIEL, Edward **14**:407, 409, 440
 Francis **13**:636; **14**:125, 432
 James **10**:660
 John **15**:25
 John (alias Donnel) **9**:715, 717
MC DE HART, Jacob **13**:758
MC DEIRMATT, Michael **4**:47
MC DERMOT, Patrick **16**:547
 Terrence **10**:302, 304-305, 313
MC DONALD, Agnus **10**:581
 Alexander **13**:153; **14**:312
 Alexander (Coudrach) **10**:581, 647
 Alexander (Son of Kingsbrough)
10:581
 Allen **10**:581, 639, 648
 Daniel **11**:127; **12**:187
 Donald **10**:581, 595
 Eleanor **13**:72; **14**:292, 299
 Elizabeth **11**:161-162, 164-165
 Francis **14**:138
 Hannah **13**:575
 James **10**:581, 697; **11**:87; **16**:422
 John **10**:581; **13**:599, 752; **16**:541
 John (alias MC DOWELL) **14**:127,
421, 489, 568, 576
 Kenneth **10**:581
 Malcolm **15**:38
 Mary **15**:606
 Patrick **14**:123, 126
 Robert **13**:643; **14**:86, 432
 William **14**:292, 299; **16**:185
MC DONALL, John **14**:489-490
MC DONNAL, --- **10**:451
MC DONOP, James **14**:301
MC DONOUGH, James **14**:433
 John **15**:31
MC DORMIT, John **14**:501
MC DOUGAL (MC DUGALL), --- (Col.)
11:151, 154, 158
MC DOWEL, Andrew **5**:3
 John **7**:493
 William **13**:613
MC DOWEL(L), John **10**:451, 717
MC DOWELL, --- **7**:232
 --- (Dr.) **16**:475
 --- (Lt.) **13**:586
 --- (Mr.) **13**:410; **15**:582
 Alexander **14**:445, 454, 471, 604,
645; **15**:358, 421; **16**:43, 225
 Andrew **5**:210; **14**:396
 Hugh **16**:190
 James **11**:208; **12**:322; **16**:191
 John **6**:434; **9**:583-584; **12**:438;
13:135, 409, 481, 527, 546, 732,
737, 740; **14**:1-6, 8-11, 15-16,
18, 23-60, 65-80, 86, 103,
105-119, 121-123, 130, 135-149,
151-154, 156-165, 167-172,
174-186, 188, 196-203, 210-211,
213-219, 224-226, 228-229, 231,
233-240, 242-246, 249-250,
252-256, 260-270, 274, 277-279,
281-285, 287-291, 311, 313-318,
321-324, 326-327, 342, 344-348,
357-363, 367-369, 371-377, ->

MC DOWELL, John (continued)
14:384-387, 396, 398-400,
404-406, 414, 431, 442, 446,
469-474, 476-484, 486-489, 501,
503-504, 508-511, 514, 516-522,
524, 526-537, 544-548; **16**:204,
225, 372
 John (Dr.) **13**:498, 717; **15**:105,
437, 623-624
 John, Jr. **9**:584
 Nathan **15**:437
 Nathaniel **14**:237, 533
 Patrick **11**:80, 135
 Thomas **5**:194
 William **11**:621; **12**:166, 245;
13:716; **15**:218
MC DUNNELL, John **14**:240
MC EIRR (MC EVER), Angus **14**:88, 419
MC ELERVETY (MC ILREVEY), Hugh
14:98, 425
MC ELHALLON, Jno. **10**:684
MC ELHATTON, William **10**:756; **13**:643
MC ELHATTON (MC ILHATTON), John
14:123, 125
 William **14**:95, 424
MC ELROY, --- **11**:151-154
 Hugh **14**:82
MC ELROY (MC ILROY), John **14**:91,
419
MC ELVAINE, Thomas **13**:709
MC ELWAIN(E) (MC ILWAINE), Joseph
11:32, 44, 96, 301, 330, 340
MC ENTIRE, Daniel **14**:128
 Thomas **10**:450
MC EVER, Angus **13**:581
MC FABRICK (MC FATRICK), John
14:305-306, 434
MC FABRIDGE, Archibald **12**:188
MC FADDEN, John **15**:48
MC FADEIN, Mary **5**:385
MC FAILAN, William **14**:124, 128
MC FALANE, John **12**:521, 523, 635
MC FALL, Archibald **13**:568; **14**:413
MC FARLAINE, James **14**:190
MC FARLANCE, James **13**:639
MC FARLAND, Elizabeth **12**:588
 James **13**:690, 715
 John **12**:576; **16**:187
 William **13**:740; **16**:194, 509
MC FARLAND (MC FARLEN), William
15:552, 589
MC FARLANE, Andrew **14**:63, 300, 423
 Daniel **15**:617, 625
 James **14**:123, 126, 194, 300, 414,
436-437
 Malcolm **14**:308
 Walter **13**:705
 William **14**:427, 444
MC FARLEN, William **13**:135
MC FARLIN, Alexander **11**:761
 William **13**:135
MC FARLING, John **12**:333
MC FARNEN, William **11**:633
MC FARREN, John **13**:343; **14**:68
 John, Jr. **12**:767
 Samuel **14**:191, 196, 610
 William **12**:506; **13**:112
MC FATRICK, John **11**:117
MC FATRIDGE, Daniel M. **14**:61, 98,
431
 John **10**:536; **12**:507
MC FEE, Matthew **13**:300
MC FERSON, Samuel **10**:451
MC FITRUM, --- (Capt.) **11**:117
MC GAGHAN, Joseph **16**:92
MC GARATY, Arthur **15**:13

MC GARRAUGH, James **11**:220
MC GARY, Joseph **13**:158
MC GASKEY, Hugh **13**:534
MC GAUGHAN (M'GAHAN), Michael
 14:292, 299, 416
MC GAUGHEY, --- (Mr.) **13**:647
 Arthur **15**:198, 600; **16**:32, 212
 Thomas **15**:600; **16**:212, 498, 518
MC GAUGHY, Andrew **13**:638
MC GAW, Robert **13**:112
 William **12**:483; **16**:32
 William (Dr.) **13**:716
MC GAWEN (MC GOWEN, MC GAWAN), John
 10:765-767
MC GEE, Barnabas **7**:344
 James **4**:102; **15**:178, 202-203, 209,
 213
 Robert **11**:279-280; **12**:141
 Thomas **12**:526, 730; **13**:757
MC GEE (MAGEE), James **14**:294-295,
 301-302
 Thomas **14**:86, 416
MC GEE (MC KEE), Thomas **5**:138, 401,
 407, 761-762
MC GENNIS, Mary **10**:734
MC GERRAUGH, Joseph **14**:346
MC GHEE, Nathanl. **7**:500
MC GIGHEN, Alexander **15**:102
MC GILL, Andrew **3**:612
 Charles **5**:210
 James **11**:472
 John **15**:576; **16**:79
MC GILSON, Bruce **14**:366
MC GILVIVRAY (MC GILLIVRAY),
 Alexander **16**:395, 404-406, 410,
 524-525
MC GINLEY, --- (Capt.) **12**:80, 83
 John **11**:136, 142
MC GINLY, Duncan **11**:154-155
MC GINNET, John **11**:88
MC GINNIS, Arthur **5**:269, 277
 Susanna **12**:253
MC GINTY, Alexander **5**:626-628 (See
 MAGINTY)
MC GLAUCHLIN, Elizabeth **15**:32
MC GLAUGHLIN, --- (Capt.) **6**:764
 George **14**:233, 253, 255; **15**:347
 James **15**:486, 498-499; **16**:402-403,
 509
 John **13**:669
 Owen **14**:133, 435
 Patrick **13**:615; **14**:101, 434
 William **15**:8
MC GOCHAN (MC GAUGHAN, MCGUICHEN),
 Alexander **16**:73, 380, 509
MC GOFFIN, --- (Mr.) **13**:764
 Joseph **13**:112, 737
MC GOMERY, John **12**:85
MC GONAGHY, David **13**:737
MC GOWAN, --- (Maj.) **16**:409-410
 John **12**:119, 321, 633, 675, 693;
 13:620, 709
MC GOWAN (MC GOWEN), John **11**:65,
 73, 84
MC GRADY, Samuel **13**:292
MC GREGGIN, Anne **13**:552
MC GREGON, John **13**:568
MC GREGOR, John **14**:128, 438
MC GREW, Archibald **6**:144; **9**:201,
 731; **10**:163
MC GUFFIN, James **13**:93
 Joseph **13**:397
MC GUICHEN, Alexander **14**:537
MC GUIRE, Barnabas **14**:96, 424
 John **15**:143

MC GUIRE (MAGUIRE), George **14**:119,
 151
 James **14**:153
 Mary **14**:151
 Matthew **14**:91, 421, 425
MC GUNNIGLE, George **10**:736
MC GURNEY, Edward **11**:152
MC HARG, Joseph **11**:762
MC HATTON, Samuel **14**:125, 429
MC HENRY, Charles **10**:449;
 11:418-419, 593
 Francis **12**:426, 505
 John **13**:684
 Matthew (Dr.) **10**:541
 Thomas **10**:703
 William **10**:648; **11**:340; **13**:82;
 14:500, 532; **15**:540
MC HOGE, William **14**:365
MC HUGH, Matthew **11**:483-485
MC ILHADDON, John **11**:740
MC ILHANEY, Robert **15**:460; **16**:13
MC ILHATTON, John **12**:456
 Samuel **14**:63
 William **12**:51, 89, 267, 279, 338,
 372, 397, 421-422, 448, 466,
 492, 527, 555, 588, 599, 603,
 633, 675, 693
MC ILHINNY, James **14**:208
 Samuel **14**:208
MC ILHOSE, Isaac **13**:604
MC ILMAY, Catharine **15**:58
MC ILROY, John **13**:607
MC ILVAINE, Abigail **14**:173
 Ferguson **11**:342
 John **13**:589
 Joseph **13**:748
 Samuel **16**:295
 William **14**:200, 203
 William (Dr.) **16**:174-179
MC ILVANE, --- (Dr.) **12**:386
MC ILWAINE, --- (Capt.) **10**:629
 Robert **5**:468
MC INTIRE, --- (Widow) **13**:778
 Daniel **13**:778; **14**:611
 James **14**:97, 424
 Thomas **15**:356
MC INTOSH, --- (Gen.) **12**:75
 Donald **13**:568; **14**:91
 Laughlin **15**:113
MC INTOSH (MACKINTOSH), --- (Gen.)
 11:526, 679, 699, 773-774
MC K(E)IM, Thomas **10**:81, 217
MC K(N)EE, Thomas **8**:113, 117-118,
 122-123, 383, 385-386, 429, 433,
 489, 709
MC KAW, David **10**:235
 John **10**:235
MC KAY, --- (Capt.) **6**:51
 --- (Mr.) **12**:37
 Abigail **11**:236
 Alexander **10**:581
 John **12**:29
MC KAY(S), James **14**:311, 365
MC KEAN, --- (Chief Justice) **13**:762
 --- (Mr.) **12**:60
 Adam **11**:748
 Thomas **10**:81, 83, 217, 548, 616,
 639, 648; **11**:254, 271, 304,
 561-562, 566, 574, 600, 603,
 630, 653, 659, 694; **13**:3, 15,
 25, 41, 543; **14**:167, 318-319,
 357, 359, 484, 543, 554, 603,
 669; **15**:45, 89, 138, 186, 211,
 233, 280, 360, 419, 452, 479,
 501, 507, 553, 629, 631, 636;
 16:39, 87, 105, 114, 128, ->

MC KEAN, Thomas (continued) **16**:165,
169, 192, 204, 240, 312, 349,
352, 389, 465, 546
William **10**:685
MC KEE, --- **7**:154-155
--- (Capt.) **6**:153, 648, 650, 657;
7:46-47, 51, 182, 484, 486, 507,
509, 513, 516, 544, 546, 550,
597-598, 619, 622, 666, 669,
672, 675, 684, 689, 697, 702,
705, 708, 735-736, 768
Alexander **9**:215, 223, 227, 250,
252, 264, 515, 517, 519, 521,
534, 730; **11**:515, 517-518; **12**:76
David **14**:214
James **12**:76; **14**:607
Robert **14**:214, 443
Samuel **14**:215
Thomas **4**:630, 633-635, 640-643,
646 (See MEGHEE); **5**:247 (See MC
GEE); **6**:35, 650, 658, 669, 762;
9:27, 29, 89
MC KEE(S), Robert **11**:63, 83, 101
MC KEEB, Owen **5**:443
MC KEECHEN, Alexander **16**:216, 220
MC KEEGAN, Edward **12**:244
MC KEEVER, Henry **10**:642; **12**:730,
735, 779; **13**:153
Isabella **16**:382
MC KEGGAN, Edward **14**:465
MC KELLER, Peter **6**:491
MC KELTON, Margaret **14**:534
MC KENNY, Nathaniel **11**:160
MC KENSEY, Thomas **10**:688
MC KENSIE, Mary **14**:581
MC KENSY, Daniel **12**:187
MC KENZIE, --- (Capt.) **10**:341
Duncan **11**:771
Elizabeth **14**:378
Samuel **10**:530
Thomas **11**:67
MC KEWN, Thomas **11**:43
MC KEY, Alexander **3**:468-469, 472,
476
MC KIE, James **10**:450
MC KIGHAN, George **16**:218
MC KILLAM, Edward **13**:709
MC KILLAN, Edward **14**:89
MC KIM, John **13**:250-251; **14**:61
William **15**:143; **16**:322
MC KIN, James **13**:109
MC KINLEY, --- **11**:315-316
--- (Gen.) **10**:598, 651, 743
Henry **10**:756; **11**:97, 126, 684
John **5**:194; **10**:669; **13**:602
Peter **13**:601
MC KINLY, John **8**:403
MC KINNEY, Andrew **14**:90, 426
David **11**:528
John **13**:581, 710, 717; **14**:83-84,
422-423
Mordecai **10**:725; **11**:120, 398
MC KINSEY, Duncan **12**:188
Elizabeth **15**:488
MC KINSTRY, Henry **11**:281
Samuel **12**:350, 381
MC KINSTRY (MC KENSTRY), John
15:279-280
MC KINZEY (MC KINZIE), Neil
(Nicholas) **14**:100, 440
MC KINZIE, John **10**:581
Unity **11**:150
MC KISSACK, William **11**:2; **13**:639
MC KISSACK (MC KESSACK), William
14:132, 437
MC KNIGHT, Anne **15**:413

MC KNIGHT, David **12**:428, 550;
13:716; **14**:259
James **11**:199, 676
John **9**:201, 487
Paul **10**:577
Robert **14**:497; **15**:171, 272
Will. **4**:468
William **5**:186
MC KOWN, John **5**:247
MC KOY, James **14**:311
MC KULLER, --- (Lt.) **6**:491
MC KUVAN, Benjamin **16**:533
MC LANE, James **11**:633; **13**:234
Joseph **10**:661
Samuel **14**:583
MC LAUGHLIN, Francis **12**:85
John **14**:95, 424
MC LEAN (MC CLEAN, MC LENE), ---
(Capt.) **16**:8
--- (Mr.) **10**:603; **11**:491
Alexander **16**:27, 51, 257, 340,
444, 466, 476-477, 531
Allen **11**:561
Archibald **11**:187, 191, 219, 274,
348, 388, 556-557, 582
James **13**:713; **15**:39, 135, 436,
447-448, 556, 573, 633, 640
John **13**:556; **14**:414, 421; **15**:567,
569
Samuel **13**:85
Thomas **16**:210
MC LEES, Edward **11**:114
MC LEISH, Everhard **11**:63
MC LENE (M'LENE, M'LANE), --- (Mr.)
13:106
--- (Mrs.) **15**:72
Brannon **13**:529
Daniel **14**:442
James **12**:227, 371, 483, 517;
13:112, 133, 415; **14**:201, 213,
236, 342, 344-345, 347-348,
364-365, 367-369, 371-382,
384-387, 393-396, 398-402,
404-406, 441-442, 480-484,
486-489, 491-502, 562-568, 571,
573, 577-582, 584-593, 595-598,
600-603, 646-655, 657, 659-672;
15:1-5, 59-61, 63, 65-88, 90-92,
104, 106-116, 118-130, 165-190,
192-195, 197-204, 206-208,
220-230, 232-237, 239, 258-267,
269-271, 273-280, 282-285, 287,
303, 306-307, 318, 364, 552,
584; **16**:261, 541
Joseph **13**:85
Lazarus Brown **15**:279, 536,
541-542, 588, 599, 601, 603,
620-623; **16**:161, 169
Thomas Brown **15**:91; **16**:231, 261
MC LEOD, David **10**:581
John **10**:581
Murdock **10**:581
MC LINE, James **10**:610
MC LOCHLIN (MC GLOCHLIN), George
14:431, 433
MC LOCHRY, Archibald (See Lockry)
11:
MC LONEN (MC LONON), Daniel **9**:337,
600
MC LOUGHLIN, James **5**:247
MC MA(C)HAN, Richard **14**:62, 88, 428
MC MAHAN, James **14**:465
MC MAHON, James **12**:379
MC MALHAN, James **13**:646
MC MANUS, James **16**:310
John **13**:636; **16**:335

MC MASTER, John 12:680
MC MASTERS, --- (Maj.) 10:763
 James 12:762-763
 John 13:273; 14:199
MC MEAR, James 11:281
MC MEEHEN, James 5:210
MC MEEN, William 14:30
MC MEKIN, John 11:507
MC MICHAEL, Daniel 10:428
 Edward 11:515, 517-518
 Eleanor 12:343
 James 11:181; 13:715, 766
 John 6:254, 757, 759-760; 8:231,
  576
MC MICHEN, John 15:375
MC MICKEN, Andrew 11:281
 John 10:748
MC MIMARY, Darby 15:90
MC MINN, Robert 12:443
MC MORDIE, Robert (Rev.) 14:129,
  435
MC MULLAN, William 5:247
MC MULLEN, Daniel 7:282-284
 Hugh 14:297, 304
 Margaret 15:166
 Robert 5:210
 William 10:685, 692, 710; 11:24,
  251
MC MULLIN, James 5:55
MC MULLIN (MC MULLEN), William
  12:261, 263-264, 331, 695
MC MULLOUGH, --- (Mr.) 6:561
MC MURDY, Francis 14:118
MC MURPHY, James 16:114
MC MURRAY, James 14:478, 485
 William 13:601; 14:128, 433
MC MURREY, William 11:494
MC MURRY, Levy 12:410
MC MURTRIE, David 8:576
 William 11:645
MC MURTRY, John 12:355
MC NABB, John 4:102
MC NAIR, Archibald 13:593
 John, Jr. 12:343, 345-346; 15:248,
  638
 Robert 11:78, 749
 William 11:212, 479, 504; 12:344;
  13:303; 14:200, 362
MC NAIR (MC NEER), Andrew 8:436,
  614
MC NALLY, Matthew 14:160
MC NAMAIRA, Morgan (alias Morgan
  O'BRYAN) 15:27
MC NARY, --- (Capt.) 10:693
MC NAUGHT, John 7:637
MC NEAL, Ann(e) 15:403, 513
 Anne 16:481
 Dominick 11:610-612
 Henry 12:490
 Jno. 10:456-457, 462, 474-475, 524
 John 11:602
 Laughlin 15:403
MC NEALE, --- 6:491
MC NEALY, Arthur 9:387
 Mary 9:387
MC NEIL, Larie 10:384
 Robert 11:744, 760
MC NEIL(L), Laughlin 10:506, 544
MC NET, --- (Mr.) 13:191
MC NOTT (MC NOLT), George Will
  14:97, 419
MC PHE, Jon. 10:446
MC PHERLAND, Andrew 11:69
MC PHERSON, --- 12:705
 --- (Mr.) 13:672, 732; 15:583
 Alexander 12:463

MC PHERSON, Frederick 16:395
 James 13:715; 16:54
 John 12:38-39; 14:24, 31, 385,
  522, 582; 15:246; 16:210, 395
 Robert 9:731; 10:101, 163, 687,
  710, 720, 771; 13:93, 112, 397,
  415, 737, 745
 Robt. 8:781
 William 13:764; 14:63, 132, 410
MC PHERSON (MACPHERSON), Jno.
  11:51, 121, 655
MC PIKE, James 14:303, 418
 John 14:296
 Thomas 14:294, 301, 429
MC QUEAD, John 13:708; 14:95, 424
MC QUISTON, James 14:199
MC REILY, Robert 11:281
MC SHERRY, Patrick 16:321
 Patrick, Jr. 13:480
MC SORLEY (MC CORLY), John 14:295,
  302, 410
MC SPARREN, James 15:31
MC SWAIN, George 14:295, 302
MC SWAINE, George 7:395
MC TEER, James 5:210
MC TENNET, John 11:52
MC VEAGH, --- (Col.) 13:189
MC VEAUGH, --- (Col.) 11:301;
  13:190-191
MC VEY, Daniel 14:191, 195, 414
MC VEY (MC VEIGH), Mary 11:153-154
MC VICAR, Elizabeth 15:56
MC WILLIAMS (MC WILLIAM), James
  14:145
 Joseph 11:149
 Richard 9:12, 203-204, 206, 267,
  384, 581, 671-672, 698; 10:108,
  217
MC WRIGHT, James 16:444
 Thomas 16:216
MCKEY, Alexander 11:24
 Isaac 11:271, 344, 346-347,
  349-351
MEAD, --- (Capt.) 11:65
 David 13:29, 684
 Eli 15:51
 Samuel 10:528
MEAD & COY 10:305
MEAD(E), David 14:319-320, 358-359,
  398, 497, 499, 508, 541, 572
MEADE, --- (Mr.) 13:554, 733
 Daniel 9:768
 David 13:398
 George 10:671; 12:351, 505
MEADE, GEORGE & CO. 12:44, 141,
  428
MEADOWS, Th. 2:403
MEAKE 6:143
MEAKING, Thomas 1:383
MEALLY, Edward 14:296, 303, 437
MEANS, --- 11:740
 D. William 12:136
 Hugh 13:168
 William 11:32, 372
MEAR(E)S, John 12:594, 603
MEARS, John 10:490, 681, 713;
  15:283
MEAS, James 10:281
 John 5:621, 655; 7:760; 10:281
MEAS(E) & CALDWELL 11:10, 47,
  50-52, 54, 56, 60-61, 64-66,
  88-89, 119, 575, 683
MEASE, Ann 12:235, 243
 James 10:358-359, 373-374,
  376-382, 384-385, 387-390, 395,
  398-401, 403-405, 408, ->

MEASE, James (continued)
    10:410-412, 415-420, 422-429,
    433-446, 448-449, 451-473,
    475-481, 483, 487-488, 491-492,
    498-499, 503-504, 506-507, 509,
    512, 514-515, 518-519, 522, 524,
    527, 529-537, 539, 542-544, 546,
    550-554, 557, 559, 566, 570,
    573, 575, 585-586, 589-590,
    592-596, 599-601, 605-607,
    610-611, 621, 623, 628-629,
    636-641, 647-649, 661, 674,
    687-688, 690, 710, 773; 11:462,
    575, 752; 12:465, 591, 599, 604,
    630, 706; 14:38, 225, 393, 477;
    15:50
  John 11:15, 344; 12:159, 256;
    13:236; 14:38, 190, 194, 403,
    440; 15:31, 50, 152-153, 166,
    186
  Matthew 14:38
  Michael 13:246
  Robert 10:773
  Thomas 13:87
MEASE, CALDWELL & CO. 12:679
MEASON, Isaac 13:157, 162, 730;
    15:72-73, 75-83, 85-89
  John 14:134 (See MASON)
MEAT, Alexander 14:146
MECANOPPY 13:467
MECHELOKEETY 2:557
MECHLEN, Jacob 12:182
MECHLIN, John 13:564
  Samuel 12:131
MECHTOCHRAWAY 8:644
MECK, Georg. Michal 3:456
  John 14:608
MECKELING, Jacob 3:332
  Teobald 3:332
MECKLI, Johan Jacob 3:517
MEDDAGH, Peter 14:299
MEDDIS (MIDDIS), William 14:294,
    301, 416
MEDER, Henry 3:516
MEDICK, Peter 12:715
MEELAN, Musha 4:745
MEEMEEIVOONNOOK 3:102
MEETACHUCHAY 13:467
MEETER, Thomas 11:402
MEETHAM, --- 9:689, 694
MEGHEE, Thomas 4:630 (See MC KEE)
MEHAFF(E)Y, James 14:124, 128, 610
MEHN, Johannes 3:516
MEIDLEMAN, Elias 3:385
  Voldrick 3:385
MEIGHTONG 8:750
MEIKLE, Henrich 3:524
MEIN, Patrick 1:194 (See MIEN)
MEINOR, John 6:161 (Alias Jack
    Cork)
MEINTZGER, Jonas 15:388
MEINZ(I)ES, James 1:560-561
MEISTHER, Gregorius 3:569
MEKICKACHPE 7:188
MELANCON, Philip 7:446
MELANSON, Pierre 7:240
MELCH, Joan Pieter 3:328
MELCH(I)OR (MELCHOIR), Isaac 11:35,
    51, 55, 63, 66, 77, 79, 94, 100,
    112, 116, 120, 150, 269, 271,
    301, 408, 428, 453; 12:170,
    208-209, 249, 709-710
MELCHER (MELCHOR), Adam 14:552
  Isaac 10:497, 516; 13:632, 767;
    14:552; 15:559-560, 597, 612,
    626; 16:301, 529

MELCHIN, Isaac 12:88
MELCHIONAR, Lutwig Joh. 3:467
MELCHIOR, Adam 12:249
  Isaac 14:551
  Leonard 7:62
  Nicolas 4:59
MELHANY, Robert 15:615
MELLAR, Conrad 3:410
MELLEN, Phoelix (Felix) 16:498, 532
MENAHACHTAY 3:504
MENAKIKICKON 4:447
MENANZES 1:447-448
MENATOCHYAND 7:725-726, 731
MENDENHALL, John 3:260, 289, 332,
    620; 4:182, 248, 267-268, 272
  Thomas 10:688; 12:505
MENDIES (or DAVIS) 9:228
MENG, Christopher 3:328
  Jacob 11:494
  Melchior 12:639
  Wolery (Wollry) 11:17, 36
  Wollore (Wollery, Wolere, Wollery)
    10:529, 705, 709, 774
MENIGEN, Matthias 3:452
MENSER (MEINZER), David 11:381-382,
    385
MENTGES (MENTZES, MINTGES), ---
    (Col.) 13:14, 28
  --- (Lt. Col.) 12:774; 13:23
  Christian 14:191, 195
  Francis 10:678, 768; 13:32, 713;
    14:84, 89, 411, 417, 421, 559,
    596; 15:14, 77, 135, 483, 544;
    16:92
  J. P. 11:732
  Matthew 13:272
MENTZ, Georg. 3:452
  Hans Jacob 3:414
  Johan Philip 4:60
MENTZELL, George 3:569
  Melchior 3:569
MENTZES, --- (Lt. Col.) 13:14
  Francis 11:180
MENTZGES, Francis 13:676
MERCER, --- (Col.) 7:101, 230-231,
    772; 8:265, 292-293, 296-297,
    305-306, 309, 311, 313-314, 378,
    382-386, 388-392, 394-395;
    15:481
  --- (Dr.) 7:77
  --- (Gen.) 10:657, 660-661, 680,
    712, 734, 777
  --- (Mr.) 13:529, 746
  George 13:758; 14:86, 412
  Hugh 4:7, 12
  Hugh (Capt.) 7:260-262, 289, 553,
    637
  J. (Lt. Col.) 6:142-143, 294 594,
    604
  James 11:78, 104-106, 134, 188;
    12:393, 406; 13:88, 393, 415,
    722, 737; 14:54, 396
MERCH, Thomas Ashelton 11:284
MERCHANT, Frederick 12:336
  Samuel 3:607; 4:72, 172-173
MERCIE, --- (Monsieur) 6:10
MERCIER, --- (Capt.) 7:132
  Joseph 16:95
MERCK, Henry 3:593
MERCKLEY, John 13:523-524
MEREDETH, David 1:438 (See
    MERIDETH)
MEREDITH, --- (Mr.) 13:242, 365,
    500
  James 5:209
  John 13:94; 15:153

134

MEREDITH, Jonathan 10:720; 14:649
  Mary 15:518
  Rees 7:202; 16:185
  Robert 3:486, 490
  Samuel 10:460, 477, 506, 533, 544;
    11:199, 617, 633; 13:85, 112,
    391, 415; 15:184, 224, 265, 339,
    545; 16:146, 184-185
MEREDITHS, --- 10:262
MEREE, Bastian 3:285
MERIDETH, David 1:209 (See
  MEREDETH)
MERIDITH, Simon 4:272
MERIS, Jno. 1:503 (See MIERS)
MERKEKOWON 13:463
MERKLE, Bernard 15:9
  Lawrence 5:577
MERRICK, John 16:177
  Robert 13:640; 14:120
MERRISS, George 1:375
MERRITT, Marmaduke 15:482
MERRYWHEATHER, Marie 1:576
MERSCHOTTZ, Laborious 4:59
MERTIN, Christian 3:455
MERTZ 1:450
MERTZ, David 3:519
  Hans Michael 3:519
MERVIN, Miles 16:138
MESAKEENAN 8:484
MESCA, Francisca 13:704
  Francisco 13:720, 725
MESCHTER, David 3:569
  Melchior, Jr. 3:569
MESHEMETHEQUATER 4:337, 341,
  346-347
MESLING, Nicolas 4:73
MESNARD, --- (Capt.) 5:93, 216,
  330, 343-344
MESS, Georg. 3:466
MESSEMER, John 16:479
MESSER, James 12:372
  John 5:454
MESSERLY, Daniel 11:219
MESSERSMITH, Daniel 13:89
  John 10:656
  Peter 13:632; 14:86, 416
MESSINGER, Johannes 3:453
MESTERLY, Daniel 11:696
MESTON, Arth. 2:129
  Arthur 1:601
METAMEQUANN 13:463
METASCHICHAY 2:606
METASHEECHAY 2:603
METASHICHAY 3:320-321
METASHICKAY (KING) 13:466
METAWEYKOMAN 4:307
METCALF, Timothy 1:64, 68
METCALFE, --- (Mr.) 7:501
METCYIKON 3:316
METGESS, Francis 13:778
METHAWENNAH 3:45
METHECONGA 13:465
METHEEGUEYTA 3:150-151
METLER, Hans George 3:332
METOTONICA, John 16:143
METS, Balser 3:517
  Hans Jacob 3:517
METSCHER, John Gottlieb 11:409, 413
METTAMICONT, Richard 13:465
METZ, Jacob 9:558; 10:765
  John 14:63, 133
METZER, John 16:377
METZGER, Jacob 15:113
  Johannes 3:410
MEWDY, Adam 10:498
MEYER, --- (Lt.) 7:377, 756

MEYER, Casper 3:458; 4:59
  Christian 3:290
  Christofall 3:414
  Conrad 3:593
  Daniel 4:59
  Egedian 15:522
  Fredrick 3:386, 454
  George 3:569
  Hans 3:328, 593
  Hans Jacob 3:452
  Hans Ulrick 3:390
  Hendrick 3:284
  Henrich 4:73
  Henrick 3:287
  Henry 13:47
  Jacob 3:284, 386, 593; 4:72
  Johan Georg. 3:414
  Johan Jost 4:100
  Johan Thomas 3:414
  Jorig 4:72
  Lutwig 4:59
  Martin 3:454
  Michael 3:414
  Philip 16:411
  Samuel 3:454
  Simon 3:456
  Unicus 3:284
MEYERS, Adam 11:93
  Andrew 14:294, 301, 430
  George 11:576; 12:477
M(E)YERS (MIERS), Jacob 10:267,
  346, 490, 520, 665, 737, 764,
  773; 14:90, 430; 16:362
MEYLER, Jacob 7:303
MEYRE, Mary 12:479
MEYSER, Johannes 3:457
MEYSLER, Ulrich 3:607
MICATHIE 8:723
MICHAEL, --- (Mr.) 9:222
  Everhart 11:479, 504, 599
  Valentine 3:385
MICHAL, Ulrick 3:417
MICHEALL, Rich. 1:149 (See MIRCHELL
  & MITCHELL)
MICHEGUENOTHA 5:685
MICHELL, --- 10:488
MICHL. 6:749
MICHOL, Jacob 3:417
MICHTY, Joseph 7:174, 220
MICKEY, Daniel 16:230
MICKLE, Hans 3:288
  John 11:219
  Samuel 3:545
MICKLYN, Johan Georg. 4:100
MICKTY, Jos. 8:616
MIDCAFF, Abraham 13:590
MIDDAGH, Peter 13:758
MIDDLE, Joannes 3:368
MIDDLECALF, Peter 3:328
MIDDLETON, Daniel 2:102
  John 16:392
MIDDOCK, Peter 14:434
MIDLEDORF, Hendrick Peter 3:369
MIEN, Hans Jorig 4:60
  Patrick 1:337 (See MEIN)
MIER, Jacob 3:414
MIERKEN, Peter 12:317
MIERKIN, Peter 9:727, 730
MIERS, Jno. 1:507 (See MEIRS)
  John 10:481
MIFFLIN, --- (Gen.) 13:511; 15:438
  --- (Maj.) 11:97
  --- (Mr.) 6:174; 12:109, 545;
    13:2, 60, 62
  Charles 12:253
  George 12:139

MIFFLIN, Jno. **2**:277
John **4**:769; **5**:258-259, 572; **6**:533,
   666, 672, 680, 682, 688, 691,
   696, 702, 729, 736, 742, 745,
   751, 765, 770-771, 773, 775-776,
   778; **7**:10, 33, 37, 46-47, 50,
   55-56, 58, 61, 63-64, 70, 73-74,
   78-79, 83, 87, 91-92, 110, 118,
   120, 122, 127, 135, 137, 144,
   148, 153-154, 163, 168, 181-182,
   186, 192, 201-202, 204-207, 216,
   220, 222, 228, 230, 236, 238,
   241, 246-247, 249, 251, 256-257,
   266-268, 296, 305, 308, 338,
   344, 349, 352, 361, 364, 367,
   370, 374, 380, 382-383, 392-394,
   396-397, 401, 403, 407, 409,
   416, 429, 434, 441, 443, 459,
   463-465, 468, 495, 497, 499-500,
   517-518, 522, 526-527, 552, 558,
   566-567, 572, 578, 592, 595,
   618, 637, 649, 652, 656, 660,
   663, 665, 671-672, 679-680, 687,
   692, 694, 714, 716-718, 720,
   722-723, 725, 729, 732, 734,
   739-741, 750, 753, 759, 769,
   776, 780; **8**:1, 11, 19, 21, 24,
   26, 30-31, 35, 37, 63, 66, 68,
   70, 79-81, 101, 112, 116, 125,
   146, 165, 171-175, 211, 223-224,
   226, 231-232, 236, 241-242, 259;
   9:561
John F. **12**:139
Jonathan **7**:312; **11**:294, 335, 385;
   14:230
Sam(p)son **7**:571-572, 579, 593
Samuel **7**:769; **8**:39, 172, 231, 575;
   9:205, 672, 723; **11**:121, 220,
   222-223, 225, 227, 231, 538;
   14:506
Thomas **10**:266, 418, 612; **11**:633;
   12:508, 632, 636, 740, 748, 766;
   13:524, 550, 587, 747; **14**:3, 52,
   70, 78, 147, 555, 647, 662;
   15:98, 235, 307, 531-532, 537,
   540, 542, 547, 550, 567-569,
   571-573, 577-581, 583-584,
   586-590, 592, 594-600, 602-608,
   610-617, 620, 625-629, 632,
   634-640, 651-658, 660; **16**:1-7,
   9-17, 19-22, 24-29, 31, 33-35,
   37, 39-44, 46-48, 50-60, 62-64,
   74-78, 80-91, 93-94, 96-104,
   106-109, 112-117, 124-127,
   129-138, 140-146, 148-149, 151,
   153-156, 158-160, 162-166,
   168-169, 171-173, 175-178, 185,
   188, 190, 199-202, 204-205, 207,
   209-211, 214-216, 218-220,
   222-224, 209b-212b, 225-227,
   229, 231-233, 235-244, 251-252,
   254-264, 267-274, 276-291, 293,
   295-307, 309-313, 315-318,
   320-324, 326-327, 329, 336,
   338-341, 344-350, 356-366,
   368-373, 376-384, 386, 388-390,
   392-397, 399, 401, 404, 418,
   420, 423-424, 428-429, 431-435,
   438-442, 445, 455-459, 461-465,
   477, 479-485, 487-494, 496-501,
   507-528, 530-531, 534-535,
   537-540, 543, 545
W. **6**:559
Warner **9**:645; **10**:9; **11**:426-427

MIFFLIN (MIFFLEN), Samuel **10**:46,
   215, 308, 312, 327, 340, 375,
   415, 594, 599, 708, 712, 718,
   724, 784
MIHM, Johannes **3**:518
MIL(L)EY, Abraham **12**:19, 147, 556
MIL(L)SON, William **11**:514, 516-517
MILDER, Hans Jerig **3**:284
MILE(S), Griffith **2**:520, 541, 543
MILER, James **3**:288
MILES, --- (Col.) **13**:477, 510;
   14:532
  --- (Mr.) **13**:744
Samuel **1**:48; **9**:440; **10**:330,
   373-375, 380-382, 387-389, 395,
   398-401, 403-404, 431-433, 435,
   442-446, 448-449, 451,453, 469,
   473-475, 483-484, 486, 488, 490,
   501, 524, 527, 530, 534,
   537-538, 540, 544, 546, 549,
   551, 553-554, 557-558, 560,
   570-571, 573-574, 577-578, 580,
   583, 595, 598-599, 601, 605,
   615, 623, 625-626, 628-629, 632,
   635-638, 640, 642-643, 647, 653,
   656, 672, 678, 683, 692, 694,
   697, 708, 710-712, 730, 732,
   744, 750-751, 755-756, 762, 777,
   782; **11**:6, 43, 45, 47-48, 55,
   62, 65-66, 96, 100-101, 119,
   130, 139, 150-158, 160-165, 167,
   169, 215, 320-321; **12**:65, 451,
   466, 487, 498, 512, 543, 558,
   680, 689, 693, 696, 709; **13**:41,
   293, 305, 376, 550-551, 721;
   14:66, 229, 449; **15**:70, 72, 99,
   137, 266, 302, 537, 567, 569,
   571-584, 586-590, 592, 594-604,
   606-608, 610-620, 622-623,
   625-629, 632-641, 643-653,
   656-658; **16**:1-7, 9-17, 19-22,
   24-29, 31, 33-35, 37, 39-44,
   46-48, 50-57, 59-60, 62-68,
   70-78, 80, 82-83, 85-91, 93-120,
   122-127, 129-138, 141, 143,
   145-149, 151-160, 162-166,
   168-169, 171-173, 175-176,
   190-194, 196-202, 205, 209-216,
   218, 221-224, 209b-224b,
   225-227, 229-233, 235-236,
   238-244, 251-252, 254-264,
   267-274, 276, 278-289, 291, 293,
   295-297, 299-302, 304-307,
   309-315, 317, 322, 324, 326,
   329-332, 337, 339, 341, 344-345,
   347-350, 352-360, 362-366, 368,
   370, 373, 375-376, 389-394, 396,
   399, 401, 403-406, 408-410,
   412-420, 423-425, 429, 433,
   435-436, 439, 441-442, 445-450,
   452-458, 461-465, 477, 479,
   481-484, 487-494, 496-501, 507,
   510-516, 518-521, 523-528,
   530-531, 534, 539-540, 543, 545
Thomas **10**:405, 692, 706-707, 717,
   736, 749
William **4**:102
MILES & WISTER **10**:501
MILEY, Abraham **10**:728; **13**:400, 730;
   14:244
Abram **11**:363
George **14**:65
Jacob **15**:309; **16**:216
MILLAR, Daniel **3**:452
John **2**:577
Philip **11**:340

MILLAR, Samuel **13**:219
MILLAR (MILLER), William **12**:170,
 208
MILLARD, Joseph **8**:562; **9**:172
 Mordecai **16**:122
 Tho. **1**:95
 Thomas **10**:685
MILLBEY, William **11**:190
MILLBURGER, Johannes **3**:410
MILLE, Samuel **14**:292, 299
MILLEGAN, James **11**:569
MILLER, --- **14**:109, 112
 --- (Capt.) **11**:2, 154, 464
 --- (Col.) **12**:107
 --- (Lt.) **6**:491; **11**:529; **16**:542
 --- (Miss) **11**:571, 577
 --- (Mr.) **6**:34
 --- (Widow) **15**:331
 Abraham **3**:517; **7**:620-621; **10**:728
 Adam **16**:227
 Adreas **12**:484
 Alexander **12**:611
 Andrew **5**:210; **16**:455
 Ann **12**:611
 Anthony **9**:5; **14**:615
 Arthur **10**:685
 Benjamin **10**:450; **11**:349, 514,
 516-517; **15**:502; **16**:210b, 212b,
 483
 Bernard **13**:743
 Catharine **16**:167
 Catherine **15**:13
 Charles **13**:34, 307, 389, 506;
 14:97, 425; **15**:454
 Christian **3**:285, 389; **13**:635, 757;
 14:126, 192, 432, 435
 Conrad **3**:457
 Debalt **10**:746
 Elizabeth **10**:26, 42, 105, 375
 George **13**:641; **14**:296, 303, 415;
 16:122
 Gerard **3**:368
 Hans **3**:285, 288, 329
 Hans Adam **3**:284, 458
 Hans Jacob **3**:328
 Hans Jerig **3**:290
 Hans Lendert **3**:328
 Hans Martin **3**:327
 Henry **9**:651; **10**:54, 267, 548;
 11:6, 11, 31, 179-180; **12**:411,
 513, 627, 710; **13**:93, 397, 584,
 723, 737, 756; **14**:85, 234, 415,
 557; **15**:17, 65; **16**:356, 541
 Hugh **5**:209
 Isaac **13**:759; **14**:300, 433
 Jacob **4**:72; **9**:559; **10**:283, 778;
 11:36, 297, 479, 504, 564;
 14:520; **15**:556
 James **2**:103; **14**:114-115; **15**:65
 Jerem **3**:290
 Joan Nicolas **3**:452
 Joannes Kits **3**:328
 Johan Andreas **3**:570
 Johan George Antony **3**:570
 Johannes **3**:432
 John **1**:390; **3**:285, 367-368;
 5:209-210, 387, 436, 443, 572;
 7:417; **8**:42, 403, 573;
 9:102-103, 205, 510-512; **10**:447;
 11:644; **12**:150, 275-276, 576,
 660, 773, 779; **13**:18, 71, 88,
 677, 739; **14**:67, 70, 190, 193,
 259, 368, 439, 473, 556-557,
 576, 579; **15**:98-99, 296-297,
 372, 556, 581; **16**:32, 61, 90,
 157, 216, 325, 351

MILLER, John Solomon **13**:770
 John, Jr. **13**:773
 Jorgan **3**:284
 Joseph **3**:285; **10**:689, 715; **14**:158,
 270, 307, 616, 672; **15**:81
 Leonard **13**:631; **14**:100, 428
 Magnus **13**:543
 Margaret **16**:40
 Mark **14**:191, 195, 416
 Martin **13**:461
 Mary **10**:715; **11**:6, 642; **12**:190,
 337
 Michael **3**:288; **12**:513
 Nicholas **9**:44; **10**:741; **13**:4, 155;
 16:447
 Oliver **10**:142
 Paulus **3**:456
 Peter **10**:15, 46, 420; **11**:385, 482,
 484-485; **12**:133, 145, 149;
 14:556-557; **15**:100-101; **16**:195,
 210, 212, 498
 Peter (Rev.) **13**:510
 Philip **15**:216
 Robert **3**:366; **9**:201, 448, 451,
 491, 673, 732; **10**:212, 768;
 13:726; **14**:558; **15**:300
 Samuel **3**:395, 522-523; **11**:46, 49
 Solomon **3**:515
 Warwick **9**:673
 William **4**:107; **10**:451; **12**:337;
 13:368; **14**:114-115, 320,
 407-408, 438; **15**:102, 407
MILLERON, John **10**:76
MILLICAN, William **5**:444
MILLIGAN, James **9**:673, 730; **12**:328,
 363, 395-396; **13**:7, 716; **14**:399
 Robert **15**:2
 William **14**:61, 82, 417
MILLIQUET, --- (Mr.) **6**:14
MILLIS, John, Jr. **12**:654
MILLS, --- (Capt.) **11**:163
 Alexander **12**:378-379
 Elisha **16**:79
 John **5**:573-574
 Samuel **7**:717; **14**:63, 88, 612
 William **11**:154
 Willm. **4**:468
MILNE, Edmund **13**:44, 96, 217, 275,
 309, 340, 382; **14**:66, 68, 171,
 176, 618, 624; **16**:137
 Edward **15**:123
MILNER, Edward **12**:571-572
 William **13**:320
MILNOR, John **14**:600
 William **10**:144; **13**:35, 142, 171,
 217
MILOTT, Joshua **11**:302
MILTON, --- (Mr.) **11**:198
MINDHARD, Hans Jorig **3**:453
MINEHOLD, John **3**:227
MINES, John **15**:340
MING, Melchior **11**:494
MINGER, Jacob **3**:593
MINGLE, Stophel (Stopple) **14**:63,
 93, 413
MINGO **2**:489, 508
MINHART, Friedrick **4**:59
MINICH (MINICK), Conrad **16**:427, 487
MINICHER, Johan Herb **3**:429
MINICK, Conrad **15**:254
MINIER, Christian **3**:458
MINIGH, Hans **3**:385
MINKOTTOHA **5**:691
MINOR, John **13**:264; **14**:223; **16**:219b
 William **13**:537
MINOT, --- (Commander) **7**:152

MINSHAL, Joshua **4**:156, 160
MINSHAL(L), Joshua **3**:472, 548, 550,
  555, 561
MINSHALL, John **3**:356, 543
 Thomas **9**:201, 731
MINSHAR (MINSHER), Jacob Mathias
  4:134, 256
MINTZ, Benjamin **11**:141
MINTZER, Englebert **14**:649
MINVEAL, Gabriel **1**:143 (See
  MINVIELLE)
MINVIELLE, Gabriel **1**:143-144 (See
  MINVEAL)
MIRANDA, George **4**:88, 341, 347, 443
MIRCHELL, Richard **1**:111 (See
  MITCHELL)
MIRE, Hans Adam **3**:329
 John **3**:586
 Philip **3**:519
 Roody **3**:381
MISEMEATHAQUATHA **5**:570
MISHIKINOUGHWEE **5**:523
MISKEPALATHY **8**:723, 736-737
MISSEMEDIOUEETY **4**:641
MITCHEL **2**:403-405
MITCHELL (MITCHEL), --- **10**:404, 505
 --- (Capt.) **12**:741
 --- (Col.) **13**:223; **14**:528
 Alexander **3**:612; **4**:135; **12**:336;
  15:271
 Amie **12**:177
 Ann **3**:240
 Deborah **13**:249
 George **11**:103
 Henry **5**:577
 James **3**:184-187, 189, 219, 372,
  380-382, 504, 575, 615; **4**:135,
  247, 352, 500; **13**:593; **14**:299,
  610; **16**:428
 John **3**:387, 612; **4**:135; **5**:210;
  10:504, 510, 522, 562, 594, 599,
  651, 660, 710, 738, 759, 775;
  11:18, 42, 69, 81, 101, 113,
  119, 131, 423, 559, 672, 674,
  706-709, 720, 726, 759; **12**:18,
  132, 269, 315, 318, 321, 340,
  360-361, 385, 427, 442, 459,
  664; **13**:747; **15**:404, 606, 617,
  649; **16**:456
 Jonn **3**:240, 370
 Joseph **12**:447; **13**:330, 355;
  15:388, 397, 409, 413, 423, 437,
  440
 Nathaniel **12**:493
 Read **5**:693-693, 702
 Richard **1**:116 (See MIRCHELL);
  4:313, 482; **5**:3, 388, 573; **7**:437
 Robert **5**:385-386
 Thomas **5**:247, 692-693; **9**:470, 521;
  14:61, 82, 411
 Thomas, Jr. **5**:692-693
 William **5**:247; **11**:98, 371,
  680-681, 703; **12**:19, 65, 83,
  513, 526, 688; **13**:208; **14**:459,
  462; **15**:75, 248, 282, 302, 392
MITCHENER, Isaac **11**:513, 516-517
MITCHINS, John **13**:381
MITSHELL, Randle **12**:430
MIXELL, Andrew **4**:268
MOAK, Johannes **3**:466
MOCK, Hans Peter **3**:516
MODDY (MOODIE), Robert **10**:43, 85-86
MODENA, --- (Duke of) **5**:379-380
MODEWELL, John **16**:334
MOESER, Martin **3**:332
MOESSER, Hans Adam **3**:332

MOFFAT, --- (Mr.) **10**:762
 Solomon **4**:88-89
 Susannah **9**:666
 Thomaas **13**:87
 Thomas **13**:445
MOFFATT, Mathew **11**:27
MOFFITT, Thomas **7**:282-284
MOHICKONS (INDIANS' NAMES) **9**:516
MOHLER, Henry **12**:277
MOHOCK INDIANS **13**:464, 468-470
MOHOCKSEY **1**:447-448
MOHOLIECAN **8**:31
MOHOWTICKON **8**:32
MOHR, Rudolf **4**:255
MOISE, Cutlieb **14**:669
MOLAND, John **5**:59; **8**:291, 339, 342,
  349, 360-362, 369, 397, 399-400
 William **11**:482, 484-485, 564;
  13:516; **15**:382
MOLE, Nicola **10**:748
MOLER, Lutwig **3**:385
MOLESSWORTH, James **11**:197
MOLESTINE, Alexander **1**:48 (See
  MOLESTON)
MOLESTON, Alexander **1**:82 (See
  MOLESTINE)
 Henry **2**:136
MOLESWORTH, James **13**:385
MOLICH, Johannes **3**:594
MOLINA, Solomon **13**:54
MOLINEAUX, James **13**:629
MOLINEUX, Frederick **12**:209
MOLINO, John **14**:484
MOLK, George Detrick **16**:478
MOLL **1**:109
MOLL, Bartol **3**:467
 Christofoll **3**:414
 Johan Michael **3**:413
 John **1**:47, 57-61, 63-72, 87-88,
  233, 580-582, 584, 586-587, 589;
  2:9, 18, 109
 Peter **3**:368
MOLLASTON, William **11**:264
MOLLESTON, Henry (Henrie)
  1:547-548, 552, 568, 590, 595,
  615
 William **10**:363, 376-377
MOLLEY, --- **8**:500
MOLLISTON, Alexander **3**:258-259
 John **5**:55
MOLLOY, Edward **10**:545
MOLLY (INDIAN GIRL) **9**:104
MOLONEY, Thomas **7**:717
MOLSINOUGH(K)O **5**:523-524
MOMMA, Leonhardt **3**:454
MOMPESSON, Roger **2**:68, 117-118,
  120-122, 134-136, 138, 140-141,
  143-147, 157-158, 239-240, 294,
  310, 312, 325, 564
MONACATOOTHA (MONEKATOOTHA,
  MANOQUETOTHA), Half King **6**:46,
  130, 141, 161-162, 178, 181,
  184, 456, 654-655, 670, 672
MONAGHAN, Daniel **12**:56
MONAKATOOTAH **5**:635
MONCKTON, --- (Col.) **6**:447, 480
 Robert **8**:495-496, 506, 509-511,
  578, 592
MONDAY, Beniah **9**:732
 Benijah **14**:311
MONDEATICKER **9**:228
MONE, Jesse **14**:89, 422
MONEY, John **9**:282
MONGEEST **7**:220
MONGTOMERY, Samuel **14**:86, 89, 421,
  431, 453

MONIGHOTOOTHA **5**:615
MONINGTON, Willm. **3**:298, 301
MONK, James **14**:265
MONKTON, R. **2**:403
MONRO, Nathaniel **10**:375
MONROE, John **11**:163
 Sanford **11**:762-763
MONROW, John **12**:433
MONSER, Jacob **11**:470
MONSETTO, George **14**:316
MONSEY, James **3**:486, 490
MONSON, --- **4**:357
--- (Lord) **4**:254, 483; **5**:66
MONTAGU **5**:361
MONTAGU, --- (Duke of) **4**:483-485
MONTAGUE, --- (Mr.) **6**:264
 Edward **9**:48, 51
 Jno. **2**:469
MONTAWNY, Joseph **14**:320
MONTGOMERY, --- (Col.) **8**:233; **9**:48,
 119, 486
--- (Lt.) **11**:42, 77, 85, 150, 152,
 154-155
--- (Mr.) **12**:631, 633, 636, 638,
 649, 693, 727, 740, 750, 754,
 760; **13**:62, 123, 217-218, 351,
 356, 420, 425, 497; **15**:472
--- (Mrs.) **10**:398
 Alexander **13**:353; **15**:199
 Daniel **12**:138, 513, 554; **13**:71,
 92, 117-118, 146, 186, 255, 303,
 329, 370, 436, 697; **14**:155, 250,
 256, 442, 457
 David **11**:109
 George **12**:317, 329, 339, 427
 Hugh **10**:329, 353, 437, 488, 514,
 579, 642, 776; **11**:225, 520-521,
 527, 530; **12**:4, 7, 19, 44, 86,
 111, 150, 155, 159; **14**:608
 J. **13**:509
 James **5**:186; **10**:328, 335-336, 379,
 449, 586, 665, 706; **11**:730, 747,
 782; **12**:296; **13**:637; **14**:96, 423;
 15:337
 John **10**:212, 231-232, 260, 280,
 300, 341-342, 346-348, 371,
 373-375, 377-378, 380, 382, 384,
 388-390, 398, 401, 404, 414,
 443-446, 448-449, 452, 455,
 483-484, 487, 490, 499, 524,
 595, 597, 599-600, 658, 686,
 768, 770; **13**:112, 133, 184, 242,
 511, 521, 547, 598, 625, 734;
 14:41, 56, 233, 289, 298, 304,
 416, 485; **15**:216; **16**:229, 324,
 509
 Joseph **12**:308, 544-545, 586, 635,
 692, 778; **13**:84, 201, 288, 354,
 393, 407, 410, 415, 420, 424,
 430, 431, 511; **14**:221, 364,
 377-378; **15**:41, 221; **16**:444
 Moses **10**:244
 Samuel **10**:451; **13**:710, 717; **16**:543
 Thomas **5**:210
 W. **13**:509
 William **10**:527, 592, 613, 715,
 717, 737, 739; **11**:363, 402;
 12:58, 137, 513, 537; **13**:92,
 112, 118, 132, 184, 354, 371,
 382, 398, 410, 415, 423,
 426-427, 431, 444, 503, 584;
 14:203, 213, 221, 233, 253, 255,
 261, 396, 400-441, 457, 485;
 15:27, 85, 248, 539, 636;
 16:229, 235, 539
 William, Jr. **14**:457, 544

MONTOUR **2**:451
MONTOUR, --- (Capt.) **9**:88
 Andrew **5**:290, 307-312, 318,
 349-350, 354, 358, 431, 433,
 435, 438-441, 449, 455, 460,
 485, 488, 496-497, 518, 520-524,
 528-530, 532-533, 536, 539-540,
 543, 547, 566-568, 607-609, 630,
 634-647, 665, 668-670, 677,
 682-683, 685, 688, 690-691, 693,
 698, 702-703, 707-708, 712,
 730-735, 750, 756-760, 762-763;
 6:21-22, 46, 56-57, 85, 130,
 143, 149, 151, 160-161, 397-398,
 522-523, 566-567, 588-590,
 654-655, 658, 669, 673, 675,
 681-682, 685, 697, 727, 783;
 7:4, 12-14, 19, 21, 46, 57,
 64-65, 67, 72, 74, 81, 92,
 94-95, 98, 106, 155, 171, 225,
 481, 641; **8**:201, 209, 211, 214,
 257, 263-265, 270-271, 618-619,
 700, 702, 757
 Henry **6**:616, 699; **8**:176-177, 190,
 218-219, 383, 385-386, 390,
 429-431, 433
 Lewis **5**:692-695, 702-703, 733-734;
 6:149; **7**:157, 301, 429, 436,
 490, 506, 511; **8**:415
 M. **3**:271, 295-297, 337, 501, 572
MONTRESEUR **6**:490
MONTUR, Andrew **4**:641, 680, 778 (See
 Andrew, Son of Mm. MONTOUR)
MOODY, --- (alias John HOLLAN)
 15:431
 Alexander **5**:194
 Baltzer **10**:365
MOOG, Hans Michl. **3**:452
MOON, James **3**:69
 Jno. **1**:162, 189
 Martha **1**:231
 Nathaniel **10**:746
 Peter **12**:601
MOONEY, Elizabeth **13**:18, 275;
 16:75-76, 479
 Henry **13**:634; **14**:102, 426
 John **15**:464
 Peter **15**:194
MOOR, James **10**:746
 John **1**:545-546, 551, 602; **10**:46
 John Adam **3**:367
 Lambt. **7**:195
 Mordecai **7**:417
MOOR(E), Henry (Sir) **9**:301, 569,
 642, 645
 James **11**:44, 84, 373, 624
 John **8**:403, 506, 564, 566; **9**:206,
 237, 308, 750; **11**:110, 127, 215,
 220-221, 235, 340, 363, 398,
 424, 501-502, 538, 601, 603
MOORE, --- (Capt.) **7**:406, 408;
 11:129, 680
--- (Maj.) **12**:92; **14**:319
--- (Mr.) **13**:768; **14**:508, 522;
 15:583, 657
 Abraham **10**:687
 Adam **11**:135
 Alexander **16**:306
 Allen **10**:210, 214, 296, 303, 328,
 335, 354, 379, 442, 546; **11**:56
 Andrew **15**:282
 Anne **13**:105
 Anthony **13**:103; **15**:391
 Benjamin **14**:233, 253, 255
 Catherine **16**:199

139

MOORE, Charles **5**:186; **8**:23, 25,
287, 399, 512; **10**:53-54, 216,
266, 282, 374, 389, 406, 495,
538; **15**:100; **16**:540
Fergus **14**:62, 305, 428
George **4**:102, 108; **10**:705; **16**:493
Guyon **5**:186
Hannah **7**:739-740; **12**:522; **14**:510
Henry **14**:259, 266, 605
Israel **15**:98
Jacob **10**:216
James **4**:135; **9**:673; **10**:447, 613,
659, 665, 671-672, 675, 685;
12:610, 660, 688, 705, 774;
13:9, 87, 112, 118, 258, 413,
674, 680, 697-700, 703, 706,
716, 720-721, 761, 772; **14**:18,
23, 29, 31-32, 37, 41, 80, 110,
134, 145, 154, 156, 158-159,
164-165, 180, 185, 213, 228-229,
246, 248, 258-280, 302, 311,
319, 347, 394, 414, 417, 462,
495, 555, 567, 621-622;
16:291-292
James F. **11**:95, 382
James Francis **10**:675, 767
Jesse **13**:637; **14**:89
John **1**:477-478, 580, 617; **2**:11,
62-63, 92, 97, 113, 115-116,
121-122, 151, 179-180, 183, 238,
240, 259, 386, 390, 407, 428,
488; **3**:108; **6**:160; **10**:655, 658,
660, 664-666, 670-671, 675,
677-678, 680-683, 687, 691-694,
696, 698-702, 707, 709, 711,
717-718, 721-724, 726-728,
731-735, 764; **12**:85, 262, 561;
13:207, 592, 710; **14**:93, 142,
429, 459, 561; **15**:109, 119, 381,
383-384; **16**:163, 224, 385
John Joseph **1**:29
Joseph **16**:530
Levi **5**:454
Mary **12**:175
Michael **15**:252
Mordecai **5**:572; **13**:327
Moses **5**:444; **14**:266; **16**:459
Nancy **13**:710
Nicholas **13**:49, 322, 326-327;
14:464
Nicholas (Dr.) **1**:58-59, 61, 73,
76, 78, 105, 119, 121, 129-130,
135-141, 145, 152-153, 189-190,
476
Philip **10**:536; **12**:296; **13**:210
Phillip **14**:492
Prudence **12**:23
Rebecca **13**:327
Richard **3**:50
Robert **3**:108; **4**:102; **12**:544;
14:511, 571
Rudolph **3**:367
Samuel **10**:448; **11**:44, 363; **12**:147,
320, 544; **13**:213; **14**:217; **16**:71
Samuel Preston **7**:86, 312, 728-729,
739-740; **9**:395, 649; **11**:213,
235, 307; **13**:9, 49, 295, 319,
321, 326, 501, 509; **14**:323, 447,
458, 464
Sarah **13**:327
Sheby **13**:327
Stephen **14**:503
Thomas **3**:43, 142, 227, 523; **4**:102;
8:728; **10**:363, 379; **13**:604;
14:92, 298, 305, 312, 358, 420,
431, 470, 475

MOORE, Thomas L. **13**:713; **14**:130,
434, 510
Thomas Ll'd. **13**:680
Thomas Lloyd **10**:448
Thomas, Jr. **14**:470
Walter **13**:204
William **4**:98, 248, 267, 272, 482,
495, 503; **5**:3, 185, 387, 572;
7:62, 417, 741-742, 750-751,
764, 768, 776-779, 781-783;
8:1-2, 5-6, 8-9, 11-12, 16-17,
103, 161-162, 283, 287, 439-442;
9:205, 673, 702; **10**:116, 271,
765; **11**:41, 45, 47-51, 54-55,
58, 60, 67-69, 72-73, 75, 77-78,
83-84, 87-88, 90, 93, 95, 97,
99, 101, 103-105, 107-108, 111,
113-114, 118, 124-125, 127-128,
131, 134-135, 139-140, 142, 181,
210, 301, 756; **12**:133, 136, 141,
144-145, 147, 150, 153-155,
158-166, 169, 171-174, 176-177,
179, 181-182, 185-186, 189,
192-194, 197, 200, 217, 226-232,
247, 288, 333, 364, 376, 388,
395, 397, 415, 417, 420,
451-452, 454, 456, 460, 462-468,
491, 496-497, 508, 540-541, 543,
547-548, 552, 559, 588, 598,
604, 622, 685, 690, 693,
695-696, 699, 701-702, 705-708,
711-713, 715, 717-723, 725,
727-729, 731-738, 741-742, 744,
746-747, 749-752, 754-755,
758-761, 764, 766-768, 771, 773,
776, 778; **13**:50, 78, 95, 108,
112-114, 124-125, 129-131, 146,
193, 199, 213, 249, 262,
267-268, 285, 308, 312, 333,
338-339, 349, 364, 375, 377-378,
389, 535, 615, 674, 707, 715;
14:84, 229, 250, 422; **15**:246,
581; **16**:32, 396-397
William (Col.) **6**:729
MOORHEAD, --- (Capt.) **14**:295, 302
Fergus **11**:79
Thomas **12**:551
MOOSELBACK, Carol Arant **3**:368
MOOSER, Philip **11**:89
MOOTS, Jerig **3**:329
MOPPESSON, Roger **6**:529
MOR(E)TON, John **8**:573, 719, 725,
729
MORALES, Francis **14**:484
MORAN, Charles **11**:513, 516-517
MORAN (SEE FULLERTON &) **10**:686
MORANG, --- (Mr.) **6**:10-12
MORARITY, Dennis **13**:600; **14**:294,
301
Timothy **16**:198
MORCOTTAWCOLLO **4**:147
MORDACK, Joseph **14**:260
MORDEN (MERDEN), Ralph **12**:535, 549
MORDIE, Robert (Rev.) **13**:581
MORE, Francis **11**:432
George **1**:336
Jno. **1**:202, 439
MORE(S), Marie **1**:476
Rebecca **1**:476
Samuel **1**:476
MOREHEAD, Samuel **10**:346
MORELAND, Hugh **13**:602; **14**:83
William **16**:519
MOREY, Jacob **14**:584
MORFEY, Charles **1**:84

MORGAN, --- (Capt.) **8**:386; **10**:315,
555-556, 717
--- (Col.) **11**:86, 578
--- (Ens.) **8**:386
--- (Mr.) **5**:280; **9**:302;
10:358-359; **16**:503
Abel **12**:298; **13**:262; **15**:107;
16:71, 166, 463
Abel (Dr.) **11**:124; **14**:205
Benjamin **12**:616; **16**:76
D. **10**:712
David **1**:453; **11**:330, 479, 504, 717
Enoch **11**:124
Enock **14**:229
Evan **5**:729; **6**:679, 775; **7**:64, 79,
153-154, 201, 760; **8**:19, 24;
11:152
Frances **13**:523
George **11**:486; **14**:562; **15**:526;
16:499
Jacob **7**:35; **9**:712, 673; **10**:773;
11:31, 76, 194, 203, 208-209,
218, 221, 251, 256, 287,
290-291, 293, 297, 300, 302-304,
306, 308-309, 311-322, 325, 328,
341, 344, 346-347, 349-351,
357-372, 374, 384, 387-388,
402-403, 405, 408-412, 414-415,
417-419, 421-423, 428, 430,
432-438, 440-441, 452-453, 455,
457, 466, 490-491, 499, 531,
550; **12**:46, 53, 63, 114,
116-117, 256, 299, 303, 306,
308, 412, 453, 460, 478, 484,
486, 493, 566, 594, 596, 606,
612, 615, 631, 658, 660, 668,
672, 678, 680, 686, 692, 695,
705, 712, 723, 743, 775, 779;
13:7, 31, 74, 142, 178, 201,
208, 218, 262, 269, 298, 311,
315; **14**:226-227, 555; **15**:99;
16:89, 211b, 367
Jacob, Jr. **13**:43, 92, 103, 264,
295, 311, 374, 514, 695
James **11**:372, 537; **12**:243, 410,
510
John **10**:448; **13**:64, 543; **14**:277,
624
John (Dr.) **16**:499
Mary (Mrs.) **11**:386
Mordecai **14**:612
Mordicai **16**:432
Morgan **3**:260, 289, 332, 370
Moses **11**:515-516, 518
Robert **11**:772
Sarah **12**:518
Susanna **13**:282
Thomas **3**:225, 230-231; **4**:269, 669,
748, 782; **13**:431; **16**:312
William **5**:135, 454; **11**:472
MORGESTERN, Joannes **3**:328
MORITZEN, Erasmus **11**:772
MORPOOLE, Richard **12**:619
MORR(E)Y, Humphrey **1**:167, 209, 267,
382, 559, 614-616 (See MORRIE)
MORREAU, Peter **1**:452
MORRELL, --- (Mr.) **15**:443, 455
John **12**:507; **16**:4, 122
Robert **5**:186; **16**:465
William **14**:506
MORREY, Jacob **10**:156
John **1**:559
MORRIA, Alexander **10**:748
MORRIE, Humphrey **1**:589 (See
MORR(E)Y)
MORRIS, --- **8**:576

MORRIS, --- (Capt.) **11**:150; **13**:310,
661
--- (Gov.) **5**:1; **8**:10, 88, 92, 261,
568-569, 623, 661; **11**:673, 690;
12:337
--- (Mr.) **12**:60; **13**:279, 425
Abel **10**:450, 501
Alexander **10**:720
An'y. J. **10**:415
Antho. **7**:86
Anthony **2**:34, 82-83, 86, 104, 106,
151, 161, 411; **3**:366; **11**:31;
13:167
Anthony (Anthonie) **1**:371, 382,
451, 475-476, 479, 481-485, 488,
493, 495, 498, 500, 502, 504,
507, 531, 543-545, 547-548, 552,
565-571, 575-576, 578, 592-594,
601-602
Anthony James **11**:180
Anthony, Jr. **6**:174
Anthony, Sr. **6**:174
Cadwallader **13**:389, 698, 747;
14:29, 261
Daniel, Jr. **10**:523
Deborah **13**:599
Elizabeth **13**:246
Enoch **11**:610-612
Frederick **6**:263
Governieur **13**:585
Israel **11**:473
J. **15**:363
Jacob **12**:487, 528, 567, 589, 593,
606, 609, 614, 622, 633,
637-639, 644-645, 717; **13**:115,
243, 296, 547
James **3**:465; **4**:363-364, 523, 619;
5:90, 210, 416; **9**:203; **10**:767;
13:391, 415, 721, 737; **14**:215,
218, 230, 504; **15**:233; **16**:138
Jno. **2**:434
John **4**:669; **5**:327, 506; **9**:701;
10:652, 655-656; **12**:38, 95, 103,
118, 323, 458, 576; **14**:378, 518;
15:297, 506
John (Dr.) **16**:193, 492
John, Jr. **10**:735; **11**:25, 97, 104,
187-188, 228, 246, 258, 276,
285, 294, 310, 321, 357, 385,
441, 585, 719; **14**:110
Jonathan **14**:555
Joseph **7**:394, 637; **8**:487; **9**:751,
767, 769, 771; **10**:2; **11**:656;
13:130, 326
Joshua **5**:729; **7**:148-150; **8**:242,
262; **9**:704; **13**:204
Luke **9**:699, 781; **10**:47, 88, 283,
412; **11**:538; **12**:458; **13**:100
Luke, Jr. **16**:183
Mary **15**:35
Morris **3**:28
Philip **1**:82
Richard Hill **15**:96; **16**:176, 190
Richd. **1**:340
Robert **9**:293, 366; **10**:280,
282-283, 285-288, 290-292,
295-296, 298-302, 304-307, 312,
314, 321-323, 327-330, 334-336,
338-343, 345-347, 352, 354-355,
357, 359-363, 365-368, 371,
373-375, 377-378, 380-382, 384,
387-390, 395, 397-400, 402-405,
407, 416, 421, 424, 433,
442-446, 458-459, 469, 473, 483,
494, 508, 543, 556-557, 559-562,
566, 571-572, 574-575, ->

MORRIS, Robert (continued)
10:578-579, 586, 589, 597, 601,
605, 607, 610-612, 615, 631,
638, 642, 647, 719; 11:126, 272,
346, 385, 548, 552, 580-581,
633, 653, 771, 784; 12:2, 16,
493, 507, 581-582, 632, 636,
648, 680, 779, 783; 13:6-7, 18,
73, 83, 96, 100, 110, 128, 173,
193, 195, 199, 211, 280, 282,
374, 385, 404, 427, 492, 541;
14:119, 182, 464, 466, 468, 473,
481-482, 488, 495-496, 506, 550,
555; 15:5, 98, 107, 151, 342,
657; 16:100, 540
Robert Hunter 6:143-145, 164-165,
167-168, 170, 176, 181, 186-190,
193, 203-204, 215, 220, 223,
226, 236, 240, 243, 247,
252-255, 259, 261-262, 267-269,
276-278, 281, 285-287, 290,
293-301, 303, 305-310, 318-320,
322-323, 325, 327, 329-332,
334-335, 338-340, 344-345,
352-354, 358, 364-365, 370, 372,
377, 382, 388, 394-399, 401,
404, 406, 408, 410-412, 414,
416-417, 419-423, 426, 428-430,
432-433, 438-439, 441, 443,
445-446, 450-453, 455-457, 459,
462-465, 467-468, 475-477,
480-485, 487, 489, 492-493,
495-496, 498-499, 502-503, 505,
509-512, 514-517, 519-523, 526,
533-536, 546, 548-551, 554-555,
558-561, 564-567, 587-588,
591-592, 595, 597, 599, 601-607,
613, 615, 617, 623, 637,
639-640, 643-645, 647, 649,
651-653, 656, 661-662, 665-666,
670, 672, 676-677, 680-682, 685,
688-689, 691, 696-697, 700-703,
706, 711-714, 720, 724, 729-730,
733-734, 736, 738, 742, 744-745,
747, 750-751, 753-755, 760,
762-763, 765, 769, 771-775,
777-779, 781, 783; 7:1, 3, 5, 7,
9-11, 13-16, 18-20, 23, 29,
31-33, 35-37, 40-42, 44, 46,
55-56, 58-62, 64, 70, 72-74,
78-79, 83-84, 87-88, 90-93,
96-97, 100, 105, 110-113,
116-117, 122-123, 127-128,
131-137, 142, 144, 148, 151-153,
156, 158, 160-162, 164-165,
167-170, 172-173, 179-182,
186-187, 189-193, 196, 202-207,
220-223, 226, 229-231, 233-234,
246, 263, 270, 279, 284, 306,
312-313, 325, 335, 377, 447,
463, 635, 640-641, 643, 724
Roger 6:488-489
S. 13:60, 161, 483
S. C. 13:509
Samuel 4:271, 762; 5:388, 562,
597, 602, 662; 6:144; 7:10;
8:402, 505; 10:280, 282-291,
294-297, 299-302, 304, 306-307,
312-314, 334-336, 338-339,
343-344, 351, 367-368, 373-374,
382, 384-385, 388-390, 395, 401,
403-404, 407, 411, 415, 424-425,
429, 431, 433, 435, 438,
442-446, 448, 451-453, 455-456,
464-465, 468-474, 476, 478,
480-481, 483, 489-491, ->

MORRIS, Samuel (continued)
10:495-496, 498-499, 509, 515,
517, 519, 524, 526, 530-532,
535, 539, 541-544, 548, 550-553,
557, 559-563, 566-567, 570, 572,
574-575, 578-580, 584, 586, 590,
592-596, 599, 603, 605, 610,
615-617, 621, 623, 626, 631,
636-639, 642, 644, 645, 649-653,
655-660, 662, 664-666, 668,
670-672, 675, 677-678, 680-683,
686-687, 689, 691-702, 704-705,
707-711, 713, 716-718, 721-733,
735-736, 738-742, 744, 746-748,
750, 752-756, 758-762, 764, 766,
768-775, 777-778, 782-784;
11:1-14, 16-20, 22-28, 30,
32-33, 36-37, 39-40, 47, 49,
67-68, 72-73, 75-77, 81, 83-87,
90, 92-95, 97, 99, 103-109, 111,
113, 122, 134-143, 145, 181,
186-187, 194, 198, 246, 258,
564, 656, 716; 12:29, 161, 210,
507; 13:304, 391, 721; 15:430,
442; 16:247, 401
Samuel C. 11:1-12, 14-20, 22, 25,
45-46, 102-104, 107-109, 111,
114-115, 117-118, 120-122,
124-128, 130-143, 145, 181-182,
658, 747, 751; 13:737
Samuel Cadwalader 10:281, 717,
720, 722-733, 735-741, 744, 746,
748-750, 752-756, 758-764, 766,
769-775, 777-779, 783-784
Samuel, Jr. 13:85, 112
Staats 6:292-293, 304
Thomas 16:497
William 10:211; 11:9, 11, 35, 44,
65, 74, 91, 513, 516-517
William W. 15:340
MORRIS (SEE WILLING &) 11:1, 7,
10; 12:38
MORRIS CADWALADER 12:142
MORRISON, Ann 13:329
Daniel 13:91; 16:238
Hans 10:771; 15:348
Hugh 10:377, 481
James 10:303, 523, 708; 11:62;
12:31; 13:160, 168, 302; 14:296,
302, 322-323, 420; 16:204
John 5:506; 15:502
Joseph 13:668; 14:132, 413; 16:498
Larkin 14:613
Margaret 15:652
Obadiah 12:188
Robert 5:662; 6:638; 7:267; 9:337,
600; 14:557
Samuel 14:34, 189, 192, 418, 428
Thomas 10:705, 707
William 11:587; 13:294
MORRISSON, --- (Ens.) 13:168
MORROW, --- (Capt.) 11:210
Abraham 15:374, 406, 422, 456,
468, 519; 16:14, 197-198, 209b,
222b
Abram 11:358
Charles 5:210
John 4:102; 11:368
William 11:368
MORRY, Jacob 14:208
MORSE, Joseph 11:606
MORTIMER, John 16:45
Robert 12:333; 13:568
MORTIMORE, Robert 14:91, 415
MORTON, Jno. 11:31

MORTON, John **7**:417; **9**:375, 398,
442, 547, 657, 673, 703, 705;
10:66, 70, 113, 117, 173, 241,
254, 256, 266, 268, 272, 281,
357-358, 647, 708; **13**:481
Robert **13**:481
Sketchly **10**:656, 666, 682; **12**:131
Thomas **13**:730, 737
William **2**:34, 50, 129, 136
Wm. **1**:503, 510, 547, 601, 615
MORTONSON, Morton **2**:480
MORTZ, Bartholomius **3**:454
MOSEKE, Henry **3**:594
MOSEMAN, Andreas **3**:518
Christian **3**:518
MOSER, Abraham **16**:162
Andreas **3**:458
Jerig **3**:455
Leonhard **3**:456
Michael **3**:456; **15**:254; **16**:90
Paulus **3**:456
Tobias **3**:456
MOSES **8**:132
MOSES, --- **5**:686
Isaac **11**:108; **12**:424, 427, 464;
13:507
Philip **11**:109
MOSES (THE MOHOCK) **7**:64, 70
MOSES (THE SONG) **6**:141, 159, 161,
614
MOSES CONTJOCHQUA **6**:160
MOSES Jr. **8**:132
MOSIMAN, Hans **3**:432
MOSLEY, Increase **9**:571
MOSS, --- (Mr.) **11**:654
Joseph **4**:102; **9**:584
Mathew **5**:107
Thomas **10**:716; **11**:53
Vester **11**:158
MOSSE, Tho. **1**:95
MOSSER, Jacob **11**:665
Philip **11**:310, 665
MOSSON, Susannah **11**:154
MOTHOWANA (METHAWANA) **4**:588
MOTHS, Michel **3**:414
MOTT, Ashet **7**:394
Samuel **1**:83
MOTTACHA PETER (MATTACKA PETERS)
8:383, 386
MOULD, William **7**:186
MOULDER, John **10**:327, 339, 353,
362, 478; **11**:514, 516-517;
14:248
Joseph **10**:407, 409, 422, 430, 478,
489, 567, 592, 596, 616, 622,
630, 632, 640; **11**:82, 110, 223
Robert **7**:560; **14**:475
William **10**:484, 541, 544, 671,
675, 781; **11**:17, 595; **12**:131
MOULDER & COATS **10**:723
MOUNCE, Luke **5**:248
MOUNT, Thomas A. **14**:265-266
MOUNTFORT, --- (Count) **11**:487
MOUNTS, Providence **12**:482
MOUNTY, John D. **13**:679; **14**:96, 424
MOURER, Frederick **13**:432
MOUSER, --- (Capt.) **11**:99
MOWHORTER, Thomas **14**:250, 556
MOY, George **15**:570; **16**:195, 495
MOY(E)S, John **11**:573, 636, 752
MOYER, --- (Capt.) **11**:99
Adam **14**:190, 194, 434
Egedius **14**:226
Henry **11**:775
John **10**:730
Matthias **15**:378

MOYER, Nicholas **11**:212
Philip Melchoir **3**:467
Valentine **12**:601
MOYES, John **10**:745; **13**:324, 517,
520; **15**:272
MOYLAN, --- **13**:577, 589, 624;
14:191, 195
--- (Col.) **11**:647; **13**:44, 221,
504, 542
Jasper **12**:656
John **15**:301
Stephen **12**:81, 293, 332, 576, 609,
642, 647, 740, 758; **13**:555;
14:126, 430; **16**:356
Steven **13**:712
MOYSER, Christian **3**:287
Hans **3**:287
MOYSTEN (MOSTYN), --- (Adm.) **6**:457,
461, 712, 729
MRISES, --- (Mrs.) **1**:412
MSTON, John **13**:171
MUCK, Jacob **10**:273-274
MUCKLEHENNY, Dennis **6**:648
MUHLENBERG, Frederick A. **13**:85,
352, 391, 744
Frederick Augustus **13**:112, 414,
721; **14**:2, 23, 54, 163, 210,
213, 229, 279; **15**:636, 639, 644,
658; **16**:423, 438
Peter **14**:568, 571, 573-575,
577-581, 588-592, 596, 604,
606-607, 626-629, 631-635,
637-643, 646-661, 663-672;
15:1-12, 14-17, 21-22, 24-45,
47, 49-63, 67-71, 75-76, 78,
83-89, 92-94, 97, 99, 101-116,
118-178, 180-190, 193-195,
197-204, 206-209, 211-222,
224-230, 232-267, 269-275,
278-279, 284, 287-290, 294-304,
306, 308, 311-317, 320-328, 331,
337-353, 356-358, 360-362,
364-391, 394-404, 406-410,
414-421, 424-427, 430-436,
438-473, 475-477, 479-480,
482-492, 494-506, 508-509, 513,
516-518, 520-527, 530-545,
547-551, 554-563, 566, 636, 639,
658; **16**:193
MUHLENBERG (MULENBURGH), Michael
11:437, 481, 724
MUHLENBURG (MUHLENBERGH), Frederick
12:61, 78, 172-173, 263, 311,
349, 351, 371, 390, 507, 531,
541, 568, 580-581
MUHLHAUS, Casper **3**:515
MUIR, James **13**:742; **14**:58, 166,
467, 626; **15**:294; **16**:515
MUIRS, James **13**:741
MUK, Robert **5**:210
MULCHSLAGER, Frederick **3**:432
MULELR, Hans Michael **3**:455
MULHALLEN, John **15**:428
MULHOLLAN, Hugh **14**:425
MULHOLLIN, Hugh **13**:638
MULHOLM, Hugh **14**:96
MULL, Johan Henrick **3**:453
MULLAN, Thomas **9**:390, 392
MULLAR, Fulk **3**:466
Jacob **3**:516
Simon **3**:458
Valtin **3**:466
Wolfgang **3**:516
MULLEN, Charles **12**:671
James **16**:132
John **13**:757; **14**:427

MULLEN, Patrick **14:**3
 William **13:**622
MULLER, Andreas **3:**432
 Anthony **3:**386
 Christian **3:**414
 Fredrick **3:**454
 Georg. **3:**457
 Hans **3:**593
 Hans Georg. **3:**415
 Hans Jacob **3:**453
 Herman **3:**414
 Hieronimus **3:**456
 Jacob **3:**386, 453, 456
 Johan Georg. **3:**453
 Johan Nicolaus **3:**458
 Johannes **3:**454
 John **14:**90
 Johs. Philip **3:**454
 Leonhard **3:**458
 Martin **3:**386
 Matthias **3:**455
 Peter **3:**385
MULLERY, Edmund **16:**393
MULLIGAN, James **14:**386
 William **5:**469
MULLINAX, Nathaniell **1:**390, 437-438
MULLONEY, John **14:**506
MULLOWNY, John **11:**156, 158-159
MULLOY, Edward **10:**388
 James **10:**450
MULVANEY, Patrick **13:**636
MULVARY (MULVANEY), Patrick **14:**90,
 426
MUMMA, Jacob **3:**413
MUMMEY, Jacob **13:**577
MUMMEY (MUMMAY), Jacob **14:**193, 438
MUNDAY, Henry **4:**101-107, 109, 147
MUNDELL, John **4:**245
MUNDY, Beniah (Benejah) **14:**172, 495
MUNEER, Joseph **7:**14
MUNN, Mary **11:**703
MUNRO, George **9:**337, 600
 Mary **14:**316
MUNRO(E), George **5:**551, 597, 662
MUNROE, Mary **15:**532
MUNROW, John **16:**382
MUNTZ, Johan Casper **3:**414
MURCHISON, John **10:**581
MURDOCH, John **14:**600
MURDOCK, Samuel **15:**155
MURDOCK (MURDOCK), Samuel **11:**284,
 289, 296-297, 525
MURFEY **1:**104, 115
MURPHEY, Edward **15:**142
MURPHY, --- (Lt.) **11:**63
 Archibald **13:**645, 756; **14:**87, 427
 Catherine **11:**250, 530
 Daniel **10:**340; **11:**76, 119; **12:**187
 Edward **3:**592-593
 Elizabeth **15:**119
 George **13:**135
 Henderson **15:**457
 James **16:**8
 John **9:**713; **12:**188; **13:**580, 614;
 14:432; **15:**119; **16:**87
 Joseph **13:**635; **14:**88, 414
 Martin **11:**117
 Philip **14:**293, 300, 422
 Susannah **12:**760, 778-779
 Thomas **12:**450, 776, 779
 Timothy **14:**108; **15:**119
MURPHY (MURFEY), Roger **5:**444, 469
MURR(A)Y, Mary **12:**365-366
MURR(A)Y (SEE BUNNER &) **12:**474
MURR(E)Y, Humph. **1:**162, 190, 322,
 371

MURRAH, John **7:**154
MURRAN, William **11:**782-783
MURRAY, --- **11:**481
 --- (Capt.) **6:**20
 --- (Gov.) **8:**505
 --- (Lt.) **12:**356
 --- (Mr.) **5:**640
 Alexander **14:**465, 487, 517
 Alexander (Rev.) **11:**502-503,
 564-565, 579
 Edward **10:**235
 Eleanor **13:**394
 Francis **10:**162, 766; **11:**116;
 13:277, 594, 686, 745-746;
 14:102, 139, 207, 212, 293, 300,
 410, 439, 596
 Humphrey **2:**9, 11-13, 18-20, 24-30,
 32-33; **13:**321
 Ja. (Gen.) **9:**290-291
 Jacob **11:**212
 James **5:**443; **10:**101, 212; **11:**85,
 87-88, 120, 367, 719; **12:**42;
 13:752; **14:**361, 380, 465
 John **4:**154; **10:**451; **11:**57, 89,
 703, 732; **12:**195; **13:**569,
 614-615; **14:**130, 134; **16:**309
 Joseph **5:**8; **6:**57, 67-68, 72-73,
 75, 82, 92-93, 96, 105
 Lackey **13:**544
 Martha **12:**322
 Noah **15:**606; **16:**126
 Patrick **15:**171
 R. **1:**29
 Simon **11:**111, 130, 139
 Tho. **2:**114
 Thomas **13:**568; **14:**82, 91, 102,
 125, 130, 189, 192, 415, 429,
 431
 William **9:**127-128, 214, 250-256,
 259, 262-263, 322-323; **14:**151,
 296, 303, 609; **16:**332
 William, Jr. **15:**326
MURREN, William **12:**632; **13:**708,
 717, 758; **14:**87, 102, 410, 420
MURREY, Alexander **15:**325-326
MURROW, William **12:**307, 572
MURROW (MUNROW), Andrew **14:**371, 376
MURRY, Alexa. **11:**453
 James **10:**701
 John **10:**765-757
MURS, Hans Simon **3:**385
MURTHWAIT, Richard **12:**374
MURTHWAITE, Richard **13:**148
MURTZ, Georg. Henrich **3:**516
MUSER, --- (Capt.) **11:**143
MUSGENUNG, Anthony **13:**706; **16:**453
 Jacob **14:**202
 Joseph **12:**33
MUSGRAVE, --- (Mr.) **11:**153
 Aaron **12:**320
 Aron (Aaron) **15:**500, 502
 John **3:**263, 345, 356
MUSGROVE, John **11:**515-517, 549
MUSHET(T), Thomas **10:**8-9, 14
MUSKETNESS, Adam **13:**708; **14:**94, 415
MUSQUANAKO **5:**685
MUSSAUSE **8:**750
MUSSELMAN, Christian **13:**337
 Peter **14:**50
MUSSEMEELIN, John **4:**675-676,
 680-684
MUSSER, John **13:**328; **14:**485
MUSTARD, Archibald **14:**131-132, 609
MUSULBURGER, Hans **3:**386
MYER, Giddy **11:**251
 Jacob **16:**495

144

NEWLIN, Nathl **2**:34, 103, 106, 156,
536, 577, 585
 Nich. **1**:125-130, 135, 137-138,
140, 148-149, 169-171, 176-179,
181-184, 186, 190-191, 196-198,
203-206, 208-211, 320, 622-623
NEWLIN(E), Nathaniel **1**:547-548, 614
NEWMAN, Christopher **3**:569, 619
 John **13**:615; **14**:303, 432
 Melchior **3**:569
 Paine **10**:734; **11**:113
 Wingate **10**:605; **11**:24, 37, 61, 223
NEWMEITER, Christopher Erhard **3**:594
NEWMOCH **6**:37
NEWOLEKA (NEWALEKA) **9**:78-79, 86,
88, 656
NEWS, Thomas **3**:293
NEWSWANG, Christian **3**:328
NEWTIN, Nichoals **1**:79
NEWTON **2**:179; **3**:478
NEWTON, Edward **15**:164
 Henry **3**:416, 465, 521, 575, 615
 John **3**:473-474; **15**:571
 Richard **15**:228, 230
NEYES, Hans **2**:549
NEZLEY, Henry **15**:174
NI(C)HAS **8**:175, 177-178, 189-191,
196, 205, 218
NIC(H)OLA, Lewis **10**:156, 491, 517,
724, 728, 732, 736, 740-741,
744, 746, 752, 761, 774, 781;
12:10, 22, 37-38, 51, 58, 62,
66, 68, 92, 107-108, 177, 250,
267, 279, 332, 338, 358, 372,
375, 391, 397, 400, 422, 431,
438-439, 448, 450, 455, 458,
464, 466, 492, 515, 527, 550,
555, 588-589, 603, 605, 622,
633, 639, 641, 649, 675, 693,
780
NICE, --- (Capt.) **13**:189, 191, 212,
228
 John **10**:767; **11**:180; **13**:562;
14:100, 316, 406, 408, 429, 436,
672; **15**:432
NICES, William **11**:156
NICHAQUANTAQUEAH **8**:218
NICHOL(L)S, Francis **14**:447, 635
NICHOLA, Lewis **13**:15, 620, 712;
15:633; **16**:17, 37, 70, 75, 167
NICHOLAS **5**:685
NICHOLAS, --- **12**:255
 Edward **3**:620; **4**:182
 John **14**:207, 446
 Lewis **10**:283-284; **13**:185
 Sampson **16**:42
 Samuel **11**:26; **14**:230
NICHOLEAU, Lewis **10**:739
NICHOLES, William **10**:451
NICHOLL, James **14**:311
NICHOLLS, Ebenr. (Maj.) **6**:608, 611
 Francis **12**:137
 Martha **13**:253
 Richard **6**:263
 Samll. **1**:521
 Scudamore **13**:253
 William **12**:70, 647
 Wm. **1**:203-204, 401
NICHOLS, --- (Col.) **10**:127
 Amos **2**:22
 Francis **11**:51, 91, 113, 267
 John **14**:214
 Samuel **16**:210b
 William **13**:550, 724, 768, 770;
15:45, 315, 367; **16**:157,
268-269, 291

NICHOLS, Williams **14**:49, 667
NICHOLSON, --- (Mr.) **13**:547, 673
 Ann **12**:159
 Coll. **2**:450-451, 532, 534, 538
 Francis **1**:515-516, 527, 533
 James **4**:104
 John **10**:333, 335, 458, 633, 651;
11:103; **12**:219, 494, 646, 652,
654-655, 703, 705-709, 714-715,
723, 732, 752-753, 763, 780;
13:1, 24, 71, 117, 138, 149,
187, 202, 242, 265, 269,
271-272, 275, 277, 292, 300,
334, 364, 373, 380, 385, 395,
407, 417, 423, 431, 439, 443,
454, 461, 478-479, 493, 498,
504, 515, 522, 530-531, 541-542,
545, 557, 562, 571, 581, 592,
625, 645, 667, 671, 679, 694,
703, 706, 718, 753; **14**:2, 7, 34,
47, 50, 66, 71, 75, 97, 105,
118, 139, 148, 160-161, 178,
206, 231, 248, 277, 315, 325,
403, 419, 454-457, 466, 476,
497, 500, 503, 548, 550, 554,
582, 602, 619, 625, 627, 642;
15:6, 49, 67, 96, 114, 148, 193,
204, 224, 230, 239, 243, 285,
294, 320, 347, 349, 370,
373-375, 380, 394-395, 399, 413,
425, 438, 465, 486, 509, 519,
539, 550, 561, 565, 618,
621-622; **16**:2, 31, 54, 56, 86,
94-95, 97, 110, 112, 174, 179,
191, 197-198, 201, 216, 256-257,
266, 298-299, 318, 323, 326,
330, 336, 342, 359, 362, 383,
385, 403, 416, 494, 357-358,
503-506, 508, 511, 513-514
 Samuel **15**:58; **16**:352, 356
 William **14**:189, 192, 435
NICHOLSON (NICHOLLS), Samuel
10:436, 441, 443, 447, 452
NICHSHOMPEYAT **3**:316
NICHTAMSKAKOW **3**:310
NICKAS **5**:470
NICKELSON, James **4**:102
NICKIPHOCK **5**:570
NICODEMUS, --- **7**:169, 173-174, 186,
191, 220, 357, 478, 774
 Christian **7**:174
 Dorothea **7**:174
 Gashatis **7**:174
 Justina **7**:174
 Nathan **7**:174
 Thomas **7**:174
 Zacharias **7**:174
NICOLA, Lewis **14**:89, 411
NICOLA (NICHOLA), Lewis **11**:24, 26,
33, 38, 48, 56, 68, 81, 101,
134, 222, 256, 266, 284, 286,
289-290, 296, 299, 305-306, 528,
538, 567, 637, 647, 741
NIESBIT, John **11**:373
NIGHLINGER, Samuel **13**:632
NIGHTLINGER, Samuel **14**:418
NIHANIUCHSA **5**:685
NILNET, --- **11**:123
NIMHON (NIMHAM, NIMEHAM) **8**:176,
208, 221, 667
NIMISHA **9**:229
NINGER, Mark **3**:389
NINING, John **10**:108
NISEWANGER, Christian **3**:429
NITTARUNTAQUAA **4**:663
NITZILIUS, Matthias **2**:480

148

149

OWEN, Griffith (continued) **2:**95-98,
101, 103-104, 107-109, 111-112,
114, 117-118, 120-125, 128-129,
134-135, 138, 149-141, 144,
146-148, 150-158, 161, 163-166,
168, 170-174, 178-187, 190, 194,
198, 200, 204, 206, 209-210,
212-220, 222, 234, 237, 239-242,
247-248, 251-253, 259, 276, 281,
297, 321, 343, 362, 364-365,
373-373, 378, 386, 391, 393-397,
403, 407, 468, 472, 478, 482,
484, 489, 493, 509, 513,
516-517, 524-539, 541-542,
544-545, 550-552, 557, 559-568,
571, 573-574, 577-579, 582,
584-587, 589, 591-592, 594-595,
599, 601, 603, 607, 609,
613-614; **5:**209; **6:**529; **13:**536;
14:55, 395, 654; **15:**174, 414,
618; **16:**29, 180, 197
John **3:**370, 387, 416, 615; **6:**160;
9:635
Owen **3:**260, 289, 332, 370, 387,
416, 464, 520, 575, 614
Rich. **1:**127
Robert **5:**175
Robt. **1:**123, 438, 441, 517
Thomas **5:**3, 388
William **16:**385
OWEN(S), John **4:**86, 247, 669, 748,
782; **5:**411, 464, 532, 536, 550
Owen **4:**85, 247, 309, 352, 469
William **4:**271
OWENS, David **9:**190, 215, 222, 228,
280
Francis **10:**273-274
Mary **15:**367
Matthew **15:**362
OWER, Hans Erick **3:**287
OWINGS, Robert **5:**584-586, 588, 593
Samuel **5:**585
OWISTOGAH (Capt. Peter) **8:**293
OWISTOGO **7:**67
OWNER (SEE LITTLE &) **10:**758
OXLEY, Margaret **13:**285
OXMAN, Lazarus **3:**329
OYAGHTAWNIGH-ROANU INDIANS **4:**586
OYANOWHACHSO **3:**102
OYSTER, Christian **16:**403
OYUCHSERAGARET **5:**686
OZEAS, Peter **11:**640; **13:**35, 81,
171; **15:**98, 571

P(E)ARIS, Richard **7:**272, 503-505,
527-529, 532, 535, 552-557, 598
P(H)RAHL, Lewis **10:**380, 399, 458,
461, 467, 493, 503, 550, 556,
600
PA(I)CA, --- (Mr.) **11:**677, 679,
702, 737
PA(R)TRIDGE, Oliver **6:**57, 67, 71,
82, 96, 100, 505
PAAL, Tobias **3:**458
PAALT, Johan Jacob **4:**60
PABOUL, Stephen **16:**137
PABST, Henrick **3:**456
PACHT, Johan Peter **3:**323
PACKENAH **13:**465
PACKER, James **13:**18; **15:**84
PACKMAN, George **3:**542, 587
Jacob **11:**527

PACKSENOSA **6:**360
PADON, --- (Capt.) **10:**690
PAESCHAL, Joseph **4:**482
PAGE, Stephen **1:**228; **15:**388
PAINE, Edmd. **1:**186
Thomas **12:**65, 286, 366, 503, 595;
14:275, 402; **15:**529
PAINTER, Christopher **13:**516
Henry **1:**180
Richd. **2:**129
PAISLEY, Robert **11:**549; **16:**391-392
PAISLEY (See BAISLEY), Robert
15:558
PALAKACOUTHATER **4:**347
PALESKE, Charles **15:**371
PALFREY, John **12:**194
William **12:**382
PALMER, Anthony **2:**429, 432,
434-435, 437, 439, 441, 443,
446, 449, 451, 463, 468-470,
473, 482, 484-485, 489, 506,
510, 513, 517-518, 520-522,
524-531, 534-536, 538, 540;
3:14, 16-19, 21, 25, 28, 30-31,
33, 38-39, 44, 50, 57-58, 62,
64, 67, 75, 90, 107, 109, 111,
113, 115, 138, 140, 158, 160,
162-163, 171, 175, 180, 196,
203, 222, 228-230, 233, 238,
242-243, 245-246, 254, 257-259,
261, 264, 266, 269, 321, 384,
387, 390, 393, 395, 399-400;
4:47, 51, 71, 73, 82, 85, 100,
104, 165, 232, 247, 274, 285,
288-290, 304, 306, 336, 341,
350, 356, 387, 381-382, 395,
421-422, 429, 432, 443, 461,
468-469, 496, 506, 524; **5:**29,
39, 52, 61, 65-68, 70-74, 76-78,
80, 82-83, 89, 94-96, 100-101,
104-105, 107-112, 120-121,
123-125, 127, 131, 134, 136,
140, 143-145, 148-149, 152,
154-159, 162-166, 168-176,
181-183, 186-190, 192, 196,
198-199, 201-203, 205-209,
211-212, 215-216, 220-223,
225-229, 232, 234-235, 238, 245,
248, 252, 256, 258-259, 265-270,
272-274, 280-282, 284, 287, 289,
293-294, 296-300, 304, 306, 319,
323-326, 328, 330, 332, 338-340,
343, 347, 359-362, 380
Elizabeth **13:**523
George **11:**83; **12:**157, 568; **13:**89,
395-396, 723-724; **14:**458; **16:**9,
288
John **1:**521; **9:**213; **11:**513,
516-517, 605; **12:**277; **14:**214-215
Richard **11:**610-611
Sarah **15:**478
Thomas **10:**503, 528, 633-634, 653;
11:605
PALMER(S), John **10:**260, 267, 368,
371
PALMERSTON, --- **9:**343
PALTZ, Johannes Jorig **3:**454
PAMYLACHAD **8:**9
PANCAKE, George **13:**196
Philip **12:**451; **15:**98
PANCOAST, David **11:**30, 34, 36, 44,
104, 129, 142, 602
PANNEL, James **12:**86
PANNEY, Tho. **1:**129
PAPLEY, John **12:**49, 236
Susanna **12:**236, 251; **13:**554

POMEROY, John 14:313, 656
 Ralph 11:749, 752
 Robert 10:327
POMFRET, --- (Earl of) 9:761;
 10:103
POMPUNAGH 9:135-136
POMROY, Seth (Lt. Col.) 6:608, 611
POMSHIRE (PUMPSHIRE, PUMPSHARE),
 John 7:152, 174, 176, 189, 192,
 199, 200, 204-207, 220, 296,
 307, 309, 313, 431, 477, 514,
 587, 589, 649-650, 654, 657-658,
 663, 665-666, 669, 672, 675-677,
 681, 684, 689, 694, 697, 702,
 705, 707-709, 713, 770-771
PONGUIS, Henry 10:746
PONNE, Andreas 3:368
PONNEAL, --- (Gov.) 8:483
PONSLER, John 13:777
POOL, Johan Snider 6:125
 N. 2:562
POOLK, John 5:454
POOR, John 11:514, 516-517
POORHAM, John 14:611
 John (alias Casper Kerkler) 15:149
POPAUCO 8:189
POPE, --- (Mr.) 6:675
 John 9:543, 731; 10:163; 11:133
 Nathaniel 2:566-567
 Richard 4:102
POPHAM, William 11:772
POPPLE, --- (Gov.) 7:202
 Alfred 3:262
PORROGALLI, Gaetano 13:773
PORTER, --- 15:116
 --- (Capt.) 12:210, 245, 266
 --- (Col.) 11:52, 84, 110; 13:479,
 616
 --- (Maj.) 13:456
 --- (Mr.) 14:539
 Alexander 5:194
 Andrew 13:145, 223, 233, 246, 320,
 367, 492, 573, 601, 714; 14:69,
 88, 104, 114, 119, 134, 285-286,
 308, 359, 399-400, 418, 454,
 457, 507, 586; 15:19, 106, 175,
 220, 340, 356, 382, 642, 644;
 16:43, 49
 Charles 14:225
 David 10:772; 12:703
 James 10:717; 13:88, 112; 14:485
 Jno. 11:58
 Nathaniel 10:687, 689
 Robert 10:685, 688; 13:456, 573,
 715; 14:88; 15:401
 Samuel 13:778; 14:610
 Stephen 13:538, 542; 14:403, 441,
 443, 445, 460, 623, 643; 15:16,
 108, 120; 16:209b
 Thomas 10:657, 678, 683, 686, 688,
 704-705, 707-709, 711, 715, 717
 William 5:210; 11:93; 12:164;
 14:296, 303, 415; 16:103
PORTEUS, George 5:245-246
PORTH, John 13:276
PORVEY 13:465
POSKETS, Christiana 11:679
POSSART, Jacob 3:368-369
POST, Frederick 8:132-133, 142,
 145, 147-148, 173, 187, 206,
 212, 223, 297, 301, 341, 419,
 425, 434, 455, 463-464, 466-469,
 474, 485, 490-491, 676, 690-691,
 724, 730
 Nicolas 4:60
POSTLETHWAITE, John 5:3, 378

POSTLETHWAITE, Samuel 13:133, 396,
 726; 14:236, 567; 16:328
POSTLEWAITE, Samuel 10:770; 12:721
POTANG, --- (Lt.) 12:357
POTE, Edward 11:141
POTOM, --- (Lt.) 12:546
POTT, Degenhart 3:569
 Wilhelm 3:569
POTTENGER, --- (Lt.) 6:490
 James 12:219
POTTER, --- (Gen.) 11:646; 12:70,
 584; 13:70, 72, 83-84, 86, 362,
 376, 382, 384, 386, 409, 444,
 493, 567, 638
 --- (Gen./Mr.) 13:70, 73-75,
 82-84, 86-87, 90-96, 98-104,
 106, 109-111, 4127-419, 421,
 430-432, 435, 437, 439-444, 446,
 448-449, 491, 493-496
 --- (Maj. Gen.) 13:371, 374, 380,
 514
 --- (Mr.) 13:74, 82, 87, 90-91,
 447
 Andrew 13:456
 David 11:28
 James 9:481, 483, 506, 508; 10:43,
 730, 735; 11:66-68, 85, 101,
 199, 209, 248, 266, 277, 346,
 361, 372, 478; 12:365, 490, 492,
 513, 541, 543, 546-552, 554,
 556-564, 566, 568-570, 572-573,
 575, 578, 582-584, 586, 591-593,
 596, 604, 611, 618, 620,
 622-623, 626-634, 636-637,
 639-640, 642, 644-646, 648-654,
 657-658, 660-665, 667, 669-670,
 672, 674, 678-681, 769; 13:29,
 98, 104, 112-114, 132, 137,
 150-152, 157, 160, 165, 225,
 269, 289, 292, 309, 366, 370,
 372, 400-401, 408, 413-414,
 422-425, 429, 436, 447, 499-500,
 503-505, 508-510, 513-516,
 518-519, 522, 524-527, 530-532,
 534, 536-538, 540, 544-547,
 632-635, 637-642, 645, 647, 666,
 668, 670-673; 14:165, 199, 212,
 441-442, 485, 655; 15:91;
 16:168, 257-258, 266, 538
 John 5:210, 468; 6:144, 397, 435,
 638, 673-674, 706; 7:77, 230,
 631, 637; 13:386
 Joshua 7:725
 Matthew 12:320
 Nicholas 11:330
POTTS, --- 13:34
 --- (Adj.) 13:189
 --- (Mr.) 13:744
 David 10:297, 373, 733, 764;
 11:494; 12:694
 James 10:643, 701, 705-706, 709;
 15:141
 Jesse 11:163
 John 4:762; 5:388, 444, 524, 572;
 6:667; 7:249, 769; 8:575, 586,
 719; 9:672; 10:46; 11:163, 494,
 745, 772, 783; 12:114, 116, 137,
 577, 694; 13:505, 517, 759;
 14:580; 15:15-16, 93; 16:490
 Jonathan (Dr.) 10:395, 462, 537;
 11:42, 50, 633; 12:48, 100-101,
 139, 576-577
 Joseph 10:100, 212, 448; 11:379;
 14:159; 16:179
 Margaret 11:783; 13:545
 Nathaniel 12:138

POTTS, Robert 9:335
  Samuel 10:46, 412, 463, 476, 530;
    11:244; 12:576, 694; 13:517,
    544; 15:656, 658
  Thomas 10:710-711, 714, 721, 738;
    11:46-48; 12:576; 13:675, 722,
    737; 14:238, 250
  Thos. 2:541
  William 11:50; 13:552, 760;
    14:298, 305, 427
  Zebulon 10:770; 11:215, 601, 603;
    14:230, 313, 555, 596;
    15:100-101, 564, 569, 571-584,
    586-590, 592, 594-596, 600, 602,
    606-608, 610-620, 622-623, 625,
    635-658; 16:1-7, 9-17, 19-29,
    31, 33-35, 42-44, 46-48, 50-52,
    54-57, 59-60, 62, 64-78, 80,
    82-91, 93-94, 96-101, 104-111,
    114-116, 118-120, 122-127,
    130-138, 144-146, 148-149, 151,
    153-155, 162-166, 168-169,
    173-173, 175-176, 180-183,
    187-188, 190, 192-194, 196-197,
    199-202, 205, 209-211, 214, 216,
    218-220, 222-224, 209b-212b,
    215b-223b, 225, 230-233,
    235-236, 238-239, 244, 251-252,
    254-264, 267-274, 276, 278-291,
    293, 295-307, 309-313, 315-316,
    318, 320-326, 329-332, 336,
    339-341, 344-358, 360, 364-366,
    368-369, 371-373, 375-382, 384,
    386, 388-389, 392-396, 399-406,
    408-421, 423-429, 432-433, 435,
    439, 441, 445-447, 449-459,
    461-465, 477, 479-484, 487, 489,
    492-494, 496-501, 507, 511-528,
    530-531, 534-536, 539-540,
    542-543, 545-546
POTTS (SEE BUTLER &) 10:770
POUCH, --- (Capt.) 9:508
POUCHET, --- (Monsieur) 8:504
POULSON, Barbara 12:696
POULTNEY, Benjamin 10:496, 528;
    11:19, 53, 74, 137; 13:534
  Thomas 14:583
POVEY, Jno. 2:89
  John 6:267
POWEL, David 2:277, 289
  John 2:276
  Robert 4:504
  Samll. 2:541
  Thos. 2:510
  Wm. 2:111, 203, 277
POWELL (POWEL), --- 15:112
  --- (Capt.) 11:156
  --- (Mr.) 10:231; 12:43
  David 1:155; 3:601
  Giles 9:513-514 (See BOWER)
  Isaac 11:111, 602, 605
  Jeremiah 11:690, 728
  John 3:612-613; 7:186; 14:109, 111
  Joseph 8:335; 12:147, 164, 544
  Robert 14:308
  Sam'l. 3:428, 431
  Samuel 7:84, 86; 10:47; 12:348,
    709; 13:19-20; 16:53, 123, 490
  Thomas 10:114; 13:636; 14:87, 414
  William 1:29, 380-381, 390,
    437-438, 478; 5:626-627,
    663-664; 9:702; 10:116; 13:543
POWER, Alexander 13:384-385, 521,
    557; 15:185
  John 12:2
  Michael 14:441

POWER, Nicholas 13:759
  William 13:30, 456, 563, 713;
    15:421
POWER(S), Alexander 14:87, 197,
    292, 413, 462
  William 14:97, 101, 127, 197, 414,
    423-424, 454
POWERS, --- 11:648
  --- (Capt.) 12:266
  Alexander 12:775, 783; 13:183
  Elizabeth 12:309, 420
  Sarah 13:757
  William 13:757
POWERS (SEE EDES) 11:648
POWLE, John 5:87-88
POWNAL, Thomas 7:717
POWNAL(L), John 7:738, 740
  Thomas 6:110, 118, 267, 314, 549
POWNALL, --- (Capt.) 9:515
  Jno. 8:514
  John 6:118
POWTOWMACK INDIANS 13:467
POYADE, Peter Henry 14:67, 70
POYNTEL(L), William 14:513, 538,
    543
POYNTELL, --- (Mr.) 15:648
  William 16:221b
POYNTER, Henry 1:322
POYNTZ, Stephen 4:254, 484-485
POYTON, James 14:512
PRAHL, Lewis 12:514; 15:375
PRATHER, Henry 9:673, 732
PRATT, --- (Mr.) 7:272
  C. 8:621-622
  George 13:614
  Henry 4:500, 601, 669, 748, 782;
    5:55, 120, 345; 13:343, 543
  James 14:295, 302, 411
  John 12:357, 427, 545, 573;
    13:568, 717; 14:98, 415
  Thomas 10:384
PRAUL, John 15:256
PRAY, Job 12:551, 581
PREEST, Peter 5:318
PREMIR, Adam 16:308
PRENTICE 1:118
PRENTICE, --- (Capt.) 8:386
  --- (Dr.) 7:77
PRENTUP, William 7:507, 509,
    519-520, 533, 536, 539, 643
PRESCOT, James 13:528
PRESEL, Johan Valentine 3:518
PRESLY, --- (Mr.) 16:225
PRESMALL, Robert 13:327
PRESTON, --- 6:490
  --- (Mrs.) 12:425
  Ann 11:106
  Nathan 12:381
  Samuel (Sam., Saml.) 1:321, 479,
    578, 580, 596, 601, 612; 2:34,
    183, 429, 432, 434-435, 437,
    439, 441, 443-444, 446-449, 452,
    459, 461, 463, 466-470, 472-473,
    477, 479-480, 482, 484-487,
    489-491, 493-494, 502-503, 506,
    508-511, 513, 516-518, 520-522,
    524-532, 534-543, 545, 553,
    556-557, 561, 566-568, 571-573,
    576-580, 582, 585-587, 589,
    594-596, 604-614; 3:14, 16-18,
    25, 28, 30-33, 38-39, 43-45, 47,
    50, 55-58, 62-64, 67 , 71, 75,
    81-82, 90, 92, 98, 107-109, 111,
    113-115, 120, 130, 134, 138,
    141, 143-144, 147, 156, 158,
    160, 162-163, 165-167, ->

PRESTON, Samuel (Sam., Saml.)
(continued) **3:**170-172, 175, 178,
180, 187, 189-192, 196, 203,
209, 212, 216, 221, 225-230,
233-236, 242-251, 253-254,
256-257, 259, 261, 266, 269-271,
276, 279-282, 284, 289-290, 292,
294-295, 298, 302, 307-309,
315-316, 321, 326-327, 332-333,
336-337, 340, 343, 345-347, 354,
365-366, 369, 372, 375-376,
379-380, 382, 384, 387, 390,
395, 400-401, 404, 406, 410,
413, 415, 428, 435, 437-438,
442, 446, 459, 463, 466-467,
474, 479, 500, 505-506, 520-521,
524, 529, 534-535, 537-540, 542,
544-545, 563, 571, 573-574,
588-589, 591, 595, 598-599, 604,
607, 609, 612, 615, 617; **4:**17,
19-21, 23, 32-34, 39-41, 47, 49,
51, 53, 56, 71, 73, 80-82, 87,
90, 96-97, 100, 104, 106, 109,
112-113, 115, 119-120, 124, 129,
136, 140, 143-144, 147, 149-150,
152, 155, 158, 165, 167, 171,
175, 181, 186, 190, 195-198,
201-206, 209, 215, 219, 223-229,
232-233, 235, 238, 241-243, 245,
247-249, 256-257, 259, 262-264,
273-274, 277, 280, 283-285,
288-290, 292-297, 301-302,
304-307, 309-310, 312-314,
317-318, 321, 329-331, 333-334,
336, 341, 343, 345, 347, 350,
352-355, 359, 364, 387, 391,
393-395, 402, 413, 422, 429,
432, 435, 443, 461, 469,
479-483, 496, 501-503, 506, 548,
560, 566, 569, 572-573, 575-577,
583, 587-588, 618, 620, 626,
630, 639, 646, 651-652; **14:**447,
449; **16:**212b, 325
PRESTON, William **13:**622; **14:**99, 429
Wm. **2:**65, 101-102
PRETTYMAN, Thomas **9:**203
PREUS, Jno. **1:**499
PREVOST, --- (Maj.) **9:**214
PRICE, --- (Mr.) **7:**502
Aaron **5:**570
Benjamin **9:**337, 600
Edward **15:**110, 119
Elisha **13:**671; **16:**303, 498, 512
Elizabeth **13:**422
Henry Yelverton **10:**503, 524
John **8:**573; **9:**205, 673; **10:**384;
13:295; **14:**305, 475; **15:**424,
442, 478, 480-481
Joseph **10:**172; **16:**303
Pelitiah **15:**122
Peter **11:**514, 516-517; **13:**315
Philip **11:**244; **12:**245-246, 257,
426, 592, 651, 727
Rece **3:**620
Rees **16:**118, 299
Reese **15:**439
Rice **4:**182
Richard **14:**290
Samuel **13:**383; **14:**248
Tho. **1:**188, 321
William **11:**494; **13:**3, 9, 748;
14:68, 669; **15:**261; **16:**18, 23
PRICHARD, Joseph **4:**294
William **13:**558
PRICHET, --- (Mr.) **11:**51
Wm. **2:**148

PRICHETT, Thomas **14:**488
PRIDE, Chetmall **2:**513
PRIDE (THE) **7:**382
PRIEST, David **4:**135
PRIESTLY, John **5:**110; **10:**448;
13:580
PRILL, Martin **3:**284
PRINCE, Caleb **7:**168
John **3:**102
PRINCELAND, Christian **3:**386
PRINGLE, --- (Dr.) **6:**174
John **10:**407, 420, 425, 441, 744,
760; **11:**21, 119; **12:**130; **16:**466
Thomas **12:**206-207, 220
William **11:**664
PRINGLE(R), Tho. **1:**132, 140,
145-146
PRIOR, Lydia **13:**327
PRIOR (PRYOR), Thomas **10:**281, 531,
769
PRIS, Johan Peter **4:**100
PRISMAL, Robert **13:**322, 326
PRISSER, Henry **9:**508
PRITCHARD, John **13:**94
Joseph **11:**661, 670; **13:**94
PRITCHETT, John **11:**163
Rowland **11:**127
Thomas **15:**322
William **13:**64
PRIZGARD, Thomas **13:**254, 258
PROBST, Johs. Michael **3:**515
Matthias **11:**212
Michael **3:**515
PROCTER, Thomas **13:**296
PROCTOR, --- (Col.) **12:**631, 686,
727; **13:**115, 299, 367, 561, 571
Francis **10:**416, 423-424, 620,
742-743; **11:**156, 165; **12:**570;
13:244, 713; **14:**86
Francis, Jr. **13:**632
George **5:**248-249, 252-255
James **13:**456
John **10:**59, 106, 603; **11:**110, 118,
134, 173-175, 177-178, 181-182,
184-188, 190-191, 193-198, 200,
202-203, 205-210, 212-217, 219,
221-223, 225-238, 241-243,
245-250, 256-265, 267-268,
270-278, 280, 283, 285-287,
290-291, 293-295, 297, 300,
302-304, 316, 330, 392, 477,
479, 504, 511, 521, 531, 576,
662, 703, 722, 739-741, 756,
766, 774, 776, 781; **12:**7, 9-10,
14, 22, 102, 123, 182, 210, 215,
238, 245, 247, 250, 255, 266,
333-334, 439, 605, 618; **13:**112,
157-158, 162, 766, 775; **14:**449
John, Jr. **9:**779
Joshua **11:**515-517
Thomas **9:**678; **10:**167, 382-383,
390, 394, 402-403, 405, 416,
423-424, 438, 452, 467-468, 472,
494, 504, 507-=508, 512, 516,
526-527, 552, 560, 571, 630,
643, 685, 716-717, 719, 722,
734, 742-743, 749, 753, 756,
758, 769, 772-773, 775-777;
11:1, 7, 25, 27, 33, 44, 47, 53,
63-64, 67, 83, 90, 96, 112, 116,
139, 568; **12:**622, 645-646;
13:391, 555, 722-725; **14:**85,
120, 143, 158, 230, 423, 430,
456; **15:**116, 246, 269, 372;
16:391, 449, 481, 485, 510, 522

PROCTOR, William **12**:455;
   13:388-389; **16**:36, 77, 448
William, Jr. **9**:730; **10**:78, 163
PROLE, John **10**:459, 508, 579
PROPST, Matthias **14**:586
PROSSER, Philip **12**:85
   Stephen **16**:386
   William **13**:597; **14**:97, 424
PROSTLY (PRIESTLY), John **14**:94, 427
PROTHERO, Evans **1**:438
PROUD, Charles **16**:335
PROUT, Charles **16**:333
PROVENCE, --- **9**:508
PRUDDEN, Nathaniel **12**:1
   Thomas **10**:636; **13**:153, 389
PRUDYARD, Thomas **1**:29
PRUNDER, Johannes **3**:369
   Joseph **3**:368
PRY, --- (Capt.) **12**:278, 712
   Thomas **13**:568, 712; **14**:100, 424,
   428
PRYCE, --- (Capt.) **8**:582
PRYER, Antho. **1**:90-91
PRYOR, --- (Capt.) **10**:398, 531
   Charles **12**:146, 636; **16**:79
   Silas **3**:382
   Thomas **11**:601, 603; **12**:477-478;
   14:107, 403
PUCKLE, --- (Capt.) **2**:32
PUFFENBERGER, John **14**:296, 303, 430
PUGH, --- (Capt.) **11**:215, 227
   --- (Lt.) **11**:647, 753; **12**:14, 51,
   267, 279, 338, 372, 377, 422,
   448, 466, 492, 527, 555, 588,
   603, 633, 675, 693
   Abraham **13**:139
   Hugh **2**:613, 615; **3**:40-41; **11**:483,
   484-485
   James **11**:483, 484-485
   John **11**:67, 75; **15**:564, 647;
   16:501
   Jonathan **13**:713
   Joseph **6**:638; **7**:266
   Samuel **10**:674
PULASKI, --- (Count) **12**:76
PULLE(Y)N, --- (Capt.) **2**:99-101
PULTENY, J. **2**:403
PUMPHIRE, John **8**:156
PUNICHECKAN **8**:435
PUNNER, Elizabeth **13**:384
PURCEL(L), John **14**:406, 408, 437
PURCEL(L) (PURSELL), Henry D.
   14:85, 103, 420-421, 470
PURCELL, Henry **13**:680
   Henry D. **12**:355; **13**:669, 716
PURDEN, Fergus **11**:136
PURDY, --- (Col.) **13**:222
   James **11**:90, 340, 648
   Robert **12**:131, 411
   William **16**:294-295
PURRINS, John **5**:247
PURSEL, Thomas **12**:733
PURSELL, Jonathan **15**:645
PURSLEY, Benj. **9**:509
PURTLE, John **14**:82, 101, 426, 512,
   613-614
PURVIANCE, John **10**:281, 781;
   11:286, 476, 601, 603, 664, 667,
   756, 782; **12**:468, 487;
   13:490-491, 768
   Michael **10**:707
PUS(S)EY, Caleb **1**:87, 324, 454,
   475, 481-485, 488, 491, 503,
   507, 509, 513-521, 525-526,
   547-548, 552, 555, 557-559, 561,
   563, 565, 567-568. 571, 575, ->

PUS(S)EY, Caleb (continued) **1**:578,
   580, 589, 591-593, 595-596,
   601-602, 606, 611-612, 614,
   616-617, 622, 624; **2**:13, 17-22,
   27-30, 32-34, 36-37, 39-40, 43,
   45-47, 49, 52-55, 60-61, 67-69,
   71, 74, 78-79, 81, 86-87, 90-91,
   94-98, 101, 103, 105, 108-109,
   112, 116-119, 121-125, 128-129,
   131-132, 134-135, 138, 140-141,
   144-150, 152-156, 164-165,
   167-174, 179, 181, 186-187, 190,
   194, 198, 200, 204, 209, 226,
   236, 243, 253, 256, 258-259,
   280, 309, 315-316, 318, 320,
   356-357, 361, 364-365, 372-373,
   377, 397, 427-429, 434-435, 437,
   439, 441, 443, 446-447, 452,
   459, 461, 463, 473, 478,
   484-487, 489-490, 494, 502-503,
   508-510, 531, 533, 540, 545,
   560-561, 572, 579-580, 596, 606,
   608; **3**:122-123, 258, 603; **4**:340;
   6:529
   Ellis **11**:347
   Joshua **5**:547, 572
PUTNAM, --- (Gen.) **4**:6
   --- (Maj. Gen.) **11**:46, 59, 203-204
PUTS, William **2**:494
PUTZ, Michel **3**:456
PYAT, Jacob **4**:757
PYATT, Jacob **5**:444, 532, 536, 750;
   6:460-461
   Jacob, Jr. **5**:444
PYFER, John **12**:187
PYKE, Richard **13**:18, 33
PYLE, Caleb **11**:494
   Isaac **13**:576-577, 691
   Joseph **9**:673
   Nicholas **1**:614; **2**:33, 82, 85, 106,
   173, 536, 575-576, 586-588, 596;
   3:381
   Ralph **4**:482
   Robt. **1**:324, 337, 601; **2**:34, 209
   Wm. **3**:256
PYMM, William **5**:3, 387
PYTERHAY **13**:463

QUALITY, Joseph **11**:576; **14**:81, 101,
   418
QUANT, Thomas **5**:89
QUARE, Daniel **15**:413, 442, 481, 485
QUARREL, James **15**:401
QUARRELL, James **12**:333, 576
   Joseph **12**:410
QUARRIER, Alexander **12**:338; **13**:621;
   16:529
QUARRIER & HUNTER **15**:77
QUARRY, Robt. **1**:541, 544-546, 550,
   561-562, 565-566, 575, 580,
   602-604
QUARY, Robt. **2**:89, 92-93, 115-116,
   428, 517
QUASSENUNGH **3**:459, 463, 507
QUEBEC, Nicholas **6**:151
QUEE, Seth **11**:215, 218, 601, 603
QUEEN, Daniel **11**:139
QUEEN MARY **1**:49-50
QUEENSBERRY, --- (Duke of) **9**:637,
   640, 761; **10**:103
QUENAMEQUID (ALIAS CHARLES) **13**:466
QUEQUEDAGAYTHO **9**:523, 525

QUEQUEDAGDUEDO 9:537
QUEWRCHLAH 7:478
QUICKELL, Johan Phillippus 4:100
QUICKLE, Hans Jerig 3:432
 Johan Georg. 4:100
QUICKSALL, John 11:105
QUIDAHICKQUNT 4:742
QUIGG, Charles 5:662
 John 14:611
QUIGG (QUICK), Jacobus 11:472-474
QUIGLEY, Christopher 15:373
 Henry 16:193-194, 509
 James 15:605
QUIN, Francis 11:695
 Hugh 12:342
 Samuel 10:756
QUINCY, Josiah 6:314, 329-330,
 334-335
QUINN, Elinor 12:217
 Patrick 16:71, 79
 Samuel 12:769, 773; 13:16; 14:582
QUIRK, Gilbert 14:610
QUITHEYYQUENT 4:684
QUNKLE, Johan Michal 4:100
QUYASYCAMON (AUDOWROFF) 8:594

RAAN, Hendrick 3:328
RAB, Andrew 11:45
RABB, Eliza 11:679
RABE, Christopher 3:570
RABSON, John 11:23
RADDEN, --- (Capt.) 11:560
 Francis (Mrs.) 11:560
RADES, James 1:134
RADFANG, George 11:380
RADLER, Joannes 3:288
RADWITZER, John 2:493
RAFER, Feltin 3:369
RAHM, Jacob 16:500
 Michael 15:570; 16:195, 498, 500
RAIN(S) (RAINE), Samuel 10:679,
 697, 712, 732, 735
RAINEY, John 13:457
 William 15:216
RAKESTRAW, Joseph 13:279; 14:380;
 16:90, 215, 355, 394
 William 2:11
RALCHICKOP 13:464
RALPH, James 9:556
 Thomas 10:729; 14:146
RALPH (NEGRO) 11:565, 570; 12:113
RALSTON, --- (Capt.) 10:689
 John 10:728; 11:365, 434, 451,
 574, 579, 633; 13:144; 14:217,
 250
 Paul 14:196
 Robert 11:79, 251; 13:293, 376;
 14:238, 250, 555; 16:24
 William 13:431; 16:316, 320
RALSTON(E), John 12:134, 164,
 361-362, 630, 646
RAMAGE, William 5:444
RAMBACH, Asimus 3:520
RAMBO, Gunner 1:95, 156
 John 1:156
 Peter 1:156; 10:51
RAMMAGE, Josiah 15:2
RAMSAUR, Henrick 3:432
RAMSAY, --- (Maj.) 6:10
 James 11:455; 12:513
 John 3:233; 11:281, 339, 493;
 12:5, 491

RAMSDALE, Daniel 11:432
RAMSEY, Alexander 11:282, 358;
 15:300; 16:210, 527
 James 13:93
 John 6:143
 Thomas 13:14
 William 5:209
RAMSTON, Nicholas 7:474
 Simon 13:192
RAN(C)KIN, --- (Capt.) 11:159-160
RANDAL, Job 9:571
RANDALL, John 12:332
RANDALS, John 5:210
RANDLE, Enos 14:320
RANDOLPH, --- (Mr.) 10:620
 Benjamin 10:745; 12:357, 587;
 13:250-251
 Beverly 15:660
 Edmund 14:651
 Edmund (Gov.) 15:416, 465
 Edward 1:528, 535-536, 538, 551;
 11:487, 665
 Isham 5:255, 264-265
 Payton 6:163
 Peyton 10:332
RANHARD, Michael 3:517
RANK, John Philip 3:367
 Michael 4:268
RANKIN, Abigail 12:494
 Ann 11:582
 David 14:365
 Elizabeth 14:15
 James 10:271; 11:307, 582, 745;
 12:82, 174, 218-219, 560, 577,
 680; 13:98, 273, 385; 15:468
 John 11:483-485, 565, 570-571,
 745; 12:82, 113, 342; 13:384;
 14:15, 217; 16:24, 297
 Robert 14:81, 94, 433
 Thomas 14:214, 365; 16:174
 William 9:731; 10:163, 615, 659;
 12:174, 710-711; 14:214; 15:425
RANNAX, Alexander 11:99
RANNEL(L)S, John 14:236, 369
RANNELS, John 11:229
RANNINSTON, John 12:58
RANSAILER, Jacob 3:456
RANSCH, Johan Adam 4:100
RANSELEAR, John 6:61
RANSELER, Hans Philip 3:456
RANSEY (RAMSEY), Robert 11:179, 372
RAPE, Christian 3:456
RAPER, Stephanus 3:288
RAPP, Elizabeth 12:163
RAPPALL, George 13:441
RAPPE, Gabriell 1:81
RAQUIER, Jacob 1:81
RARBETT, --- 7:192
RASH, Nicholas 13:604
RAT, Hans 3:517
RATCLIFFE, James 14:124, 128, 429
RATGAL, Hans Jacob 3:593
RATSELL, Frantz 3:517
RATSLUE, Hans Jacob 3:367
RATTER (RUTTER), Moses 14:103, 425
RATTLE, French 6:638
RAUB, Michael 3:457
 Philip 3:457
RAUCH, Peter 3:456
RAUDEBUSH, Isaac 3:466
RAUP, Michael 10:722
RAUSHER, Jacob 3:515
RAVAN, William 13:704
RAVENSCRAPT, Thomas 13:445
RAWLE, --- 5:60
 --- (Mr.) 15:572; 16:215, 218, 440

RAWLE, Francis **2**:154, 160, 163,
321, 397; **3**:232, 246
RAWLE(S), Francis **1**:320, 330, 371,
573
RAWLIN, --- (Col.) **11**:156
RAWLINGS, Wm. **1**:439
RAWLINS, --- **11**:758
RAWSON, Walto. **1**:311
Wm. **1**:159
RAY, George Michael **3**:457
John **15**:577
Richard **10**:273-274
Samuel **10**:156
RAYMEL (RYMEL), John **11**:515-516,
518
RAYMOND, --- (Lord) **7**:277
Benjamin **11**:165
John **11**:165
RAYNOR, Catharine **15**:119
RE, Johan Nicolas **3**:413
RE(A)DWOOD, John **1**:203, 207,
539-540
REA, --- (Mr.) **13**:739
James **10**:446
John **11**:111; **13**:726; **14**:563
Samuel **10**:100; **12**:317, 336, 374,
391, 485, 488, 607, 623, 737,
739, 767
REA (RAY), Samuel **11**:212, 453, 479,
504
READ (REED, REEDE, REID), ---
(Capt.) **5**:708; **8**:140
--- (Col.) **13**:661
Adam **6**:650, 657-659; **7**:302-304
Andreas **13**:381
Casper **12**:601
Charles **1**:559; **2**:23-24, 106, 153,
164; **3**:50, 157, 257, 370, 387,
416, 430, 491, 529, 534,
537-538, 540, 544-545, 563, 571,
574, 579, 585, 589-591, 594-595,
598-599, 612, 614, 617; **4**:17,
20-21, 32, 47, 49, 51, 53, 56,
58, 62-63, 66, 82, 86-87, 95-97,
151, 172-173, 243; **5**:499-501;
8:156, 175, 179, 194-195, 219;
10:216; **14**:616; **16**:8-9, 14-15,
25, 27
Colberson **11**:146
Collinson **10**:727; **15**:656, 658;
16:130
Francis **14**:540
Franklin **13**:628
George **10**:217; **12**:601
Henry **10**:168; **14**:616
Jacob **12**:601
James **1**:139, 218; **5**:8, 106,
264-265, 269; **6**:503, 650-652,
667, 703; **8**:562; **9**:172, 192,
673; **10**:667, 670, 684, 717;
11:195, 197, 203, 206, 358, 374,
394, 424, 500, 515-531, 533,
537, 544, 550, 571-574, 576-580,
582-584, 586-594, 596, 620, 625,
628-629, 632-633, 638, 640,
642-645, 650, 652, 655-656,
658-661, 664-669, 672-679,
682-685, 691, 693, 696-698,
701-702, 706, 748-749, 773, 776,
778-779, 781, 783; **12**:1, 3-5,
7-11, 17-20, 22-25, 30-33, 35,
37, 39-40, 42, 46, 48-49, 51,
57, 64, 67-71, 77, 80, 82,
84-94, 100-102, 107, 109,
111-115, 117, 119, 123-125,
127-128, 130, 136, 141, ->

READ (REED, REEDE, REID), James
(continued) **12**:144-145, 147-148,
150, 152-155, 158-164, 166-167,
169, 171-174, 176-177, 179,
181-182, 185-186, 189, 191-194,
197-198, 200-201, 203, 205, 207,
209-210, 212, 215-217, 220-221,
223-224, 226-233, 235, 237,
240-244, 246, 248-249, 251, 253,
256-259, 263, 265, 268-269,
271-274, 276, 279, 288, 292,
296-297, 301-302, 307, 309,
311-313, 315, 317-322, 324, 326,
330-331, 333-334, 338, 340-341,
343, 347-348, 350-352, 354, 358,
360-361, 449-450, 452, 454-456,
458-460, 462-468, 478-479,
486-489, 493-494, 497-500,
503-506, 508-510, 512, 514-515,
517-518, 520, 522-523, 525-526,
528, 531, 533-536, 538-541,
543-544, 546-547, 550-552,
554-561, 564, 566, 568-569, 572,
575, 578-579, 582-584, 586-588,
591-592, 594-595, 597-599, 601,
603-607, 609-611, 614, 616, 618,
620, 623-624, 629, 631-633,
636-637, 639-640, 642, 651,
654-655, 657-658, 660, 663-664,
669-670, 674, 676, 679-681, 683,
685-686, 688-690, 693, 696, 699,
701-702, 705, 707, 711-713, 715,
717-719, 721-723, 725, 727-729,
731-738, 741-742, 744-745, 748;
13:255-256, 720; **14**:7, 25, 147,
176, 202, 213, 223, 235, 417,
445; **15**:294-306, 308-317,
320-328, 331, 337-353, 356-380,
386-388, 390-391, 394-395,
398-401, 403-412, 414-427,
429-436, 438-456, 458-464,
466-473, 475-476, 479-480,
482-483, 485, 490-492, 494-496,
498-500, 502-506, 508-509,
513-518, 520-527, 533-536,
538-541, 543, 548-551, 554,
556-562, 564, 566-569, 571-584,
586-590, 592, 596-604, 606-607,
611-620, 622-623, 625-629,
631-635, 637-641, 643-651,
654-656; **16**:1-7, 9-13, 15-17,
19-22, 24, 26-29, 31, 33, 35,
37, 39-48, 50-57, 62-63, 66-68,
70-78, 80, 82, 84-91, 93-94,
96-97, 102-103, 106-116,
118-120, 122-127, 129-138,
141-146, 148-149, 151, 153-158,
160, 164-166, 168-169, 171-173,
175-178, 180-183, 186-188,
190-194, 196-202, 205, 209-211,
214-216, 218-220, 222-224,
209b-212b, 214b-222b, 224b,
225-227, 229-233, 235-236,
239-243, 252, 254-255, 258-264,
267, 274, 276, 278-290, 293,
295-307, 309-313, 315-318,
320-324, 326-327, 329, 331-332,
336, 339-340, 344-346, 357,
359-360, 362-363, 365-366, 368,
370-373, 375, 378-384, 386,
388-390, 392-396, 399-406,
408-418, 420-429, 432-433, 439,
442, 445-447, 450, 453, 458-459,
461-464, 479-484, 487-488, 546

REED (READ), Peter **14**:407, 409, 439
  Samuel **12**:65, 587, 676; **13**:717;
    14:320
  William **5**:210; **13**:602; **14**:100,
    131, 134, 414, 432
REED (READ, RIED), James R. **15**:339,
  351, 449, 505, 508, 568
REED (REID), --- (Maj.) **12**:262,
  711-712
REEDER, David **13**:180
REEHM, Adam Peter **5**:318
REEL, Simon **3**:368
REEMER, Philip **3**:290
REEP, Johannes **3**:457
REES, --- (Maj.) **13**:661
  --- (Mr.) **13**:356, 420
  Adam **6**:668
  Daniel **4**:277; **7**:500; **11**:730;
    12:599; **13**:71, 117-118, 146,
    186, 191, 255, 262, 303, 329,
    370, 436; **14**:18, 572
  David **13**:48
  George **5**:454
  John **5**:248, 325
  Joshua **13**:758
  Thomas **13**:85, 112, 304, 415, 580,
    721, 737; **14**:555; **15**:428
  William **5**:248; **9**:701; **14**:446, 458,
    469, 483, 497, 510, 521, 534,
    549, 586, 601, 626, 666; **15**:4,
    30, 47, 57, 76, 99, 135, 172,
    202, 349
REESE, --- (Mr.) **13**:425
  Christiana **11**:38
  Daniel **16**:185
  John **10**:447
  Joshua **14**:421
  Peter **13**:624; **14**:249
  Thomas **13**:391
  William **10**:114
REESER, William **9**:674
REEVE, Peter **9**:293, 366; **10**:283,
  296, 412; **13**:104; **14**:609
REEVES, --- (Capt.) **5**:551
  Enos **13**:708, 716
REEVES (REWES), Enos **14**:126, 422
REGAN, Allan **9**:745
REGENSBERGER, John Stephen **3**:367
REGISTER, Daniel **11**:516-517
REGRE, --- (Dr.) **5**:327
REH(E)RER(S), Jacob **16**:460, 542
REHSH, Matthias **3**:519
REIB, Mary **16**:298
  Nicholas **13**:580; **14**:98, 429
REICHART, Adam **15**:297
  Henry **16**:234
REICHEL, John Frederick **12**:782
REICHENBACH, Johannes **3**:520
REID, --- (Col.) **9**:227, 267-269,
  271-276
  Daniel **3**:517, 570
  George **11**:784
  James **12**:611
  James R. **10**:448
  John **13**:183, 204, 273, 277, 295
  Joseph **15**:583
  Thomas **3**:256, 359
  William **3**:387 (See READ)
REIDNER, Nicholas **13**:346
REIFF, Jacob **15**:100
REIGART, Adam **11**:223, 447, 451,
  476, 489; **12**:508; **13**:639;
    14:264, 519, 557; **15**:99
  Henry **15**:31
  Jacob **11**:77; **14**:254-255, 264
REIGER, Jacob **15**:173

REIGER, Jacob (Dr.) **10**:765
REIHM, --- (Capt.) **11**:76
REIL(E)Y, Richard **10**:280, 288-289,
  296-299, 332, 374, 459
REILEY, --- (Mr.) **16**:272
  Barnabas **14**:296, 303, 426
  Richard **11**:251
REILY, --- **8**:142; **10**:168
  Isabella **12**:271
  John **10**:756; **11**:154; **13**:712
  Richard **9**:205, 648, 673
  Thomas **5**:612; **9**:365, 369
REIM, George **14**:383
REIMER, Fredrick **3**:385
  Jacob **14**:415
  Peter **10**:42
REIN(E), John **12**:80, 237, 674
REINE, George **11**:483-485, 745
  John **11**:483-485
  Mary **13**:184
  Michael **13**:184
REINECK, Christian **14**:609
REINECKER, Casper **14**:488
REINER, Hans Nous **2**:493
  Jacob **13**:755
REINHARD, Michael **12**:85
REINHART, George **11**:145, 693;
  16:478
  Joh. Phillipus **3**:467
  Michael **15**:97
REINHART (REINHARD), Michael
  11:364, 378, 392
REINICK, Catharine **15**:185, 249,
  276, 480
  Catherine **16**:174, 361
  Christian **16**:361
  Christian (Dr.) **15**:249, 276, 480
REINWALT, Christopher **3**:569
REIS, Michael **6**:705
REISH, Johan Arnolt **3**:570
REISIN, Christiana **13**:395
REISNER, Michael **4**:110, 256
REITERSON, Arnold **3**:457
REITHMEYER, John **10**:491, 560
RELFE, --- **8**:576
  John **9**:621-622, 762-763
RELYEWSAN, --- **4**:338
REMER, Johan Nicolaus **3**:457
  Stephen **3**:385
REMINGTON, John **4**:276-277
REMISS, Lawrence **16**:388
RENDON, Francisco **12**:398
RENEHART, Frederick **16**:73
RENN, Bernard **3**:385
RENNARDS, John **3**:38
RENNER, Hans Valent **3**:453
RENNETS, John **15**:121
RENNICKS, Henry **5**:247
  William **4**:154
RENSHAW, Richard **5**:175, 184
RENSSELAR, John B. V. **6**:276
RENSSHAW, Benjamin **12**:187
RENTHART, Michael **11**:321
RENTSH, Peter **4**:60
REOSE, John **13**:708
REPE, --- **7**:191
REPTON, Bernard **10**:172
RESBERG, Gustavus **10**:703, 721, 727;
  11:35, 58, 88
RESER, Bernard **3**:374
  Georg. Adam **3**:457
  Hans **3**:290
  Hans Jurig **3**:457
  Matthias **4**:60
RESSAR, Ulrich **3**:455
RETELSBERGER, Christian **3**:520

RETER, Hans Jerig 3:284
RETMAN, Johannes 3:457
RETSEL, Johan Adam 3:517
RETZ, Henricus 3:466
REVAN, John 1:162
REVEL, Thomas 2:113, 179-183, 185
REVERD(D)IE, Peter 1:370, 435
REVERS, Henry 15:69
REW, Matthew 4:313, 482
REX, Abraham 12:445; 13:381
 George 7:769
REY, Jaquelin D. 12:483
REYBOLD, Daniel 10:755
REYER, Hans Hichl. 3:457
 Johan Carl 3:457
 Johan Martin 3:457
REYL, Hans 3:467
 Hans Jacob 3:467
REYLENDER, Philip Jacob 3:284
REYMERT, Johannes 3:413
REYN, Michael 3:452
REYNALS, William 3:176
REYNELL, John 7:86; 11:292
REYNOLD, John 8:487
REYNOLDS, --- 14:243
 --- (Capt.) 7:164, 313
 Catherine 5:612; 12:106
 Elihu 14:81, 95, 416
 George 6:755
 Henry 1:157-159, 161, 199
 James 11:753; 12:441; 14:224, 265;
  15:443
 John 4:348, 483; 8:22; 9:201, 673,
  732; 10:42, 424, 465;
  11:266-267, 750; 12:106, 778;
  14:164, 242, 259, 359, 413;
  15:424, 469, 516; 16:102, 211b,
  222b, 375, 455, 478-479, 481,
  528
 Joseph 14:609
 Martin 13:601; 14:92, 419
 Nathan 12:187
 Richard 1:253, 521, 607
 Robert 14:465
 Thomas 13:24; 15:346, 499
 Waddy 1:444
REYNOLDS (See KLINE &) 15:457, 518
REYSER, Jacob 3:367
REYTER, Hendrick 3:452
 Paulus 3:452
RHEA, --- (Mr.) 16:429
 Adley 14:311
 David 14:506
 John 8:24; 14:237, 294, 301, 416,
  506; 15:155
 Samuel 13:738; 15:249
RHEIM, George 16:533-534
RHEINER, John 15:191, 197, 201,
  208, 246, 248, 254, 415, 423,
  446, 452-453, 525
RHERER, Godfred 9:557
 Jacob 9:557
RHINE, George 12:327
 John 13:138
 Michael 12:327
RHINEDOLLAR, Elizabeth 12:346
RHO(A)DES, Henry 11:432, 608, 616,
  633
RHOAD(E)S, William 9:197, 203, 339
RHOADS, --- (Capt.) 12:9
 Daniel 13:309
 Henry 10:728
 Joseph 12:175, 323
 Peter 10:762; 12:134, 506; 13:762;
  14:226; 16:48

RHOADS, Samuel 8:719, 723, 725,
  729, 757, 774; 10:53-54, 266;
  11:290; 12:196
RHODDEN, William 12:28, 731
RHODES, --- (Mr.) 12:740
 Adam 1:438
 Jno. 1:166, 438
 William 8:506, 781; 10:9, 217
RHODES (RHOADS), Peter 11:53,
  92-93, 101-105, 107, 127-135,
  365, 579, 633
RHODT, George 12:608
 Matthias 12:608
RHOORBACH, Margaret 13:418
RHOORBACK, Margaret 13:249
RHOR, Jacob 3:415
RHULAND, Jonathan 13:292
RI(T)CHIE(S), Craig 14:216, 371
RIBBELL, Nicholas 15:77
RIBBLE, Johan Georg. 3:520
RIBOULEAU, Nicholas 1:81
RICE, --- (Capt.) 12:22, 297
 Adam 13:302; 15:502; 16:296
 Benjamin 10:464
 David 11:162
 Edmund 12:482
 Evan 5:248; 9:203, 707, 742, 744;
  10:276
 George 9:40
 James 5:604 (See DILLON; 11:364
 John 3:367; 9:557; 10:287, 335,
  379, 514, 516, 535, 556, 570,
  606, 702, 725, 772, 777; 11:2,
  8, 80, 113, 117, 358; 13:449,
  737; 14:298, 393, 417, 461
 John Jeremiah 13:100
 Joseph 11:139; 13:272, 554; 14:85,
  430
 Patrick 10:482; 11:679, 683
 Peter 13:577; 14:608
 Robert 11:563, 573
 Thomas 13:383, 506
 William 10:643; 11:63, 66; 13:108,
  168, 278; 14:665
RICH, Johan Georg. 3:457
 Patty 1:82
RICHALL, Matthias 3:455
RICHARD, Anthony 5:325
RICHARD(S), John 15:295, 454, 566;
  16:49, 192, 501
RICHARDS, --- (Mr.) 6:263
 Adam 12:459
 Ann 2:20
 Catharine 13:431
 Henry 15:55
 Ja'c. 11:255
 John 2:20; 11:215; 12:187; 14:149,
  244, 375
 Jonathan 12:553
 Mathias 15:376, 407, 520
 Peter 12:132, 298, 301; 14:66,
  230, 250, 555
 Phill. 1:267, 343, 450-451
 Robt. 1:84
 Sam. 1:317
 William 10:489, 510, 515, 523,
  549, 561, 576, 583, 598, 609,
  617-618, 658, 660, 673, 692,
  694, 700, 704, 725, 759, 763,
  775, 779, 783; 11:5-6, 13, 24,
  29, 33, 40, 46, 118, 133;
  12:387; 14:42, 230
RICHARDSON, --- 3:51
 David 1:218
 Edward 13:687-688
 Franc. 1:143

170

RICHARDSON, Francis 10:231; 11:146
  George 13:710; 14:132, 411
  Isaac 8:562; 9:172
  Jacob 11:202, 216, 226, 494
  John 1:47, 57-73, 84, 87, 89-90,
    101, 103-104, 149, 210, 212,
    218, 227, 252, 337, 342, 518,
    619; 3:254, 270; 10:448; 13:578;
    14:102, 430
  Joseph 5:621, 655; 8:22;
    10:99-100; 12:270, 272-273, 339;
    13:550-551; 14:506
  Rebeckah 2:114
  Richard 3:254
  Saml. 2:10, 34, 65, 85, 106,
    110-111, 156, 159, 203, 284,
    308, 318, 321, 397, 539
  Samll. 1:213-226, 228-235,
    238-240, 242-244, 246, 268, 270,
    280-282, 293, 312, 319, 321-327,
    329-338, 340-343, 454, 460,
    475-476, 479, 481-485, 488, 491,
    493, 502, 507, 517, 519,
    522-523, 531, 544-545, 547-548,
    552, 578, 601
  T. L. 1:319
  Thomas 10:563, 565, 591, 632, 652,
    686; 14:203
  William 12:375-376, 390
RICHART, Rudolph 3:455
RICHE, Anne 12:257, 284
  David 14:191, 196, 413
  John 14:47
  Thomas 7:394; 9:673; 10:162
  Thos. 8:576
RICHER, Bernhart 3:570
RICHEY, David 15:347
  Gideon 11:363, 608; 12:556, 610;
    13:675
  James 5:209
  Robert 14:205
  William 14:407-408, 439
RICHEY (RITCHIE), Matthew 16:223b,
  225
RICHIE, William 10:76
RICHISON, Richard 5:186, 387
RICHITTS, William 14:85
RICHLEY, William 12:120
RICHMOND, --- (Capt.) 3:29
  --- (Duke of) 4:484-485
  Elizabeth 12:44
  John 3:545
RICHNER, Daniel 14:81, 95
RICHOUMEACK 9:229
RICHTER, George 14:647
  Jongr. 3:518
RICK, Charles 13:305
RICKETT, William 15:240
RICKETTS, William 13:759; 14:418
RICKEY, Catherine 12:156
RICKEY (REIKEY), Alexander 11:514,
  516-517
RICKS, --- (Capt.) 5:100
RICS, Ulrich 3:618
RIDDICK (REDDICK), William 14:64,
  90, 412
RIDDLE, George 12:188
  James 11:494
  John 11:75; 13:545
  Robert 14:37
RIDEOUT, --- (Mr.) 7:556
RIDER, --- (Capt.) 11:89
RIDG(E)L(E)Y, Chas. 9:203, 339,
  655, 742, 744
RIDGLEY, Charles 10:9, 217
RIDGWAY, Richd. 1:173

RIDGYARD, William 9:769-770
RIDLEY, Richard 13:477
RIDT, Hans Jacob 3:515
RIECH, Gottfried 3:520
RIED, J. R. 14:157
  James 13:756
RIEGEL, Daniel 3:518
  Johannes 3:518
  Johannes, Jr. 3:518
RIEGER, Jacob Hendrich 3:569
  Johannes Bartholomay 3:414
RIEHL, Conrad 16:160
RIEL(L)Y, --- (Capt.) 12:88-89,
  355, 466, 492, 527, 555, 588,
  603, 633, 675, 693
RIELY, Edward 10:707
  Philip 12:410
RIEN(E), George 12:279, 552
RIES, David 4:505
RIFE, Jacob 13:621
RIFFE, Jacob 14:190, 194, 410
RIFFET, Paul 9:578, 580
RIFFETS, Philip 15:482
  Rebecca 15:523
RIGART, Adam 9:623
RIGBY, Nathaniel 4:109-110, 149,
  231
  Richard 9:629, 637, 640
RIGDEN, William 11:602
RIGER, Hans Jurig 3:329
RIGHT, Andrew 12:78
  Charles 14:407, 439
RIGHTER, Jno. 11:64
  John 12:572
  Michael 14:610
RIGHTON, Wm. 2:275, 405
RIIM, Christian 3:457
RILES, Robert 1:129
RILEY, John 14:69
  Richard 10:679; 14:475
RINCK, Hans 3:288
RINDERSMITH, George 14:426
RINE (RHINE), Michael & John
  15:193, 205
RINEDOLLAS, Elizabeth 12:311
RINGER, Abraham 15:297
RINGLAND, Jane 12:110
RINHALT, Christian 6:171
RINKER, John 7:266
RINN, John 15:350
  Michael 16:8, 103
RINNALD, George 3:569
RIORDON, John 11:240
RIPLEY, Peter 13:604; 14:85, 302,
  416
RIPPEY, Hugh 10:50
  William 11:609; 13:133-134, 396;
    15:122
RIPPIE, William 10:451
RIPPON, William 12:250
RIPSON, John 14:102, 411
RISBIE, James 1:439
RISE, Christopher 3:453
  Fredrick 3:453
  John 13:720
RISHIL, Casper 3:329
RISK, --- (Mr.) 14:621
  Charles 12:477-478; 13:40, 389;
    14:67, 70; 15:574
RISNER, Michael 4:134
RISTEAN, Abraham 12:134
RITCHEY, Gideon 13:301-302
  John 10:230, 232
RITCHIE, Ann 13:448
  Helena 13:527

ROBERTS, George 10:267; 11:283,
288; 16:53
Huge 3:332
Hugh 1:370, 438; 4:270; 5:107,
131, 729; 8:244-245, 487; 9:627;
10:267; 11:283, 288; 14:123;
15:98; 16:330, 337
Hugh, Jr. 12:710
Isaac 13:204
James 10:357, 363, 376-377;
11:160; 12:375
Jane 13:671; 14:174, 538; 15:17,
225, 467; 16:65, 350
Jehu 12:374
Jno. 2:322, 397
John 3:304, 387, 416, 464, 520,
542, 575, 587, 590, 614, 619;
5:193; 7:769; 8:575; 9:343, 592,
595; 11:167, 482, 484-485, 494,
600-603, 606-607, 613-614, 745;
12:38, 324, 374, 572; 14:174,
538; 15:17, 225, 467; 16:65,
191-192, 350, 490
Jonathan 14:456
Joseph 13:535, 706
Josteph 13:511
Mordecai 15:426
Nathan 12:28; 13:108
Owen 3:30-31, 56, 69, 108; 4:269;
11:483-485; 13:180
Peter 16:419
Phineas 13:191, 228
Robert 1:147; 3:524
Thomas 12:333, 441, 576; 14:365;
15:448
William 10:721, 754; 11:42, 69,
108, 135, 508; 12:548, 619;
13:392, 577; 14:115, 294, 301,
555; 15:98-99, 296-297
William (alias EDWARDS) 15:413,
442
Wilson 12:441
ROBERTS, FISHER & 14:492, 570
ROBERTSON, --- (Capt.) 9:120
--- (Mr.) 10:605
Grizzle 16:35
James 10:626
John 3:575; 11:96
Lawrence 13:565
Patrick 13:146
Robert 3:416, 465; 16:35
Robt. 1:174
ROBERTSON & SMITH 15:429
ROBERTUS, Hans Adam 3:458
ROBESON, --- (Capt.) 13:204, 214,
567
--- (Mr.) 11:290
Andrew 1:365-368, 370-373,
375-381, 383-384, 389-391,
393-396, 398-399, 401, 404,
407-409, 416-418, 422-426, 428,
442-444, 446-450, 453, 458-470;
12:14, 316, 582, 745, 769;
13:678
Andrew, Jr. 3:50, 520, 575
David 3:146
Hugh 14:609
Israel 3:112
James 3:587; 15:512
John 2:136; 3:50; 11:56; 12:28,
187; 13:309; 16:136
Jonathan 4:312, 482; 11:494
Jonathan (John) 15:136, 205
Peter 11:494
Philip 7:303

ROBESON, Thomas 13:213, 215, 477,
522, 564; 16:223b, 536
William 11:17
ROBESON (ROBISON), Peter 8:402,
505, 781
ROBI(N)SON (ROBESON), George 9:386,
673, 732
ROBIESON, Joseph 3:270
ROBIGLIO, Hanna 13:373
ROBIN NANTICOKES 9:66
ROBINETT, Joseph 13:51
ROBINS, Ezekiel 13:458-459; 14:73
John 13:581
Samuel 3:114, 116, 118, 162
ROBINS, DUN & HAIL 11:29
ROBINSON, --- (Capt.) 5:257-258;
9:110-111, 113; 13:72, 117, 132,
200, 292, 303, 313, 427, 436,
439, 497, 546, 653, 678, 766;
14:347, 394, 538; 15:171, 246
--- (Col.) 8:140
--- (Mr.) 9:755; 15:133
--- (Mrs.) 11:569
--- (Widow) 2:297
Abraham 10:275
Alexander 13:7
Andrew 1:166, 365, 421; 13:679;
14:102, 437
Benjamin 13:263, 271
Ebenezar 10:286
Edward 1:561-563
Elizabeth 1:587-588; 5:506; 16:259
Frank 5:107
George 11:70, 85, 367
Humphrey 8:576
Isaiah 10:713
Jacob 13:585
James 3:542; 9:711; 10:677;
11:779; 13:332, 679; 14:82, 191,
195, 411, 414; 15:73, 598, 602,
606, 609; 16:378
Jeremiah 16:461
John 3:52, 83; 9:711-712; 11:358,
679; 12:380-381, 392, 572; 14:3,
37, 79, 105; 16:530
Jonathan 4:762; 5:388; 15:135
Joseph 15:372
Nicholas 16:49
Parker 9:374; 10:81, 218
Patr. 2:32, 297
Patrick 3:159-160
Peter 9:779; 10:56; 13:580
Richard 12:440; 15:570
Robert 13:580, 630; 14:133, 608
Robt. 1:340
Septimus 3:464, 520, 574; 4:309,
352, 391-394, 469, 762; 5:60,
107, 131, 175, 388, 572-573;
7:769; 8:575; 9:205
Thomas 4:674; 9:203, 711-712, 777;
10:81, 106, 217, 447; 11:67,
179-180, 301, 639; 12:371, 584,
622-623, 679; 13:104, 165, 211,
423, 437, 503, 555, 699, 716;
14:52, 80, 126, 152, 318, 437,
618, 660
Thomas (Sir) 5:618; 6:176-177,
191, 200, 202, 211, 214, 233,
246, 294-295, 303, 311, 322,
325, 327, 333, 366, 373,
394-395, 449, 451, 509, 512,
599, 640, 644, 719, 730-731;
7:24, 179, 340, 363; 8:23, 438
William 10:490; 14:555
William, Jr. 15:98

RONGER, Hans Martin **3**:455
RONY, James **11**:79
ROODT, Hans Dirik **3**:328
　Laurence **3**:413
　Pieter **3**:518
ROOKEN, John **12**:662, 667
ROOKS, Sarah **12**:767
ROOLE, Peter **3**:288
ROOMFULT, Jacob **3**:569
ROONEY, Peter **15**:13
ROOP, Peter **4**:59
ROOSEN, --- (Mr.) **11**:149
ROOT, --- (Mr.) **11**:677, 737;
　12:131-132; **13**:291
　Jonathan **9**:571
ROOTELIE, Hans **3**:452
ROOTS, Samuel **8**:617-618
ROPENHEVER, --- (Capt.) **11**:110
ROREMAN, --- **10**:723
ROSBOROUGH, John **12**:261, 294-295
　Robert **12**:261
ROSBOTHEM, --- **11**:123
ROSBRUGH, Jno. **11**:63
ROSE, --- (Capt.) **6**:304, 481
　Allen **12**:147
　Daniel **14**:554
　Francis **14**:459
　James **12**:480
　John **13**:202, 717, 770; **14**:41, 64,
　　67, 82
　Polycarpus (P.C.) **1**:396, 397, 435
ROSEBOROUGH, Jane **15**:234, 442, 485,
　643; **16**:407
　John **14**:538
　John (Rev.) **15**:234, 442, 485, 643;
　　16:407
ROSEHER, Gabriel **3**:415
ROSELL, William **16**:528
ROSENBERRY, Elias **14**:480
ROSENCRANGE, Jacob **15**:35
ROSENSTEEL, Johannes **3**:519
ROSIKRANS, Herman **9**:666
ROSS, --- **3**:553; **13**:692
　--- (Capt.) **6**:490
　--- (Col.) **11**:82
　--- (Lt. Col.) **13**:70
　--- (Mr.) **5**:233; **7**:398, 558;
　　10:528; **15**:166; **16**:264
　--- (Mrs.) **11**:599
　A(e)neas **9**:337, 600
　Alexander **10**:142; **12**:665-666;
　　13:766; **14**:290, 472, 498, 532;
　　15:242; **16**:155
　Allen **13**:134
　Charles **14**:66
　Edith **15**:366
　Elizabeth **15**:399
　George **10**:280, 282-283, 285-286,
　　290-291, 297, 299, 301-302, 304,
　　306-307, 323, 327-331, 334-335,
　　339, 341-342, 346-347, 355, 357,
　　360, 373-374, 377, 380, 384-386,
　　389, 453, 501, 503, 512, 530,
　　550, 554, 578, 582, 597, 602,
　　606, 610-612, 615, 617-618, 623,
　　644, 653, 657, 683, 700, 705,
　　729, 772; **11**:76, 78, 341, 343,
　　349, 384, 447, 458, 476, 713,
　　755; **12**:46, 49; **14**:276, 320,
　　385; **15**:296-306, 308-317,
　　320-329, 337-353, 356-368,
　　396-401, 403, 405-412, 414-426,
　　458-463, 465-473, 475-477,
　　479-480, 482-488, 490-491, 495,
　　499-501, 503-506, 508-509, 513,
　　515, 518, 520-526, 534-536, ->

ROSS, George (continued)
　15:538-541, 543-545, 548-551,
　554, 556-564, 566-569, 571-584,
　586-590, 592, 594-596, 598-600,
　602, 618-620, 623, 625-627,
　634-637, 639-650; **16**:7, 9-17,
　19-22, 24-29, 31, 33-35, 37,
　39-48, 50-57, 59-60, 62-68,
　70-73, 97-107, 110-111, 113-116,
　118-120, 122-127, 129-133,
　135-138, 141-143, 145-146,
　148-149, 151-158, 160, 162-166,
　168-169, 171-173, 175-178,
　181-183, 187-188, 190-194,
　196-202, 205, 208-211, 214-216,
　218-219, 223, 216b-223b,
　225-227, 229-230, 232-233,
　235-236, 238-239, 241, 243-244,
　251-252, 254-261, 288-291, 293,
　309, 318, 324, 326-327, 329,
　339-341, 344, 350-360, 362-366,
　368-373, 375, 395-396, 398-406,
　408-427, 429, 433-435, 439,
　441-442, 447, 449-459, 461-465,
　477, 479-485, 495
　J. **6**:293
　James **11**:66, 179-180, 500; **13**:735,
　　746; **14**:264, 509; **15**:98, 289,
　　409, 570; **16**:24, 31, 193, 399,
　　464, 493-494
　John **4**:135, 210, 255; **5**:174; **7**:59,
　　378; **8**:113-114, 339, 342, 349,
　　360-361, 457; **9**:491; **10**:338,
　　355, 361, 427, 430, 457, 465,
　　686; **11**:146; **13**:550; **16**:155, 335
　Jonathan **16**:42
　Joseph **11**:35; **14**:588
　Loetita **14**:593, 606
　Malcolm **11**:494
　Oliver **12**:343
　Robert **14**:191, 195, 414; **15**:366,
　　429
　Thomas **10**:50
　William **10**:363, 376-377, 717,
　　729-730; **11**:223, 334-335,
　　610-611; **12**:298; **13**:313;
　　15:543-544, 546-548, 551, 604;
　　16:196
ROSS & EGA **10**:722; **11**:16, 48
ROSS(E), William **14**:223, 298, 305,
　311, 429
ROSSEN, Wm. **1**:499
ROSSMAN, Johannes **4**:59
ROTCH(E), Isaac **10**:344, 383, 488
ROTCHFORD, Dennis **1**:48, 69 (See
　ROCHEFORD)
ROTH, Francis **16**:530
　Jacob **7**:620
　Johannes **3**:415
　Mathias **15**:454
　Philip **13**:758; **14**:91, 414
ROTHERWELL, Daniel **11**:195
ROTHROCK, Jacob **12**:513; **13**:93
　Johannes **3**:520
　Philip Jacob **3**:520
ROTHWELL, Jared **3**:548, 550, 556,
　560
　Jerrard **5**:194
　Thomas, Jr. **3**:548, 550, 556, 560
ROTROKE, Johannes **4**:60
ROTT, Daniel **3**:517
ROTTER, Jacob **11**:682
ROTTON, John **10**:302, 304-305, 313
ROUDEBUSH, George **16**:491
ROUDS, Jno. **1**:72
ROUF, Conrad **3**:517

ROUGET, Stephen Jos. 11:282
ROUGH, Michael 12:540; 13:158;
   14:33
ROUP, Conraad 3:466
 Hans Georg. 3:457
 Michael 7:492-494; 9:732
ROUSCH, Jacob 3:453
ROUSE, Tho. 1:87, 340
ROUSENBURGEN, Joh. Fred. 3:457
ROUSS, Johan Frantz 3:454
ROUST, Jacob 3:287
ROW, George 15:112; 16:518
ROW(E), George 16:224
 Mary Magdelena 16:224, 420
ROWAN, Charles 16:371
 Flaval 14:79
 George 15:517
 James 12:229, 320, 487, 525, 695,
   775
 John 15:517
 William 10:682; 11:371, 422, 599;
   12:145, 161
ROWAN (ROVAN, REWAN), John 14:295,
   301, 434
ROWDENBASH, Henrick 3:458
 Peter 3:458
ROWE, Mary 15:652
ROWELL, --- (Capt.) 5:297
ROWERDON, Alexander Mathiew 5:75,
   79
ROWHIGH, Peter 11:223
ROWLAND, David 5:248
 James 13:624
 Jno. 1:169, 521, 523; 10:692, 699
 John 12:508
 Jonathan 15:106
 Robert 4:102
 Saml. 2:98-99
 Samuel 3:254, 259, 270; 5:226;
   8:781
 Samuel, Jr. 5:226
 William 5:210; 5:226; 10:682
ROWLES, Mary 1:440-441
ROWLING, William 12:278
ROWLWAGEN, Frederick 10:643
ROWNEY, Thomas 12:671-672
ROWSTON, Bartholomew 1:390
ROXBURG, --- (Duke of) 3:71
ROXBURY, Mary 11:582
ROYAL, Samuel 10:737
 Wm. 1:576
ROYER, Jno. 1:143
 Samuel 11:229; 14:237, 668-669
ROZEN, William 11:650
RUBELL, Johannes 4:59
RUBER, Leonard 16:536
RUBICHON, Matthias 3:467
RUBLE, David 14:324
RUBY, John 13:19
RUCH, Michael 15:269
RUCHTER, George 14:8
RUCK, Hans Georg. 3:515
 Hans Jacob 3:515
 Hans Jurg. 3:515
RUDI, Bastain 3:454
RUDISELL, Jacob 13:397
RUDISILL, Jacob 12:513; 13:723;
   14:201, 208, 229, 256
RUDISILL (RUDISELL), Jacob 15:474,
   615
RUDMAN, Andrew 2:147, 149
RUDOLF, T(h)obias 10:706, 711
RUDOLPH, Christopher 4:60
 Jacob 11:55, 328; 12:352; 15:261;
   16:18, 413

RUDOLPH, John 10:450; 11:476;
   13:557; 14:101, 426
RUDY, James 4:353
RUE, Benjamin 12:391, 570; 13:392,
   722
 Lewis 5:247; 15:204, 216, 225,
   236, 365
 Mathew 5:3
 Matthew 12:614
 Richard 13:539, 720, 737
RUELL, Elizabeth 12:563
RUFF, Adam 13:603; 14:9, 156, 571
RUGGLES, Timothy 6:608, 611
 William 14:94, 415
RUGH, Michael 10:142; 12:182;
   13:419
 Peter 15:85
RUHT, Michael 3:516
RUITER, Hans Michael 3:332
RUKENS, John 12:779-780
RUMBLE, Jacob 16:450
RUMFORD, John 3:112
RUMHART, George 11:10
RUMMEL, Nicholas 15:514, 521
RUMSEY, Charles 1:253-254, 320, 340
 Nathaniel 10:470
 William 3:591-593
RUND, Gottfried 5:576
RUNDES, Peter 11:139
RUNDLE, Daniel 7:394; 13:96, 132
 George 13:132
 Richard 13:96
RUNDLE (RUNDEL), Daniel 8:22, 24,
   573-574, 576, 583
RUNER, Jacob 14:94
RUNKLE, Andrew 16:373
 Siegmund 13:306
RUNTZ, Johan Yorg. 3:569
RUNYON (RUNGAN, RUNGON), George
   14:191, 195, 413
RUPER, John 11:37
RUPERT, Adam 13:623; 14:96, 419
 Leonard 10:771
RUPPELT, Johan Adam 3:415
RUPPLE (RUPPELE, RUPPELL), Augustus
   (Augustine) 11:10, 38, 64
RURNER, Robt. 1:298 (See TURNER)
RUSH, --- (Mr.) 7:129; 11:680;
   13:188, 192, 194, 410, 430, 509;
   14:29, 31
 Benjamin (Dr.) 10:347, 361-362,
   409, 412, 545, 549, 553, 614;
   11:543; 14:634; 15:316, 340,
   616, 654; 16:77
 Catherine 16:295
 Hutchinson (Dr.) 15:315
 Jacob 11:544; 13:200, 391, 415,
   721, 737; 14:42-43, 70, 175,
   319, 481, 540, 602, 626; 15:43,
   89, 135, 184, 217, 233, 276,
   358, 434, 477, 545, 632; 16:31,
   90, 102, 114, 129, 165, 189,
   192, 243, 305, 349, 389, 458,
   546
 Jno. 1:85, 89, 207
 Jos. 14:193, 230
 Joseph 11:720, 739, 751; 12:507;
   13:85, 391, 709, 722-723, 727
 Nicholas 14:551
 Richard 10:452
 William 5:135, 175; 10:478, 544,
   556, 580, 668, 721; 11:16, 38,
   91, 606, 697, 770; 12:688;
   13:141, 164, 170, 181, 209;
   15:26, 143-145
RUSHOUT, John (Sir) 5:618

SCHOCKNEY, Thomas **16**:481
SCHOLEFIELD, William **15**:71
SCHOLL, Johannes **2**:494
 Peter **2**:494
SCHOLLTZ, George **3**:417
SCHOLMEYER, Gerhard Michel **3**:454
 Johan **3**:454
SCHOLTZE, Melchior **3**:597
SCHONBERGER, Baltzar **3**:455
SCHONFELDT, Johan **3**:518
SCHONHOVEN, John **3**:329
SCHONOVEN, Nicholas **3**:309
SCHOOK, Johannes **3**:467
SCHOONHOVEN, --- (Capt.) **11**:65
SCHOTT, --- (Capt.) **12**:217, 221,
 255, 297; **13**:755
 --- (Mr.) **15**:303
 John Paul **15**:540
SCHOTT(S), John Paul **14**:176, 415
SCHOUP, Martin **3**:328
SCHOVETT, Abraham (Dr.) **13**:398
SCHR(E)INER, Jacob **10**:671, 675
SCHRADER, Jacob **14**:638
 William **14**:137
SCHRATZ, Jacob **3**:457
SCHRAWDER, --- (Capt.) **13**:424, 532,
 645, 653, 678, 733
 --- (Col.) **13**:519
 Jacob (Capt.) **14**:102, 429, 659
 Philip **10**:679; **12**:297, 309;
 13:136, 522-523, 575, 581, 593,
 697, 731; **15**:169
SCHRAWTON, Philip **13**:450
SCHREFLER, Christina **15**:323
 Henry **15**:324
SCHREIBER, Jacob **16**:434
SCHREIDER, Jacob **13**:758
SCHREINER, Jacob **12**:156, 160, 164
SCHREMER, Johan Sebalt **3**:432
SCHRICAK, Christian **4**:59
SCHRINER, Jacob **11**:17, 31, 65, 93,
 116, 123, 330, 504
SCHRIVER, George **14**:620
 Henry **11**:119, 469
 Samuel **10**:450
SCHROF, Johan Adam **3**:570
SCHROTER, Johan Adam **3**:415
SCHRYVER, George **15**:100, 297, 570
SCHUBER, Hendrich **3**:593
SCHUHL, Daniel **3**:453
SCHULLER, Frantz **3**:519
 John **11**:691
SCHULTZ, Chris'r. **11**:195
 Christian Otto **3**:570
 Christopher **12**:357
 George **12**:634
 Hans Martin **3**:413
 Johannes Christian **3**:456
 John **16**:84
 Valentine **3**:414
SCHULTZE, Godfrey **3**:390
SCHUMANN, Ludwig **16**:49
SCHURGH, Joseph **3**:284
SCHURTZ, George Michael **12**:345
SCHUSLER, Hans Jacob **3**:457
 Henrich **3**:457
 Jerig **3**:457
SCHUST, Stefan **4**:72
SCHUTZ, Martin **3**:613
SCHUYLER, --- **3**:82
 Myndt. **6**:61-63, 77
 Peter **3**:199, 453; **6**:410-411, 419;
 7:24, 29; **8**:240
 Reyendert **6**:129
 Wynder **6**:276
SCHWARTZ, Georg. Wilhelm **3**:415

SCHWARTZ, George **11**:11
 Henrie Ludwic **3**:415
 Peter **12**:601
SCHWAUB, Peter **3**:597
SCHWEITSER, Caspar **3**:593
SCHWEITZER, Jacob **3**:454
 John **12**:601
S(CH)WOOPE, Peter **12**:222, 257
SCHWOP, Justice **5**:377
SCHYLER, Col. **5**:474
SCHYP, Valentine **3**:455
SCHYWER, Conrootz **3**:454
SCISSEL (See CECIL), William **15**:241
SCKILES (SKELES, SKYLES), Henry
 11:446-447
SCLAUGH, Jacob **5**:327
SCOBALECTIC **9**:194
SCOBY, James **14**:169, 267
SCOFFIELD, Haunce **13**:496
SCOGGIN, Jacob **10**:504
SCOLFIELD, Nathan **16**:191-192, 492,
 530
 William **14**:610
SCOLLITCHY **2**:546, 557
SCONOVER, Ezekiel **16**:450
SCOONOVER, Ezekiel **14**:311, 320, 495
SCOOT, James **5**:186
SCOT(T), John **5**:387, 443, 572
SCOTOSH, Chief **15**:58
SCOTT, --- **8**:576
 --- (Capt.) **10**:689
 --- (Mr.) **12**:75; **13**:672, 764;
 15:533
 Abraham **13**:33, 88, 112, 393, 415,
 682, 722, 737; **14**:556; **16**:480
 Alexander **16**:41, 494, 537
 Emon **13**:431
 Hugh **13**:531; **15**:589
 James **10**:762; **11**:261; **12**:330, 515;
 14:538; **16**:42, 515
 Jere **1**:322
 Jeremiah **12**:576
 John **3**:267; **7**:261, 417; **10**:116;
 11:89, 145, 157, 160, 166;
 12:333; **13**:92, 332, 751;
 14:256-257, 581, 610; **15**:49,
 118, 487
 Joseph **15**:279, 483; **16**:150
 Josiah **10**:209; **11**:219; **15**:646
 Matthew **11**:180, 418-419, 452, 474,
 534
 Moses **13**:177; **14**:379
 Patrick **13**:397, 415
 Philip **11**:339, 351-352, 624;
 12:461; **14**:260, 321; **16**:68, 88
 Robert **11**:302; **13**:748; **14**:471
 Samuel **4**:135; **7**:597; **13**:182;
 15:413
 Thomas **9**:751; **10**:142; **11**:373,
 378-393, 395-396, 398-399,
 402-403, 405-412, 414-415,
 417-419, 421-423, 425-426, 428,
 430, 432-438, 440-445, 499,
 501-503, 506, 508-512, 518-521,
 556, 608-609, 612-619, 624, 626,
 628-633, 635-639, 641-651, 653,
 655-665, 668-669, 672-675,
 677-680, 683-685, 691, 693-695,
 702-703, 705-709, 713, 716-717,
 734, 773; **12**:182, 187, 198, 234,
 334-335, 337-343, 347, 352, 354,
 357-358, 360-364, 367-368,
 370-373, 375-376, 378-379,
 384-389, 391, 465-469, 473,
 476-479, 481-485, 487-488, 681;
 13:403, 586, 703; **14**:259; ->

SHELLHAMER, Abraham **14**:262
Philip Jacob **16**:364
SHELLIG, Philip **3**:466
SHELLMAN, John **12**:222
SHELLY, Daniel **11**:307-308
SHELP, Peter **14**:348
SHELTON, John **1**:208
SHENEKENWHOA **2**:33
SHEPARD, John **16**:541
SHEPERD, Thomas **11**:620
SHEPHERD, --- **13**:167
 David **14**:214
 John **10**:142
SHEPPERD, John **11**:494
 William **5**:444, 452
SHEPPERD (SHEPHERD), Robert **12**:333,
 576
SHEPPERD (SHEPPARD), John **12**:182,
 540
SHERBURNE (SHERBORNE), Henry, Jr.
 6:57, 67, 71, 73, 82, 90
SHERER, --- (Widow) **11**:72
 Hans **3**:519
 Henry **11**:647
 Johannes **3**:385
 John **11**:72; **12**:662; **13**:515
 John Justice **3**:385
 Jos. **10**:703
 Richard **14**:441, 443
 Robert **15**:189
SHERGELD, John **13**:115
 Richard Cooke **13**:115
 Robert **13**:115
SHERIDAN, Abraham **14**:638; **16**:419
 James **16**:333
 John **15**:243
SHERKEY, Neal **13**:476
SHERLOCK, James **8**:630, 632, 644,
 652
SHERMAN, --- (Mr.) **12**:198
 Conrad **14**:201, 486
 Roger **10**:120
SHERMAN & LEWIS **11**:105
SHERNER, Hans **3**:454
SHERRED, John **10**:746
SHERRMAN, Margaret **13**:367
SHERRON, Roger **5**:249
SHERRY, William **12**:187
SHERWOOD, Joseph **9**:48, 50-51
SHETLER, Andrea **3**:432
SHETZLY, Adam **15**:648
SHEUFFLEY, Matthew **11**:340
SHEWELL, --- (Capt.) **12**:520
 Joseph **11**:31; **13**:209, 294, 297
 Robert **10**:372; **11**:669-670, 680;
 14:162, 506
 Stephen **11**:31; **15**:524; **16**:210b,
 232
SHI(C)KALAMY **5**:83-88, 136-139,
 162, 167, 190, 212-214, 222,
 284-285, 440
SHIBE, Martin **3**:515
SHIBLEY, --- (Capt.) **10**:710
SHICK CALAMY **8**:212
SHICK CALAMY, John **6**:35, 110,
 112-113, 119, 215-217, 250, 256,
 258, 274, 287, 420-422, 444, 495
SHICKALAMY, Jonathan **6**:495
SHICKEY, Daniel **14**:92
SHIED, Christian **14**:230
SHIELD, Luke, Jr. **10**:264
SHIELDS (SHIELD), Francis **13**:159
 James **15**:119
 John **11**:149-153, 156-157, 149,
 163, 373, 377, 394, 448, 633,
 738; **12**:123

SHIELDS (SHIELD), Luke **5**:112-114,
 226; **10**:341
 Thomas **11**:605; **12**:170, 208;
 13:306-307, 721; **14**:521; **15**:538;
 16:251, 344
SHIELL, Hugh **12**:591, 630
 Hugh (Dr.) **14**:35
SHIFLER, --- (Capt.) **11**:47
SHIKALAMY (SHICK CALAMY,
 SHICCALLAMY), John **7**:34, 46-48,
 50, 54, 65, 148, 171, 176, 244,
 282, 768
SHIKELLIMO (SHIKELLIMY) **4**:641-644,
 646-647, 650-653, 661-662
SHIKILLIMA (SHIKELLIMA) **3**:316,
 330, 333-334, 337
SHILGAS, Henry **15**:466
SHILLEBERGER (SHELLEBERGER), Simeon
 14:125, 429
SHILLING, Peter **3**:288
 Philip **10**:693
 Sohan Martin **3**:453
SHINEBERGER, George **14**:66
 Jacob **16**:411
SHINEY, Lawrence **10**:54
SHINGAS **6**:163, 675-676 (See
 CHINGAS); **7**:230, 242, 381;
 8:189, 310, 383, 386, 676, 690,
 707
SHINGASS **5**:734-735
SHINGER, Johan Christfel **4**:100
SHININGS, John **14**:192, 432
SHINNARD, Abraham **13**:479
SHINNEY, Lawrence **12**:631
SHINNINGS, Barbara **13**:631
 John **13**:631
SHIPE, Casper **14**:81, 88
 Martin **11**:251
SHIPPEN, --- (Judge) **16**:204, 443,
 526
 Edward **1**:490, 495, 498, 500, 502,
 504, 507, 509, 511, 514-518,
 526, 531, 536, 539, 545-547,
 549, 551-553, 555, 559, 561,
 565, 567-568, 571, 57 3,
 575-576, 578, 580-584, 586-587,
 589, 592-593, 595-596, 601, 612,
 614, 617, 620, 622; **2**:9-13,
 17-22, 24-27, 32-24, 36-37, 40,
 43, 45-49, 52-55, 60-63, 66-67,
 69-71, 74-75, 78, 81, 86-92,
 95-98, 101, 103-104, 107-109,
 111-112, 114-125, 128, 131-132,
 134, 138, 141, 143-148, 150-154,
 156-161, 163-166, 169-174, 176,
 178-187, 190, 194, 198, 200,
 204-205, 217, 226, 232, 236-237,
 239-244, 247, 251, 253, 258-259,
 261-262, 266, 276, 280, 297-299,
 308-310, 315, 318, 320-321, 323,
 328, 336-337, 343, 356-357, 361,
 396-397, 403-404, 406-407, 410,
 412-414, 426-429, 434-435, 437,
 439, 441, 443, 446-449, 451-452,
 463, 468, 478-479, 482-486,
 489-491, 493-494, 503, 506,
 508-511, 516-518, 520-522,
 529-531, 534, 539, 543-546,
 550-553, 555; **3**:603; **5**:119, 388,
 572, 635, 659, 661; **6**:394, 402,
 431, 459, 493, 521, 529, 653,
 655; **8**:113-114, 171, 231, 562;
 9:5, 89-90, 100, 172, 282, 292,
 419, 438, 448, 673, 704-705,
 707-708, 721, 723-724, 727,
 730-731, 733, 745-746, 748, ->

SHOEMAKER, Benjamin (continued)
8:360, 362, 402, 407, 409, 412,
415, 422, 436, 460, 484, 487,
501, 505, 516, 560, 563,
573-574, 677, 692, 719; 9:25,
31, 57, 63, 66, 71, 85, 88, 93,
100-101, 108, 119, 125, 135,
146, 149, 172, 201-202, 204-205,
293, 316, 571, 573, 584; 12:616,
782; 13:241, 545, 674
Benjamin, Jr. 9:584
Charles 10:703; 11:251;
14:226-227; 16:122
Daniel 9:732
Geo. 2:493, 520, 539, 543
George 3:332
Henry 9:651, 670; 12:308; 13:77;
14:32, 288, 311, 319, 495;
15:570; 16:195, 495
Isaac 2:493
Jacob 2:493; 6:175-176; 9:547,
623, 634, 688; 10:720; 11:52-53,
156, 195, 598; 12:103, 333, 413;
13:217, 584
John 14:296, 303, 426
Jonathan 15:279
Joseph 11:494
Peter 2:493; 3:569; 12:448
Rebecca 13:544
Rebecca (Mrs.) 11:770
Samuel 8:575; 9:205, 672; 10:46,
53; 11:284, 288, 745; 12:49,
185, 265, 271, 352, 413, 430,
553, 613, 737; 13:246, 674;
14:650
Samuel (Mrs.) 12:271, 352
Thomas 9:634; 11:3; 12:202
William 11:124
SHOEMAN, Mary 15:474
SHOLL, Frederick 3:331
SHOLTS, David 3:518
George 3:518
SHOLTZ, Johanness 3:456
SHOLTZE, Christopher 3:569
George 3:569
Gregorius 3:569
Melchior 3:569
SHONE, Hugh 1:438
SHOO(C)K, Peter 16:38-39
SHOORK, Hans Jacob 3:458
SHOOT, Conraad 3:516
SHORCROSS, Leonard 9:628
SHORE, Wm. 1:83
SHORT, Adam 1:394
David 11:335
James 16:492
Samuel 10:256, 258
William 13:669; 14:95, 424, 609
SHORTALL (SEE BROWN &) 16:8, 121
SHORTER, Eliza. 1:207
SHORTS, Thomas 11:153
SHOTT, Andrew 12:601
Benjamin 11:195
Paul 14:130
SHOUFLER, --- (Capt.) 12:52
SHOUSE, Christian 14:247
SHOVER, Jacob 14:412
SHOWMAN, Philip 3:329
SHRAM, Christian 3:385
SHRATER, William 14:146
SHRAUDER, --- (Capt.) 12:717
SHRAWDER, --- (Capt.) 13:137, 363,
374, 380, 421, 427, 497
Philip 12:623; 13:132, 223, 247,
316; 14:195, 229, 239-240, 436
SHRAWSS, Engelbrod 3:410

SHREUER, --- (Col.) 11:676
SHREWER, George 16:192
SHREWSBURY 1:302
SHREYACK, Hans Michl. 3:518
Jacob 3:518
SHRIEVE, Jesse 14:104
SHRINER, Jacob 12:129
Philip 13:111
SHRISTIE, James 13:716
SHRIVER (SEE LASKY &) 11:469-470
SHRIVER, SUMMERS & LASKY 11:449
SHROD, George 11:131
SHROPP, Matthew 7:460, 495
SHROUDY, Ann 12:157, 256
SHRUPP, Henry 12:728
SHRYOCK, --- (Capt.) 10:461
SHUB, Jacob 3:516
SHUBART, --- (Monsieur) 14:9, 573
Michael 12:129, 164, 486; 13:36,
46, 64; 15:29, 34
SHUBEL, Theobald 11:755
SHUBERT, John 13:191
Michael 11:633, 727
SHUFARD, Johan Georg. 3:519
SHUFFELN, Joh. 3:467
SHUGART, Elizabeth 11:567
Peter 8:403
Zachariah 8:506
Zacharias 13:680; 14:133, 438
Zachary 11:567
SHULER, Adam 3:386
SHULTAS, Georg. Peter 3:456
SHULTS, John 11:614
SHULTZ, Hendrick 3:285
Martin 4:181
SHUMAKER, Joseph 3:519
SHUMAN, Johannes 3:457
SHUMAN(N), John Ludwig 16:49, 126
SHUMBUR, Hans Jacob 3:518
SHUNCK, Christian 16:43, 49
SHUPE, Jacob 15:101
SHUPERT, John 10:688
SHURK, Joannes 3:328
Uldrick 3:327
Uldrick, Jr. 3:328
SHURLOCK (SHERLOCK), Simon 10:486,
495
SHURLOW, Wm. 2:153
SHURMER, --- 3:473-474
Benjamin 3:253-254, 269
SHUTE, Attwood 7:359, 367, 769
Atwood 5:174
Edward 1:521
Thos. 2:276-277
Wm. 1:80
SHUTES, --- 10:267
SHUTTEN, Derrich 4:100
SHUTZ, D. 15:400
SHWARZ, Godfried 7:460
SHY KELUNG 6:126
SHYMER, Isaac 13:676; 14:129, 436
SHYROKTZ, Johannes 3:458
SIBBALD, John 12:110
John (Capt.) 5:267, 284
SIBER, Hans 4:72
SICALAMY, John 6:616, 648 (See
TOCHNECTORAS T.)
John Petty 6:616
SICALAMY (SCKALAMY), James Logan
6:616
SICHAIS 13:465
SICHERNE, Michael 3:455
SICKEL, David 6:171
SICKLE, Lawrence 13:85
William 13:340
SIDDENS, Deborah 14:15

SKAR'ONYADA (SKAROEYADE,
    SKARONYADE) 6:183, 470, 472,
    474
SKATATCHI 2:600
SKATCHEETCHOO 3:153
SKAYANANNEGO 3:310
SKAYANAS 7:68
SKEETOWAS 3:123
SKELLINGER, Enos 13:49
SKELTON, James 15:552
SKENE, --- (Col.) 12:52
SKERRET (SKERRITT), Joseph 16:72,
    516
SKERRETT, Joseph 14:669; 15:575
SKETANUS 13:464
SKETCHLEY, John 5:108, 303
SKIDMORE, Henry 1:82
  Thomas 3:260, 289
SKILLING, John 13:477
  William 12:187
SKILTON (SKELTON), William 11:514,
    516-517
SKINNER, A. (Dr.) 12:638
  Daniel 8:566
  James 1:162; 11:775; 12:775
  John 15:121, 123, 196, 227, 322,
    324, 330, 370, 394, 431, 519,
    543, 635; 16:27, 466, 477
  Margaret 16:222b
  Reuben 13:530, 685
  Richard 13:597; 14:308; 15:17, 346
  Richard C. 16:479-486
  Robert 11:162
  Stephen 9:543-544
  Timothy 8:566
SKIROONIATTA 6:616
SKULL, John 1:148-149
  Nicholas 1:187-188, 536; 8:211,
    250, 260
SKY(L)ES, Henry 11:483-485, 494,
    745
SLABACH, Johan Henry 3:520
  Johannes 3:520
SLACEY, Richard 7:168
SLACHTEN, Christian 4:72
SLACHTER, Hans 3:369
SLACK, Abraham 5:444
  Cornelius 11:281
  Samuel 12:222
SLADE, Samuel 10:342, 351
SLAGLE, --- 13:692
  --- (Mr.) 13:670
  Henry 10:735; 12:145, 298, 647,
    703, 714; 14:182, 208, 234;
    15:420, 474, 615
SLATER, John 11:535; 16:363
  Thomas 10:563
SLATTERLY, Thomas 14:100, 415
SLATTERY, Thomas 13:582
SLAUGHTER, George 10:332
SLAURE, Hans Jacob 3:332
SLAY, Daniel 14:541
SLAYMAKER, Henry 14:149, 196, 259,
    269
  John 12:134
SLEAS, John 11:156, 159
SLEEPMAN, John 14:414
SLEGLE, Henry 10:163
SLEIGEL (SLEGLE), Henry 9:201, 731
SLEISMAN (SLEESMAN), John 14:63,
    128
SLER, Johannes 4:100
SLEWBELLS, --- (Capt.) 9:508
SLICE, John 10:723
SLIGLOFF, Hendrick 3:368
SLINAGER, Michael 3:452

SLITTER (STILLER), John 14:91, 421
SLOAN, David 10:678; 15:545
  John 14:613
  Lawrence 14:96, 424
  Mary 15:545; 16:318
  Samuel 10:78, 142; 12:182, 373,
    540; 14:33; 15:186
  William 12:443
SLOANE, Lawrence 13:637
SLONE, Samuel 11:373
  William 14:217
SLOPER, W. 7:739; 8:552
SLOSSHER, George 10:315
SLOTTENBERG, Henry 13:353
SLOUGH, --- (Col.) 11:78
  --- (Mr.) 13:110, 123
  John Philip 3:458
  Mathias 9:57, 89, 100, 199, 285,
    333, 398, 547; 15:252
  Matthias 6:638; 7:266; 8:402, 506,
    780; 10:503, 538, 540, 554, 580,
    583, 606, 726, 734, 746, 763,
    778; 12:411, 508, 576, 748;
    13:88, 112, 393, 415, 722, 737;
    14:15, 33, 72, 76, 109
  Yost 12:608
SLUBY, Sarah 14:464
  William 14:464
SLUMMERFELD, Zacharias 3:570
SLUNACKER, Stephen 3:518
SLUYS, Adrian Vander 2:493
  Vander 2:493
SLY, Michael 14:581
SLYDER, Jacob 14:81, 100
SLYLE, Michael 15:122
SMALL, --- (Maj.) 9:206; 10:418,
    500
SMALLMAN, --- (Capt.) 8:386
  --- (Maj.) 10:141
  Thomas 7:553; 9:194, 223
SMALLWOOD, --- (Col.) 11:150-155,
    158-159, 162
  --- (Gen.) 12:548
  --- (Gov.) 14:589, 651; 15:463
  John 11:663
  Peter 16:85, 116, 196
SMARL, Lydia 13:327
SMART, James 15:119
SMEIT, Johan Casper 3:385
SMEYER, Philip 3:518
SMIDT, Christian 3:414
  Johan George 3:414
  Johan Hendrick 3:414
  Peter 3:467
SMIEDT, Johannes 3:415
SMIET, Johan Nicolas 3:417
  Michael 3:515
SMILERS (SMEILER), William
    11:149-150
SMILEY (SMILIE), --- (Mr.) 12:237;
    13:744
  John 11:633, 695; 12:134, 164;
    13:730; 14:16-17, 206, 213,
    258-260, 344, 371, 385;
    15:109-116, 118-149, 151-153,
    156-164, 168-173, 177-190,
    192-195, 197-201, 224-230,
    232-238, 240-245, 247-267,
    269-279, 282-285, 287-290, 292,
    294-305, 308-318, 320-327, 331,
    337, 339-340, 342-344, 349-353,
    356-361, 396-401, 403-412,
    414-429, 431-436, 438-443,
    446-460, 533-536, 538-545,
    548-551, 554, 556-564, 566-570,
    572-582, 584, 586-590, ->

SMILEY (SMILIE), John (continued)
15:592, 594-596, 612; 16:6-7,
9-17, 19-22, 24-29, 31, 33-35,
37, 39-44, 46-48, 50-57, 59-60,
62-68, 70-78, 80, 82-91, 93-94,
96-101, 104, 137-138, 141-146,
148-149, 151-160, 162-166,
168-169, 171-173, 175-177, 445
William 15:590
SMIT, Christian 3:413
Hans Jerig 3:452
Hendrich 3:519
Joan Joost 3:328
Peter 3:518
Pieter 3:413
SMITH, --- 7:9, 497, 630; 11:548,
550-554, 557-567, 569, 571-572,
625-626, 628-629, 632
--- (Capt.) 3:102-104; 6:491;
7:303; 11:56, 164
--- (Col.) 11:629; 12:156; 14:662
--- (Dr.) 13:199
--- (Ens.) 12:88-89
--- (Lt.) 9:281; 11:185
--- (Mr.) 5:640; 6:20, 149; 9:121;
10:615, 630; 11:268; 12:60;
13:448, 494, 764; 14:621;
15:133, 135
--- (Rev. Dr.) 9:611-612, 615;
16:122
Abraham 10:451, 765; 11:340, 343;
12:166, 322, 358, 488-489, 737;
13:246, 314, 726, 737; 14:236,
250, 400-401, 563; 15:86,
301-306, 308-318, 320-328, 331,
337-353, 356-361, 380-391,
394-401, 403-412, 414-430,
432-436, 438-461, 464-473,
475-477, 479-480, 482-488,
490-492, 494-506, 508-509,
513-518, 520-523, 525-527,
530-536, 538-540, 542-545,
548-551, 554, 556, 581-584,
586-588, 590, 592, 594-597, 600,
602-604, 607-608, 611-620,
622-623, 625-627, 631-658;
16:1-7, 9-17, 19-29, 31, 33-35,
37, 39-48, 50-57, 59-60, 62-68,
70-78, 80, 82-91, 108-116,
118-120, 122-127, 129-138,
141-149, 151-160, 162-166,
168-169, 171-173, 175-178,
180-182, 186-188, 190-194,
196-202, 205, 209-212, 214-216,
218-224, 209b-215b, 217b-224b,
225-227, 229-233, 235-239, 241,
243-244, 271-274, 276, 278-291,
293, 295-307, 309-313, 315-324,
326-327, 329, 331-332, 363-366,
368-373, 375-379, 384-386,
388-390, 392-396, 399-406,
408-429, 432-435, 439, 441-442,
445-447, 449-459, 461-465, 477,
479-484, 495, 497, 516
Alexander 11:610, 745; 13:11
Andrew 4:135; 11:610-612
Anne 16:222b
Baltzer Cline 15:545
Baltzer Kline 16:16
Benjamin 16:79
Brice 15:178-179
Buchanan 11:101
Charles 16:225, 396, 398, 494
Charles (Alias GORDON) 14:492, 630
Christopher 3:21-23, 84-85
Cinrad 14:84, 415

SMITH, Conrad 13:632
Daniel 13:601, 624; 14:92, 300,
419
David 3:270; 9:396, 398-399, 510
Devereaux 12:286
Devereux 10:142, 169-171, 235
Dirik 3:328
Ebenezer A. 15:41
Edward 14:520; 16:61
Edward Brice 13:527-528, 546
Elizabeth 13:517
Ezekiel 8:403, 506
Felix 5:699
Francis 1:241, 243; 14:131, 410
Francis (Dr.) 13:502, 532
Garret 15:514
George 5:245, 262, 318; 11:348,
538, 608; 12:189, 298, 326, 347,
507, 630; 13:85, 207; 15:153,
179, 199
George Linder 14:90, 230, 250,
263, 358, 395, 447, 463
Glentworth W. (Dr.) 13:170
Hannah 11:152-153
Hans Michael 3:287
Henry 1:77, 323; 3:330, 333,
343-344, 506-507; 9:549; 10:668;
12:48, 563
Hooker (Dr.) 14:110, 308
Indian 3:123, 181-182, 187, 197,
202, 219
Isack 1:89
J. 13:60
Jabbel 13:49
James 3:370; 4:675, 680-684;
5:247, 378, 600; 6:466; 9:219,
270, 293, 297; 10:234-235, 671,
724, 726, 749; 11:103, 126, 177,
326, 341, 373, 385, 535; 12:174,
411-412, 513, 548, 560, 577,
579-580, 718, 723; 13:222, 311,
352, 383, 514, 632, 669, 698,
715; 14:85, 99, 189, 193, 420,
430, 574, 662; 15:13, 399;
16:73, 270, 335
James B. 13:356; 15:267
Jane 12:197, 648, 694
Jer. 10:668
John 1:180; 2:494; 3:309; 4:102,
104; 5:210, 247, 388, 572;
6:131, 142, 379, 425, 434, 481;
7:86, 120, 637; 8:475, 566;
9:89, 104, 201, 584, 731,
769-771; 10:163, 384, 581;
11:12, 242, 259, 276, 347, 482,
484-485; 12:247, 349-350, 362,
405, 531, 632, 636, 684, 731;
13:608, 624, 638, 708; 14:82,
84, 96, 130, 214, 411, 416,
420-421, 436, 471, 555, 585,
614-615, 636, 654; 15:119, 411,
464, 482; 16:8, 224b, 335, 388,
434, 4356
John (Dr.) 10:150, 461, 469
Johnston 10:518-519, 524, 527, 546
Jonathan 12:86
Jonathan B. 11:45, 102-103, 115,
119-121, 124, 126, 128, 130-137,
197-198, 202, 225, 276, 325-326,
349-352, 385, 425, 461, 465,
527, 534
Jonathan Bayard 12:589, 593, 600,
606, 609, 614; 14:15, 110, 143;
15:325, 595; 16:446
Jonathan, Jr. 15:11

SMITH, Joseph **5**:210; **13**:3; **14**:543,
545, 581; **15**:3
Katharine **4**:47, 209, 224 (See
CONNOR)
Lawrence **16**:333, 335
Mary **11**:585; **14**:649
Mary Cline **16**:16
Matthew **9**:138, 142, 147; **10**:688;
11:34, 180, 502, 506, 508, 512,
518-520, 522, 524-526, 570,
614-620, 622-623, 633, 635-641,
644-650, 652-653, 655-661,
664-667, 669, 672-675, 682,
715-724, 727-728, 730, 732-734,
751, 779-781, 783; **12**:1, 3-5,
7-8, 11, 13, 15-20, 72, 88-91,
94, 100-102, 104, 106-115, 117,
119, 121, 123-125, 127, 130,
132-133, 136, 139, 141, 144-146,
148, 194-195, 197-198, 200-202,
205, 207, 209-210, 212, 216-217,
220-222, 243, 461, 493, 567,
573, 576, 581-584; **13**:29,
446-447, 492-494, 696
Meriwether **11**:613, 669
Michael **11**:393; **14**:207; **16**:352
Moses **14**:310
Nathaniel **12**:427-428, 550; **13**:593,
717; **14**:610
Peggy **9**:89, 104
Peter **12**:355, 544; **13**:569, 600,
623, 714; **14**:84, 91, 415, 423;
16:528
Pleasant **15**:195
Richard **10**:9, 217
Robert **3**:332, 387, 524, 575;
5:247, 444; **10**:290, 299, 462,
603, 605-606, 630, 641, 645,
700, 705, 708, 750, 762; **11**:2,
6, 66, 79, 84, 98, 101, 107,
195, 222, 225, 229-230, 234,
238, 255, 257, 282, 286, 318,
321, 330, 340, 370, 479, 492,
504, 555, 574, 596, 624, 662,
775, 781; **12**:110-111, 185, 298,
349-350, 360, 362, 405, 460,
505, 513, 515, 554, 569, 574;
13:141, 341, 344, 547, 722;
14:42, 123, 385, 465, 486, 555,
619, 647, 651, 657-658, 663-665,
670; **16**:32, 92
Robert, Jr. **15**:205, 216, 239, 246,
363, 366, 370, 373, 598
Samuel **3**:615; **4**:66-69, 86, 117,
135, 247, 313, 483; **5**:3, 378,
436, 443, 452-453; **6**:433, 435;
7:135-136, 186; **8**:19; **9**:126;
10:448, 554; **11**:125, 194, 260,
330, 340, 380, 393, 397, 476,
633; **12**:687; **13**:392, 714,
719-720, 778; **14**:9, 62-63, 84,
98, 109, 126, 176, 203, 213,
238, 313, 405, 410, 421, 435,
615
Sarah **11**:770; **16**:222b
Thomas **1**:374, 438; **3**:60; **5**:597;
6:144; **10**:78, 163, 461, 658,
672; **11**:35, 89, 256, 372-373,
461, 466, 555, 630, 633, 726;
12:8-9, 70, 104, 124, 457, 551,
556, 563, 667, 694, 740; **13**:1,
6, 24, 186, 297, 354, 399, 423,
548, 585, 600; **14**:7, 29, 149,
160, 450, 457, 466, 476, 483,
505, 546, 589, 604, 656; **15**:5,
11, 54, 205, 219, 230; ->

SMITH, Thomas (continued) **16**:32,
158, 324
Thomas Duncan **15**:330
Timothy **3**:332, 370, 387, 575, 615;
4:85-86; **7**:400; **8**:250, 253, 260
Walter **12**:124-125
William **2**:11, 397; **3**:416, 464;
5:210, 411, 464, 550; **6**:57, 67,
72-73, 75, 82, 93, 96, 105, 131,
404, 467; **7**:637; **8**:402-403, 506;
9:201, 269-273, 276, 281,
292-293, 297, 302, 731; **10**:163,
684, 687-689, 693, 697, 703,
717, 738; **11**:28, 31, 43, 140,
219, 284, 289, 515-517; **12**:43,
157-158, 268, 299, 612, 775-776;
13:54, 121, 151, 196, 296, 335,
393, 404, 429, 449, 462, 514,
529, 624, 633; **14**:47, 97, 101,
418-419, 454, 510, 598-599;
16:237, 407
William (Dr.) **11**:124; **13**:562
William (Rev.) **8**:11, 17, 438,
442-443, 445-446
William D. D. **11**:284, 288, 296,
309, 460, 472, 525
William Drewett **11**:284, 288, 296,
309, 460, 610
William Hooker **14**:80, 94, 395-396;
15:35-36, 212, 489
William Moore **12**:30; **14**:247;
15:295, 428
Wm. **1**:241, 243, 438
SMITH (See BROOK), William **15**:164,
212, 407, 628
SMITH (See ROBERTSON &) **15**:429
SMITHER, James **15**:387
Rachel **15**:387
SMITHER (SMYTHER), James **11**:214,
513, 516-517
SMITHER(S), George **15**:450
John **9**:689, 778
SMITT, George **3**:619
Johan Hendrick **3**:385
Johan Philippus **3**:516
SMITZ, Johannes **3**:454
SMOUT, Edward **3**:416, 521-523, 531;
4:69, 75, 131, 135, 142, 152,
313, 483; **5**:3, 318, 378
SMULLER, John **15**:66
SMYCER, Michael **14**:224
SMYSER, --- (Capt.) **11**:93
Jacob **16**:214, 444
Michael **12**:513, 662
SMYTER, --- (Capt.) **5**:319
SMYTH, James **1**:83
John **9**:571
SMYTHERS, --- (Capt.) **10**:649
SNABLEY, Hans **3**:517
SNAKE'S AON **8**:293
SNATHERLY, Georg. Philip **3**:466
Hans Michl. **3**:466
SNEAD, Robert **1**:510, 550, 562
SNEBLER, Ultiner **3**:367
SNEIDER (SNEYDER), --- (Mr.) **7**:447
Catharine **12**:607
Frederick **11**:10, 42, 78, 84, 146,
151, 307, 319, 388, 507, 594,
606, 622, 668, 778; **12**:48-49,
119, 153, 185, 218, 241, 266,
304, 335, 338, 357, 373, 406,
443, 466, 494, 504, 509, 523,
533, 550, 558, 592-593, 601,
615, 645, 681, 696, 715, 777;
13:20, 49, 73, 91, 101, 137,
165, 183, 208, 247, 252, ->

SNEIDER (SNEYDER), Frederick
(continued) **13**:258, 262, 276,
298, 320, 340, 359, 381, 386,
407, 445, 545, 566, 588, 615,
633, 677, 700, 734, 760; **14**:1,
8, 27, 37, 46, 61, 79, 123, 154,
170, 196, 227, 231, 245, 269,
307, 327, 370, 395, 450, 470,
490, 508, 529, 542, 589, 616,
630, 648, 671; **16**:16, 44, 67,
87, 105, 124, 145, 162, 169,
180, 209, 220b, 234, 252, 270,
291, 313, 353, 372, 391, 414,
439, 480, 488, 509, 529
Henry **13**:565
Jacob **13**:402
John **12**:607; **13**:445-446; **14**:558
Simon **12**:279; **14**:322, 325, 493;
16:495
SNELL, Adam **7**:620-621
Jacob **14**:614
John **16**:192, 491
Nicholas **16**:542
SNEPPELEN, Jacob **3**:290
SNEPPELEY, Henry **3**:290
SNEVELY, Jacob **13**:302
SNEYDER, David **13**:37
Frederick **13**:462, 495, 520
Johannes **3**:287
SNIDER, Abraham **4**:60
Conrad **14**:563
Fred. **10**:765
SNIDER (SNYDER), Conrad **10**:697, 719
SNIEDER, Jacob **10**:765
SNIFF, Martin **15**:499
SNIVELY, --- (Capt.) **11**:46
Jacob **3**:417
SNOBBLE, George **6**:648
SNODDY, Michael **16**:221b
SNODGRASS, Benjamin **11**:281, 741
James **14**:364, 393, 459
SNOLT, Philip **3**:328
SNOODGRASS, James **5**:247
John **5**:247
SNOWDEN, Christopher **1**:148
Isaac **10**:93; **12**:636; **13**:64, 334,
340; **15**:85
Jedediah **11**:58, 640; **13**:63, 369
Jedidiah **12**:116
Jno. **2**:596
John **3**:28
Joseph **16**:281
Leonard **10**:359, 361, 371, 397,
408, 455-456, 467
Samuel **10**:506; **11**:53
Sarah **13**:369
SNYDER, Casper **16**:117
Christian **3**:368
Conrad **14**:407, 409, 440
Daniel **11**:212
David **11**:601, 603
Detrick **13**:586
Detrick (Detrich) **14**:97, 424
Jacob **3**:368; **13**:495
John **11**:305-306; **13**:584; **15**:570;
16:335
Matthias **3**:368; **11**:638
Michael **11**:131
Peter **11**:515-516, 518
Simon **11**:334
Valentine **3**:413, 516
William **11**:576
SNYDER (SNEIDER), Philip
11:272-273, 559
SNYDER (SNIDER), Conrad **15**:120, 301
SOACHKOAT **2**:553

SOAMES, Thomas **3**:390
SOAN, Peter **7**:493-494
SOANES, Daniel **1**:83
SOBER, --- **5**:79
Charles **1**:531
Charles (Dr.) **2**:120
John **11**:37
SOBERS, John **12**:324
SOCK, Betty **8**:113
William (Billy) **8**:112-116, 118,
121-122, 134, 138
SODEN, Benjamin **12**:200
SODER, --- (Capt.) **11**:99
SODORARANGCHESE **3**:435
SOFFMAN, Andreas **3**:390
SOFFRENZ, Johannes **3**:454
SOGEHOANNA **7**:507
SOGOGOCKIATHER **5**:284
SOHAES, --- **10**:257
SOHAIS, Connedechto **3**:102
SOHAISE (SHAHAISE) **8**:116-118,
121-123
SOHAYS, --- **9**:89
SOIGLE, Benjamin **11**:504
SOLCONWANAGHLY **5**:467
SOLDERMAN, Christian **3**:288
SOLDNER, Hans Georg. **3**:459
SOLO(O)BY, Wm. **2**:168, 181-183
SOLOMON, --- **7**:461
Haym **13**:166, 389; **15**:458
Joseph **14**:311, 495
Rachel **15**:458
SOMERS, Catherine **16**:295
Richard **15**:259
SOMERSETT, Israel **7**:168
SOMERVILLE, John **13**:601
SOMERVILLE (SOMMERVEILL), John
14:92, 420
SOMEY, Hans Jacob **3**:519
Hans Peter **3**:519
Hans Peter, Jr. **3**:519
Otto Frederick **3**:519
SOMMERFIELD, --- (Esqr.) **1**:550
SONACHCHREGI **3**:571
SONACHQUA **5**:355
SONAGARIS, N. Lowrens **6**:122
SONAHRAWANO **6**:588-590
SONATZIOWANAH **5**:311
SONDAY, Jacob **4**:59
SONGHURST, John **1**:48, 92-93,
109-110, 112, 123, 162, 168, 178
SONMAMS, Bethian **13**:18
SONMANS, Arent **15**:379, 382-383
SONONGUA **8**:384, 387
SONOYEYOUGH **8**:293
SONTSINGER, Hans Paulus **3**:455
SONYTOWANA **3**:609
SOOHAYESSE **3**:45
SOOTER, Christian **3**:520
SOOTERA, Hendrick **3**:368
SORIHOWANEY **5**:686
SOROR (SEE FRATER &) **10**:358, 362
SORRELL, Isaac **12**:395
SOSANNAN **2**:557
SOT(A)YRIOTE **2**:606, 613
SOTAYYOGHT **2**:574
SOTCHER, Jno. **2**:21, 488, 630-631
SOTEERYOLE **2**:604
SOTERWANACHTY **5**:475
SOTEYOTE **2**:607
SOTSHIYITSHIYGWANOE **6**:291
SOUDER, Charles **10**:730
Johan Philip **3**:456
John **14**:71; **16**:144
Lawrence **11**:33
Peter **3**:456

191

SOUDER, Thomas 3:454
SOULANGES, --- (Monsieur) 14:560
SOULDER, Hans Adam 3:287
SOUR, Peter 11:513, 516-517
SOURMILG, Lutwig 3:410
SOUTH, Humphrey 1:29, 202
  Jacob 14:311
SOUTH(E)RIN, Edward 1:64, 72-73,
  79-82, 84, 105-106
SOUTHBE(E), Wm. 1:530-531, 556,
  559, 576, 582
SOUTHERLAND, Daniel 4:280
SOUTHERN, William 15:325
SOUTHERS, John 10:244
SOUTHERSBY, Wm. 1:104-110, 115,
  132-133, 135, 137-138, 140,
  145-147, 153, 165-171, 173,
  175-193, 195, 208, 453
SOUTHREN, John 1:193
SOUTHWELL, Robert 1:534-535, 538
SOUTHWORTH, John 1:48
SOVER, Johan Philip 3:516
SOVERHILL, Abraham 6:648
SOWER, Christopher 13:126, 207
  Daniel 12:303, 771
  Elizabeth 13:208
  Henrich 3:520
  Luke Thomas 13:208
SOWERMAN, Rosanna 16:320
SOWERS, Christopher 13:34
SOWTER, Nicolaus 3:520
SOWYER, Adam 3:414
SPAFFORD, George 5:175
  William 3:115, 545
SPAG, Adam 3:524
SPALDING, --- (Mr.) 16:440
  John 14:49, 160
SPALL, William 13:91
SPANGENBERG, --- (Mr.) 7:107, 109,
  118-119, 151, 165, 173-174, 189,
  190, 353; 8:84, 147, 304
  --- (Rev.) 6:358, 756-757
  Joseph 5:575-576 (alias Augustus)
SPANGLER, Baltzer 10:729; 12:390
  Charles 11:150-151
  George 10:640, 775; 11:74, 105,
    311, 513, 516-517; 12:412
  Leonard 14:295, 302, 417
  Mary 12:412
SPANGLER & BALSER 11:42
SPANGLER & WILEY 11:17
SPARHAWK, John 10:740, 770; 15:40,
  234-235
  John (Dr.) 11:765; 13:306
SPARKE, William 6:548, 594
SPARKS, --- (Maj.) 6:490
SPEAR, --- (Capt.) 11:12
  Edward 13:202, 716, 731; 14:409,
    440, 559; 16:41
  Hugh 16:29
  Joseph 10:78, 142, 166, 168;
    12:446
  Robert 11:315-316
SPEARING (SPERING), John
  11:515-516, 518
SPEARS, John 11:180
  Joseph 9:269
SPECHT, George 15:230
SPECK, Johan Wilhelm 4:60
  Mathias 4:60
SPECKERT, John 15:91
SPEEDY, William 9:715, 717
SPEER, --- (Sgt.) 12:681
  Edward 13:710; 14:63, 83, 130,
    422, 431
  Hugh 15:382

SPEES, Henry 12:139, 305
SPEIGHT, Jacob 11:10
SPEIKER, Daniel Ultree 11:330
  Henry 12:557
SPELLER, John 14:541
SPELTER, Daniel 4:100
SPENCE, Douglas 11:202
  James 16:8, 382
  Mary 14:573
SPENCER, --- (Col.) 12:53
  David 14:292, 295, 299, 302, 426,
    437
  Francis 14:56
  James 9:509; 10:564
  Nicholas 11:79
  Saml. 2:104
  Samuel 7:717
  Timothy 16:228
SPENDELOW, --- (Lt.) 6:491
SPENDER, John 9:203
SPENE, Peter 15:350
SPERGER, Wolfer 3:385
SPERING, Henry 13:252; 16:542
  John 13:252
SPICER, Jacob 2:275; 8:175, 179
  Robert 4:468
SPICKER, Benjamin 6:657
SPICKER (SPYCKER), Peter 6:650,
  703-704
SPIDER (SPEDER), Jacob 12:333, 576
SPIEGEL, Jacob 13:636; 14:422
  John 13:636
SPIES, Ulrich 3:569
SPIKEMAN, Randal 1:576
SPIKER, Henry 14:554, 604
  Peter 12:546
SPIKER (SPYCKER), Henry 16:82, 195,
  523, 538
SPINGLER, Balzar 3:465
  Georg. 3:465
  Henrich 3:465
  Jacob 3:520
SPINHOUSE, Anthony 14:416
SPITLER, Hans 4:72
SPITTLEMAYER, Hans Adam 3:518
  Martin 3:518
SPLITDORFF 6:491
SPOGENER, Aran 3:517
SPOHN, Adam 3:519
  Henry 15:294, 565
  John 10:447; 11:596; 12:131;
    13:88; 16:122, 192
SPONSELLER, Andrew 12:76
  Jacob 12:537
SPOONER, Ward 13:572
SPOTS, George 9:778
SPOTSWOOD, --- (Capt.) 7:604
  --- (Gov.) 4:396, 428, 439, 591,
    717
  Alexander 3:21, 23, 30, 89, 116,
    118-119, 202-203, 205-207,
    209-211
  William 15:366, 374; 16:189
SPRAY, Christopher 1:438
SPRECHER, Hans Georg. 3:467
SPRIGG(S), Samuel 14:294, 301, 306,
  410
SPRING, --- (Capt.) 8:234; 10:341,
  345
  --- (Widow) 11:54
  Cornelius 4:578, 580
  Lethea 13:517
  Nicholas 11:89
SPRINGER, Charles 3:254, 270
  Dennis 14:312
  Harbert 1:29

192

STANWIX, John (Col.-Earl of)
(continued) 7:715-716, 732, 737,
772
STAPLER, John 9:203; 10:81, 217
STAPLETON, William 10:303
STAR, Frederick 5:445
John 4:107
STAR(R), James 4:102, 107
Moses 5:210, 729
STARCHERS, Lewis 15:248
STARGES, Jonathan 13:708
STARK, --- (Mrs.) 12:425
John 16:92
Rose 13:337
STARLEY, Ann 12:681
STARMAN, --- 14:47
STARR, Arthur 1:576
Elijah 14:64, 126, 437
Jeremiah 4:523; 6:241
Moses 4:102
STAUFFER, Daniel 3:454
Jacob 3:432
STAUP, Johan Wilhelm 3:454
STAUT, Yost 12:608
STAWYUNTIS 4:501
STAYMAN, Hans 3:517
Peter 3:517
Peter, Jr. 3:517
STAYNER, Roger 10:457
STEAD, John 14:406, 408, 437
STEALLY, Baltzer 14:262
STEBEY, Daniel 12:608
STEDAFORT, Garait 10:480
STEDDICORN, Simon 15:462
STEDDIFORD, Garret 13:202
STEDHAM, Jonas 10:218
STEDHAM (STEDMAN), Joseph 10:56,
211, 270
STEDIFORD, Garret 12:215, 240
STEDLER, Christopher 3:452
STEDMAN, --- (Mr.) 5:100
Alex'd. 11:284, 287, 289, 610-611
Alexander 6:175; 7:62, 93, 96,
367, 769; 8:322, 339, 342, 360,
575; 9:172, 192, 235, 282, 286,
292, 334, 387; 12:204; 13:695
Charles 11:284, 287, 289, 494;
12:204
Jno. 3:413, 452
John 3:518, 568
STEECHER, Hans Melchior 3:456
STEEDEL, Frantz 3:455
STEEL (STEELE, STELL), --- (Capt.)
10:718
--- (Mr.) 6:675; 12:486
Archibald 13:722; 14:233, 615
Arthur 3:486, 490
Ephraim 11:64, 229, 267, 691;
15:570
James 3:107, 111-112, 157, 161,
259, 544, 547, 573; 13:634
John 10:139, 147, 237; 11:444-445;
13:604; 14:83, 130, 421, 426,
494, 550, 572
John (Rev.) 7:241; 9:451, 464,
481, 483, 485-486, 506-510, 540,
622, 762
Peter 11:113
Robert 13:687-688
Samuel 9:515
Thomas 15:196, 218
William 12:301; 13:514, 584;
16:461
STEELE, Andrew 1:120
Archibald 12:306
Benjamin 13:597

STEELE, Ephraim 12:166
James 12:751; 13:23; 14:608, 671
Mary 14:465
Robert 14:359, 558
William 14:514
STEELE, KAMMERER & GLENTWORTH
14:571-572
STEELMAN, --- 5:384-385; 13:252,
262
James 12:553, 585
John 12:574
John Hans 2:17, 21, 434
STEELS, --- (Capt.) 11:113
STEEN, John 15:183
STEENE, Hans 14:72
STEER, Aaron 14:190, 194, 428
Christian 14:47, 50
STEETS, W. 1:209
STEFFER, Johan Casper 3:331
Johan Casper, Jr. 3:331
STEGER, Henrick 3:456
STEGGER, Hans Peter 3:456
STEHELY, Jacob 13:309
STEHLER, Ludwig 15:589
STEIGLE, Valentine 14:127, 421
STEILEY, Ulrick 3:455
STEIMETZ, --- (Mr.) 10:528
STEIN, Hans 14:50
Leonhardt 4:73
Mary 14:50
Philip 14:252
STEINBACH, Barnhard 3:569
STEINBACK, Christian 3:452
Jacob 13:582
STEINEBACH (STEINEBACK), Jacob
14:91, 412
STEINER, --- 13:445
Jacob 3:413
Melchior 13:24; 14:400, 581;
15:375; 16:126
STEINER & CIST 11:177, 200
STEINHAWER (STEINHAUER), George
William 15:209, 525
STEINIGER, Jurg 3:284
STEININGER, Henry 13:273; 14:34
STEINMEITZ, John 11:602
STEINMENTZ, --- (Mr.) 13:511
STEINMETZ, --- (Mr.) 13:509, 537
John 12:507, 545; 13:85, 112, 304,
306, 391, 415, 576, 646, 721,
737; 14:583; 16:529
STEINMITZ (STINEMITZ), Jacob
11:558, 616
STELFELT, Henry 3:329
STELLERAN, Jno. Hans 4:340
STELLERS, Charlotte 13:398
STELLING, Casper 4:59
STELLMAN, Jut Hans 3:603
STELLY, Jacob 3:607
STELWELL, John 10:701
STEMPEL, Nicalaus 3:457
STEMPUL, Jacob 3:457
STENBARD, Hans Michl. 3:518
STENCHEON, James (Alias BURGES)
14:477
STENINGER, Henry 12:28
STENS, Henrich 3:516
STEPHANNS, Baltzer 4:59
STEPHANS, Friend 5:541
STEPHEN, Michael 16:61
STEPHEN(S) (STEVEN), Adam (Col.)
7:289-290, 381, 502
STEPHENON, Stephen 11:548
STEPHENS (STEVENS), --- (Capt.)
6:491
--- (Gen.) 10:754, 757

194

STEPHENS (STEVENS), Arent 5:462,
 624-625, 644; 7:115, 625
Benjamin 9:571
Daniel 15:613, 625
James 14:407, 409, 439
John 8:156, 179, 219
Jno. 1:90
Phineas 14:223
Richard 10:40, 42; 15:571; 16:427
Tho. 1:92 (See STEVENS)
Thomas 10:172
William 16:547
William (Dr.) 11:89
STEPHENSON (STEVENSON), --- (Mr.)
 12:64
James 13:778; 12:185, 646, 652,
 654-655, 701, 703, 708,
 717-718, 723, 752-753, 763;
 14:194
John 13:740
Richard 15:576
Robert 11:219, 330, 479, 504, 782;
 15:176
Stephen 13:202, 624, 714; 14:71,
 82, 123, 414, 428
STEPNEY 2:403
STERETT, James 13:102; 14:312
Robert 11:77
Samuel 13:108, 123, 128
STERIT, --- (Capt.) 7:342
STERITT, Samuel 13:102
STERLING, --- 6:491
--- (Gen.) 4:6
John 14:589
STERLING (STIRLING), Isaac
 11:152-153
James 10:645-647
STERNFIELD, John 12:201
STERRAT, John 4:135, 748, 782
William 14:469
STERRAT (STERRETT), James 5:55, 120
STERRET, Samuel 13:454
STERRETT, William 14:482, 542
STERRETT (STERITT), Samuel 12:462,
 580-581, 694, 740, 771
STERTZELL, Henrich 3:455
STESNINGER, Johan Adam 3:415
STEUART, Christopher 12:356
Geo. 5:586
STEUBEN, --- (Baron) 12:72
--- (Gen.) 4:6
STEVENS, --- (Gen.) 11:158-159, 162
--- (Lt.) 6:610
Alexander 7:155
Daniel 12:515
Dennis 14:312
James 11:494
Nehemiah 6:143
Richard 14:217
Tho. 1:92 (See STEPHENS)
William 14:384 (See John FISHER)
STEVENSON (STEPHENSON), --- (Capt.)
 8:171-172
Charles 14:608
Cornelius 11:5
Elizabeth 13:338
George 5:431, 435, 438, 443;
 6:640; 8:322; 10:768; 11:307,
 330, 365, 479, 504; 12:8, 201,
 296; 13:718; 14:95, 437
George (Dr.) 13:568
James 5:135; 6:114, 118, 122, 127,
 248, 474, 563; 11:482-485;
 13:71, 117, 138, 149, 177, 202,
 295, 470, 696; 14:139; 15:221
John 11:363; 13:38, 248; ->

STEVENSON (STEPHENSON), John
 (continued) 14:244-245, 247, 250
Robert 10:730; 13:741
Stephen 12:356, 705
Thomas 2:106, 132, 456, 458, 528,
 544, 560, 587, 596
Thos. 3:28
STEVER, Casper 4:268
STEWARD, Charles 14:100
David 5:194
Francis 4:135
James 10:616; 11:234; 15:283
Samuel 15:406
Story (Dr.) 11:130
William 10:781
STEWARD (STEWART), George 11:102,
 330, 378, 479, 504, 547, 570,
 572
STEWART, --- 14:312
--- (Capt.) 6:491, 502
--- (Col.) 13:626; 14:296
--- (Lord) 9:761
--- (Mr.) 9:503
Abraham 16:423
Alexander 13:145, 153, 183, 272;
 14:132, 609; 15:64
Alexander (Dr.) 13:593, 714
Andrew 10:256
Archibald 16:185
Catherine 12:607
Charles 5:247; 9:569, 572-573,
 575, 583-587, 606-607, 612, 615,
 620, 663, 675-676, 751, 756;
 10:50; 11:303; 14:62, 413;
 16:146, 183, 185
Christopher 13:33; 14:451
David 7:500; 9:3-5; 14:614;
 16:225, 444, 541
Elizabeth 12:79
George 10:383, 421-422; 14:321,
 385
I. 11:232
Jacob 15:188
James 9:711, 715, 717; 13:159,
 282; 14:131, 295, 302, 427, 435;
 16:196
James A. 13:509
John 12:488, 519; 13:636;
 14:558-559, 662; 16:214, 117b,
 428
Lazarus 9:675-676, 682-685,
 687-688, 710-717, 749, 757-758,
 767, 769-772, 780; 10:2
Lazarus (the younger) 9:711
Robert 5:325, 411, 464; 11:591;
 13:589, 667; 14:36, 215
Walker 11:526
Walter 10:447; 11:225, 227, 231,
 421, 456, 459, 782-783; 12:7,
 116, 368; 13:573, 713; 14:195,
 611; 16:185
William 9:51, 199, 715, 717;
 11:195; 12:411; 13:635, 712;
 14:133, 608; 16:24
STEWERT, John 11:363
STEY, Peter 3:432
STEYER, Hans Jerig 3:432
STEYMUTZ, Johan Nicolas 3:413
STEYNER, Ulrick 3:385
STEYNER (STEINER) & CIST 12:387,
 404, 440, 448, 456
STICKER, Adam 12:636
STICKLER, Andreas 3:332
STIDHAM, Jonas 9:337
STIEGAL, Henry William 10:225, 227
STIEGEL, William 10:54

STIEGLE, Valentine **13**:759
STIELT, John **13**:713
STIESS, Georg. Adam **3**:467
STIFFELL, Jacob **3**:385
STIGER, Stephen **11**:494
STIL(B)FORD, Thomas **12**:672, 620
STILEES, --- (Capt.) **13**:670
STILES, --- (Capt.) **8**:436; **13**:335,
 663
 Danll. **1**:175
 Edward **10**:414; **11**:494; **12**:196;
 13:146, 448; **15**:277; **16**:179
 George **1**:376, 379
 Henry **11**:54
 Joseph **10**:728; **11**:47, 105, 125,
 130, 137, 141, 143, 242, 252,
 310, 470, 538, 546, 552, 564,
 579, 490, 606, 630, 635-636,
 638, 642, 653, 662, 667, 669,
 682, 696, 716, 735, 747, 760,
 765, 772, 774-775, 784; **12**:3, 7,
 10, 20, 24, 45, 72, 104, 111,
 139, 145, 172, 266, 287, 313,
 322, 330, 340, 367, 385,
 390-391, 404, 428, 433, 457-458,
 464, 469, 481-482, 485, 488-489,
 493, 501, 549, 587, 614, 641,
 647, 662, 664, 702, 712-713,
 774, 777; **13**:1, 19-20, 28, 44,
 48, 68, 70, 76, 82, 96, 110,
 130, 137, 149, 178, 213, 232,
 239, 247, 263, 310, 318, 329,
 341, 344, 363, 412, 485-486,
 508, 522, 567, 603, 611, 614;
 14:29, 72, 154, 159, 183, 186,
 199, 206, 231, 349, 366, 375,
 401, 403, 441, 449, 469, 477,
 520, 552, 588, 620, 655; **15**:12,
 15-16, 23, 46, 61, 83, 110, 204,
 235-236, 277, 289, 307, 339,
 433-434, 447, 449, 453, 456;
 16:70, 92, 154, 270, 355, 408,
 513
 William **14**:550
STILFORD, Thomas **12**:620
STILL, Henrich **3**:516
 Isaac **10**:256; **14**:88, 430
STILL(E), Isaac **8**:30-32, 51, 87,
 89, 101, 133, 140, 147-148,
 175-176, 202, 205, 211-212, 292,
 297, 305-306, 308, 341, 346,
 403, 405, 419, 425, 497, 594,
 618-619, 633, 654-656, 660-661,
 667, 707-708, 724, 757; **9**:6,
 611-612, 620, 694, 738
STILLE, --- (Mr.) **13**:558; **14**:442
 Edward **10**:451
 Isaac **11**:111
 John **13**:150; **16**:320
STILLER, John **10**:722; **11**:133
STILLIE, --- (Mr.) **11**:157
STILLWAGGON, John **9**:398
STILLWAGON, John **11**:244
STILLWALL, Elias **10**:78, 163
STILLWELL, Daniel **3**:51
 John **11**:610-612
STILWELL, Elias **5**:454
 John **10**:271
STIMAN, Johan George **3**:453
STIMMAN, Hans **3**:453
STIMMELL, Mathias **12**:92
STIMROD, Simon **11**:633
STINE, John **16**:478
STINNINGER, Henry **11**:89
STINTON, --- **9**:140
STIRLING, --- (Earl of) **9**:73, 121

STITES, Benjamin **11**:77
 Henry **11**:112
 Thomas **13**:449-450
STITLER, John **13**:557
STITZ, Jacob **11**:75-76
STO(C)KL(E)Y, Thomas **16**:36, 124,
 444, 515
STOAKLIE, Jno. **1**:490
STOBEL, Samuel **10**:414
STOBO, Robert **6**:53, 140-142, 146,
 161, 163
STOCK, Joannes **3**:328
 John **15**:337
STOCKDALE, Wm. **1**:152, 268-270, 272,
 275, 277, 280, 282-286, 290-292,
 312, 317, 320-327, 335-338, 340,
 342-343
STOCKER, Anthony **12**:594-595; **15**:141
 Clement **12**:594-595; **15**:141
 Michel **3**:415
 Peter **3**:524
STOCKER & WHARTON **10**:339; **15**:647;
 16:4, 223
STOCKIE, Hans **4**:73
STOCKINS **2**:488
STOCKLEY, Benjamin **9**:203
 Paynter **6**:638
 Thomas **15**:266, 405
STOCKLY, Thomas **13**:143
STOCKTON, --- (Maj.) **11**:201, 216
 --- (Mrs.) **11**:216
 Thomas **11**:340, 479, 504
STODDARD, Benjamin **5**:462, 624;
 11:533
 John **5**:8
STODDERT, Benjamin **5**:550
 Thomas **14**:223
STOEVER, Caspar **13**:454
 Casper **10**:703
 Frederick **13**:454
 Philip **14**:654
STOHL, Andrew **10**:513
STOKEL(E)Y, Nehemiah **14**:533, 609,
 637
 Thomas **14**:33, 38-39, 41, 44, 48,
 225, 245, 259-260, 357, 455
STOKELEY, --- (Capt.) **13**:591
 Nehemiah **13**:427-428
 Thomas **13**:473-474, 529, 642
STOKELY, --- (Capt.) **13**:484, 593,
 745
 John **13**:577
 Nehemia **13**:423
 Nehemiah **11**:469, 617; **13**:244, 415,
 419, 527; **16**:297
 Thomas **12**:367, 623; **13**:53, 288,
 445, 461, 527
STOKER, --- **8**:576
STOLTZ, Henrich **3**:570
STONE, --- (Capt.) **6**:491
 Abraham **14**:74
 Andrew **4**:486-487, 489, 671, 675
 Conrad **13**:593; **14**:84, 411
 Frederick **9**:689, 778; **10**:56;
 16:322
 John **1**:92; **10**:757; **11**:81; **16**:335
 Lodowick **11**:223
STONEBURNER, Leonard **10**:637; **11**:21
STONEMATZ, Daniel **10**:778
STONER, --- (Capt.) **11**:110
 Jacob **13**:634; **14**:125, 432
STONY, Matthew **11**:770
STOOPS, Elizabeth **12**:746
STOP, Nicolas **4**:100
STORER, John **11**:85
 Thomas **7**:220

STRETTEL(L) (STRETHIL, STRETTLE),
Robert (continued) 6:412, 423,
430, 450, 459, 480, 485, 498,
510, 523, 533, 558, 567,
587-588, 591, 601, 638-639, 653,
662, 666, 670, 672, 680, 682,
685, 688-689, 691, 696, 701,
711, 714, 728-729, 736, 742,
744, 751, 755-756, 762, 765,
769-771, 773, 776, 778; 7:10,
18, 33, 37, 41, 46, 50, 55-56,
58-60, 63-64, 70, 72, 78, 83,
87, 91, 96-97, 105, 110, 120,
122, 127, 130, 137, 148, 163,
167-168, 172, 181-182, 192, 220,
222, 228, 230, 236, 238, 241,
246-247, 249, 251, 256-257,
264-268, 280, 296, 305, 308,
338, 344, 346, 354, 361, 364,
367, 370, 374, 382-383, 391-392,
396, 401, 403, 407, 409-410,
412, 416, 429, 434, 441, 443,
453, 459, 463-465, 468, 484,
495, 500, 552, 558, 565-566,
572, 578, 592, 595, 618, 637,
714, 716-718, 720, 722-723, 725,
727, 729, 732, 734, 739-741,
750, 753, 757, 759, 769, 776;
8:19, 21, 26, 29-30, 35, 40, 42,
58, 63, 65-66, 70, 74, 77, 81,
84, 86, 100-101, 116, 124-125,
139, 146, 163, 165, 171-173,
223-224, 229, 231-232, 242, 261,
263, 269, 271, 282, 285, 288,
297, 299, 301, 304, 315, 329,
335-337, 339, 342, 347, 353,
357, 360, 397, 399, 402, 407,
409, 412, 414-415, 449, 460
STRIBER, Michael 11:162-163
STRICHER, Hen. 1:168
STRICKER, Adam 11:262
Henrich 3:517
Henry 10:757; 16:543
John 13:562, 573, 715, 717; 14:63,
85, 90-91, 422-423, 425, 435;
16:543
STRICKLAND, Amos 5:55, 120,
345-346; 8:170, 175; 10:270
Ann 13:431
STRICKLER, Elias 3:520
Henry 3:290; 16:166
Johannes 3:520
STRICKMAN, --- (Mr.) 13:189
STRIDE, Joseph 11:41
STRIEKER, John 12:355
STRIKEBELT, --- (Capt.) 9:508
STRINGER, James 15:143
William 11:569; 14:511
STRINGFELLOW, John 15:389
STRODE, Richard 11:402
STROHAVER, Hans Georg. 3:515
STROHBOGH, --- (Capt.) 11:4
John Martin 10:567, 571, 619, 742
STROHM, Christian 3:455
STRONG, Jedediah 10:118-121,
123-124, 129, 133, 138
Matthew 10:230, 363, 376-377, 556;
11:700
STROOP, Adam 14:64, 88, 428
Henry 14:305, 428
STROUD, --- (Col.) 11:29, 717
Daniel 16:523
Edward 11:12, 44, 74, 105, 248,
274, 307

STROUD, Jacob 11:28, 93, 95;
12:64-65, 100-101, 312; 13:89,
112, 395, 415, 421, 427, 723,
737
James 11:330
John 14:608
William 11:514, 516-517
STROUDMAN, Mary 8:728
STROUP, Andrew 15:570
STROUP(E), Andrew 16:195, 495
STROUS, Albrecht 3:458
STROUSE, Henry 12:467
STROW, Jonathan 11:611
STROWD, Jacob 10:728, 773
STRUBEL, Fredrick 3:414
STRUVEL, Casper 4:100
STTELE, James 13:167
STUART, --- 6:491
--- (Capt.) 9:214
Alexander 13:154
Charles 5:444; 10:706
Christopher 10:447
James 11:82, 114; 14:133, 175;
15:46
John 11:453
Robert 5:551
Thomas 12:598
William 10:424
STUBER, Frederick 14:608
Henry (Dr.) 15:286
STUBERT, Elizabeth 12:36
Jacobine 12:36
Rachel 12:36
STUDDYBAKER, John 16:518
STUDEBECKER, Philip 8:728
STUFER, Henry 12:774
STUKLY, Christian 4:59
STULI, Jacob 3:456
STULL, Ludwick 9:513
STULTZ, Charles 10:692
Christian 14:525
STUMP, Frederick 9:328, 414-420,
422, 424, 429, 436, 438,
441-446, 448-451, 453-454, 458,
460-464, 468-470, 479-480,
484-491, 500, 510-512, 517
Joseph 13:255
Mary 12:722
STUMP(S), George 12:722
STUPP, Leonard 12:601
STURGEON, Alexander 14:443
Jeremiah 13:595
Thomas 15:143
William 7:741
STURGIS, --- 8:58
Jonathan 14:96, 424
STURMFELS, George 15:51
Paul 14:649
STURTZEBACH, Michael 3:515
STUVER, Baltzar 3:455
STYER, Stephen 11:513, 516-517
STYNER, Christian 3:458
STYNER & CIST 11:146, 319
SUBER, Christian 3:458
SUBZEY, Lot 13:504
Luz 13:504, 508, 527
SUCCOMABE 7:531
SUCHRACHERY (SUCHRAQUERY)
5:317-318
SUCK(E)Y (NEGRO) 12:377, 750
SUDER, Christian 4:60
SUFFOLTZ, David 3:386
SUGARS, Zachariah 6:638; 7:267
SULGAR, Stephen 12:399
SULLAVAN, Dennis 5:532, 536
SULLENGER, Christopher 3:328

SWO(O)P(E), Michael 10:212, 280,
  340-342, 344, 346-348, 351, 364,
  366-367, 375, 377, 380, 382,
  390, 406, 502, 511, 524, 558,
  735; 14:129, 610, 612
SWOOP, --- (Col.) 11:150
  Michael 12:647
SWOOP(E), Mich'l. 9:301, 237, 731
SWOOPE, --- (Mr.) 13:692
  Mich'l. 8:781
  Michael 13:422, 586
SWOPE, George 5:378
SWORDS, High (Hugh) 14:80, 90, 411
SWORT, Daniel 3:390
  Nicolas 3:389
SWYZER, Mathias 3:290
SYBERT, Conraat 3:413
SYBOOT, Lorentz 3:516
SYDER, George 16:452
SYFRET, Conrad 12:338
SYFRET, Anthony 16:185
S(P)YKES, Mary 9:337-338
SYKES, James 9:337, 339, 600; 10:9,
  217
  Nathll. 1:185, 382
  William 11:233-234, 237-238, 241;
  14:108, 111
SYMCOCK, Jno. 1:70-74, 76-77,
  79-82, 84, 86-89, 92-93, 95-97,
  99-110, 115-120, 124-130, 133,
  135, 137-138, 140, 142, 148-149,
  151, 153-154, 156, 160-163,
  169-171, 173-174, 176, 193,
  196-198, 200-207, 210-228,
  233-234, 238-240, 242, 252,
  258-262, 268-270, 272-273, 275,
  277, 279-281, 283-286, 290, 292,
  298, 300-301, 303-304, 312, 317,
  321-327, 329-333, 335-338,
  340-344, 503, 506-507, 509,
  515-518, 526, 536, 539, 541, 546
SYMES, James Smyth 10:377-378,
  385-389, 410-411, 418, 455, 500
SYMMONDS', --- (Lt.) 10:437
SYMONDS, --- (Capt.) 13:612,
  664-665
  Jonas 13:714
SYMONEL, Jaques 3:288
SYMSON 1:175
SYNG, Charles 13:138, 246; 15:193
  Philip 3:176-177; 9:237, 240, 440;
  13:760
SYPE, Frantz 3:459
  George 3:459
  Lutwig 3:459
SYSLOOF, George Nicolas 4:59
  Johan Baltzer 4:59
  Yorig 4:59

TAAF(E) (TAFFE), Michael 5:614,
  628, 669, 684, 701
TAAFE, --- 6:150
TAAFES 7:95
TABAS, Johan Henrich 3:516
TABLEMEYER, Johannes 3:466
TACAOGON 5:686
TACH-NECH-DOARUS 5:431, 435
TACHANOONTIA 4:698, 710
TACHNECKDORUS 7:51
TACHNICHTOROUS 3:500
TACKER, John 14:614
TACUTTELENCE 3:163

TAEDYSCUNG 6:380
TAEF (TAAFE), Michael 7:34, 144
TAFFE (TEAFF), Michael 6:193-194,
  649
TAFFER, Catherine 15:44-55
TAG(A)SHATA (TAEGASHATAE)
  8:176-179, 181-182, 190, 194,
  196, 205, 208, 210, 218
TAGANAYESY 5:355
TAGART, --- (Capt.) 16:337
TAGAWARA 9:505
TAGEE-ISKATT-A 8:159
TAGG, John (Sir) 15:485
TAGGART, Joseph 15:654
  Robert 10:328
TAGHESHATA 8:152
TAGHNEGHDORRUS 5:84
TAGHUTTALESSE 2:604
TAGINCHUNTEE 4:80
TAGMAN, Hans Michael 3:284
  Peter 3:290
TAGOLELESS 3:102
TAGOTELESSAH 2:613
TAGOTOLESSA 3:45-46
TAGOUUSEDAY (TAGAUUSADAY) 8:383,
  386
TAHACHDACHQUEESERY 5:686
TAHASCHWUCHDIOONY 5:476-477, 480
TAHASHWANGARORIS 6:126
TAHASHWANGO 6:126
TAHATI 6:199
TAHTAHQUEESA 5:637
TAINY, Nicholas 4:173-174
TAKASHWANGARORAS 4:80
TAKECHSADON 5:686
TAKEGHSADO (TAKEAGHSADO) 8:176-177
TAKEGHSATU (TAKEGSATA) 6:120-122
TAKENTOA 5:523-524
TAKYEWSAN 2:15; 3:601, 603; 4:340
TALAWSIS 13:463
TALBATT, William 13:669
TALBERT, John 15:56
  Joseph 5:186
  Lamv't. 11:109
TALBOT, --- (Mr.) 6:491
  Geo. 1:104, 113-115, 120
  J. 7:275
  James 11:281, 704
  Jeremiah 15:120, 343; 16:63, 279
  John 11:514, 516-517
TALBOT(T), Jeremiah 14:134, 237,
  423, 434, 563
  William 14:94, 416
TALBOTT, Jeremiah 13:580
  John 15:123
  Margaret 15:68
TALCOOT, Eleazor 9:571
  Samuel 9:571
TALFORD, Bedney 11:155
TALMAN, Samuel 15:567, 569
TALSE, Henry (Sir) 1:129
TAMANEE 1:447, 449
TAMANEN 13:463
TAME, John 13:758; 14:420
TAMINENT (KING) 13:466
TAMINY (KING) 13:466
TAMISON, Richard 14:96
TAN WESON 5:685
TAN(U)AGHDORUS (TANNAGHDORUS)
  6:120-122
TANACHAHA 3:199
TANACHARISSON 6:85, 147, 150-151,
  158-159, 193, 784
TANACHARRISON (HALF KING) 7:5
TANANGHSAGOUGHTA, Zacharias 6:122
TANEY, Jacob 12:271

200

THOME, Durst 4:171-172, 226
  John 11:450; 16:514
THOMOND, Earl 8:40
THOMPSON, --- 11:776, 778-779, 781,
  783
--- (Capt.) 11:320
--- (Col.) 12:111
--- (Gen.) 15:338, 381
--- (Justice) 7:59
--- (Lt.) 10:503
--- (Mr.) 7:510, 557; 13:23-25,
  27-28, 30-33, 35-38, 41-45,
  47-48, 76; 16:136
Andrew 11:219; 15:420, 474
Arch'd. 10:692
Archibald 12:131, 188
Benjamin 10:335, 353; 11:199
Catherine 16:341, 465-466
Charles 7:648-649, 665-666,
  680-681, 683, 694, 702, 707,
  724-725; 10:294, 317, 343, 357,
  385-386, 410, 414, 418, 432-433,
  440, 444, 450, 454, 458, 463,
  466, 484-485, 502, 508, 510,
  540-542, 547, 563, 564, 567,
  571, 591-592, 595, 602, 621,
  628, 638-639, 647; 12:6, 26,
  115-116, 148, 188, 211, 214,
  433, 473, 501, 516, 783; 13:105,
  319, 412; 15:104, 106, 215, 268,
  391, 455, 458, 474, 480, 496,
  515, 521, 529-530, 535-536, 542
David 11:513, 516-517, 745;
  12:195, 222; 15:66
Edwrd 10:166, 168
George 1:579; 10:330; 13:303
Isaac 16:353, 461
Isaiah 13:771
James 9:487; 10:755; 11:698, 744,
  750; 12:5, 49, 75, 216, 304-306,
  469, 486, 511-512, 570, 653;
  13:25, 28, 77; 16:72
Jesse 11:747, 775
John 5:210; 10:56, 100, 211, 275,
  765, 778; 11:162, 179, 234, 249,
  372, 378, 398, 596, 661; 13:303,
  308, 453, 557, 583, 769; 15:125,
  260; 16:116, 212b
John (James) 12:34-35, 37, 39-40,
  42-43, 46, 54-57, 74, 77-78,
  123-125, 127-128, 130-133,
  136-137, 139, 141, 186, 190,
  192-195, 197, 200-203, 205, 207,
  209-210, 212, 215-221, 223-229,
  274-276, 279, 281, 283, 288,
  292, 296-302, 304-305, 392-395,
  397, 399-402, 404-407, 409, 413,
  464-469, 473, 477-487, 490-491,
  493-495, 497-500, 502-506,
  508-510, 512, 514-515, 517-518,
  632-634, 644, 649, 652, 736-738,
  741, 744, 746-747, 749-751,
  753-755, 758-761, 764, 766-768,
  771, 773
Jonathan 15:399, 422
Joseph 7:266; 16:352, 356
Joseph (Dr.) 13:712
Joshua 4:495, 503; 6:144, 638;
  8:402, 506; 11:514, 516-517;
  11:715-716
Lucy 12:32
Margaret 13:336
Martha 15:548
Mary 15:503
Peter 11:549; 15:399, 442, 481,
  486, 520, 524; 16:457, 462, 477

THOMPSON, Rebecca 16:294
  Richard 1:438
  Robert 4:748; 5:601; 8:562; 9:172;
    12:2; 13:38; 15:338, 381, 437
  Samuel 11:572; 12:70; 13:187, 748;
    15:300
  William 8:111; 9:728, 732; 10:78,
    142, 260, 267, 280, 291; 12:576,
    609; 13:221, 579, 712; 16:341,
    465
THOMPSON (See MC ALPINE), James
  15:56, 204, 398, 400, 402, 417
THOMSON, Charles 13:123, 406
  David 11:5
  James 13:547
  Joshua 5:550
  Mary 13:413
  Thomas 4:107
  William 10:589
THORN, John 11:189; 12:646; 16:313
  Robert 16:322
THORN(E), William 11:58, 301
THORNBURGH, Joseph 15:300
THORNBURY, Francis 12:534; 13:717
THORNE, --- (Rev.) 12:334
  William 12:232
THORNHILL, Israel 13:579
THORNTON, Harminus 16:332
  Jane 14:3
  John 12:187
  Joseph 3:387; 8:402, 505; 16:153
THORP, George 1:116
THORPE, William 11:286
THRAPE, Benjamin 16:455
THURN, Abraham 3:284
THURSTON, Edward 2:112
THUTCATANY, John 6:551
THUUIN (THUAN), --- (Mr.) 14:77,
  104
THWEIGHTS, Thomas 3:109
TIAGONNEAROUT 3:571
TIAHANSOREA 7:507
TIBANDO, Batute 7:240
  Joseph 7:240
  Olwig 7:240
TICHIBACHQUEY 3:435
TICOUT, Francis 16:333
TIDD, --- 7:621
  James 6:759-760
  Mary 8:750
TIDDEMAN, George 10:735
TIEBERT, Michael 12:506
TIETS, Peter 13:593
TIFFIN, --- (Capt.) 5:113
TILBURY, Jacob 14:311, 395
  John 14:320
  Lena 14:320
TILDEN, John B. 13:717
  John Bell 13:604
TILDEN (TELDEN), John B. 14:300,
  437
TILDON (TILDEN), John Bell 12:572,
  632
TILG(H)MAN, Tench 11:389, 683
TILGHMAN, --- (Col.) 13:94
  Edward 15:116, 372
  James 9:354-356, 359, 362, 375,
    378, 385, 388, 394, 397,
    399-400, 402, 404, 406, 412,
    426-427, 430, 432, 438, 446,
    449-450, 459, 465, 481, 488,
    490, 492, 510-514, 543, 545,
    551, 554, 556, 561-563, 565,
    567, 569, 576-577, 581, 583,
    589, 592, 594, 601, 603-604,
    609-610, 622-623, 626, 629, ->

TOLBERT, Samuel **10**:457; **11**:418-419,
424; **13**:716
TOLCOT, Samuel **6**:260
TOLL (TOLE), --- (Capt.) **11**:151,
165
TOLL(E)Y, John **11**:513, 516-517,
745; **12**:114, 260
TOLLET, Benjamin **9**:571
TOLLIBOIS, Jacque **13**:143
TOLLY, Catherine **12**:21
John **13**:146
TOLOWSIS, George (alias
Seegaghtachman) **13**:467
TOM (NEGRO) **16**:313
TOMA, Dierich **4**:72
Durs **4**:72
Hans Jacob **4**:72
TOMACKHICKON **13**:463
TOMAGO **8**:723
TOMAKER, Michael **12**:608
TOMAQUIOR (TAMAQUI) **8**:499, 618
TOMENEBUCK **4**:336-337, 341, 346-347
TOMENIBUCK **5**:685
TOMKIN(S), John **14**:599
Joshua **14**:93, 420
TOMKINS, Robert **13**:567
TOMLINSON (THOMLINSON), John **9**:48,
50-51; **13**:394, 399, 431
Joshua **10**:289, 533, 602, 648
William **14**:613
TOMPOH, George **16**:227
TONASPECK, Johan Jacob **4**:60
TONELAGUESENA (TONELAGUESONA)
5:685, 734
TONG(U)E, William **2**:66, 97, 102,
122-123, 386
TONINGTON, --- (Viscount) **4**:298
TONKELBERG, Pieter **3**:328
TONKLEBERG, Clement **3**:328
Frederick **3**:328
TONRY, Ann **12**:342
TOOACHTACHKOUT (TIOCHTACHKOUT)
3:435, 513
TOOK (NEGRO) **13**:530
TOOMB, --- (Col.) **11**:301
TOONEY, Darby **12**:188
TOONIS **13**:464
TOOPLE, Isaac **8**:629
TOPHAM, Daniel **12**:311; **13**:85;
14:506, 611
TOPPAM, Daniel **10**:556
TOPY, John **9**:328, 330-331
TORAGHYORAS, X William **6**:122
TORASOUGHKO **5**:538
TORBETT, John **16**:174, 179-180
TORRINGTON, --- (Viscount)
4:484-485
TORT, L. **1**:340
TORTNER, Robert **12**:10
TOSSWEYCHIMON **3**:316
TOST, John **1**:57, 60, 67
TOTALES **4**:53
TOTIENARO **3**:435
TOTINIONTONAH **8**:773
TOTONRNIHIADES **5**:355
TOTTEN, William **15**:34
TOTTEN (TODDEN), John **14**:306, 435
TOTTINYANTRINGO (TOTTINYANTUNGO)
8:264-265
TOTYONONTONHA **8**:698, 700
TOUGHACHENA **8**:634
TOULKE, Judah **6**:714
TOUTASARIAGA **3**:500
TOWACHDACHIOAT **5**:686
TOWEENA **3**:149

TOWERS, Robert **10**:298-301, 304,
306-308, 312-314, 322-323,
327-328, 330-331, 333, 338-339,
341, 343, 346-347, 350-354, 360,
365-366, 371, 373, 375, 379,
382-383, 394, 398, 400, 402,
404-407, 409, 411, 415-417, 421,
423, 426, 428, 430-431, 433,
435-438, 441, 443, 447, 452-453,
456, 458, 461, 463, 468, 471,
475, 478-479, 484, 486-487,
493-494, 496-498, 501-508,
510-513, 516, 520, 522, 524,
526-527, 529-531, 533, 535-537,
540-542, 546, 551, 554-556, 558,
560-561, 563, 566, 571, 573-575,
580, 583, 585, 589-590, 592-593,
595, 597-602, 604-605, 607-608,
610, 613-614, 620-623, 626-627,
629, 632, 634, 636-642, 644,
647, 649-651, 653, 656-660, 662,
664-666, 670-678, 681-684, 686,
688-692, 695, 697-698, 700-704,
706-713, 715, 717, 719, 721,
723-279, 732, 734-736, 739-742,
744-745, 747-749, 751-752,
754-756, 759-763, 766, 769-772,
774-776, 778-779, 781-782, 784;
11:3-7, 9-10, 12-13, 15-17, 20,
23, 26, 28, 30-33, 35, 41-42,
45-47, 49-50, 52, 54-55, 58-61,
64, 66, 68-69, 74-78, 82-83,
88-89, 92, 94, 97, 99-100,
105-107, 111, 113, 115, 119-121,
126-129, 133, 136, 138, 141-142,
278, 280, 297, 301-302, 305,
310, 313, 389
TOWERS & EVANS **16**:289
TOWIS **13**:465
TOWN, Benjamin **10**:422, 497, 511,
713, 765; **12**:253, 325, 328
TOWN(E), Benjamin **11**:61, 114, 513,
516-517
TOWN(E)HILL, James **16**:334
TOWNE, Benjamin **15**:34
TOWNLY, Henry **15**:1
TOWNS, John **16**:192
TOWNSEND, --- **10**:684
--- (Adm.) **7**:571
Ewell **14**:297, 304, 411
John **2**:9
Littleton **11**:59, 141
Lyttleton **10**:211
TOWOR, --- (Capt.) **3**:29
TOY, Ann **13**:373
TRABER, Nicolas **4**:59
TRACE, Henrich **3**:517
TRACEY, --- (Capt.) **8**:614
Elisha **8**:566
Isaac **8**:566
James **14**:293, 299, 430
TRACY, --- (Lt.) **10**:7
Godfrey **9**:515
John (See WHITE, John) **15**:398, 400
Thomas **11**:161, 164
TRAIL(L), Robert **11**:212, 260, 422,
437; **15**:100, 103-106, 140-161,
238, 240-245, 247-261, 296-306,
308-317, 320-324, 439, 460-461,
618, 642
TRAILE, Edward **12**:187
TRAILL, Robert **13**:89, 395-396, 682,
723-724; **14**:232, 248, 458, 556;
16:48, 491
TRAIN, David **10**:56

VAN CAMPEN, John (continued) 13:77, 105, 149, 225, 227, 310, 319, 380, 387, 414, 424, 427, 429, 481-482, 484-486, 490-491, 493-499, 501, 503-519, 521-524, 526-528, 530-532, 534, 536-538, 540, 544-545, 571-572, 574-589, 591-592, 646-647, 666-668, 670-673, 675, 677-681, 683-684, 687, 691-706; 14:168, 238, 343, 443; 16:323-324, 354
Moses 12:311, 622; 13:437, 439; 14:110
VAN CARTWRIGHT (CORTWRIGHT), Abraham 14:311, 375, 495
VAN COURT, John 13:456, 715
VAN COURTWRIGHT, Abraham 15:123
VAN CULLEN, Jann 1:191
VAN CULLIN(G), John 1:200-201
VAN ETTEN, --- 7:17, 214
VAN FLEA, Joseph 15:101
VAN GORDON, Jere 14:295, 302
VAN HEER, --- (Capt.) 13:188, 211
Bartholomew 16:195
VAN HIER, B. 11:757
VAN HORN, Isaac 12:89
VAN LAASCHET, Christian 4:59
Johannes 4:59
Johannes Petrus 4:59
VAN LAER, John 2:605
VAN LEER, Gerhard 3:250
VAN LINKENSDORF, Lewis 10:679, 685
VAN METTER, --- (Capt.) 14:312
VAN OPDAM, Heer 1:17
VAN PHUL, Christian 13:542
VAN SHAAK (VANSCHAAK), Sylvant 6:61, 63
VAN SICE, John 7:44
VAN SWEARENGEN, --- 11:46
VAN SWEARINGEN, --- (Capt.) 12:470
VAN SWEARINGEN (VANSWERINGEN), --- (Capt.) 10:168, 603
VAN VLECK, Henry 11:765
Isaac 13:547; 14:362-363
VAN VLET, Derrick 14:658
VAN(N)ETTEN, John 14:69, 169, 312, 461
VAN-LEER, William 12:356
VANAKIN (VANIKIN), Rebecca 10:40, 53-54
VANARSDALE, Nicholas 11:281
Simon 11:281
VANATTA, John 5:573
VANBEB(B)ER, Jacob 9:203, 206, 267, 384, 581
VANBEBBER, Jacob 5:210, 248
VANBIBBER, Isaac 11:15
VANBIBBER & USHER 11:15
VANBORSON, Jno. 1:87, 94
VANBOTT, Johan Jorig 4:59
VANBURSON, Jno. 1:94
VANCAMP, --- (Maj.) 11:62
VANCAMPEN, Aaron 9:710-711
Benjamin 11:310
John 9:573, 660, 732; 11:119, 365, 633
VANCAMPER, John 10:156
VANCE, --- (Maj.) 11:79
David 10:236; 14:289
John 5:194; 12:267-268, 272; 16:38
Patrick 11:229
Robert 14:146
VANCOURT, John 12:483
VANCUL(L)IN(G), Jno. 1:95, 200-201
VANDE(R)VEER, Catherin(e) 1:583-584
VANDEGRIFT, Abraham 14:611

VANDEGRIFT, John 14:606
VANDEN HAM, Henry 5:643
VANDEREN, John 13:538; 15:426; 16:374
John, Jr. 13:96
VANDERER, --- 14:68, 171
John J. 14:568
VANDERFREST, John 10:748
VANDERGACH, Cornelius 2:493
VANDERGRIFF (VANDERGRIFT, VANDEGRIFF), Jno. 10:313, 443, 456, 516, 607, 730
VANDERGRIFT, John 11:253, 642
VANDERGRIST, John 11:251
VANDERHAYDEN, Matthias 1:210
VANDERIN, --- (Mr.) 10:779
VANDERN, John 13:44
VANDERSLICE, Henry 10:211, 270; 14:62, 409, 439; 15:294; 16:211b
Jacob 14:277-279
VANDERSLIER, Jacob 11:577
VANDERSPIEGLE, William 6:766
VANDERVERE, Jacob 1:174
VANDERWERF, John Roclofs 2:493
Richd. 2:493
VANDIKE, Henricus 2:238
VANDRENE, --- (Monsieur) 6:313
VANDYKE, John 5:194, 411, 468
Richard 9:628; 10:51
VANELLEN, --- 8:485
--- (Capt.) 7:313
VANEMAKER, Philip 14:410
VANES, Hedges 12:577
VANETTA, John 5:490
VANETTEN, --- (Capt.) 13:343
VANGARTEN, William (Wilhelmus) 14:222-223
VANGORDEN, Jeremiah 14:411
Samuel 14:311, 495
VANHALT (VANHOLD, VANHOLT, VANHALL), Valentine 10:692, 705, 708, 715, 719
VANHORN (VAN HORN), --- (Capt.) 10:479
Barnet 11:281
Christopher 3:298
Isaac 10:450; 13:202; 14:98, 427
John 11:340
Joshua 13:431
VANHORN(E), Bernard, Jr. 5:247, 325
Isaac 15:98-99, 296, 566
VANHORNE, Barnet 5:209
C. Bernard 5:326
Isaac 13:581, 710, 713; 16:191-192
Richard 5:247
William 14:611
VANIMAHR, Philip 14:123, 126
VANKEMP, John 12:326
VANKEN, John 15:122
VANKIRK, Abram 11:472
Art. 1:601
Jacob 14:311
Sarah 12:218
VANLASHET, Christian 12:709
VANLEAR, William 13:675
VANLEER, Bernard 5:378
Samuel 11:339; 14:579, 584
William 11:468-469, 492-493, 548; 13:556, 714; 14:129, 440
VANLOVING, Joseph 14:614
VANMETRE, Henry 14:357
VANMETRI, Jesse 15:310
VANNOST, John 12:745
VANOCIVER, William 12:388
VANORMAN, Joseph 14:498
VANOSBRAND, John 13:569

VROSEN, Mason 15:481
VROSEN (VROZEN), Adrain 15:484-485
VRY, Andreas 3:518
VSHER, Thomas 1:263-264

WA(L)TERS, Thomas 14:296, 303, 415,
  611
 William 10:225, 227
WA(L)TZ, Michael 14:94, 415
WAAPEN 3:504
WAAPESSUM, George 3:102
WABADIKISY 6:152 (Alias Little
  Johnny)
WADD(E)Y, Hen(rie) 1:454, 607
WADDEL, George 14:610
WADDELL, William 11:373, 638
WADDIE, Henry 1:389
WADDLE, Francis 10:273
 William 12:182, 540; 13:730
WADE, --- (Capt.) 13:282
 Edward 14:296, 303, 430
 Elizabeth 13:17
 Francis 10:423-424, 468, 485, 514,
  520, 577, 640, 673; 13:169, 574;
  14:631, 633, 640; 15:155, 195,
  374, 384-385, 482-483, 520, 524;
  16:317
 James 13:574
 John 3:69, 108
 Joseph 11:32, 40, 56, 93, 619,
  642; 12:389
 Robt. 1:48, 63, 95, 129, 169, 440,
  477
 Terrall 12:563
 William 15:410
 Wm. 2:112
WADSWORTH, Jeremiah 12:91
WAGENER, Andreas 3:515
 Bastian 3:453
 Elias 3:455
 Hans Georg(e) 3:454, 456
 Hans Ulrich 3:455
 Matthias 3:455
WAGER, Charles 4:254, 298
 Charles, Sr. 3:525
 John 10:674
 Philip 13:28, 63; 15:98
WAGGONER (WAGGENER, WAGNER), ---
  (Capt.) 6:491, 501-502; 8:293,
  386
 --- (Lt.) 12:355
 Caspar 13:680
 Caspar (Casper) 14:93, 608
 Christopher 9:345, 308; 10:156;
  11:212, 633; 15:92
 David 16:491
 John 16:132
 Joseph 11:195
 Philip 13:384, 394
WAGHOOLALENUM (Jo) 6:360
WAGNER, Carl 3:455
 Christopher 12:134, 506
 Justus Simonius 3:515
 Malcher 3:515
WAGONER, Henry 6:755
WAHNSIDEL, Johan Georg. 3:467
WAIN, James 9:204
WAINE, --- (Mr.) 9:132
WAITE, John 16:370
WAKECAWPA 9:232
WAKEFIELD, Thomas 16:461
WAKELY, Margaret 15:68

WAL(L)N(E), Nicholas 1:48, 87, 144,
  285, 493, 502, 517, 601, 606
WALBER, Peter 3:618
WALBORN, Leonard 6:704
WALBRON, --- (Maj.) 10:464
WALCOTT, --- (Mr.) 12:614
WALD, Oswald 3:415
WALDEGRAVE, Earl 8:320-321
WALDER, Rudolph 3:368
WALE, Jno. 1:87
WALKER, --- (Capt.) 12:762
 --- (Mr.) 6:301; 7:759
 Andrew 13:680, 713; 14:85, 89,
  417, 421, 431
 Benjamin 15:374; 16:396-397, 483,
  508, 547
 Charles 12:446-447
 David 11:261; 16:461
 George 9:548; 13:306
 Gideon 13:280
 Henry 16:396-397, 483, 508, 547
 Isaac 12:28
 Jacob 12:9
 James 2:136; 5:248; 8:506, 781;
  9:286, 333, 398; 11:78
 Jane 10:44
 Jno. 1:165, 168, 174, 320, 339,
  517, 595, 607
 John 2:34, 50, 136; 10:661-663;
  13:635; 14:80, 103, 125, 432;
  15:300, 374, 577-578
 Joseph 11:503; 12:247; 14:631;
  15:31; 16:396-397, 483, 508, 547
 Nath. 1:83
 Nathaniel 14:223
 Obediah 14:311, 320, 495
 Peter 7:232
 Rachel 11:616
 Richard 3:30-31, 56, 69, 108;
  5:193, 388, 573; 7:437; 8:577;
  9:235, 672
 Richd. 2:546
 Robert 5:193; 16:174, 234
 Robt. 1:83
 Samuel 14:292, 299
 Thomas 15:454
 William 5:209; 11:157
WALKER(S), John 16:461, 509
WALL, --- (Col.) 11:636
 --- (Mr.) 13:404, 406-407, 409,
  411-413, 417-418, 430-432, 437,
  439-444, 454-455, 458-460, 515,
  589, 670
 Ann 11:585; 13:330
 George 13:628; 16:104, 309, 320,
  382, 390, 507
 George (Jr.) 11:473, 479, 537,
  558; 12:73, 78, 101, 136-137,
  156-157, 250, 268, 298, 350,
  510, 614, 754; 13:86, 94,
  182-183, 238, 295, 361, 391-392,
  395, 414, 441, 461, 471,
  476-481, 498, 515-517, 519,
  521-524, 526, 530-531, 543-544,
  572, 574-589, 591-592, 594-595,
  597-603, 605-607, 609-611,
  613-615, 617-623, 625-627,
  630-635, 637-640, 646-647,
  666-668, 670, 672, 674-675,
  677-679, 684, 686, 693-697,
  700-706, 719, 721, 724-727, 729,
  731-732, 734-746, 748, 750,
  760-766, 768-776; 14:1-6, 8-11,
  14-16, 18, 23-60, 65-70, 73-80,
  103-107, 153-155, 200-201, 205,
  211, 213-215, 224-227, ->

WALL, George (Jr.) (continued)
  14:237-239, 242-243, 246-250,
  262-264, 268-269, 281-285,
  287-288, 308-311, 313-318, 345,
  356-363, 383-387, 458-461,
  472-474, 505, 542-547, 598
John 12:626
Rebecca 16:165
Richard 12:776
Richard, Sr. 13:31
Richd. 1:85
Sebastian 13:666
Thomas 13:368; 14:181-182, 513,
  522
WALLACE, --- (Widow) 11:508
Andrew 11:81
Benjamin 10:666, 668, 714; 11:163,
  339, 381; 13:586; 14:101, 438;
  16:210, 212, 387
David 11:80
Elizabeth 14:471
George 10:737; 14:118; 15:550,
  560; 16:150, 360
James 10:56, 375, 471-472, 475,
  511, 537; 11:253, 372, 501, 508;
  12:626; 13:167, 330; 15:438, 577
John 10:272; 11:80
Joseph 14:444-445
Joshua Maddox 14:55
Michael 11:281
Nathaniel 11:37
Richard 10:720; 13:324, 730, 745;
  14:15, 32-33
Robert 5:55; 6:669; 9:699
Solomon 9:333, 398, 548
Thomas 13:567; 14:96, 420
William 10:408; 15:103, 300, 483;
  16:212, 514, 437, 538
WALLACE (WALLICE), James 9:509,
  547, 623, 688, 778
WALLACE (WALLIS), --- (Capt.)
  8:163-164
WALLER, James 9:508
Johan Fredrick 3:386
John Peter 3:386
WALLIAM(S), James 1:127, 206, 285,
  335-338
WALLICE, John 10:450
Joseph Jacob 15:307
Thomas 10:450, 765
WALLINGTON, Charles 16:333
WALLIS, Francis (alias Willis)
  15:68, 440
James 1:166
Joseph 14:441; 16:211b
Robert 14:647
Samuel 9:151, 161; 11:613; 13:543;
  14:369, 445, 449, 485; 16:211b,
  390
WALLON, Thomas 14:588
WALLS 1:68
WALLS, Richard 2:520
WALMAN, Michael 14:663
WALN, George, Jr. 11:504
Nicholas 2:34, 65, 106, 110,
  576-577, 586-587; 15:478
Richard 13:23
WALNE, Rich. 2:561
Richard 3:573
WALOOPIES 8:151
WALOTS, Hans Michl. 3:457
WALPOLE, Horatio 3:525; 4:484-485;
  5:618
WALSH, James 11:756; 12:252
Sarah 13:300
WALSTELLER, Lutwig Tretler 4:100

WALSTON, Samuel 10:720
WALTER, --- (Capt.) 3:204
--- (Mr.) 10:589, 595
Bernhard 3:457
Earl Fitz 4:254, 298, 483
Ephraim 16:279
George 13:357
Henry 12:218-219
Jacob, Jr. 3:285, 458
Jacob, Sr. 3:285, 458
Mathias 3:455
Michael 3:518
Rebecca 8:728
Rudolph 3:593
WALTER (SEE BEDWELL &) 10:608
WALTER (See FREDEHER), Jacob 15:145
WALTER(S), Ephraim 15:120
WALTERS & BEDWELL 10:712, 754
WALTHAM, Jno. 2:136
WALTHER, Conrad 3:457
WALTHOE, N. 7:570
WALTMAN, Frederick 14:306, 436
William 10:668
WALTON, --- (Col.) 11:129
--- (Mr.) 9:121
Albertson 12:673
Albinson 11:482, 484-485
Amos 15:587
Banjamin 11:565
George 3:259, 270
Jacob 12:12
William 16:191
WALTONE, Christian 3:287
WALTS, Cato 13:542
WANAMAKER, Georg. 3:415
WANCCHATUCKA 5:685
WAND, Egidius 13:496
WANDUNY 5:355
WANGER, Lazarus 3:607
WANNER, Jacob 3:288
WAPATYKEETY 6:160
WAPEMASHEHAWEY (WAPEMASHAWAY)
  8:723, 737
WAPYMAGAN 4:643
WARBURTON, --- (Gen.) 6:491
Matthew 9:390, 392
WARD, --- (Capt.) 8:294, 386
--- (Ens.) 6:28
Benjamin 12:8
Bernard 10:765; 13:543, 562;
  14:89, 418
Edward (Capt.) 7:230, 232, 561
Frances 3:472
James 12:5
John 12:31; 13:715
Joseph 10:289
Maycock 9:571
Moses 11:576
Ralph 1:476-477
Richard 13:330; 15:379, 423, 459,
  480-481
Thomas 5:532, 536; 11:37; 13:595
Tillghman 3:549
William 5:155, 158, 163-164,
  210-211
WARDEL, Ann Read 16:14
Thomas 15:390
WARDEN, Samuel 10:235
Thomas 15:119
WARDER, Jeremiah 7:391, 637; 8:487,
  750; 10:210; 11:284, 289; 12:191
Willoughby 2:596
WARDNER, Wm. 1:162, 176
WARE, Catharine 13:304
David 11:78
WARMER, Edwd. 1:83-84

WARMSDARFF, --- (Ens.) **8**:292
WARNER, --- (Col.) **11**:301
--- (Mr.) **5**:657; **7**:475
--- (Widow) **13**:640
Edmund **1**:48
Edward **4**:355, 523; **5**:416, 492-493;
  6:176
George **10**:528
Hendrick **3**:368
Isaac **9**:711; **11**:633
Jno. **2**:277
John **3**:524
Jorig Adam **4**:60
Joseph **12**:755
Joseph Remsey **15**:217-218
Ludwick **13**:680; **14**:424
Martin **13**:640; **14**:94, 435
Peter **11**:74, 91
Philip **14**:612
William **12**:553, 737; **13**:545, 643;
  14:126, 428
Wm. **1**:438
WARRACHYAGO **6**:291
WARRAGHIYAGEE **5**:508, 510
WARRAGHIYAGEE (WARRAGHIYAGEY,
  WARRAIGHEYAGEY) **7**:43, 115, 538,
  545
WARRAGHIYAGEY, Gorah **9**:497, 504-505
WARRALL, John **2**:82
WARRAWS, Jno. **2**:510
WARRELL, James **11**:610
WARREN, --- (Admiral) **5**:4, 6, 28
--- (Commodore) **4**:762-766
James **11**:641
John **8**:402
Peter (Sir) **6**:313
William **13**:756; **14**:91, 421
WARRUCHYOCKON **7**:490-491
WARTH, Thomas **12**:410
WARTMEN, Casper **3**:432
WARTSMAN, Hans Adam **3**:410
WARTZ, Hans Jacob **3**:457
Jacob **3**:457
WASHASCANTANT **8**:189
WASHINGTON, --- (Col.) **8**:56, 62,
  225
--- (Gen.) **10**:303-306, 330-331,
  340, 345, 565, 604, 632, 703,
  757; **13**:39, 41, 51, 94, 131,
  173, 177, 184, 188, 195, 199,
  202, 211, 221, 301, 362, 380,
  399, 419, 446, 457, 482, 484,
  497, 502, 765; **14**:130, 265, 275
--- (Maj.) **5**:714-716, 720, 731,
  756-757
Eve **15**:477
G. **6**:28-29, 37, 46, 50-51, 55,
  137, 140, 151-152, 177, 181,
  195, 288, 376, 420, 488-489,
  492, 507, 509, 683
G. (Col.) **7**:70, 601-604
George **4**:7, 12; **12**:8, 26, 32, 36,
  43, 63, 91-92, 99, 114-115, 120,
  123-124, 129, 140, 144, 156,
  203-204, 210, 219, 227, 252,
  254, 262, 276, 313, 316, 321,
  330, 352, 370, 387, 389, 392,
  394, 403-404, 419, 428, 439,
  446, 460, 474, 476, 480, 483,
  496, 498, 517, 545-546, 574-575,
  591, 706-707, 727, 742, 753,
  759, 761, 768, 778-779; **13**:130,
  767; **16**:25, 60, 203, 227, 436
George (Gen.) **11**:22, 24-25, 27-28,
  33, 35, 38-39, 43, 46, 49, 54,
  67-70, 73-75, 80, 83, 94-95, ->

WASHINGTON, George (Gen.)
  (continued) **11**:117, 154, 169,
  178, 189, 197, 202, 216,
  227-228, 232, 237, 241, 250-251,
  253, 275, 287, 301, 305, 313,
  348-350, 401, 404, 418, 420-421,
  428-431, 436, 442, 446, 457,
  473, 476, 480, 490-491, 520,
  523, 568, 581, 587, 607, 626,
  650, 654, 671, 673, 682, 723,
  732, 755
WASLEY, Michael **13**:275
WASSELLS, Peter **1**:390
WAT(T)SON, Luke **1**:48, 69, 76-78,
  82, 86, 89, 97, 99-116, 118,
  122-124, 128-133, 135, 137-138,
  140, 176, 178, 180, 205, 213,
  222-226, 267, 269-270, 272, 275,
  277, 284-286, 290-291, 294, 297,
  302, 304-307, 310, 321-327,
  329-333, 335-338, 344, 369, 458,
  460, 517-518, 521, 540, 548,
  601, 615
Luke, Jr. **2**:31, 34, 50, 136
WATERHOUSE, --- **10**:230
WATERMAN, Humphrey **1**:372
Robert **15**:434
WATERS, Thomas **11**:84
WATKEES, Elizabeth **13**:214
Kitty **13**:214
WATKIN(S), William **10**:583, 656;
  12:14, 21, 33-34, 570
WATKINS, Joseph **10**:569, 573; **11**:44,
  55, 74, 117, 129, 272, 280, 301,
  313, 440
William **14**:298, 305, 427
WATNELL, John **4**:47
WATS (WATT), Frederick **11**:88, 93,
  97, 99, 105, 122, 149, 158, 453
WATSHAM **6**:490
WATSON, Benjamin **11**:244; **16**:535
Catherine **15**:503
David **11**:219, 334, 340, 423-424,
  444, 462, 489; **12**:231, 307;
  14:616, 618, 672; **15**:183; **16**:204
Isaac **9**:203
James **11**:340; **15**:1
John **5**:577; **8**:218-219; **11**:128,
  484; **15**:171
John, Jr. **5**:573
Joseph **9**:589, 591
Luke, Sr. **2**:101, 136, 183
Mark **4**:482; **5**:3, 388
Moses **11**:662; **12**:182; **13**:158
Patrick **5**:378; **10**:746; **14**:465
Robert **13**:474
Samuel **10**:423, 438, 447, 686
Thomas **2**:520, 542, 596; **3**:28, 233,
  241, 415; **9**:592-593
WATT, David, Jr. **14**:260, 454
David, Sr. **14**:260, 455
Frederick **13**:248, 293
George **10**:235; **15**:357
James **14**:436
John **11**:137, 139, 143
WATT(S), David **15**:368
Frederick **12**:166, 170, 322;
  14:236, 248, 250, 348, 455, 485;
  15:300, 304, 306, 308-317,
  320-328, 331, 337-353, 356-391,
  394-401, 403-412, 414-417,
  520-527, 530-536, 538-539, 554,
  556-569, 571-575, 578-584,
  586-587, 589-590, 592, 594-600,
  602-604, 606-608, 612, 640-658;
  16:1-7, 9-17, 19-22, 24-29, ->

WATT(S), Frederick (continued)
16:31, 33-35, 37-39, 50-57,
59-60, 62-67, 70-78, 80, 82-86,
133-138, 141-146, 148, 151-158,
160, 162, 164-169, 171-173, 175,
178, 180, 205, 209-211, 214-216,
218-220, 222-224, 209b-212b,
214b-219b, 221b-224b, 225-226,
229-233, 235-236, 238-244,
251-252, 254-264, 266-274, 276,
278-291, 293-307, 309-313,
315-316, 318, 320-324, 326-327,
329, 331-332, 336, 368-371, 373,
375-384, 386, 388-390, 419-429,
432-435, 441-442, 445-447,
449-459, 461-465, 477, 479-483,
487-488
WATTMAN, Jno. 1:95
WATTOM, John 9:57
WATTS, Arthur 11:253; 12:136, 164
Cato 13:368
Frederick 10:688; 13:726, 737
James 13:737; 16:288
John 9:497
Samuel 9:390, 392
WATZ, Michael 13:669
WAUGH, Patrick 12:187; 16:485, 497,
519-520, 536, 542
WAUGHHAUGH(H)Y 7:529, 553-554
WAUNTAUPENNY 7:531
WAWHAP (WAWHUP), Edward 11:29
WAWIABIESSANAGH 3:598
WAY, Caleb 14:58, 224
George 11:31
William 9:127
WAYAJOE-QUAS 8:484
WAYNE, --- 7:15-17
--- (Gen.) 4:6; 12:97, 124, 135,
191, 437, 483, 550, 571, 587,
593, 599, 719, 739; 13:25, 671
Anthony 10:280, 285, 287-288,
291-292, 297-300, 305-307, 314,
323, 331-332, 340-341, 347-348,
355, 357-358, 360, 362, 373-374,
382, 384, 403-404, 410-412,
419-420, 426, 430-431, 433-434,
441-443, 446, 448, 452-453, 455,
458-460, 463, 473, 478-480, 484,
518, 529, 532, 551, 749; 11:48,
68, 116, 253, 464, 468, 477,
491, 559, 582, 619, 710; 13:710,
712, 722; 14:18, 52, 127, 166,
213, 238, 248, 250, 430; 15:402
Henry 10:445
WAYTSKONOWAS 9:228
WE(A)THERBY, Benjamin 10:631, 645
WEAMS, John 12:769
WEAR, Ralph 14:189, 192, 433
WEAR(E), Meshec(h) (Mesheck) 6:57,
67, 71, 82, 90
WEATHERBY, Benjamin 5:186
William 14:41
WEATHERHOLT, --- (Capt.) 7:313
WEATONA 8:723
WEAVER, --- (Dr.) 12:693
Adam 15:99, 206, 297
Casper 10:765
Christian 13:510, 512
Christopher 14:576
Conrod 11:24, 83
Frederick 13:604; 14:305, 426
George 16:490
Henry 10:701, 712; 14:539, 592
Henry (alias FISHER) 9:548-549
Jacob 4:268; 8:402, 506; 9:57,
199; 11:190, 195, 464; ->

WEAVER, Jacob (continued) 12:635;
13:580, 622; 14:226, 299, 373,
439, 557; 15:419, 424, 439, 454,
482; 16:436
Johannes 3:452
John 6:737; 14:208
Martin 14:477
Matthias 12:608
Michael 10:746
Nicholas 9:17; 11:118, 528; 14:10
Peter 15:38
Valentin 10:714
WEAVERLIN, Catherine 12:577
WEAYOUGH 8:293
WEB(B), Joseph 10:675, 713
WEB(B)ER, Christian 3:285, 607
WEBB, Ezekiel 10:730
George 8:562; 9:172, 651, 670, 674
Henry 4:413, 420-421, 446-447
James 5:378; 7:180, 372, 379, 511,
525, 606-607, 629, 714; 8:723,
750; 10:60, 66, 113, 117
James, Jr. 9:398, 442, 547, 556,
623, 657, 703
John 2:103, 410; 9:651, 670;
10:354-355, 503, 606, 643
Joseph 13:404
Richard 2:596
Robert 1:515, 541, 543-545, 563,
566, 602
Thomas 13:778; 14:193, 439
William 4:102-103, 482, 573-574;
5:3; 10:557; 11:137, 663; 13:13;
15:502; 16:539
WEBBER, Thomas 10:699, 735
WEBER, Christian 15:124
Johan Herbert 3:570
Johan Philip 3:429
Johannes 3:519
Ludwig 12:277
Mathias 3:429
WEBERN, Lorentz 3:453
WEBSTER, --- (Sergeant) 10:429
James 11:586, 609
John 5:566
John B. 13:456, 611, 715; 14:85,
89, 419, 423
Pelatiah 10:458; 12:228, 316
WEDBURN, John 13:673
WEDER, Augustin 3:288
WEEAYWAIS 3:45
WEED, Elija(h) 12:354, 451, 570
Elijah 11:423; 13:54-55, 552, 680,
743; 14:447; 15:315-316, 401,
413
WEED(E), --- (Dr.) 11:150-151
WEEDON (WEIDEN), --- (Col.) 11:149,
151, 153, 155-160
WEEGAR, Peiter 3:368
WEEKS, --- (Capt.) 12:385
WEEMS, Thomas 11:340
WEENEPEEWEYTAH 3:151
WEER, Ralph 14:433
Samuel 11:96
WEERAOOCHWEE 7:220
WEESE, Peter 8:772
WEESER, William 7:284
WEEVER, Michael 3:367
WEEWHINJOUGH 2:15; 3:601, 603;
4:340
WEGERLIN, Paulus 3:453
WEGERLY, Adam 13:12
WEHEELAND 13:466
WEHEEQUECKHON (ALIAS ANDREW)
13:466
WEIAND, Henry 15:33

215

WEIB, Jon'n. 11:106
 Jon'o. 11:106
WEIBERT, --- (Lt. Col.) 13:744
WEICHER, George 15:516
WEICKART, George 14:270, 281
WEIDEL, George 13:383
WEIDLE, Dirick Adam 3:367
WEIDLEY, John 16:193
WEIDMAN, Abraham 3:593
 Jacob 3:593; 14:189-191, 193-195;
  16:335
 John 10:643; 12:782; 13:170, 586;
  14:98, 418
 Matthias 14:610
 Rudolph 3:593
WEIDNAR, Hans Georg. 3:517
WEIDNER, Daniel 13:580
WEIGALL, Mardin 3:432
WEIGHTMAN, Joannes 3:369
WEIGLER, Jacob 14:225
WEIGNER, Christopher 3:568
 George 3:569
 Hans 3:569
 Melchior 3:569
WEIKERT, John 15:509
WEIMER, George 16:299
 Peter 16:333
WEINHEIMER, Wendel 3:453
WEINTZ, --- (Capt.) 10:679
WEIR, Robert 11:281
 Robt. 2:97
 Samuel 11:281
WEIR (WIER), Thomas 10:581, 771
WEIS, Casper 3:415
 Daniel (Dr.) 15:482
 Jacob 3:329
WEIS(S), George 11:11, 35, 38, 56,
  130
 Jacob 14:83, 348, 415
WEISER, Benjamin 9:557; 10:43, 634;
  11:405; 12:112, 374; 13:88
 Conrad 4:7, 12, 79, 81-82, 86, 88,
  96, 203-204, 245, 432, 443, 483,
  501, 566, 575-577, 580, 583,
  587, 601, 634-635, 637, 640,
  642-643, 646-647, 649-653, 655,
  660, 676, 678-680, 698-699,
  702-703, 705, 709, 711, 713,
  715-716, 719-720, 722-723,
  726-727, 729, 731, 733, 735-736,
  747, 751, 757-759, 768, 776-778;
  5:2-3, 6, 19-22, 24, 73, 83,
  88-89, 97-98, 119-121, 132, 136,
  139-140, 145, 148-150, 162, 167,
  185, 188, 190, 193, 197,
  212-214, 222-224, 229, 232, 257,
  284, 286-290, 293-294, 298, 304,
  307, 311, 318, 327, 329,
  347-348, 358, 378, 388, 393,
  396-398, 402, 406, 431, 435,
  437, 440, 442-443, 445, 447,
  455, 467, 470, 480, 485, 487,
  517-519, 526, 528, 530, 532-533,
  541, 543, 547, 566, 576, 628,
  632, 634, 636, 639-642, 647,
  665, 669-670, 676, 685, 688-700,
  702, 731, 747, 758, 760, 775;
  6:24, 34, 36, 38, 49, 84-85, 89,
  110, 112-115, 117-119, 122-127,
  143, 145-148, 150, 160-161,
  186-188, 216, 243, 248, 250,
  277-278, 284-285, 291-292, 331,
  340, 352, 361, 403, 443, 445,
  457, 467-468, 493-495, 503-504,
  522-523, 533-536, 551-552,
  566-567, 588-591, 612-613, ->

WEISER, Conrad (continued) 6:615,
  640-641, 647, 649-653, 656,
  659-661, 664-665, 667-668, 670,
  681-683, 685, 688, 690, 697,
  699, 703, 727, 729, 744,
  760-763, 771, 779-780, 782-783;
  7:1, 3, 5-6, 33, 35, 46-48, 50,
  78, 83, 87, 90, 92, 95, 103-104,
  106-107, 137, 141, 144, 146,
  182, 184, 206-207, 209, 216-217,
  220, 222, 244-245, 282, 296,
  298, 302-303, 307-308, 311,
  313-315, 317-318, 326-327, 336,
  431, 462, 465, 487-489, 517-520,
  533-534, 536, 539, 543, 549,
  581, 603, 621, 640-641, 649,
  652, 655-656, 658, 663, 666,
  669, 671-672, 675, 683-684,
  688-689, 692-694, 697, 702, 705,
  708, 713-714, 734-736, 772;
  8:50, 112, 115, 118, 121, 128,
  149-150, 172, 176-178, 180, 190,
  201, 204-205, 211, 214, 218-220,
  255, 260-261, 458, 631-632, 638,
  652; 9:145, 618-619; 10:177;
  13:470
 Frederick 6:459, 649; 9:440, 561,
  618-620
 Jacob 12:601
 Jno. 6:704
 Peter 6:649, 651
 Sam (Capt.) 7:296, 303
 Sammy 5:518, 543, 643; 6:35, 122,
  127, 468, 640, 651, 656
 Samuel 8:458, 630, 632-633, 638,
  644; 9:57, 199, 285; 15:306
WEISNER, Henry 16:143
 Jacob 14:63, 413
WEISS, --- (Col.) 11:452-453
 Frantz 3:516
 George 13:565
 Henry 13:778
 Jacob 13:778; 15:187
 Johannes 3:593
 Justice 16:119
 Lewis 13:8, 389; 14:400, 445;
  15:23, 26
 Philip 11:650; 14:120, 164, 184
WEISSER, Benjamin 13:112
WEITHWRIGHT, Matthias 14:371
WEITNER, George 11:611
 Henry 11:611-612
WEITZEL (WEITZLE, WETZELL,
  WEITZELL), Casper 10:767
 Jacob 12:534; 13:620, 716; 14:128,
  431; 16:408
 John 10:262, 274, 658, 660, 662,
  666, 668, 675, 681-683, 686,
  691, 693, 696, 699-701, 704-705,
  710-711, 713-715, 717, 725, 730,
  733-734; 11:218, 222, 257, 278,
  409, 538, 705-706; 13:427-429,
  519, 628, 635, 703, 741, 743,
  766; 14:111, 113, 218, 342-343,
  345, 347, 558; 16:99, 323, 354
WEKERLEY, Abraham 3:593
WELAPACHICKIN 9:212
WELBORNE, Christian 12:601
WELBROGT, Joseph 3:284
WELCH, Jacob 9:584
 James 9:201
 Thomas 16:221b
 William 14:82
 Wm. 1:96-97, 99-114, 116-119, 121
WELCH (WELSH), Francis 10:230, 232
WELDEN, Matthew 11:258

216

WELDONE, Is. 1:607
WELFING (WELFLING), Henry 11:513,
 516-517
WELFLANG, Henry 13:402-403
WELFLING, Henry 12:669
 Margaret 12:669
WELGAR, Daniel 14:80, 90, 412
 David 13:675
WELHANTZ, Jacob 12:219
WELLS, Alexander 14:365
 David 16:373
 George 12:10
 Henry 16:111
 Isaac 16:492
 James 9:398, 548, 624; 11:432;
15:24
 Jane 13:315
 Jno. 1:500
 John 3:465, 524, 531; 4:313, 482;
 5:3
 Jonathan 16:259
 Joseph 16:24
 Phililp 6:266
 Richard 5:248; 6:136; 9:203;
 10:567; 11:70; 13:9, 49, 319,
 321, 326, 503, 509; 14:327, 359,
 458, 464; 15:215, 242, 344-349,
 352, 355-356, 359, 481, 486,
 520, 524, 538, 622; 16:27-28,
 33-34, 40, 47, 49, 52-53, 55-56,
 251
 Richd. 1:90
 Robert 10:340
 Rosewell 15:484
 Samuel 5:8; 6:64, 67-68, 72-73,
 82, 92, 109
 William 8:403
WELNER, --- (Col.) 12:305
WELPAR, George Godfrey 13:271
WELPERT, --- (Capt.) 10:685
WELSH, Carret (Garret) 14:295, 302,
 426
 David 15:134
 James 10:723; 11:501; 12:187;
 13:641; 14:97, 197, 419
 John 13:676; 14:96, 424; 16:368
 Margaret 11:135
 Nicholas 16:461
 William 13:710, 778; 14:95, 153,
 411, 424
 Wm. 1:103
WELTNER, --- (Col.) 12:309
 Ludwick 12:595
WELTZ, Andreas 3:515
WELTZHOOVER, Jacob 16:255
WENCIL, John 11:582
WENCIL (WENSEL), Daniel 11:582, 608
WENDAL, Jacob 5:8, 296
WENDALL, Abraham 3:609
WENDEL, Augustus 3:432
WENDOCALLA 8:723
WENDSHALE 8:386
WENDTZ, John, Jr. 11:340
WENEYWALIKA 7:677, 681
WENRICK, John 14:383
WENSEL, Hans Adolf 4:73
WENSER, Jac. Matthias 3:467
WENST, Joest 3:410
WENTELWOLFE, George 12:601
WENTWORTH, --- (Gen.) 4:499
 --- (Gov.) 6:19, 53
WENTZ, --- 13:190-192, 210, 212,
 228-229
 Georg. Carl 3:410
 John 12:46
WENTZELL, John 11:582

WEQUEALA 3:330
WERBEL, Philip 3:432
 Wendel 3:432
WERCHMAN, Henrich 3:597
 Johannes 3:597
WERFLLE, Hans Melchoir 3:455
WERGONNER, Johan Philip 4:59
WERKBELL, George 15:409
WERKEISER, Charles 13:318, 350
WERLIE, Deitrich 4:72
WERNER, Hans Adam 3:454
 John Adam 3:520
WERNESS, Conrad 3:367
WERNON (SEE VERNON), Elias 11:515
WERNS, Jacob 12:277
WERT, Christian 10:705
 Martin 10:584, 673
 Mary 16:382, 384, 427
 Philip 10:709
WERTMAN, George Philip 13:278;
 14:666
 Philip 12:28
WERTZ (WORTZ), Christian 11:78,
 236, 318, 335-336, 357, 433,
 442, 459; 12:116, 174, 302, 306,
 310, 364, 411, 435, 457, 484,
 570, 660
 Henry 13:446
 Johannes 3:458
 John 16:543
WERVELL, Hans 3:515
 Hans Jurg 3:515
WERWHINJOUGH 4:338
WESEHANNAS 8:484
WESHBACH, Johan Henrich 3:570
WESKEKITT 13:463
WESLY, Henry 12:336
WESSEL, Grunadus 1:123
WESSELL, John 12:4
WEST, --- 3:76; 14:243
 Adam 14:647
 Charles 10:289; 12:577; 13:26
 Edward 12:468
 Francis 7:637
 Gregory 12:402
 James 5:581; 16:387
 Jno. 2:42
 John 14:260
 Robert 3:224
 Thomas 12:391
 William 5:747, 751, 758-762;
 6:590; 7:93, 96, 469, 518,
 635-636, 715; 8:19, 311; 10:447,
 627, 768
 William, Jr. 12:496, 558, 599,
 604, 706
WESTBY, Henry 16:80
WESTCOAT, George 14:453, 462
 Joel 10:450
 John 13:305
 William 12:501-502, 504, 506, 516
WESTHEBER, Valentine 3:429
WESTL(E)Y, Richard 2:468, 506
WESTLAND, Nath 2:113
WESTMORE, Joseph 13:462
WESTMORELAND, --- (Earl of) 3:70
WESTON, Anto. 1:92
 Richard 11:610-612
WESTRON, Abra. 1:90
WETCHYWALIKON 3:316
WETHERILL, Joseph 10:467
 Richard 13:96
 Samuel 13:346
 Samuel, Jr. 13:447
WETHERS, Ralph 1:72

WETHERSPOON, David **5**:89 (See
    WITHERSPOON)
WETMER, Peter **11**:349
WETTERHOLT (WETTERHOLD), --- **7**:15,
    17
WETZEL, John **10**:156
WETZELL, Hans Martin **3**:415
WETZLE, Casper **14**:532
    John **11**:207; **13**:536
WETZLE (WIETZLE, WEITZELL), John
    12:57, 64, 243
WETZSTAIN, Peter **3**:432
WEVER, --- (Sergeant) **10**:760
WEY, G. M. **3**:284
WEY & YALLY **2**:628
WEYAND, Nicholas **14**:383
WEYBER, Jacob **3**:467
WEYBRECHT, Martin **3**:456
WEYBRIGHT, Hans Martin **3**:457
    Martin **14**:570
WEYBURN, Samuel **9**:584
WEYER, Leonard **3**:454
    Peter **4**:73
WEYES, Jacob **3**:432
WEYGALL, Johannes Michael **4**:59
WEYGANDT, Cornelius **4**:59
WEYHELM, Joannes **3**:328
WEYMAN, Bernard **3**:613
WEYMER, Bernard **4**:251-252
WEYMOUTH, --- (Viscount) **9**:629,
    637, 640
WEYNANDT, Johan Philip **3**:518
WEYNARD, Johan Jacob **3**:415
WEYNEPREEWEYTA **3**:150
WEYS, Andreas **3**:455
    George **3**:569
WEYSAR, Christian **3**:413
WEYSEL, Michal **3**:467
WEYSER, Conrad **3**:425, 435, 438,
    440, 445-447, 451, 503, 507-508,
    511, 577, 598, 608, 610
WEYSOW-WALOW **3**:310
WEYSS, Johan Leonhart **3**:516
WEYTCHOLECHING **4**:307
WHARBURT, John **9**:584
WHARRY, Robert **14**:123, 126, 422
    Robert (Dr.) **13**:714
WHARTMAN, Adam **13**:191
WHARTON, Carpenter **10**:408, 665,
    762; **11**:513, 516-517
    Charles **16**:185
    Elizabeth **13**:707
    Isaac **10**:451; **11**:513, 516-517;
        12:317; **16**:185
    James **9**:723; **10**:566, 571, 649, 707
    John **3**:387, 416, 464, 575, 615;
        4:86, 247; **10**:283-284, 289, 296,
        306, 314; **11**:12, 31, 762;
        12:186; **13**:707; **14**:499
    Joseph **3**:547; **4**:294; **12**:441, 501;
        14:381; **15**:452, 499
    Samuel **7**:760-761; **8**:19, 575;
        9:302-304; **13**:439, 442, 447;
        14:108
    Thomas **8**:22, 24; **11**:4-6, 10-13,
        26-30, 32-34, 36, 40-42, 45,
        47-48, 50-51, 54-55, 57-58,
        60-64, 67-69, 73, 75-79, 81, 83,
        87-88, 90, 92-93, 95, 97, 99,
        101-102, 104-105, 107-109,
        113-115, 117, 121-124, 126-128,
        130-131, 133-139, 173-178, 181,
        184-188, 190-191, 193-198, 200,
        202-203, 205-210, 212-214,
        216-217, 219-223, 225-226,
        228-238, 241-243, 245-253, ->

WHARTON, Thomas (continued)
    11:255-265, 267-268, 270-278,
        280, 282-283, 285-288, 290-291,
        293-295, 297, 299-300, 302-304,
        306, 308-309, 311-322, 334, 346,
        353, 357-387, 390-391, 394-396,
        398-400, 402-403, 405-411,
        413-415, 417-419, 421-423,
        425-426, 428-430, 432-445,
        447-453, 455, 457-466, 468-469,
        471-472, 474-475, 477-479, 481,
        485-489; **12**:283, 441, 594;
        13:385, 707; **14**:155; **15**:141;
        16:185
    Thomas, Jr. **10**:280, 282-291,
        294-302, 304-307, 312-315,
        322-323, 327-332, 334-336,
        338-342, 344-347, 351, 354-357,
        360, 362, 365, 367-368, 371,
        373-382, 384-385, 387, 390, 396,
        399-401, 403-404, 406-408,
        410-411, 415-417, 420-428,
        430-431, 433-436, 438-439,
        441-443, 445-446, 448-449,
        451-453, 456-461, 463-464,
        466-471, 473, 476, 478, 480-481,
        483, 486-492, 499, 501-502,
        504-505, 509, 511, 513-515,
        519-520, 523-526, 529-537,
        539-540, 543-547, 552, 554-557,
        559-562, 560-570, 572, 574-575,
        578-580, 582-583, 585, 589-590,
        592-600, 602, 606-607, 610-611,
        614, 616-617, 620-621, 623,
        627-629, 633, 635-637, 640,
        642-634, 647-648, 650, 655-659,
        664-667, 670-672, 674-675,
        677-678, 681-682, 687, 689,
        692-694, 696-698, 700, 702, 704,
        707, 709-711, 713-714, 716,
        718-721, 726-729, 732-733,
        736-738, 742, 744-746, 749-750,
        753-756, 760, 762-763, 766,
        768-772, 775, 777-779, 781-784
WHARTON (SEE STOCKER &) **10**:339;
    15:647; **16**:4, 223
WHATRON, James **13**:707
WHAWYAYGAMEN **3**:361
WHEADON, --- (Col.) **11**:70
WHEALON, --- (Capt.) **10**:689
WHEATON, Israel **10**:679
WHEELEN, Israel **14**:555
WHEELER, --- (Mr.) **15**:648
    Adam **15**:176-177, 443
    Gilbert **1**:375, 512, 586, 588
    Isaac **15**:567, 569
    Israel **16**:329, 337, 450
    John **15**:217
    Robt. **2**:113
    Samuel **10**:298, 741; **11**:5, 44;
        15:100-101
    William **16**:224
WHEELER & WILEY **11**:109
WHEELWRIGHT, J. **5**:420
WHEET, John **9**:584
WHELEN (WHEELIN), William **14**:297,
    304, 426
WHELLAN, Israel **11**:339
WHERRY, Joseph **15**:103
WHEUNCLOWO **8**:124
WHIBBLE, George **13**:756; **14**:436
WHIEDMAN, Matthias **3**:516
WHIPPLE, William **13**:474
WHIPPLE(S), William **11**:673, 690
WHIT(E)MAN, Adam **11**:68, 101, 358

WHIT(E)PAIN(E), Zachariah **1**:143,
187, 246-247, 249, 396
WHITALL, Benjamin **10**:289
WHITCOMB, Job **16**:500
John **15**:489, 603
WHITE, --- **4**:67, 69, 107, 109
--- (Capt. Widow) **5**:240
--- (Rev.) **11**:300
Alex'a. **11**:472
Amos **13**:687-688
Bishop **15**:614
Charles **12**:187; **13**:142
Christopher **14**:593-594
Collo. **5**:220
Fane **12**:199, 206
Francis **1**:521; **12**:356; **14**:406,
408, 437
Frederick **14**:453
George **1**:228; **14**:123, 126, 433
Hanna **16**:61
Isaac **14**:407, 409
James **5**:261-262; **10**:698; **11**:756;
13:773; **14**:81, 98
John **1**:87, 108-110, 137, 139, 142,
145, 147, 150-151, 163-164,
179-180, 188-189, 204, 206, 226,
253-254, 259, 261, 327, 329,
333, 341, 365, 367, 378, 387,
406-407, 416-418, 420-421,
425-429, 445, 514, 607; **3**:545;
8:492, 614, 616; **10**:684, 694;
11:101, 109, 141, 263, 266;
12:187, 513; **13**:38; **14**:145, 157;
15:514, 519, 563, 572, 637, 649;
16:189, 206
John (alias John TRACY) **15**:238,
398, 400
Jona. (Maj.) **6**:608, 611
Mary **1**:444-445
Nicholas **12**:356, 483
Peter **13**:773
Rachel **10**:720; **13**:202
Robert **1**:147, 150; **7**:507; **8**:176,
194, 218, 492-493, 595, 598,
617, 655, 661, 756, 770; **11**:80,
610-611; **12**:199
Samuel **14**:411
Sarah **13**:482
Stephen **4**:102
Thomas **4**:102; **5**:572; **10**:217;
14:365
William **5**:441-442, 445; **11**:330;
12:351; **13**:135; **15**:390
William (Dr.) **14**:399
WHITE (SEE CHALONER &) **12**:411
WHITE (WHYTE), Robert **10**:280,
282-291, 294-302, 304-307,
312-215, 322-323, 327-331, 334,
335, 338-339, 344-345, 360,
367-368, 373-374, 376, 385, 388,
390, 395-396, 399, 401, 403-404,
406-407, 410, 412, 141-415, 417,
419-420, 422-423, 425, 430,
432-433, 436-439, 442-443, 446,
448, 451-452, 455, 460, 463,
465, 467, 470-471, 473, 475,
480, 483-484, 486-487, 493-496,
499, 502, 505, 507, 510-513,
515-517, 519, 524, 526-527,
530-531, 533, 536, 540, 543-544,
546-548, 554, 556-557, 559,
566-567, 571, 575, 582-583, 586,
594-595, 597-600, 602-604, 606,
608, 610-617, 619-621, 642, 648
WHITE MINGO **6**:784

WHITE MINGO (alias John COOK)
9:428, 436-437, 470, 539
WHITEBREAD, George **11**:644
Sarah **11**:644; **13**:208
William **13**:759; **14**:140, 367-368,
525
WHITECOMB, Joseph **16**:270
WHITEFORD, Hugh **5**:247; **10**:689
WHITEHALL, Robert **13**:89
WHITEHEAD, Benj. **1**:87, 95
James **10**:429, 437, 439, 704, 765;
11:98, 358, 596, 598;
12:131-132; **14**:189, 193, 435
James, Jr. **9**:547, 623
John **11**:538
Matthew **11**:57
Richard **13**:166, 389; **15**:50
WHITEHILL, --- (Mr.) **13**:43-45,
47-48, 50-52, 54-56, 59-62,
67-70, 73-76, 82-84, 86-87, 242,
369, 672
David **11**:334, 343-344, 346-347
James **4**:152, 483; **5**:3, 247, 378,
600
John **12**:134, 156, 164, 508; **13**:88,
112, 393, 415, 722; **14**:18, 213,
267, 287-291, 307-311, 313-318,
321, 324-326, 342, 344-348,
356-365, 367-387, 393-396,
398-402, 404, 441, 462-474,
476-484, 486-488, 522, 524, 526,
531-539, 546-554, 556-568,
570-571, 573-575, 577-582,
584-590, 606, 623-635, 637-639,
644, 647-651, 653-657, 659-661,
663-672; **15**:1-12, 14, 21-47,
58-60, 62-63, 74-97, 99,
101-108, 110-114, 126-163,
169-182, 184-190, 192-195,
197-201, 242-245, 247-267,
269-285, 287-289; **16**:136
Robert **11**:208, 314, 317, 320-321,
325-326, 328, 366, 374, 434-435;
12:166, 212, 215-221, 223-233,
235, 237, 240-251, 253, 256-260,
262-263, 265, 267-276, 279-281,
283, 285, 287-289, 292, 296,
460, 462-469, 503-506, 508-510,
512, 514-515, 517-518, 520,
522-526, 528, 531, 533-534, 536,
538-544, 546-552, 554-559,
561-563, 717-723, 725, 727-729,
731-738, 741-742, 744, 746-747,
749-751, 753-755, 758-760;
13:521, 726; **14**:236, 250, 485;
15:636
WHITELY, Thomas **11**:62
WHITEMAN, John **13**:393; **16**:453
Thomas **6**:292
William **16**:491
WHITESIDE, Peter **12**:404, 477-478;
14:68
Thomas **14**:260
William **6**:755
WHITESIDE (WHITESITT), Samuel
10:227-228
WHITESIDE(S), Thomas **11**:62, 65, 85
WHITESIDES, Abraham **14**:656
James **11**:251, 265
Peter **13**:307
WHITEWELL, Francis **1**:147
WHITFIELD, Elinor (Helinor) **1**:515
WHITING, Nathaniel **6**:259, 608, 611
WHITLEY, Michael **14**:637
Samuel **14**:625
WHITLOCKE, Anne **13**:530

WILLIAMS, John (continued) **12**:187,
421, 671; **13**:7; **14**:190, 193-194,
420; **15**:330, 577; **16**:260, 333,
528
John (alias John HINES) **9**:173
Joseph **13**:139, 757; **14**:83, 410
Joshua **11**:280, 282, 357-359,
468-469
Lewis **5**:454; **10**:718-719; **11**:371;
12:146, 513
Mary **8**:629; **16**:233
Nathaniel (Nathan) **14**:125, 130,
411
Peter **14**:407-408, 437
Richard **14**:227-228, 605
Samuel **11**:24, 32; **12**:162; **13**:87
Sarah **15**:218, 339
Stacey **13**:643
Stacy **14**:93, 421
Thomas **1**:77, 83; **4**:269; **14**:296,
303, 412; **15**:414, 422
William **3**:50; **5**:209; **9**:203; **10**:81,
120, 406, 471; **11**:179-180, 513,
516-517, 732; **12**:51, 88, 187;
13:555, 635; **14**:95, 306, 417,
434, 641; **15**:77
WILLIAMS & CLINTON **10**:727
WILLIAMSON, --- **6**:491
--- (Col.) **13**:297
--- (Mrs.) **13**:760
Benjamin **10**:496
Cuthbert **11**:149
Daniel **3**:298
David **13**:759; **14**:365; **15**:646;
16:212
Edward **13**:596; **14**:85, 415
Hugh **14**:317
James **10**:741; **11**:418-419
Jeremiah **13**:759
Jesse **11**:649, 680
John **5**:186; **10**:448
Ralph **13**:440
Samuel **4**:102; **11**:340; **12**:81; **13**:38
Sarah **11**:649
Thomas **12**:201
William **12**:218, 750
WILLING, --- **5**:79, 258-259; **8**:576
--- (Mr.) **12**:43, 268
Charles **4**:517, 526, 762; **5**:174,
388, 572; **12**:120
Chas. **6**:176
Morris **12**:38
R. (Mrs.) **11**:607
Richard **10**:306, 379, 481; **13**:722,
737; **14**:238, 250, 344; **15**:303,
566-569, 571, 574-582, 584,
586-589, 597-600, 602-604,
607-608, 610-611, 613-620,
622-623, 625-629, 632, 634-644,
652; **16**:1-7, 9-17, 19-29, 33-35,
37, 39-44, 46-48, 50-57, 59-60,
62-64, 68, 70, 74-78, 82-91, 93,
96-97, 107-109, 119-120, 122,
125, 130-138, 141-146, 148,
151-158, 164-166, 169, 171-173,
180-183, 186-188, 190-191,
193-194, 196-202, 205, 209, 211,
214-215, 218-220, 222-209b,
216b-218b, 220b-224b, 225-227,
229-233, 235-236, 238-239,
241-244, 251-252, 254-260,
262-264, 267-268, 270-273, 276,
278-281, 283, 288-291, 293, 295,
299-305, 307, 309, 311-313,
315-316, 318, 320-324, 326-327,
329-332, 336, 339-341, ->

WILLING, Richard (continued)
16:344-350, 354-360, 362-366,
368-371, 373, 375-384, 386,
388-390, 394-396, 401-406,
408-414, 416-417, 420-425, 427,
442, 445-447, 449-454, 456, 459,
461-463, 477, 480-485, 487-494,
496-501, 507, 509-517, 521-528,
530-531, 534, 535, 537, 540,
543, 545
Thomas **3**:294; **6**:122; **7**:76; **8**:19,
59, 575; **9**:205, 293, 393, 398,
510, 513, 545, 548, 596, 601,
632, 666, 678, 682, 684,
711-712, 735, 745, 778; **10**:43,
53, 129, 172-173, 256, 265-266,
280, 305, 379; **11**:345-346, 349;
12:120; **13**:200-201
WILLING & MORRIS **11**:1, 7, 10
WILLING & MORRIS & CO. **10**:425-426
WILLIS, --- **11**:648
--- (Capt.) **11**:428
--- (Col.) **6**:268
Jebediah **8**:566
Jebediah, Jr. **8**:566
Joel **16**:402
John **10**:265, 422, 483, 653, 679,
764
Jonathan **16**:308
Richard (Robert) **11**:515, 517-518
Samuel **14**:63
William **11**:307, 515, 517-518
WILLIS (SEE EDES) **11**:648
WILLISBY, John **16**:451
WILLOBY, Charles **14**:610
WILLS, --- (Capt.) **11**:47
--- (Gen.) **3**:75
John **16**:286
WILLS & TOWN **10**:556
WILLSHEYT, Frederick **3**:413
WILLSON, Joseph **10**:505, 525, 533
WILMAN, John **12**:48
WILMER, James Jones **11**:703
Lambert **14**:497
WILMERTON, Attwell **1**:521
John **3**:218-219
WILMINGTON, To. Cant. **4**:471
WILMONT, Henry **9**:749, 758, 765
WILMOT, Henry **10**:164, 176, 179
WILNOR, William **13**:576
WILSON, --- **5**:75, 78; **11**:267-268
--- (Col.) **10**:170-171; **16**:283
--- (Judge) **16**:443, 533
--- (Maj.) **14**:213
--- (Mr.) **10**:140, 445; **11**:198,
202, 204, 246; **13**:417
--- (Sgt.) **11**:150
--- (Widow) **13**:756
Alexander **13**:556, 756
Andrew **14**:608
Anne **13**:480
Benjamin **12**:101
Catharine **15**:124
Christ'r. **12**:246
Christiana **14**:590
Christopher **7**:462; **11**:514, 516-517
David **7**:637; **12**:146, 446, 513;
13:282
Dorington **11**:112
Elizabeth **14**:554, 568, 586, 591;
16:34
Francis **14**:240, 265, 368, 473,
653; **16**:141
George **6**:136; **10**:78, 142, 165,
167; **14**:671; **16**:198, 542-543
Goodwin **13**:115, 169; **14**:414

WOOD, Uriah 11:153
  Wm. 1:96-97, 99-110, 119, 121,
    124-130, 132-133, 138, 140,
    145-146, 153-155, 158-159, 169
WOODBEY, Emanuel 10:740
WOODBRIDGE, --- (Mr.) 6:111-112,
    117, 128, 251, 257
  Timothy 9:571
WOODBY (WOODLY), Emanuel 11:7, 88
WOODEN, Joseph 15:570, 578
WOODHOUSE, Thomas 10:421
  William 13:290, 345
WOODHULL, Nathaniel 10:681
WOODLAND, Jonathan 12:621
WOODLEY, Ann 16:89
  John 16:89
WOODROFF, Zebulon 11:152
WOODROW, --- (Mr.) 11:12
  Simeon 4:270
WOODRUFF, Samuel 8:156
WOODS, --- 12:575
  --- (Mr.) 13:512; 15:132-133
  Archibald 8:728
  Charles 5:454
  George 9:730; 10:78, 163, 265;
    11:81, 633; 13:400, 509, 730;
    15:185, 298, 309-317, 320-328,
    331, 337-347, 478, 538-541,
    543-545, 548-551, 554, 556-564,
    566-569, 571-573, 575-584,
    586-587, 590, 592, 594-604,
    606-608, 610-620, 622-623, 631,
    652-658; 16:1-7, 9-17, 19-21,
    24-29, 31-34, 37, 39-44, 46,
    50-52, 134-138, 141-146,
    148-149, 151-158, 160, 162-166,
    168-169, 171-178, 180-183,
    187-189, 214, 220, 319, 337,
    341, 361, 385
  George, Jr. 15:91, 113
  Jacob 11:340
  James 5:210; 13:301, 701; 14:311
  John 12:34; 14:249-250, 252-270,
    277-279, 281-284, 290-291,
    307-311, 313-316, 321-327, 342,
    344-348, 346-363, 365, 367-369,
    371-376, 563-568, 570-571,
    573-575, 577-582, 584-593,
    595-604, 616-625, 628-635,
    637-643, 646-648, 662; 15:15-34,
    56-61, 64-82, 229, 239, 250,
    277, 362
  Josiah 14:34, 38, 53, 171
  Peter 16:543
WOODSIDE, John 5:247; 10:448;
    12:781; 13:573; 14:130, 610
WOODWARD, --- 6:491; 13:344
  --- (Capt.) 8:386
  David 15:489, 603
  Thomas 14:590
WOODWORTH, John 9:571
WOOLASTON, Thomas 1:207, 218, 224,
    236 (See WOLLASTON & WOOLLASTON)
WOOLFALL, Charles 11:75
WOOLFE, Reynard 11:363
WOOLFERT, Matthias 11:23
WOOLIE(N), Zil(1)a 4:662-663, 665
    (See ZILLAWOOLIE)
WOOLMAN, Jacob 9:286
WOOLPPER, --- (Col.) 15:315
WOOLSEY, John 10:679
WOOLSINGHAM, --- (Mr.) 6:298
WOOLSTON, John 6:241
WOOLVIN, Mary 3:186, 193
WOOSTER, David 6:259
WOOTERS, Jno. 1:136

WOOTRING, Abraham 3:519
WOPATHTHA 2:15; 3:601, 603
WOPEKENCY 5:685
WOPEY PLETHAY 5:685
WOPTHAMA 5:685
WOR(R)EL (SEE ALLISON &) 10:761,
    782
WORK, Andrew 5:464; 8:562; 9:172,
    636; 10:709, 711
  Henry 16:210, 495-496
  James 9:673
  John 11:229, 691; 14:237; 16:496
  Joseph 12:134, 508; 13:88, 722,
    737; 14:453, 556; 15:91, 98,
    244, 570
  Robert 12:187
  William 6:669; 10:756; 13:586;
    14:89, 417
WORKEISER, Charles 13:303-304
WORKING, Jacob 12:209
WORLEY, Francis 3:50, 176, 179,
    181-182, 184-186
  Henry 2:511-512
  John Daniel 3:367
  Nathan 3:575
WORLING, John 13:777; 14:86, 432
WORM, Joseph 14:439
WORRA, Joseph 11:178
WORRAL(L), John 2:65, 86, 630
  Peter 2:127, 190
WORRAL, ALLISON & 15:66
WORRALL, Peter 7:148-150
WORRALL (WARRALL), ALLISON & EVANS
    16:432, 486, 490-491
WORREL, Benjamin 10:490, 605
  James 11:32, 279, 293, 306
WORREL (SEE ALLISON &) 11:7, 32
WORRELL, --- (Mr.) 16:479
  Isaiah 11:515-517
  James 3:254
  Mark Bingley 13:757
WORRELL (WORRALL), Mark B. 14:93,
    421, 613, 615
WORROLA, Jno. 1:568
WORRRICK, Andrew 5:411
WORSHAM, Joshua 14:189, 193, 433
WORTH, Jno. 1:517
  John 15:123; 16:52
  Thomas 5:387, 572; 7:417; 8:573;
    9:205, 673
WORTHINGTON, John 6:57, 67, 71, 82
  Robert 5:60
WORTZ, William 11:75
WOSHTACHARY 2:469
WOTTON, Mich. 1:165
WOYL, Hans Jacob 4:60
WRAXALL, Peter 6:61, 63, 65-66,
    110, 473, 608, 611; 8:155
WRAY, John 3:450, 459, 463
WREN, --- (Mr.) 11:584
  Joseph 13:612; 14:128
WREXALL, Peter 7:115, 194-195,
    625-626
WRIGHT, --- 6:491; 9:584
  --- (Maj.) 11:340; 12:111
  Abijah 11:631, 635; 12:573-574,
    620, 672
  Alexander 13:263, 537; 14:366
  Anthony 5:247; 13:46; 15:307, 435,
    519; 16:29, 52, 84, 94, 201,
    341, 345, 365, 465
  Benjamin 2:177, 205-206, 233, 355
  Catherine 15:469
  Charles 14:408
  Eleanor 14:308, 630, 650; 15:345
  Enoch 11:110

YEATES, Jasper (continued) 2:262,
  289, 309, 393, 428, 435, 439,
  441, 449, 509, 527, 534;
  3:13-14, 17-18, 28, 32, 50,
  57-58, 65, 67, 71, 75, 143;
  12:577
John 5:551, 597
Richard 13:135
Thomas 14:611
YEATS, Joseph 7:264
YEDALL, Anthony 16:422
YEDER, Melchiors 12:672
YEGENER, Hans Francis 3:453
YEGLE, John 12:672
YEIGER, Phlip 4:251
YEIGIE, Johannes 3:467
YEILDALL, Robert 1:559
YEISER, Frederick 10:643
YELDALL, --- (Dr.) 13:297
  Anthony 11:513, 516-517; 13:516,
  519
  Anthony (Dr.) 12:496-497, 504, 509
  Esther 12:509
YELDALL (YELDALE), Anthony 15:606,
  614
YELDON, Jean 1:377
YEOMANS, Richard 14:297, 304, 422
YERIGH, Johan Philip 3:453
YETTER, Peter 14:346
YISSLER, Henry 12:577
YOCKUM, Jacob 8:661
YOCUM, Jonas 12:577
YODER, Daniel 16:30
YOKAM, Andreas 4:59
YOKE, Adam 9:723
YOKUM, Mounce 1:435
  Peter 1:396-397, 435
YONDON (IONDAN), Francis 14:594
  Peter 14:594
YONGE, Walter 1:534-535, 538
  William 4:484-485
YONGER, Martin 3:386
YONGMAN, Conrad 3:386
YONILEY, Christian 3:517
YORDE, Johannes 3:520
YORHLIG, Bendict 4:72
YORISTAGERY 7:49
YORK, --- (Duke of) 6:262-263, 271,
  273, 556-557; 8:410, 621;
  10:123, 126-127, 131
  --- (Mr.) 7:272
  Edward 13:150
  Richard 13:141
  Samuel 12:772
  Thomas 4:762; 5:193, 257, 388;
  12:28, 772
YORK (NEGRO) 13:137
YORK(E), Thomas 8:573-575, 583;
  10:407, 425
YORKE, --- (Mrs.) 11:595
  Andrew 14:385
  Edward 10:521
  John 9:40, 80
  Mary 13:529
  Richard 13:164
  Thomas 7:417, 635-636
YORKES, Thomas 14:385
YOST, Casper 10:746
  John 13:615; 14:92, 420
YOU, Hans 3:287
YOUGHLY, Benedict 4:173-174
YOUNG, --- 5:659
  --- (Capt.) 6:730; 13:191
  Ann 1:331
  Anne 15:58
  Archibald 5:325

YOUNG, Barbara 13:157
  Carolina 13:445
  Charles 12:185; 15:255
  Christian 13:641; 14:193, 608
  David 11:515-516, 518
  Edward 10:450
  Elizabeth 12:36; 13:384
  George 1:82, 188; 11:244
  Jacob 1:331; 13:607; 14:432
  James 7:34, 162, 476, 724; 8:123,
  227, 234, 287, 458-459; 9:393,
  672; 10:46, 697, 782; 11:85,
  112, 116, 123, 194, 215, 218,
  228, 236, 238, 350-351, 378,
  398, 449, 588, 601, 603, 650,
  672; 13:447
  Joanna 13:524
  Johannis 3:516
  John 5:247; 6:266, 648; 10:542,
  546-547, 641, 708; 11:91, 470,
  494, 745; 12:62, 67, 157, 268,
  283, 525; 13:53, 346
  John, Jr. 14:44
  Lazarus 9:675-676, 682
  Lewellen 12:298
  Marcus 13:248
  Matthew 11:34
  Matthias 10:731; 11:93
  Moses 11:72, 130, 133-135,
  137-141, 143, 145-146
  Nathan 9:286
  Nicholas 13:275, 295, 319, 323;
  14:268, 323, 327, 458; 15:399,
  442, 481, 486, 520, 524; 16:167,
  170, 462, 477
  Peter 9:508; 13:46
  Rebecca 13:437
  Robert 15:61
  Samuel 11:79; 14:497
  Thomas (Dr.) 10:653; 11:50, 52,
  151, 155
  W. 5:585
  William 9:711, 715, 717; 11:751;
  12:325, 328, 610; 14:320
YOUNGE, Felton 3:287
YOUNGMAN, Thomas 16:130
YOUNKEN, Henry 12:608
YSLEBACH, Joh. Christo. 3:518
YSSELL, Rhineholt 3:458
YUNDT, Nicholas 16:12
YUNG, Johannes 3:570
  Marcus 3:457
  Matthias 3:457
YUNGMAN, Johan Ditrich 3:429

ZAARTMAN, Alexander 3:329
ZAC(C)HEUS 7:284-288, 317, 429,
  461
ZACCHEUS, --- 9:435-437
ZACHA(R)IAS 7:220, 587-588
ZACHARIAS, Johannes 4:59
ZACHARY, Lloyd 3:293-294;
  4:496-498, 516-518, 522, 525,
  527, 529, 568
ZACHNECHDORUS 13:470
ZADOUSKY (ZADOUSKI), Anthony 3:330,
  344, 367, 571
ZANCK, Jacob 14:155
ZANE, Isaac 8:19, 211
  Joel 10:747; 11:12
  John 10:555
  William 15:571

ZANES, --- (Mr.) **16**:503
ZANTINGLER, Catherine **16**:148
ZANTZINGER, Adam **10**:481, 647, 689,
 736, 766
 Paul **11**:82, 223; **12**:256, 314, 317,
 339, 357, 628, 660; **14**:264, 268
ZEIGLAR (ZEIGLER), David **12**:621,
 628, 634, 684, 701, 713
ZEIGLER, --- (Capt.) **16**:535
 David **13**:170-171, 708
 Johan Leonhard **3**:432
ZEIGLER (ZIEGLER), David **14**:177,
 213, 440, 533, 549
ZEISBERGER, David **6**:736; **7**:119, 244
ZEISSBERGER, David **5**:576
ZELL, Erick Lutwich **3**:288
ZELLER, Peter **15**:259
ZENGH, Jurgh **3**:285
ZERBEN, Wandle **11**:75
ZERN, Michael **14**:610
ZEYLER, Adam **3**:453
ZIBLE, Jacob **11**:244
ZIEBER, Daniel **12**:390
ZIEGLER, Bernard **15**:227
 D. **13**:164
 David **13**:8, 76, 91, 713
 David (Capt.) **15**:13, 381, 394,
 437-439, 445, 473, 519
 Dean **12**:64, 220, 266, 278, 297,
 335, 547
 Hans Wilhelm **3**:458
 Michael **10**:714

ZIEGLER (ZIGLER), David **11**:418-419,
 710-711, 750
ZIGAREA (ZIGREA) **6**:640, 681 (see
 JAGREA)
ZIGELL, Jurg **3**:455
ZIGER, Johannes **3**:432
ZIGLER, Bernard **12**:146
ZILLAWOOLIE, --- **4**:668-669 (See
 WOOLIEN)
ZIMMER, Johan Johan **3**:515
ZIMMERMAN, Godfrey **14**:452
 Hans **3**:454
 Johan Adam **3**:455
 Matthew **2**:541
 Nicolaus **3**:454
 Sebastian **5**:612; **9**:340, 674
 Ulrick **3**:454
ZINN, Gerard **3**:385
ZISAWGEGH-ROANU INDIANS **4**:586
ZITTELL, Jacob **3**:516
ZOLL, Jacob **10**:701
 William **16**:523
ZOLLER, Hans Georg. **3**:515
ZOLLICOFFER, Matthias **3**:452
ZORN, Christian **11**:426
ZRICKETT, William **14**:666
ZUB(L)EY, Stophel **14**:63, 94
ZUGG, Peter **3**:285
 Ulrick **3**:285
ZWALLE, Hans **4**:72
ZYDERMAN, Johan Jacob **4**:60

228